Advance praise for *The Evolution of the Modern Workplace*

'At the 150th anniversary of the publication of *The Origin of Species*, it is an opportune time to ask how and why, in coping with the environmental changes of markets and legal constraints, British employment relations as a species has been transformed in the past quarter century. William Brown and his colleagues have provided a globally relevant and truly insightful picture based on WIRS/WERS.'

> TAKESHI INAGAMI, Emeritus Professor at the University of Tokyo and President of the Japan Institute for Labour Policy and Training (JILPT)

'A pioneering and unprecedented, empirically based and encompassing work by leading scholars and well-known experts on basic changes at the workplace and the fundamental shifts of employment relations in Britain. An absolute must for everybody interested in understanding the extraordinary transformation processes and their far-reaching consequences over the quarter century spanning the Thatcher/Major/Blair years.'

> BERNDT KELLER, Professor of Employment Relations, University of Konstanz

'*The Evolution of the Modern Workplace* makes excellent use of Britain's workplace surveys to capture the profound changes that have occurred in employment relations since the turbulent 1980s. This will be the standard comparative reference for assessing changes in employment relations yet to come. It is especially timely and valuable, given the likely impacts the global financial crisis will have on employment institutions and outcomes in the years ahead.'

> THOMAS A. KOCHAN, Co-Director, MIT Institute of Work and Employment Research

'This book provides the most comprehensive analysis of the major changes which have occurred in the British workplace over the past twenty-five years and the implications for work and employment relations in the future. It brings together renowned scholars who have shaped the study of the British workplace and is required reading for all who are interested in this important subject.'

> RUSSELL LANSBURY, Professor of Work and Organisational Studies, University of Sydney, and President, International Industrial Relations Association

'Workplaces and work have both changed radically in the past three decades. Professor Brown and his colleagues brilliantly chronicle the alterations using successive Workplace Employment Relations Surveys. These include the retreat from collective bargaining, voice, high involvement HRM, contingent pay, upheaval in the public sector and legal regulation. This is the definitive work on the twenty-first-century workplace.'

DAVID METCALF, Professor of Industrial Relations, London School of Economics

'This book sets the international benchmark for studies of the changing workplace. Drawing on a unique data set spanning three decades of workplace surveys, an elite research team interrogates the sources of continuity and change in the study of work and employment in the United Kingdom. This masterful blend of longitudinal data analysis, accessible prose and deep understanding of key human resources, employment law and industrial relations issues generates critical policy and practitioner insights and sets the reserach agenda for years to come.'

GREGOR MURRAY, Professor and CRIMT Director, University of Montreal

'This is a compelling read. Anyone who works in the field of employment relations, whether as an academic, HR specialist, trade unionist or student will find it a marvelous reference source. It is a comprehensive account of the changes that have coursed their way through the workplace in the recent years and points to several potential changes to come. The chapters bring to light the importance of the Workplace Employment Relations Survey – no mean feat! It's an excellent addition to the study of employment relations.'

ED SWEENEY, Chair of Acas

The Evolution of the Modern Workplace

The last twenty-five years have seen the world of work transformed in Britain. Manufacturing and nationalised industries contracted and private services expanded. Employment became more diverse. Trade union membership collapsed. Collective bargaining disappeared from much of the private sector, as did strikes. This was accompanied by the rise of human resource management and new employment practices. The law, once largely absent, increasingly became a dominant influence. The experience of work has become more pressured. *The Evolution of the Modern Workplace* provides an authoritative account and analysis of these changes and their consequences. Its main source is the five Workplace Employment Relations Surveys (WERS) that were conducted at roughly five-year intervals between 1980 and 2004. Drawing on this unique source of data, a team of internationally renowned scholars show how the world of the workplace has changed, and why it has changed, for both workers and employers.

WILLIAM BROWN is the Master of Darwin College and Professor of Industrial Relations at the University of Cambridge. He was previously Director of the Industrial Relations Research Unit of the Economic and Social Research Council (ESRC) at the University of Warwick. He was a foundation member of the Low Pay Commission, which fixes the United Kingdom's National Minimum Wage. He is a member of the Advisory, Conciliation and Arbitration Service (Acas) Panel of Arbitrators, and was an independent member of the Acas Council. In 2002 he was awarded a CBE for services to employment relations.

ALEX BRYSON is a senior research fellow at the National Institute of Economic and Social Research (NIESR). He is a visiting research fellow at the London School of Economics' Centre for Economic Performance and has been an editor of the *British Journal of Industrial Relations* since 2004.

JOHN FORTH is a research fellow at the National Institute of Economic and Social Research (NIESR). He was involved in the design and primary analysis of the 1998 and 2004 WERS.

KEITH WHITFIELD is Professor of Human Resource Management and Economics and Associate Dean for Postgraduate Studies at Cardiff Business School and Director of Cardiff University's Research and Graduate School in the Social Sciences. He was the ESRC's Academic Consultant and member of the Steering Group for the fifth WERS, and is a founding member and on the Steering Group of the Wales Institute of Social and Economic Research, Methods and Data.

The Evolution of the Modern Workplace

Edited by

William Brown
Alex Bryson
John Forth
Keith Whitfield

CAMBRIDGE
UNIVERSITY PRESS

CAMBRIDGE UNIVERSITY PRESS
Cambridge, New York, Melbourne, Madrid, Cape Town, Singapore,
São Paulo, Delhi

Cambridge University Press
The Edinburgh Building, Cambridge CB2 8RU, UK

Published in the United States of America by
Cambridge University Press, New York

www.cambridge.org
Information on this title: www.cambridge.org/9780521514569

© Cambridge University Press 2009

First published 2009

Printed in the United Kingdom at the University Press, Cambridge

A catalogue record for this publication is available from the British Library

Library of Congress Cataloguing in Publication data
The evolution of the modern workplace / edited by William Brown ... [et al.].
    p. cm.
Includes bibliographical references and index.
ISBN 978-0-521-51456-9 (hardback)
1. Industrial relations – Great Britain.   2. Work environment – Great Britain.
3. Labor unions – Great Britain.   I. Brown, William Arthur.   II. Title.
HD8391.E96   2009
331.25′60941 – dc22   2009012260

ISBN 978-0-521-51456-9 Hardback

Contents

Figures

Tables

Contributors

STEPHEN BACH: Professor of Employment Relations, Department of Management, at King's College London, University of London

ANDY CHARLWOOD: Senior Lecturer in Human Resource Management and Employment Relations at York Management School, University of York

DAVID G. BLANCHFLOWER: Bruce V. Rauner Professor of Economics at Dartmouth College

WILLIAM BROWN: Montague Burton Professor of Industrial Relations, Faculty of Economics, at the University of Cambridge

ALEX BRYSON: Senior Research Fellow at the National Institute of Economic and Social Research

SHIRLEY DEX: Professor of Longitudinal Social Research in Education, Centre for Longitudinal Studies, Institute of Education, University of London

LINDA DICKENS: Professor of Industrial Relations at Warwick Business School, University of Warwick

GILL DIX: Principal Research Adviser at the Advisory, Conciliation and Arbitration Service (Acas)

PAUL EDWARDS: Professor of Industrial Relations at Warwick Business School, University of Warwick

TONY EDWARDS: Reader in Comparative Human Resource Management, Department of Management, at King's College, University of London

JOHN FORTH: Research Fellow at the National Institute for Social and Economic Research

REBECCA KOLINS GIVAN: Assistant Professor of Collective Bargaining, School of Industrial and Labor Relations, at Cornell University

RAFAEL GOMEZ: Lecturer in Marketing at the London School of Economics

FRANCIS GREEN: Professor of Economics at the University of Kent

DAVID GUEST: Professor in Organisational Psychology and Human Resource Management, Department of Management, at King's College, University of London

MARK HALL: Professorial Fellow, Industrial Relations Research Unit, at Warwick Business School, University of Warwick

ANDREW PENDLETON: Professor of Human Resource Management at York Management School, University of York

KEITH SISSON: Emeritus Professor, Industrial Relations Research Unit, at Warwick Business School, Warwick University

JANET WALSH: Professor of Human Resource Management and Employment Relations, Department of Management, at King's College, University of London

KEITH WHITFIELD: Professor of Human Resource Management and Economics at Cardiff Business School, Cardiff University

PAUL WILLMAN: Professor in the Management Department at the London School of Economics

STEPHEN WOOD: Professor of Employment Relations at the Management School, University of Sheffield

Preface

The genesis of this project was in a series of conversations between the four investigators around the theme that the advent of the 2004 Workplace Employment Relations Survey (WERS 2004) would allow the construction of a data set that covered one of the most interesting periods in British industrial and economic history – that starting with the election of the first Thatcher government and ending at the beginning of the third term of the Blair Labour government. Moreover, the fourth survey's timing coincided closely with the change of government from Conservative to Labour, and a significant change in approach to matters in the employment and economic areas, thereby offering something of a natural experiment relating to the impact of this change. The main idea that came out of these conversations was to build on the pioneering work undertaken by members of the research team for the fourth WERS and published under the title *All Change at Work?* Two members of that team (Alex Bryson and John Forth) decided to link up with two researchers with long track records of working with WIRS/WERS and beyond (William Brown and Keith Whitfield) to extend the analysis in two main directions – first, to extend the series to incorporate the 2004 data, and to involve a wider range of researchers in the analysis of the data set so developed. Fortunately, the Economic and Social Research Council agreed to fund the study, and most of the researchers whom the team identified as potential co-authors agreed to take part and undertook their tasks with alacrity.

The product of this collective effort is presented in this book. It offers an evidence-led set of analyses of how, where and why employment relations have changed at the British workplace in the quarter century spanning the Thatcher/Major/Blair years – a period of considerable change in the area. Such an analysis is unprecedented. There can be no equivalent subject area that has been the subject of such an intensive scrutiny over such a long period of time, and certainly not one that has involved as much fundamental change as workplace employment relations in the last quarter century. However, it should be borne in mind that such a study has never been the purpose of the sponsors of the WIRS/WERS series. Their intention has always been to produce strong pictures of workplace IR/ER patterns at a point in time with, at most, a comparison with one other survey for a limited area of investigation. Moreover, survey data, no matter how well conceived and collected, can never tell the whole story of what is going on in any particular area, and is especially limited in terms of addressing the 'why' questions. Nonetheless, the WIRS/WERS sponsors have not only been especially astute in developing an extremely penetrating survey instrument, but have also been aware of their obligation to history, by keeping in place a number of questions that are closely comparable across a number of surveys and, in some cases, all five. Therefore, any failure to tell a strong and compelling story of this fascinating period is highly likely to be the responsibility of the project team, rather than the materials with which they were working.

We would like to express our grateful acknowledgements to a range of people and organisations that have helped us turn our interesting idea into the reality that is this book. First and foremost are the WIRS/WERS sponsors (various government departments, but currently the Department for Business, Enterprise and Regulatory Reform (BERR); the Advisory, Arbitration and Conciliation Service (Acas); the Economic and Social Research Council (ESRC), and Policy Studies Institute (PSI), for showing the sustained commitment to produce such a powerful data set. ESRC is also to be warmly thanked for providing the funding for the project (grant number RES-000-23-1603).

We are grateful to the National Centre for Social Research for providing access to the British Social Attitudes Survey, to Marco Ercolani for providing data on annual rates of absenteeism from the Labour Force Survey, the Institute for Social and Economic Research at the University of Essex as the originators of the British Household Panel Survey data, the Office for National Statistics as the originators of the Labour Force Survey, and the Economic and Social Data Service as the distributors of both data sets. We are also grateful to John Kelly and Citizens Advice for providing data on numbers of employment-related problems raised by visitors to Citizens Advice Bureaux; to the Centre for Longitudinal Studies, Institute of Education, for providing the data for Figure 10.1; and to Andy Charlwood for providing statistics on union membership density from the 1983 British Social Attitudes Survey.

Thanks are also due to Paul Marginson, David Nash, Andrew Oswald and Mike Terry, who have provided comments that have significantly improved the quality of the work that is reported herein. A major debt of gratitude is owed to Katy Huxley, who has provided tireless support to the project team, and has brought a degree of organisation to the project that has allowed the rest of us to concentrate on what we enjoy doing most – data analysis and writing. Our advisory board members Neil Millward and Mike Emmott have made important and insightful comments at all stages of the project, and have had a strong impact on the directions that we have taken. Phil Good of Cambridge University Press has been an excellent editor with whom to work.

WILLIAM BROWN, ALEX BRYSON, JOHN FORTH AND
KEITH WHITFIELD

Abbreviations

Acas	Advisory, Conciliation and Arbitration Service
BERR	Department for Business, Enterprise and Regulatory Reform
BSAS	British Social Attitudes Survey
CAB	Citizens Advice Bureau
CAPI	computer assisted personal interviewing
CBI	Confederation of British Industry
CEHR	Commission for Equality and Human Rights
CIPD	Chartered Institute of Personnel Development
CLIRS	Company Level Industrial Relations Survey
CPBR	collective payment by results
CRE	Commission for Racial Equality
CSO	Central Statistical Office
DCLG	Department of Communities and Local Government
DE	Department of Employment
DRC	Disability Rights Commission
DTI	Department of Trade and Industry
EC	European Community
EOC	Equal Opportunities Commission
ESO	employee share-ownership
ESRC	Economic and Social Research Council
ET	employment tribunal
EU	European Union
EUKLEMS	European Union Kapital Labour Energy Materials and Services
FDI	foreign direct investment
HIM	high involvement management
HPWS	high performance work systems
HRM	human resource management
IDBR	Inter Departmental Business Registers
IPBR	individual payment by results
ISSP	International Social Survey Programme

IWP	Institute of Work Psychology
JCC	joint consultative committee
LFS	Labour Force Surveys
MNC	multinational companies
NHS	National Health Service
OECD	Organisation for Economic Co-operation and Development
OLS	Ordinary Least Squares
ONS	Office for National Statistics
OPCS	Office for Population Censuses and Surveys
PBR	payment by results
PRP	profit-related payments
PSI	Policy Studies Institute
SETA	Survey of Employment Tribunal Applications
SIC	Standard Industrial Classification
TUC	Trades Union Congress
TUPE	Transfer of Undertakings (Protection of Employment) Regulations
UCC	ultimate controlling company
UN	United Nations
WERS	Workplace Employment Relations Survey
WES	Women and Employment Survey
WIRS	Workplace Industrial Relations Survey

1   Researching the changing workplace

William Brown and Paul Edwards

Introduction

Let us imagine, by courtesy of a time machine, that we have been able to introduce a well-informed young worker of 2004 to their counterpart in the closest comparable job back in 1980. We then suggest that the two of them discuss the way their work is managed. In most walks of life they would quickly bewilder each other. It is not just that information and control technologies have changed beyond recognition. They would probably have different experiences of how they have been trained, paid and motivated. They would almost certainly have radically different perceptions of the significance of trade unions. There would be a sharp contrast in any notions they might have of legal rights at work. There would probably be big differences in their accounts of the skills and styles of their managers, and of the extent of monitoring and appraisal. They are likely to report contrasting experience of the intensity of their work, and of the flexibility expected of them. And when they come to compare mundane matters like tea breaks, overtime opportunities, and weekend working, voices would probably rise in mutual incomprehension.

Few readers under the age of fifty will have direct experience of work back in 1980. The sharpness of these contrasts may not be self-evident. For it is not just that individual workplaces have altered, but also that structural change has altered the sorts of places where people work. This chapter will set the changing workplaces in context, and discuss the challenge of researching them. The following chapters will explore the many aspects of the changing workplace in greater detail. They will describe what has happened and, so far as is possible, discuss why it has happened.

Throughout the developed world, the management of work has changed radically over the past quarter century. Britain is not remarkable in the broad nature of this change. But few developed countries can match the pace and extent of the upheaval in Britain. Most obviously, the crumbling of trade union influence, under both market and political

1

pressures, started earlier and has gone further in Britain than in most countries; apart, it should be said, from the United States, where union decline had begun earlier, in the 1950s, and has proceeded further. In Britain, in 1980, unions were a dominating presence throughout much of the private sector and all of the public sector. Twenty years later, their influence had faded from all but a few private sector niches. It had even diminished substantially in the shrunken public sector. Britain's experience of the collapse of collectivism in employment is, in many ways, the experience of the wider world writ large. The analysis of this book thus has implications for the understanding of changing practice of employment far beyond Britain.

No other country can chart its recent experience of workplace change with anything remotely as comprehensive as the data we use here. The British workplace surveys are internationally unique as high-quality sources, chronicling this period of unprecedented institutional change. They were initially called the Workplace Industrial Relations Surveys (WIRS), and are now called the Employment Relations Surveys (WERS).[1]

The first survey, in 1980, was conducted, as it turned out, at the high tide mark of trade union influence in Britain. The survey was a direct consequence of the extent to which employment-related problems cluttered the political agenda. Strikes, incomes policies, questions about industrial efficiency, and doubts about the management of the public sector had become central issues in British politics. The 1980 survey informed the first, tentative restrictions that the Thatcher government placed on trade unions. Subsequent governments' concern to legislate on employment issues ensured that it was followed up. There were further surveys, of broadly comparable focus but increasing sophistication, in 1984, 1990, 1998 and 2004.

Cross-sectional surveys were carried out on each of these five occasions and have been the main focal point of the series. However, any series of separate cross-sections faces a problem in explaining change. Is a difference between one survey and the next due to a change in practice in continuing workplaces, or to differences in practice between workplaces that have closed down and those that have been newly established? WERS has been alive to this issue and has supplemented the cross-section surveys with a set of panel surveys covering the periods 1984–90, 1990–8 and 1998–2004 (Millward *et al.*, 2000: 248–55). Further detail on the WERS series is provided in a Technical Appendix at the end of this book.

---

[1] The 1998 survey was called 'employee' relations, although the broader term 'employment' was the intended label, and this was used in 2004.

These surveys did not spring up out of nothing. Their immediate predecessor was the Warwick Survey of 1977–8, which was the first British workplace survey based on a reasonably broad sample, although it was restricted to manufacturing workplaces with at least fifty employees (Brown, 1981). Before that had been a survey of pay bargaining, based again on manufacturing, but covering only relatively large workplaces of at least two hundred employees (Daniel, 1976). Nor was WERS unique in the development of representative surveys; its development owed much to other contemporary research. We touch below on some of these other surveys conducted since 1980, but shall not go back before 1980 in terms of survey design (for which, see Marginson, 1998).

Rich though this series of surveys is as a research resource, it has its limitations. Any attempt to chart continuity and change is unavoidably challenged by the inherent uncertainty of the future. WERS progressed from one version to another by repeating some questions and introducing new ones. They did this in response to changing circumstances and policy needs. They did so by drawing on a wide range of academic expertise. As a result, every attempt was made to incorporate newly emerging phenomena into successive stages of the survey, perhaps first evidenced by case studies or by unexpected developments, which appeared at the time to be significant for the future. Other issues that were fading from the academic or policy makers' radar could be shed. Questions, for example, about career planning and trust were introduced; questions about shop steward meetings and closed shops were dropped. As the years passed, many pathways of change opened up in unexpected directions.

The WERS data provide the basis for most of the empirical discussion in each of the chapters in this study. The authors of many chapters will be aware of questions that they wished had been asked in earlier surveys because the phenomena to which they relate gained unexpected significance later. Analysis would indeed be easier if we had a complete set of data items over the whole twenty-five year period, but that luxury is denied by the natural rise and fall of particular issues. Indeed, part of the task for the authors is a historiographic one – to reflect on how this salience has shifted, and how issues best tackled in one way in one version of the survey have to be tackled differently in its successor. The surveys have evolved because the world of work that they seek to measure has evolved. The overriding task of this book is to tell the story of the evolution of British employment relations over the past twenty-five years. Consequently, where WERS falls silent, our authors will call upon other sources of robust research evidence to guide their accounts.

In this introductory chapter, we provide the backdrop for the thirteen studies that follow. We start with a summary account of the state of employment practices and labour relations at the end of the 1970s. How were things when our story begins? It is then useful to reflect on what informed opinion at that time was expecting of the future. How far were the developments we are going to analyse unexpected? The features that emerged were shaped by a rapidly changing political and economic climate. What environment shaped this evolution? We outline some of the main changes in the structure of workplaces that can be identified. Finally, we turn to comment on the WERS series itself, as the principal research method on which our analyses are based. The way is then open for the separate expositions of how the nature of employment has evolved.

The management of employment in 1980

There is never a perfect point to break into a constantly unfolding story but, for British employment relations, the end of the 1970s is as good as one can get. It was the brink, as we shall show, of a major turning point, both in terms of the economy and of political life. It also came at a time by which it was generally evident that a once comprehensive and even acclaimed national structure of employment regulation had so degenerated as to be severely dysfunctional.

There had been a general acceptance, as the first half of the twentieth century had progressed, that employment relations were best regulated by arrangements between employers and trade unions with minimal legal intervention. Governments were largely content to encourage these so-called voluntary arrangements and to go along with established legal arrangements that, in effect, provided trade unions with rights to strike. A system of collective bargaining had developed under which, by 1950, almost all employment in the public sector, and the great bulk of it in the private sector, was covered by a patchwork of collective agreements, mostly specific to industrial sectors. Agreed between industry-defined employers' associations and the appropriate trade unions, these set out minimum wage rates, standard hours of work, holiday entitlements and in some cases grievance procedures, incentive pay schemes and much else besides. Although trade unions had only 45 per cent of employees in membership in 1950, almost all of the British workforce benefited from their agreements, or from the quasi-bargained safety-net arrangements offered by statutory wages councils.

This overtly settled system fell apart during the course of the 1960s and 1970s. A combination of tight labour markets and increasing competitive pressure in the employers' own product markets made industrial agreements increasingly ineffective in the private sector. Individual employers in many industries kicked against the restraints of agreements serving all employers, preferring to act alone in order to pay more to retain and motivate their workers. For a trade union movement with strong traditions of local activism, uninhibited by legal restraints, this encouraged informal bargaining at the workplace. It also often provoked unofficial strike activity. An accompanying feature was the exercise of considerable influence over the conduct of work by shop stewards – the elected union representatives from among the firms' own employees. We shall discuss the pattern of conflict in Chapter 8. Employers who got to grips with these problems generally did so by breaking with the industrial agreements altogether, and concluding formal agreements, specific to the firm or workplace, with their shop stewards.

By the late 1970s, more and more areas of the private sector were being affected by fragmented, strike-prone bargaining. This is not to say that such bargaining was universal or constant. Some employers, for example in the chemicals industry, were able to manage local bargaining with little overt conflict. This reflected their relatively strong product market positions, and also the comparative sophistication of their approach to industrial relations. In the car industry, by contrast, slack production and employment controls created by previously easier product markets were faced with growing competitive pressures that forced firms to contain costs. In a context of the employers' weak and fragmented approach to industrial relations, this contributed to recurrent shop floor confrontation. Chapter 2 will investigate the relationship between competition and collective bargaining.

Although employment in private manufacturing was starting to contract, the density of unionisation in the sector was rising – to 70 per cent in 1979 (Bain and Price, 1983: 11). Unionisation was increasing also amongst managerial and other 'white-collar' workers. Although unionisation was still relatively low in private services – 17 per cent in 1979 – there were sectors such as entertainment and finance where it offered a strong challenge to management. This boom-time for trade union activity in the private sector was not characterised by increased solidarity. Because bargaining was becoming increasingly fragmented, most unions were seeing their internal authority become decentralised and diffused (Undy et al., 1981: 336). Indeed, with relatively low union subscription rates, as is discussed in Chapter 4, local activists were increasingly dependent upon employers rather than trade union headquarters for their organisational resources as well as for their recognition.

The public sector had also changed substantially. In the 1950s, although highly unionised, it had been largely strike free, with the notable exception of the recently nationalised coal industry. But by the late 1970s, with public sector union density rising to 82 per cent, this had changed substantially. In part, it was because many newly nationalised industries – steel, shipbuilding, aircraft and motor vehicles, for example – brought their own traditions of turbulent workplace bargaining. But more remarkable was the new-found propensity for striking in public services, where it had hitherto been almost unknown. Local government, the health service, the civil service, teachers, postal workers and firefighters all saw substantial strike action in the 1970s. Whether this change was in response to incomes policies, or to attempts to improve efficiency, as Chapter 13 explains, the net effect was an increase in workplace activism that made public sector management altogether more challenging.

The distinctive character of workplace relations in the late 1970s is of importance to an understanding of that time. Because employment relations had become more conflictual, the welfare-related traditions of personnel management had tended to be replaced by the bargaining ethos of industrial relations management. Day-to-day labour problems were left to line managers with little or no specialist training, often selected on the basis that they had previous experience as shop stewards. When things got out of hand, efforts at resolution were often handed over to employer association officials outside the firm (Gospel, 1992: 178). It was a very combative, male, culture, metaphorically firefighting rather than fire avoiding, with little strategic thinking. By the late 1970s there had been partial reform of some of the more grotesquely dysfunctional incentive pay schemes that, a decade earlier, had caused the bulk of disputes in, for example, the docks, car assembly, shipbuilding, newspapers, and coal mining. But pay was usually still handled in a very short-term way with, for example, job evaluation used more to prevent disputes than to provide a positive basis of motivation. In both private and public sectors, the phrase 'human resource management' had not yet been heard. Its more holistic and strategic approaches to the management of employees which, as Chapters 6 and 7 describe, became routinely advocated by the twenty-first century, were largely unknown.

It is hard to exaggerate the extent to which the threat of industrial disputes dominated the management of employment. The average annual number of strikes in the 1970s – about 2,600 – was not substantially higher than for most of the previous post-war period, although the average annual number of working days lost – nearly thirteen million – was. What made a difference was that strikes were no longer concentrated in coal mining and heavy engineering, but had become a feature of manufacturing and public services more generally. At a time when much overtime working was institutionalised for manual workers, overtime bans and other non-strike sanctions were as common as strikes (Brown, 1981:

83). It should not be forgotten that the occurrence of a single strike or other sanction has far greater leverage and endurance in terms of attitudes beyond the incident itself. It is the subsequent credibility of threatened action that influences management behaviour in the longer term.

By the end of the 1970s, management attitudes were, from a twenty-first century point of view, extraordinarily defensive. Major reforms of, for example, payment systems, were perceived to be risky, expensive, and, in the case of industries such as newspapers, shipbuilding, commercial television, theatre, docks and prisons, probably impossible in the face of trade union mistrust and potential sanctions. In the great majority of workplaces where unions were recognised in the manufacturing industry, over two-thirds of managers said they negotiated with them over internal redeployment of labour, manning levels, redundancy and major changes in production methods (Daniel and Millward, 1983: 199). Substantial proportions reported the same from other sectors. For example, redeployment was a negotiable issue for at least a half of managers in unionised workplaces in government, nationalised industries, construction and services. It reflected a degree of routine local union influence over the conduct of work that is beyond the dreams of most twenty-first century trade union activists.

Another remarkable feature of the world of employment of the late 1970s in retrospect was the role of government. This was, as will be discussed in Chapter 14, both interventionist and abstentionist in ways that have become alien to more recent governments. The most conspicuous intervention had been that of the sequence of incomes policies that all governments had felt obliged to impose throughout the 1960s and 1970s. Routine bargaining over pay was heavily constrained by one-off government interventions almost every year. By the end of the 1970s, there was widespread discussion of this becoming institutionalised in some sort of 'social contract', with both the TUC and CBI cautiously discussing the possibility of an overarching procedure for deciding what pay levels the country could afford.

There was, on the other hand, little alteration to the distinctive abstention of British collective employment law. The Conservative attempt in 1971 to introduce a fundamentally new structure, including substantial rights for trade union security, had been effectively rebuffed by trade union opposition. In repealing it in 1974, Labour deliberately reverted to the status quo ante – with the important exception of the retention of protections against unfair dismissal. It thereby turned down the opportunity to retain any significant statutory protections for trade unions, should fortune ever turn against them. The most enduring and possibly most important part of an otherwise ineffective hotchpotch of Labour legislation in the later 1970s had been the creation of the Advisory, Conciliation and Arbitration Service (Acas).

It was Acas that came to play a central role in the delivery of a relatively new feature of British employment law, individual employment rights. These had started with rights to have written contracts of employment in the 1960s, followed by rights for equal pay for men and women, for health and safety protections, against unfair dismissal and against sex and racial discrimination. Chapter 8 will describe how these new rights were taken up and Chapter 10 the consequences for diversity of employment. Britain's recent membership of the (then) European Economic Community provided stimulus for these new protections. But trade unions were nervous of too much being provided by the state that they felt was best achieved through collective bargaining. They were, for example, ambivalent about wages councils and generally hostile to a national minimum wage. And there was no proposal for any proactive enforcement of individual employment rights by the sort of labour inspectorate that is normal in other countries. From the perspective of the twenty-first century, it is remarkable how little significance those involved in the late 1970s attached to the emerging array of statutory individual employment rights.

What was expected of the future?

We have the benefit of hindsight. This gives a possibly dull inevitability to our understanding of how employment relations were to develop over the next quarter century. But what happened is actually far more exciting than that. To some 1980 observers, the trip forward to 2004 in our time machine would have revealed a miraculous and desirable transformation of the British industrial scene; to others, it would have revealed an unimaginable tragedy of lost hopes and the ruins of broken institutions.

We can emphasise the extraordinary nature of the developments that this book analyses by recalling what informed observers were predicting at the time. In doing this, we should bear in mind that social scientists are not primarily concerned with prediction. Their first ambition is to shed light on current social processes and relationships. Predicting how these might change is an altogether more risky pursuit. Nonetheless, the tumultuous state of British industrial relations was so central to the concerns of politicians and business people around 1980 that there is ample evidence of what was expected. And at least as interesting is what they did not expect.

Writers of that time, whether academics or journalists, appear to have taken for granted that trade unions were firmly embedded in British

industrial governance. Whether it was Daniel advocating more imagina-
tive work organisation (Daniel and McIntosh, 1972), or Hyman (1972)
urging mass mobilisation, or McCarthy and Ellis (1973) arguing for more
industrial democracy, or Purcell (1981) analysing strategies for building
trust, or Milligan (1976) berating union power, or Taylor (1978) sympa-
thetically urging its reform, trade unions were seen as a linchpin, not just
of employment relations but of national economic life. Wherever analysts
were coming from in terms of ideology (and the list, and the range of
sympathy and antipathy, could be extended greatly), they appear to have
been in agreement on the continued strength of unions. If there was anything else on which they appeared to be in substantial agreement, it was
pessimism. They could see no end to strikes, confrontations, workplace
mistrust and acrimonious incomes policies. The prospects for employers and unions of agreeing long-term strategies for reform were seen as
wholly bleak.

Informed opinion was surprisingly unchanged even at the start of the
1980s, with a major recession under way and a Conservative government
in power which was making its hostility to trade unions increasingly clear.
In 1982 the (then) Department of Employment commissioned three
independent studies of likely developments in British industrial relations
over the following decade (Poole *et al.*, 1984). Poole approached the
issue from industrial sociology, Brown and Sisson took an institutional
approach, and Rubery, Tarling and Wilkinson adopted an economic perspective. Their predictions were much influenced by the contemporary
recession, not least because they shared a view that high levels of unemployment were likely to endure indefinitely. Nonetheless, they expected
trade union membership to be broadly sustained, perhaps growing at a
slower rate than it had in recent years. They appreciated that the new
government would legislate to inhibit trade union power, but were scepti-
cal whether it would have substantial impact on behaviour, at any rate for
many strategically important sectors. On past experience, they doubted
whether employers would be willing to take advantage of new legal
powers.

The three reports were agreed that levels of industrial conflict were
likely to remain high for the foreseeable future. But they differed over the
extent to which new forms of work organisation, worker participation,
more consultative management styles, and what at the time was being
called the 'new realism' of unions, might mitigate this. A contrary view
was that the pressure to force down wages and to make labour more
flexible would raise worker militancy to politically challenging levels.
But unions were sufficiently embedded, it was agreed, that sooner or
later there would have to be a return to a stronger form of corporatism

than was tried in the 1970s. Indeed, since inflation was still running at relatively high levels, there was support for Clegg's view that some form of continuous, permanent incomes policy, perhaps built around a 'social contract', was unavoidable (Clegg, 1979: 381).

Whatever these forecasts got right, what is more important from the twenty-first century perspective is how much they got wrong. Within a decade of 1980, trade union membership was to fall by 20 per cent, and within two decades by 40 per cent. Working days lost through strikes per year, which had averaged 460 per thousand employees in the 1970s, were to fall to an average of only 30 per thousand employees in the 1990s. Incomes policies never reappeared on the political agenda. It was to be seventeen years before the TUC and CBI were invited back into Downing Street for policy discussions, and then it was to deal with problems arising from the weakness of collective bargaining, rather than its strength. At the workplace, as Chapter 6 shows, the management of employment became the preserve of an increasingly feminised profession of specialist human resource managers. The trouble-shooting industrial relations enthusiasts of the 1970s had long since departed. The dogs that started barking after 1980 had hitherto lain silent and unobserved. What woke them was a changed economic and political environment.

THE IMPACT of NEW Technology!

The changed environment of the 1980s

To separate out the economic from the political forces that were to tear collective bargaining apart after 1980 would be a mistake. The Conservative government returned in 1979 brought with it a cautious and piecemeal initial package of industrial relations reforms, with nothing to cause trade unions much concern. But it had arrived just when North Sea oil production was about to make Britain self-sufficient. This had two consequences of far-reaching significance. First, it stopped the recurrent balance-of-payments deficits and consequent sterling crises that had dogged governments for the previous twenty or more years, not least because of the consequence that major strikes in export-related industry tended to provoke adverse currency speculation. Freed from this handicap, the Conservative government could engage with and call the bluff of industrial confrontations.

Second, North Sea oil's forcing up of the exchange rate, combined with the new government's tight fiscal policy, provoked a serious recession, which hit the manufacturing industry particularly hard. Unemployment doubled to 10 per cent and, as Figure 1.1 shows, was not to fall below it for nearly ten years, seriously damaging the confidence of unions dealing with the private sector. To the surprise of many, rising unemployment

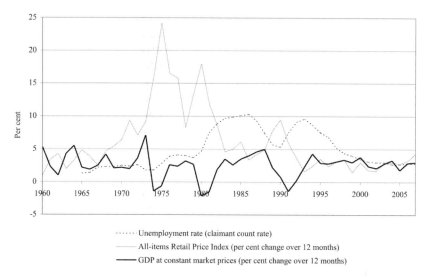

Figure 1.1 Economic growth, unemployment and inflation, 1960–2007
(Source: ONS)

did not inflict critical electoral damage when the Conservatives, greatly assisted by the Falklands War victory, won their second election in 1983.

Trade unions had underestimated how unpopular they had become. They had failed to appreciate that 'union bashing' legislation might actually win the government votes. They also failed to appreciate that, contrary to received wisdom, employers now could and would use the courts to force unions to desist from illegal action, and that this could be done independent of government and without the creation of martyrs. As a result, the government felt encouraged to produce periodic packages of industrial relations legislation. These combined to make the organisation of unions and strikes considerably more difficult and costly.

Inflation continued to be a recurrent source of disputes, as it had been in the 1960s and 1970s. As Figure 1.1 shows, it ran at high levels in the early 1980s and 1990s. But, with North Sea oil buttressing the currency, and with the discovery that the electorate would tolerate relatively high levels of unemployment, the government felt no need to embark on the interventions of incomes policies as in the previous two decades. It was left to employers to cope alone with pressures for compensatory wage increases from trade unions, or to suffer the dire competitive consequences.

The government gained the confidence to express overt support for employers faced with major strikes, as it did initially with the steel industry, and was later to do with printing, channel ferries, commercial television and, most important of all, symbolically, the coalminers. These confrontations were mostly not initiated by government. They arose from union reactions to employer responses to adverse economic and technical changes in the employers' product markets. But employers were greatly encouraged by the government's overt hostility to trade unions.

Generally, however, employers sought to avoid confrontations. There was the notable exception of the dismissal of 'Red Robbo', the senior shop steward at the massive Longbridge car assembly plant in 1979, the success of which (from the employer's point of view) reverberated through the industrial relations fraternity like a shock wave. But, more generally, employers were to withdraw effective recognition from their employees' existing union organisations by degrees, and they chose not to grant recognition when opening new workplaces (Brown *et al.*, 1998). The driving force in the private sector was ever-encroaching product market competition, which increased the pressure for labour-cost control at a pace not envisaged in the 1970s. It came with the increased internationalisation of markets, and of ownership. For the manufacturing industry, it became particularly harsh when political change worldwide during the period brought into effective competition the cheap labour and relatively high educational standards of India, China and the old Soviet bloc. Import penetration of the British domestic manufacturing market more than doubled, from 25 per cent to 58 per cent, between 1980 and 2004.[2] The implications for collective bargaining of this intensification of competitive pressure are discussed in Chapter 2.

Another fundamental change that was, perhaps surprisingly, not anticipated in the 1970s was wholesale privatisation. The transfer of ownership to the private sector, and the consequent sudden shock of product market competition, were to transform much of the highly unionised public sector. As a result, transport, communications, public utilities, steel, coal and substantial parts of manufacturing all experienced radical changes to their employment relations. Apart from the upheaval in these sectors, there were also radical changes in the management of employment in what remained in the public sector. Chapter 13 discusses how this diverged from, and how it converged with, developments in the private sector.

---

[2] Annual Abstract of Statistics, Office of National Statistics. Import penetration is defined as imports as a percentage of home demand for manufactured goods.

Table 1.1 *Distribution by broad sector*

	% workplaces		% employees	
	1980	2004	1980	2004
Private manufacturing	25	12	38	15
Private services	43	64	26	56
Public sector	32	24	36	28

Source: WIRS/WERS data. All workplaces with 25 or more employees.

This was the harshly changed environment that was about to confront the fractious, dysfunctional and curiously complacent world of British employment relations recorded in the first WERS of 1980.

The changing British workplace

Within this shifting national context, what happened to the individual workplace? For some changes, on which other studies have more to say, WERS picked up data on the consequences, rather than the immediate substance. Others have, for example, explored more directly the 'marketisation' of the employment relationship and its implications for workers in its effects on the equity and manner of their treatment, so important to our discussions in Chapters 2, 9, 10, 11 and 14 (e.g., McGovern *et al.*, 2007). Others have investigated how technical and organisational change have altered the sort of work people do and how they interact, which underlies much of what is discussed in Chapters 4, 5, 8 and 9 (e.g., Cappelli, 2008). Here we pick up briefly on some of the dynamics on which WERS sheds direct light. How did the economic role of the workplace change? How did the ownership of it change? How did the size of it change? How did the workforce within it change?

The mix of economic activity of workplaces was transformed between 1980 and 2004. The shift between the sectors in which people work is shown in Table 1.1. Manufacturing (which includes extractive industry)[3] more than halved in terms of both workplaces and workforce. It has been eclipsed by private services, in which most of the population now

---

[3] The major extractive industry in the United Kingdom used to be coalmining. By 1980 it employed a little over 1 per cent of the workforce. The industry has been the major exclusion from WERS. In 1980, as Daniel and Millward laconically point out, there was a 'failure to obtain access' (Daniel and Millward, 1983: 5). By 1984 the industry was in the midst of the strike, and thereafter it was excluded for comparability reasons and because it had declined dramatically in size to under 0.03 per cent of the workforce.

Table 1.2 *Ownership*

	% workplaces		% employees	
	1980	2004	1980	2004
Foreign owned/controlled				
All	6	14	11	21
Private manufacturing	7	30	14	37
Private services	5	11	7	17
Single independent establishment	21	22	14	18

Source: WIRS/WERS data. All workplaces with 25 or more employees.

works. The public sector declined in size, in part because of privatisation. Within public employment there has been a growth in the proportion of people working for agencies and other bodies which are at a more 'arm's length' distance from government. The decline in public ownership of workplaces has implications for employment that will be discussed further in Chapter 13.

The nature of ownership within the private sector has also changed. Individual investors have continued to decline as holders of equity shares in publicly quoted companies – the proportion of British shares listed on the UK Stock Exchange that were owned by individuals halved from 28 per cent in 1981 to 14 per cent in 2004.[4] Individuals are completely overshadowed by institutional investors, notably pension funds and insurance companies. These institutions can be expected to be more vigilant and demanding of 'shareholder value' than individual investors, and thus place workplace managements under greater competitive pressure. But, while British financial institutions have been very important as shareholders, their significance as a proportion of all shareholders has actually declined – from holding 68 per cent of all listed shares in 1981 to 49 per cent in 2004.

What has changed most over the period has been the rising importance of direct foreign investment. Between 1981 and 2004, the proportion of shares owned by investors outside Britain rose from 4 per cent to 36 per cent. Table 1.2 shows that this was reflected, according to WERS, in the growing proportion of employees in foreign-owned workplaces. Among all workplaces with twenty-five or more employees, the share of employees in foreign-owned/controlled workplaces doubled to a fifth since 1980. In private manufacturing, foreign-owned workplaces now

[4] National Statistics Online – /statbase/TSDdownload2.asp.

Micro - Firms Have not changed ownership! (handwritten annotation)

account for over one-third of employees. The implications of this for the internationalisation of employment management are discussed in Chapter 13.

What have these major shifts in sector and ownership meant for the management of workplaces? Have they increased, or decreased, local managers' autonomy? Let us look first at the extent to which workplaces are still genuinely independent. Examples could be a family-run hotel that is not part of a larger group, an independent cornershop, a single-site boat-builder's yard. Perhaps surprisingly, Table 1.2 suggests there has been little change over the quarter century. In 2004, as in 1980, about a fifth of workplaces of twenty-five or more employees were single, independent units, and they continued to employ about one-sixth of the workforce. The proportion of workers for whom the local boss is the ultimate boss has barely altered.

What about the rest? Have the remaining four-fifths of workplaces, which are part of larger organisations, come under closer control? One symptom of this on which WERS has recorded data is the question of whether there had been a move to a more disciplined approach to the collection of data for labour management. Figures available since 1990 on the collection of information on labour costs and on productivity show an upward trend in both. Tightening of controls was particularly marked in the public sector, reflecting the growth of market-like controls in parts of the sector such as the NHS Trusts. Lying behind this was the all-pervading, incremental spread of new information and comput-ing technology, which has had profound implications for automation, control, monitoring of employees, and much else besides. One of the key findings of WERS and other studies is that, while the responsibility of workplace managers seems to have increased, the use of targets and reporting to constrain them has also increased (Gallie *et al.*, 1998: 318; Millward *et al.*, 2000: 78). It is an innovation that might be characterised as 'you have more local freedom, as long as you deliver results'.

What about the size of workplaces? It has long been noted that indus-trial relations characteristics such as collectivism, conflict and control techniques are strongly influenced by the number of employees at a workplace. There is, furthermore, a common perception that in recent years the large workplace has become less common, a declining feature of a 'Fordist' past. As Table 1.3 shows, overall there has been remarkably little change in the size distribution of workplaces. But one can discern a small increase in the proportion of employees working in smaller work-places and a similar decrease in the proportion working in larger sites. This overall pattern is the sum of two contrary trends. Manufacturing plants now tend to be smaller than was the case in 1980: the proportion

Table 1.3 *Size of workplaces, overall*

	% workplaces		% employees	
	1980	2004	1980	2004
25–49 employees	50	53	15	18
50–99	25	26	15	18
100–199	13	12	16	17
200–499	8	7	19	21
500–999	2	2	13	10
1000+	1	1	22	16

Source: WIRS/WERS data. All workplaces with 25 or more employees.

of manufacturing workplaces with twenty-five to forty-nine employees rose from 34% in 1980 to 42% in 2004. But there has been an increase in size among private sector service workplaces, with the proportion that have only twenty-five to forty-nine employees falling from 62% to 56%. At the same time, there has been little change in workplace size in the public sector.

If we shift our attention from the size of workplace to the size of the owning company, there were similar trends. There has been a decline in size of the owning company in manufacturing and a slight growth in its size in private services. Of course, these figures exclude workplaces of fewer than twenty-five employees.[5] But there is no strong evidence that these small workplaces were of growing importance over the period since 1980, so the trends we have sketched can be taken as indicative.[6]

What about the workforce itself? It has certainly become increasingly female. Over the period, the proportion of employees who were women in workplaces of twenty-five or more employees rose from 38% to 48%. But this does not mean that it was also increasingly mixed in terms of gender. There was a small rise in the proportion with mixed workforces (defined as those where between one-quarter and three-quarters of workers were women). This rose from 42% in 1980 to 47% in 2004. But there was also

[5] In 2004, workplaces employing twenty-five or more employees accounted for 9 per cent of all establishments but employed 68 per cent of all employees.

[6] Consistent data on the distribution of employment by size of workplace and firm are not easy to find. The Census of Production gives information, but particularly during the 1980s the reliability of information on firms with fewer than ten employees was poor. The Small Business Service provides statistics for the period 1994–2006 on businesses (not workplaces). Taking businesses with at least one employee, those businesses with one to nineteen employees accounted for 24 per cent of total employment in 1994, a figure which fell to 21 per cent in 2006.

a rise in heavily feminised workplaces (defined as women comprising 90% and over) from 8 to 13%. This was concentrated in the public sector, where, in 2004, 31% of workplaces had this characteristic, compared to only 13% in 1980. It is exemplified by what has been happening in primary schools.

A greater increase in diversity of employment is suggested by strong trends in ethnic minority employment. In 1980, almost two-thirds of workplaces reported no ethnic minority employees, a proportion that fell to about half in 2004. This was notable in private services and the public sector, but not in manufacturing, which in fact showed a slight move in the opposite direction. Chapter 10 will discuss the dynamics of these developments.

Another aspect of the workplace that has undergone a character change is the employment contract. One national trend that, for obvious reasons, was not picked up by WERS, was the increase in self-employment. The proportion of the UK workforce for whom the main job was self-employed rose from 8% in 1980 to 13% in 2004.[7] But employment has itself altered substantially. Full-time working has given way substantially to part-time working. Part-time employment rose from 14 to 26% of workers (for workplaces of twenty-five or more employees) between 1980 and 2004, according to WIRS/WERS. This is closely associated with the rise in female employment. The proportion of workplaces where at least half the workers were part-timers grew from 13 to 28% of the total. There was an underlying contrast between manufacturing and the public sector, mirroring their different patterns in feminisation.

There has been a more complex change in the treatment of open-ended employment contracts, the traditional way in which workers have been employed, whereby the duration of employment is indefinite. There was a sharp increase in employment contracts of fixed duration – what is sometimes called 'contingent' or 'atypical' employment – during the 1990s. WIRS/WERS shows stability up to 1990 in the proportion of workplaces having employees on fixed-term contracts of less than a year: it remained at about 20 per cent. There was some evidence of a rise to 34 per cent by 1998, although the question of that year had a slightly broader definition. It is notable that the use of fixed-term contracts rose highest in the public sector. This was consistent with contemporary efforts to expose the public sector to market forces. But this increase in contingent employment may have peaked, with no evidence of increased use of fixed-term or temporary contracts after 1998.

---

[7] Office of National Statistics, Labour Market Trends.

The use of temporary workers employed through agencies showed a similar pattern, with stability between 1980 and 1984, and a higher proportion in 1998 (there had been no question on this in 1990) that remained much the same in 2004 (at 27 per cent). The growth was, again, particularly marked in the public sector. The quarter century appears to have witnessed a step-change towards more flexible employment.

The workplaces with which this study is concerned have changed substantially over our quarter century. Manufacturing and public employment have given way substantially to private services. Foreign ownership has become more important. The proportion of workplaces that are single and independent has altered little. But within larger organisations, individual workplaces have become more closely controlled, albeit through targets rather than standardisation. There has been surprisingly little change in the size of workplaces in terms of the numbers employed, although this reflects contrasting trends in manufacturing and services. Their workforces have, overall, become more feminine, more ethnically diverse, and they are employed on less open and more flexible contracts. A major challenge for the WIRS/WERS series has been to keep track of employment relations within this constantly altering context.

The research method

The survey technique that underlies this book has proved remarkably robust. We summarise the technical characteristics of WIRS/WERS in the Technical Appendix. Their distinctive features have been the use of face-to-face interviews with people in specific roles, in a large representative sample survey of workplaces, across almost the whole range of employment. In this, it has been emulated internationally, with similar surveys in countries as diverse as Australia, Norway, France, Canada, Estonia and South Korea. Lying behind this survey method has been a constant process of updating and refinement, drawing on a range of research methods and findings to make each round of the survey as sensitive as possible to the changing nature of employment relations. Strenuous efforts have been made to convert into operational questions the insights that fieldworkers have provided of contemporary changes. Sometimes, as the most recent WERS team reported of attempts to identify workplace partnership, innovations have failed (Whitfield and Huxley, 2007).

However well-trained the interviewers, there are unavoidable limits to what can be achieved by administering highly structured questionnaires to one or two respondents in a workplace. They can tell us little, for example, about the underlying power relationships and processes. That calls for deeper case-study approaches which, by their nature, place severe constraints on sample sizes. But it is significant that a substantial proportion of the contributors to this book have themselves been innovators in case-study approaches to employment relations. The WIRS/WERS approach, with its regular iteration between ethnographic fieldwork and larger-scale quantification, is part of a long tradition of British industrial relations research (Brown and Wright, 1994). Far from competing with more sensitive, qualitative methods, WERS has linked them to wider debates and other disciplines.[8] By placing magnitudes on a wide range of institutional and other relevant influences, it has opened them to investigation by a much wider range of social science analysis, from labour economics to organisational behaviour. A vast body of empirical analysis has drawn on the WERS series.[9]

The focus on the workplace has become a key link in efforts to understand the employment relationship. Looking 'downwards' from national-level surveys to studies of sectors or individual workplaces, it is now common to find studies of particular sectors that not only use WIRS/WERS-based questions but also use WIRS/WERS directly as a benchmark, rather than a mere backdrop, for the specific results.[10] The surveys have also been used in the selection of case studies, as indicators, for example, of where a phenomenon of interest may be commonly located.[11]

Meeting the need to look 'upwards', and to connect the individual workplace to the environment in which it is located, is limited by the fact that WERS itself has never engaged with informants above the level of the workplace. But linear descendents from WIRS/WERS were the two Company Level Industrial Relations Surveys of 1985 and 1992 (CLIRS1 and CLIRS2), which started at workplace level and then traced control through one or two higher levels (Marginson et al., 1988). They fruitfully connected workplaces to their budgetary context within the organisation, and with wider issues of control. A subsequent study of multinational

---

[8] The criticisms that WERS has 'crowded out' more qualitative research was discussed and dismissed by Marginson (1998). A study of publication patterns in the two main British industrial relations journals in the 1970s and 1990s also found no evidence of it (Frege, 2007: 53–8).

[9] The WERS bibliography is to be found at the website www.wers2004.info/research/home.php.

[10] For example, Gilman et al. (2002) used WERS data on pay bargaining to locate their evidence on small firms. Tsai et al. (2007) took questions on job autonomy as the benchmark for their sector-level evidence.

[11] For example, it was used to guide case-study selection in Gilman's (1998) work on performance-related pay and by Oxenbridge and her colleagues (2003) in assessing the impact of the 1999 statutory recognition legislation.

companies followed the WIRS/WERS principle of being based on a representative sample. It provided information on such issues as the global structure and organisation of the human resources function. It suggests that the character of this function is important in shaping practice, not least with respect to local autonomy (Edwards *et al.*, 2007; Ferner *et al.*, 2007). There are also increasing opportunities to link WIRS/WERS to enterprise-level data such as the Annual Business Inquiry. Looking above the workplace has proved to be a fertile and complementary activity.

Additional opportunities to look in more detail within the workplace have been provided by the two most recent surveys in the WERS series, which added a survey of employees. This major innovation – inspired by the 1995 Australian WIRS – has given a valuable new means of investigating the attitudes and experiences of workers, thereby enabling a renewed focus on the quality of work. The survey has also helped to broaden the appeal of the survey beyond its traditional base of industrial relations researchers and union-focused labour economists.

Let us return to the time machine with which we began, but think now of a time-travelling social scientist. Such a person in 1980 could scarcely have imagined the advances that were to be made in WERS by 2004. Coverage of workplaces has spread to encompass those with as few as five employees. There is panel data linking successive surveys. There is a comprehensive survey of workers as well as of managers and worker representatives. Connections have been made to objective performance data. There is every reason to suppose that WERS will continue to evolve, in step with changes in the workplaces it charts.

Conclusion

Our purpose in this chapter has been to set the scene for the detailed analyses to follow. We have emphasised the extraordinary transformation of British employment relations that has occurred over the quarter century in question. We have drawn attention to the extent to which it was unexpected, and discussed why and how circumstances brought it about. In many respects, the conduct of employment has altered beyond recognition. We have ended with a tribute to the robust research device that underpins this book, an ambitious survey that has been constantly developed to chart the pattern of change.

In what follows we first look at the crisis that faced worker collectivism. Chapter 2 charts the collapse of collective bargaining in the face of toughening competition. The diminishing impact of unions on management is analysed in Chapter 3. How this is reflected in the changing role of worker representatives is the subject of Chapter 4. It raises major questions about the extent to which employees are heard at all, which is analysed in Chapter 5.

We then turn to the changed nature of management. The emergence of human resource management is described and its effectiveness assessed in Chapter 6. Accompanying it has been what is sometimes termed 'high commitment management'; Chapter 7 explores this.

How might we assess the outcomes for employees? Chapter 8 explores the remarkable transformation of conflict and conflict resolution, while Chapter 9 looks at what altered in the individual worker's experience of work. We then turn to changes in particular aspects of the employment relationship. Developments in the equality and diversity of the workforce, the subject of considerable legal intervention, are analysed in Chapter 10. The changing ways in which workers' pay is linked to how they perform, and how their workplace performs, are discussed in Chapter 11.

We then consider the broader questions arising from the ownership of the workplace. The rise of foreign ownership was earlier identified as a major development. Chapter 12 looks at how far it altered the way labour is managed. We also noted the wholesale change in the nature of public ownership. Chapter 13 explores how far this led to differences in the conduct of employment relations in comparison with the private sector. Before concluding comments we look, in Chapter 14, at a development that has left no workplace untouched: the emergence of the law as a central player on a stage from which it had for decades been banished.

2 Competition and the retreat from collective bargaining

William Brown, Alex Bryson and John Forth

Introduction

Possibly the most remarkable feature of the period after 1980 in Britain was the collapse of collectivism as the main way of regulating employment. Collective bargaining had hitherto, for most of the twentieth century, provided the terms on which labour was commonly employed in Britain. Employers, whether or not they dealt directly with trade unions themselves, generally followed agreements that had been made with unions. But the period with which we are concerned saw this fall apart. How and why did this happen?

The theory that guides our account of this upheaval focuses on the central importance of the markets in which employers trade. The more competitive these product markets are, the smaller are the profits potentially accessible to trade unions. Having profits for unions to bargain over may be a necessary condition for collective bargaining, but it is not sufficient. What is also needed is a trade union organisation that is strong enough to make that bargaining effective. Here the product market becomes important again, because the environment in which unions are best able to flourish is one where the employers of their members face relatively slack competitive pressures. Tougher competition forces employers to tighten their control over employment, of which reducing the leeway for unions and reducing their influence over the conduct of work is a part. It was a feature of our period that product market competition tightened for much of the private sector.[1] Privatisation had similar effects in the public sector. Our story concerns the consequences for collective bargaining.

The unquestioning acceptance of collective bargaining by employers, unions and governments until the early 1980s defines the period. Proposals for reform were predicated on the assumption that, while

---

[1] As was noted in Chapter 1, import penetration of the British domestic manufacturing market more than doubled, from 25 per cent to 58 per cent, between 1980 and 2004.

collective bargaining might have to be modified, employers would continue to face trade unions across the bargaining table. In 1980, the majority of large employers entered into voluntary agreements with trade unions, not simply because unions had the bargaining power to make life difficult for them if they did not, but also because collective bargaining served the interests of employers. Even if collective bargaining entailed paying a rate for the job that may have exceeded a notional market-set wage, this was perceived to be a price worth paying if most or all competitors also paid collectively bargained rates. To use the traditional phrase, collective bargaining 'took wages out of competition', and allowed employers to focus their attention on other matters.

Our argument is that this tacit settlement between organised labour and employers was undermined by increasing product market competition. Over our quarter century, the British economy became substantially more open in terms of both trade and ownership. Employers were increasingly forced to reconsider collective bargaining habits that hitherto had been taken for granted. We start our investigation of how they did it with an overview of the changing map of collective bargaining, focusing on the private sector. Where and when did the historic retreat take place? We then move on to ask why, and to explore the part played by product market competition and, in particular, by the profitability of different industries. The chapter concludes with an analysis of the consequences of privatisation, which can be seen as an extreme case of product market change. Tougher competition in the markets within which employers compete, it will be argued, has been the driving force behind the weakening of their employees' trade unions. It lay behind the undermining of the collective bargaining arrangements that they had built up over the previous century.

Mapping the contraction of collective bargaining

The Webbs' classic definition of collective bargaining is that it occurs when the employer 'meets with a collective will, and settles, in a single agreement, the principles on which, for the time being, all workmen of a particular group, or class, or grade, will be engaged' (Webb and Webb, 1902: 173). Over a hundred years later, the term has come to be used more broadly. Collective bargaining in Britain rarely results in a single agreement. For any particular workplace, it is rather a constantly changing bundle of written and unwritten agreements and understandings.

The British experience is internationally distinctive in this respect, with none of the apparatus of legal enforcement that is to be found, for example, in the United States or many European countries. The century and

Table 2.1 *Percentage of workplaces recognising unions, 1980–2004*

	1980	1984	1990	1998	2004
All	64	66	53	41	38
Public sector	94	99	87	87	87
Private sector	50	48	38	24	22

Source: WIRS/WERS data. Workplaces with 25 or more employees.

a half during which legal enforcement was, by mutual agreement, effectively excluded from collective bargaining in Britain encouraged what has always been a relatively informal, parochial set of arrangements, varying substantially by both sector and workplace. As elsewhere, the 'principles' of engagement extend far beyond pay and hours of work. But, in the British context, any formal dialogue that takes place between employers and representatives of independent trade unions that has an influence on the employment relationship can be taken to constitute collective bargaining. It is, as a result, an elusive concept at the margin, made more so by the fact that perceptions of employers and trade union representatives differ substantially over what is bargaining and what is consultation (Brown and Nash, 2008: 100). Here we consider two different defining characteristics: employer recognition and pay bargaining.

One indicator of collective bargaining is whether or not employers say they recognise trade unions for negotiating pay and conditions. It is a question that has been asked from the start of the surveys and, as Table 2.1 indicates, there was a substantial reduction in recognition over the whole period. But the trends are very different for the public and private sectors. While union recognition remained a normal part of life for most of the public sector, in the private sector it collapsed from being a feature of a half of workplaces to under a quarter. Although fairly stable at the start and finish of our period, it is the halving of recognition in the private sector between the 1984 and 1998 surveys that stands out. This was rarely, it should be added, the consequence of employers aggressively and actively derecognising trade unions. Instead, it reflected in part a tendency not to recognise unions in newly established workplaces, and an inability of unions to extend recognition among continuing workplaces as they aged and grew larger (Millward, Bryson and Forth, 2000: 100). In part, it also reflected a process of what has been called 'implicit derecognition', whereby individual employers gradually reduced the range of issues and the intensity with which they engaged with unions to the point at which recognition was nebulous (Brown *et al.*, 1998). As the 1980s and 1990s progressed, employers, and a new generation of managers, apparently found that they could function perfectly adequately with less engagement with trade union representatives than in the past.

Change in pay fixing

Just what it means for an employer to say that they recognise trade unions for some of their employees is unclear. What action, if any, follows? Do they do no more than accept that unions may represent workers with individual grievances? Or, at the other end of the spectrum, is the union a firmly institutionalised part of the decision-making process, involved by right in pay fixing and work organisation? So let us consider the relatively concrete issue of whether employers rely on collective bargaining for the purpose of fixing pay for some or all of their employees. This reliance may mean no more than that they follow the terms of a collective agreement for their industry that has been concluded by relatively remote union and employer association officials. Or it may mean something much more proximal and immediate, with union representatives among the firm's employees taking the lead in negotiating the pay of its workforce.

The changing picture of pay-fixing arrangements since 1984 is summarised in Table 2.2.[2] This provides both the percentage of workplaces where collective bargaining is used for some part of the workforce and the total percentage of employees who are covered by these arrangements. The overall story of change for the whole economy, and of marked divergence between public and private sectors, is in line with what we have already noted for trade union recognition. Between industrial sectors, which include both private and public enterprises, there are clear variations in both the extent and timing of collective bargaining's retreat. For some sectors characterised by long bargaining traditions – engineering, metals, and other manufacturing, transport and communications – the greatest retreat from collective bargaining was in the 1980s and 1990s. There are signs of the retreat slowing or even ceasing in the 2000s, at least in terms of the proportion of employees covered. For extraction and refining, by contrast, that proportion continued to decline, despite only a small change in the workplace incidence of bargaining in this sector, implying that some large firms abandoned it. For other sectors however, notably construction, distribution and hospitality, and banking and finance, the retreat has been steady and sustained over the whole twenty-year period.

---

[2] The data on collective bargaining from the 1980 WIRS are not comparable with those from later surveys in the series, so our series here begins in 1984.

Table 2.2 *Percentage of workplaces with some collective bargaining and the percentage of all employees covered, 1984–2004*

	Workplaces with any collective bargaining				Employees in workplaces with any collective bargaining			
	1984	1990	1998	2004	1984	1990	1998	2004
Public sector	99	86	84	82	95	78	67[a]	79
Private sector	47	38	24	16	52	41	32	25
All	66	52	40	32	70	54	42	39
Energy, water supply	94	96	96	95	93	85	89	83
Extraction, metals, minerals, chemicals	53	60	47	46	72	62	54	37
Metal goods, engineering, vehicles	53	38	32	27	67	48	46	45
Other manufacturing	59	45	34	31	60	52	40	38
Construction	54	46	37	22	53	45	38	30
Distribution, hospitality, repairs	40	27	17	7	39	22	22	13
Transport, communications	88	73	60	63	91	80	63	66
Banking, finance, insurance, business services	50	44	26	12	45	38	23	17
Other services	86	73	59	53	86	68	52[a]	58

Note: [a]The fall in the percentage reflects temporary changes in the relative influence of Pay Review Bodies and collective bargaining, especially in the NHS – see Millward *et al.* (2000: 195) and Kersley *et al.* (2006: 185).
Source: WIRS/WERS data. Workplaces with 25 or more employees.

The changed incidence of bargaining

Having noted the distinctive experience of the private sector, let us explore this further. Multivariate analysis permitted us to unravel some of the many factors associated with employers' propensity to engage in collective bargaining. Some of the more substantial relationships are summarised in Table 2.3. The table presents two models estimated for the pooled years 1984–2004. The first is estimated for the whole private sector. The second focuses on 'trading workplaces' – that is, those involved in the selling of goods or services as opposed to those which are depots, administrative centres and the like. The models identify independent associations between workplace characteristics, on the one hand, and, on the other, the use of collective bargaining to set pay for at least some workers at the workplace (whatever the level at which bargaining occurs: national, sectoral, organisational or workplace). Coefficients in

Table 2.3 *The occurrence of collective bargaining within private sector establishments – regression (OLS) with specific characteristics for pooled data for 1984, 1990, 1998, 2004*

	all private sector workplaces	trading workplaces in the private sector
Establishment size (reference <50)		
50–99	n.s.	n.s.
100–199	0.10**	0.11**
200–499	0.15**	0.16**
500+	0.20**	0.21**
Single establishment	−0.08**	−0.09**
Organisation size (reference <1000)		
1,000–9,999	0.18**	0.18**
10,000+	0.30**	0.27**
Age >10 years	0.08**	0.10**
Proportion female	−0.12**	−0.14**
Proportion non-manual	−0.08**	−0.05*
Survey year (reference 1984)		
1990	−0.11**	−0.12**
1998	−0.21**	−0.23**
2004	−0.29**	−0.29**
Product market (reference 'local')		
regional		−0.12**
national		−0.11**
international		−0.12**
Observations	4507	3321
R-squared	0.26	0.29

Notes: (1) The dependent variable is available in the data set deposited at the data archive (SN 4511); (2) Models include controls for region (10 dummies), industry (9 dummies), foreign ownership, proportion of part-time employees; (3) Analyses are weighted with workplace survey weights; (4) Probit estimation made no substantial difference to the results; (5) Full models are available from the authors on request.
Source: WIRS/WERS data.
$^*p < 0.1, ^{**}p < 0.05$.

the models indicate percentage differences in the probability of coverage relative to the reference category specified in the table. In addition to these pooled year models, we ran separate year regressions to see how the association between collective bargaining and workplace characteristics had altered over time.

The models account for around one-quarter of the variance in the incidence of collective bargaining in the private sector. Although this is a sizeable proportion, and quite respectable for analyses of this sort, it does mean that roughly three-quarters of the variance remains unexplained.

Industry, region, the size of the workplace, organisation size, workplace age, and the composition of the workplace's workforce were all independently associated with the likelihood that at least some workers had their pay set by collective bargaining. The industry associations (not shown) reflect the descriptive information in Table 2.2, with workplaces in the energy and water sector most likely to use collective bargaining followed by transport and communication. Distribution, hotels and catering were by far the least likely to use collective bargaining. These industry associations are interesting for two reasons. First, they are fairly persistent over time, as we find when running the models on separate years. Second, they are independent of workplace and organisation size associations, indicating that they capture something distinctive about the working environment and industrial traditions, over and above organisational size.

Workplace size was strongly associated with the propensity of private sector employers to use collective bargaining. Although this is far from a novel finding, it merits deeper investigation. Controlling for other factors, workplaces with 500 or more employees were around one-fifth more likely to use collective bargaining than comparable (in terms of the characteristics listed) workplaces with fewer than 50 employees. Having allowed for workplace size, simply being part of a larger, multi-workplace organisation substantially increased the probability that a workplace used collective bargaining. Single-site independent organisations had an 8 per cent lower probability of using collective bargaining than workplaces belonging to multi-site firms. Furthermore, the probability that the largest organisations – those with 10,000 or more employees – used collective bargaining was 30 per cent higher than otherwise comparable organisations with fewer than 1,000 employees. Once again, the individual year regressions indicate that these size associations are fairly persistent across time. In brief, collective bargaining was continuing to play an important role in determining the pay of at least some of the workers in larger private sector organisations at the start of the twenty-first century.

The incidence of collective bargaining is also independently associated with workplace age. Over the course of the WERS series, workplaces aged ten years or more had a higher probability of using collective bargaining than otherwise comparable younger workplaces. In 1998 and 2004, we have continuous information on the age of the workplace which allows us to identify when it was born. Among private sector workplaces surveyed in 1998, 45% of those born in the 1940s or earlier used collective bargaining. The figure was half this (23%) among workplaces born in the 1960s. The percentage was half again (12%) among workplaces born in the

1980s. Assuming that employers choose whether or not to use collective bargaining to set pay early on in the lives of workplaces, these figures suggest a substantial decline in the adoption of collective bargaining between the 1950s and 1960s and again between the 1970s and 1980s. Among those workplaces surveyed in 2004, the big decline took place between the 1960s and 1970s: among those born in the 1960s, 32% were still using collective bargaining in 2004. The figure was only one-third of this (13%) among those born in the 1970s. Thus, although it is not possible from this analysis to distinguish between a pure age association and a cohort association – that is, an association linked with the historical date of birth of the workplace rather than its age per se – the evidence is suggestive of substantial declines in the adoption of collective bargaining in the three decades after the Second World War. It appears, therefore, that Margaret Thatcher's governments of the 1980s and 1990s may have taken credit for dismantling collective bargaining when, in fact, the demise of collective bargaining was already well advanced. In any event, it is clear that the 'golden age' for union pay bargaining was just after the Second World War, as Millward *et al.* (2000: 103) have suggested.

What about the workers who might be the beneficiaries of collective bargaining? Have their characteristics been related to its retreat? Table 2.3 shows that the propensity of private sector employers to use collective bargaining to determine wages does depend, in part, on the type of workers they employ. Their use of collective bargaining falls with increases in the proportion both of women and of non-manual workers they employ. The presence of part-time workers does not register as significant. We know from national surveys that trade union membership has tended to decline more in what were once characterised as manual as opposed to non-manual occupations (Grainger and Crowther, 2007: 6). Union membership has become increasingly associated with those workers with more qualifications rather than with those in less-skilled jobs. Our multivariate analysis for separate years suggests that the withdrawal from collective bargaining reflects a comparable phenomenon. That is, the effects of the occupational composition of the workforce diminished over time so that, by 2004, it was no longer a significant factor influencing the employer's propensity to use collective bargaining. For anyone concerned about the protection of employment standards, the notable implication is that it has been those workers whose comparative lack of skills made them more dependent upon collective bargaining who have been the greatest losers. It is thus not only that the protections of collective bargaining have been withdrawn from a growing proportion of the British workforce; they have been withdrawn disproportionately from the workers who needed them most.

Distinctive regional differences will be of interest to labour historians aware of deep-rooted variations in local traditions of collectivism. Collective bargaining has not been abandoned uniformly across Britain. By comparison with the South-East, and allowing for differences in industrial structure, workplace size and so on, Scotland and the North-West were significantly more likely to use collective bargaining to fix pay. The separate year regressions indicate that these differences have persisted over the last quarter century. However, there was greater regional variance in the use of collective bargaining in 1984 than there was in 2004. In 1984, employers in Wales, the West Midlands and Yorkshire and Humberside were all more likely than employers in the South-East to set pay via collective bargaining, but these differences had disappeared as early as 1990. In summary, distinctive local traditions of collectivism appear to be in decline.

A substantial change that might have affected collective bargaining has been the growth of overseas ownership. Between 1981 and 2004, the proportion of shares owned by investors outside Britain rose from 4 per cent to 36 per cent. Foreign ownership might be expected to be a relevant factor in determining whether an employer uses collective bargaining. Has the remarkable growth in foreign ownership over our period been one of the factors driving out collective bargaining? It has not. Foreign ownership was not a statistically significant factor in the incidence of collective bargaining in any of the separate year analyses, nor in the pooled years' regression.

Does the shrinking of collective bargaining simply reflect the changing structure of the economy? Is it mainly a consequence of the collapse of many of its traditional heartlands? A common assertion is that union decline is due in large part to the decline both of the manufacturing industry and of the large workplaces that were once so conducive to union organisation. We can use the separate year models to estimate the probability of collective bargaining, making the artificial supposition that variables such as industrial distribution and size remained constant over time. In this way, we can establish how much of the 29 percentage-point decline in the incidence of collective bargaining in the private sector is due to change in these observable characteristics, as opposed to change that takes place within these characteristics.

The remarkable result is that only around one-tenth of the decline in the workplace incidence of collective bargaining in the private sector is due to compositional change. The remaining nine-tenths is due to within-group change, which might be interpreted as a change in, for example, employer and employee preferences and other factors that are independent of the observable characteristics of the workplace we included in our analysis. We can thus confidently reject the proposition that compositional change in the economy has played a major part in diminishing the role of collective bargaining in Britain.

We might speculate that workplaces adopting collective bargaining in the more hostile environment of the 1980s and 1990s did so with less commitment than those where it was already established. It may be that the form of collective bargaining adopted in the late 1990s and 2000s, when 'workplace partnership' was strongly advocated by the TUC, was more shallow-rooted than the typically more confrontational form that employers had faced before. Certainly case-studies in the early 2000s suggested that, unless there were high levels of union membership, worker influence tended to be superficial and partnership fragile (Oxenbridge and Brown, 2004). Employers had adjusted to relatively settled policies towards collective bargaining. For many, it was of a more co-operative 'partnership' form than would have been the case twenty years earlier.

But, however settled this less confrontational form of collective bargaining may now appear to be, the disturbing implication of the data for private sector trade unionists is that the decline in coverage of collective bargaining does not appear to have lost momentum. This is apparent from the survey year coefficients in Table 2.3. Having accounted for observable workplace characteristics, the probability that a workplace set pay for at least some of its workers using collective bargaining fell by 29 per cent between 1984 and 2004. This is only a little smaller than the change in raw percentages presented in Table 2.2. The decline of around 8 per cent between 1998 and 2004 is statistically significant, and implies an annual rate of decline not very different from that estimated for the 1990s.[3] The decline in trade union membership that had commenced in 1980 may have been plateauing out by the start of the twenty-first century, but collective bargaining was continuing to retreat.

The coverage of workers

We have identified trends in the incidence of collective bargaining and its correlates, but how does this translate into the percentage of workers covered by collective bargaining? This is depicted in Figure 2.1. It shows a steady decline in bargaining coverage across all three major sectors of the economy between 1984 and 2004. This continued in the private sector through to 2004, whereas coverage in the public sector recovered

---

[3] Although superficially at variance with the finding of Kersley et al. (2006:188) that the rate of decline was slowing, their analysis did not take account of the other variables included in our analysis.

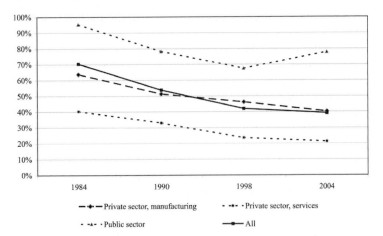

Figure 2.1 Percentage of employees covered by collective bargaining, 1984–2004. Note: workplaces with 25+ employees

a little, due in large part to collective bargaining in the National Health Service over changes in terms and conditions arising from the Agenda for Change initiative (Kersley *et al.*, 2006: 185). At the start of the period, seven in ten workers across the economy had their pay set through collective bargaining. This had slumped to four in ten twenty years later.[4] In manufacturing, coverage declined by a third over the twenty years. In the growing private services sector, it halved.

What form does the contraction of collective bargaining coverage take at the workplace? With WERS, we are able to go a stage further than household surveys such as the Labour Force Survey by observing the distribution of employee collective bargaining coverage within workplaces. Focusing once again on the private sector, collective bargaining has tended to become an 'all or nothing' feature of workplaces. As its coverage diminishes, so employers tend increasingly to polarise between those who use it for most of their workforce, and those who have abandoned it altogether. Private sector workplaces where a minority of workers are covered are becoming a rarity. Between 1984 and 2004, for example, the proportion of workplaces with any collective bargaining fell from 47% to 16%. Where collective bargaining did take place, the proportion of workplaces for which it encompassed 80% or more of the workplace rose from 58% in 1984 to 77% in 2004. But the proportion of those where fewer than 50% of workers were covered fell from 14% to 8%. It

---

[4] This figure is based on employees working in workplaces with at least twenty-five employees. Coverage is lower in smaller workplaces (Kersley *et al.*, 2006: 179–83).

has become harder for a trade union to maintain a minority presence in a workplace.

This polarisation in union presence at the workplace is partly a consequence of the change in the level at which pay-fixing decisions are made, which in part reflects a change in the structure of bargaining. On the one hand, employers have tended to move towards comprehensive pay-fixing arrangements for their workplaces, whether or not those involve collective bargaining (Kersley *et al.*, 2006: 184). On the other hand, we have seen the demise of the sort of multi-employer industrial agreements that might, for example, provide a basis for pay for a minority who are skilled craftsmen within a workplace which otherwise fixed pay without union involvement. To this we now turn.

The changing level of pay-fixing decisions

We have discussed the retreat from collective bargaining in the private sector. The closely related question is the organisational level at which decisions about pay were made, whether or not they resulted from bargaining or from management dictat. Until the 1960s, a patchwork of industrial agreements dominated private sector pay fixing in Britain. Employer organisations and trade unions negotiated agreements that covered whole sectors – carpet making, electrical contracting, shipbuilding, and so on – on behalf of their member employers. Most of these agreements were nationwide in coverage. A controversial feature of multi-employer bargaining by the 1960s had been the increasing tendency for employers to augment the industrial agreements to which they were committed with locally bargained additions. In many sectors, the pay rates arising from national agreements would be added to in various ad hoc and informal ways – such as piecework pay, merit rates, factory bonuses, questionable overtime pay and so on. Indeed, the consequent phenomenon, known as 'wage drift', and the high level of workplace disputes that accompanied it, had been a central concern of a Royal Commission of the 1960s (the Donovan Commission) into Britain's industrial relations malaise.

Then, from the 1960s onwards, and with gathering pace, employers began to break away from these multi-employer agreements to single-employer bargaining, as indeed the Donovan Commission had urged (Brown, 1981). Initially, they tended to prefer to reach agreements with their own workforces in single-employer agreements. In multi-plant companies, these single-employer agreements were sometimes at the level of the whole company, sometimes of separate divisions within it, and sometimes they were at the level of individual workplaces. Later, employer

Table 2.4 *Principal locus of pay decision-making in the private sector (by percentage of workplaces covered)*

	1984	1990	1998	2004
Collective bargaining total percentage of which	39	30	16	14
Multi-employer bargaining	18	9	3	3
Multi-site, single-employer bargaining	13	15	9	7
Workplace-level (single-employer) bargaining	8	6	4	3
Not collective bargaining total percentage of which	59	69	79	85
External to organisation (e.g., wages council)	10	6	6	2
Higher management within organisation	17	20	30	37
Management at the workplace	32	43	43	46
Don't know	2	2	5	1
Total percentage	100	101	100	100

Notes: The table identifies the level at which decisions are made for the pay method covering the most workers at the workplace. If a majority of workers at the workplace had their pay determined via collective bargaining they are identified as 'collective bargaining' workplaces, otherwise they are labelled 'not collective bargaining'.
Source: WIRS/WERS data. Private sector workplaces with 25 or more employees.

preference tended to shift away from dealing with unions at all. Table 2.4, represented in diagrammatic form in Figure 2.2, shows what happened next.

There is a clear trend after 1984 for firms to continue to bring pay determination in-house. This is evident, whether pay was fixed by collective bargaining or unilaterally by management. Where collective bargaining was the main pay-fixing method, it is reflected in the near disappearance of multi-employer bargaining. This shrank at a much faster rate than collective bargaining per se so that, by 1998, it was the dominant mode of pay setting in only 3% of private sector workplaces in Britain. Where workplaces were single and independent (the traditional client of employer associations), the proportion covered by multi-employer agreements fell from 15% in 1984 to only 1% in 2004. This is a miniscule level in historical terms, bearing in mind that thirty-five years earlier, along with the now-defunct wages councils, multi-employer agreements had covered something over 60% of private sector employees (Milner, 1995: 85). It was a change reflected in the decline of their industry-based employer associations. Between 1980 and 2004, the proportion of private sector establishments that reported being members of employer associations fell from 31% to 13%.

Further analyses revealed that bargaining at more than one level also diminished, although the main decline was not until the 1990s, a

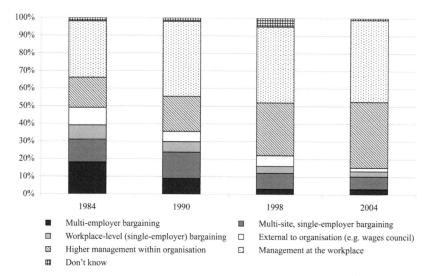

Multi-employer bargaining

Multi-site, single-employer bargaining

Workplace-level (single-employer) bargaining

External to organisation (e.g. wages council)

Higher management within organisation

Management at the workplace

Don't know

Figure 2.2 Locus of decision making within the main type of pay determination in the private sector, 1984–2004, by workplace (>24 employees)

quarter century after the Donovan Commission had criticised the practice. Private sector employers appear to have been relatively slow to break whole-heartedly away from the apparent comfort of industrial agreements. To do so was, after all, to break with long traditions of employer solidarity in the face of the trade union challenge.

The nature of the shift to in-house pay fixing becomes clearer if we separate out single, independent establishments from those that are part of larger organisations. Workplaces where management fixed pay autonomously at the workplace level, expressed as a percentage of all single, independent private sector workplaces, rose from 59 per cent in 1984 to 92 per cent in 2004. In other words, in the great majority of single-site firms, the fixing of pay has come to be almost universally the task of on-site management. But in organisations with multiple workplaces, there was a tendency from the 1990s onwards to shift the locus of decision making over pay away from the workplace. In the 1980s, fixing pay unilaterally at the establishment level was reported to be as common as at a higher level in the organisation. By 2004, it was almost twice as likely to be fixed at a higher level. Freed from trade union constraints and old worries about their 'comparability claims', employers have become both more able to respond to the opportunities and pressures of local labour markets, but also more able to follow wider corporate strategies.

It fits the picture referred to in Chapter 1, of increased local responsibility within tighter organisational targets.

Product market competition and collective bargaining

Collective bargaining has always been heavily influenced by the nature of the product market in which it occurs. The labour market is important insofar as the bargaining strength of labour, once organised, is influenced by the demand for and supply of its services. For a particular occupation within a given labour market, an increase in demand for that occupation will tend to increase its bargaining strength. The product market has a different sort of influence. In a perfectly competitive product market, there is theoretically nothing to bargain over; if a union were to force an employer to pay above the market clearing wage levels then, unless there were productivity gains not available to competitors, that employer would go out of business.

Product markets are, however, rarely perfectly competitive. Employers, to a greater or lesser degree, may have some degree of monopoly power by virtue of transport costs, brand names, consumer loyalty, patents or whatever. In such circumstances they are in a position to earn supra-normal profits, or 'rents'. Unions can be expected to target sectors and firms which have relatively high profits. By organising the workers in firms facing relatively light competition, unions seek to win a share of rents arising from partial monopoly. Such a share may, for example, be in the form of enhanced pay or of more control over manning levels or the conduct of work. Tougher competition in the product market poses a fundamental challenge to collective bargaining. This typically arises because retailers operating in a given product market get access to producers able to produce a particular good or service at lower labour cost, operating in labour markets beyond the organising reach of the trade union. Or the firms themselves may relocate to such labour markets. Without rents to bargain over, or without the organisational capacity to force the employer to concede a share, the union is denied the main economic basis of collective bargaining (Brown, 2008).

How far does the changing character of product market competition in Britain explain the collapse of collective bargaining that we have described? WERS since 1984 has asked employers in the private sector various questions about their competitive circumstances. One was whether the competition for their main product or service was primarily local, regional, national or international. This is a question of clear relevance because of the unavoidable geographical constraints on trade union organisation, and also because of the historically local origins and loyalties of employers' associations. Model 2 in Table 2.3 suggests that the probability of using collective bargaining was around 11 to 12 per cent higher among employers facing local competition than it was among otherwise comparable employers exposed to more widespread competition.

Workplaces in non-local product markets are thus significantly less likely to have collective bargaining than those in local markets. This reflects the observation of John Commons a century ago, that co-operation (or collusion) among employers in the management of labour is more feasible when they are in local competition with each other. This typically occurs when transport costs are high as a proportion of value added, or when the service is provided direct to the consumer (Commons, 1909). But this shelter for collective bargaining has been eroding. Analyses for separate years revealed the associations had diminished from 15 per cent in 1984 to 8 per cent in 2004. A local product market offers considerable support for collective bargaining, but the support it provides is declining. Solidarity among employers (as among workers) appears to be getting harder to mobilise, even at the local level.[5]

Competition from abroad has presented a challenge to successive British industries over the years – textiles, shipbuilding, coal mining, footwear and steel making are just some of the great industries it has almost wiped out. During the post-war years of trade union prosperity, those industries that were organised by unions mostly declined with their collective bargaining institutions intact, if ultimately ineffective. The encroachment of international competition on domestic product markets has increased during our twenty-five year period. It is, then, perhaps surprising that the proportion of private sector workplaces covered by WERS which reported that their market competition derived from international sources was roughly constant – 19 per cent in 1984 and 15 per cent in 2004. Furthermore, there was no evidence that international competition was more detrimental to the presence of collective bargaining than either regional or national competition.

The explanation may be that firms and sectors with earlier exposure to tougher competition from overseas were better adapted to the ever-harder competitive environment of the 1980s and later. Whether or not they had retained collective bargaining, they had fewer adjustments to make. This apparent paradox may also arise because competitive pressure can take the form of increased exposure of local firms to national and international capital markets, rather than product markets. Ownership is increasingly divorced from the locality or country. Company ownership

---

[5] This result is not sensitive to the inclusion of variables capturing the number of competitors the establishment faces.

has increasingly moved into the hands of institutional shareholders such as pension funds and insurance companies, or of foreign shareholders with no particular national allegiance. Such owners might be expected to be more demanding than the private British shareholders who dominated ownership thirty or forty years earlier. Anecdotally, this has placed growing pressure on local managers to deliver higher rates of return.

Another indicator of the competitive strain under which firms operated during the period from 1984 to 2004, wherever they were located geographically, was the number of competitors they perceived themselves to have. The surveys suggest that collective bargaining was more likely in those firms that claimed they 'dominated' the market than those where they reported up to five competitors, and that again was greater than where they reported more that six competitors. This is fully consistent with our underlying story about the dominance of product market competition. Furthermore, the pattern of collapse in the use of collective bargaining also reflected these different degrees of competition. The proportion of workplaces using collective bargaining to set pay fell by 35% between 1984 and 2004 in firms reporting they dominated their market; by 62% for those reporting up to five competitors; and by 70% for those with over six competitors. By 2004, those firms that reported that they dominated their product markets were around twice as likely to have some collective bargaining as those that reported 'a few' competitors and those with 'many' (the figures are 31, 18 and 15% respectively). Similar associations were evident for the percentage of workforces covered by collective bargaining. This sensitivity of collective bargaining to the number of the employer's competitors has been observed in previous studies (Metcalf, 2003b). That these effects cease to be evident when other factors, such as industrial sector, are controlled for, confirms that the competition association is also closely linked to sectoral and other characteristics.

A third way of exploring the influence of product markets is to see how far changes in collective bargaining were related to changes in 'rents', for which profitability might provide a reasonable proxy. Here we considered not a subjective perception of the relevant managers, but sectoral evidence of profitability from official statistics. This is provided by the EUKLEMS data set.[6] Figure 2.3 shows the percentage of employees

---

[6] The data set contains financial information collected from official national data sources for seventy-one two-digit industries over the period 1970–2004. In our analyses we use capital compensation and capital compensation/number of employees to proxy industry profitability for the fifty-one industries common to EUKLEMS and WERS. For further information go to: www.euklems.net/. We gratefully acknowledge the advice provided by Ana Rincón-Aznar on the use of the data.

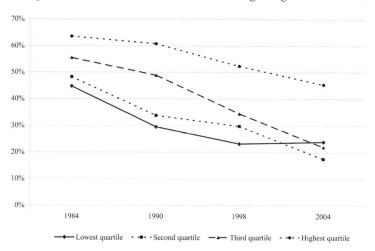

Figure 2.3 Percentage of employees covered by collective bargaining, by quartiles of the industry profit distribution at time of survey (Source: WERS for collective bargaining coverage; EUKLEMS for industry profits (capital compensation)

in WERS workplaces covered by collective bargaining, as distributed by industrial profitability. Workplaces were divided into quartiles in terms of their industry's location in the profits distribution at the time they were surveyed. Those in the lowest quartile are in the bottom quarter of the industry profits distribution, while those in the highest quartile are in the top quarter.

Collective bargaining coverage is clearly more widespread in workplaces with higher profits. Figure 2.3 shows that this is broadly evident throughout the period. This supports the view that employers are less resistant to trade unions where there are rents to share. Furthermore, the figure shows that, while collective bargaining coverage declined over the period whether profits were at high or at low levels, the decline was much less pronounced for the highest quartile. While on the retreat almost everywhere, collective bargaining has retained a foothold longer in those workplaces in sectors where profits were highest.

Let us use the same data to focus a little more on the dynamics of the profitability change and collective bargaining coverage. In Figure 2.4 we again distinguish between four groups of workplaces, but this time we categorise them according to whether they remain in the bottom or top half of the profits distribution over time, or whether they remain in the same half of the profits distribution. As would be expected from our earlier discussion, collective bargaining held up best in workplaces in

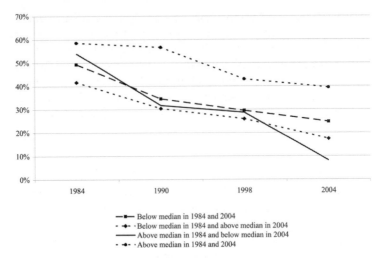

Figure 2.4 Percentage of employees covered by collective bargaining in industries above and below the median profit per head (Source: WERS for collective bargaining coverage; EUKLEMS for industry profits (capital compensation)

industries that have maintained the highest profitability over the period. They include, for example, financial intermediation, wholesale trading and food and drink manufacture. Those industries which had consistently low profitability – which include, for example, construction and non-electrical machinery manufacture – saw their bargaining coverage decline, but at about the average rate.

It is the contrasting experience of industries whose profitability fortunes changed that is of particular interest. Both saw collective bargaining decline. But those whose relative profitability improved, from being below the median in 1984 to above the median in 2004, saw much less of a decline than those whose relative profitability declined. The former, the by 2004 comparatively 'nouveau riches' industries – which include retail, and legal, technical and advertising services – saw a halving in the coverage of collective bargaining between 1984 and 2004. By contrast, those experiencing a comparative profits squeeze over the period – which include hotels and restaurants, and electrical machinery manufacture – saw bargaining coverage decline five-fold. While the revival in profitability in an industry is clearly not enough to revive bargaining coverage, profitability collapse does appear to be associated with something close to the collapse of collective bargaining.

All this confirms the intimate link between collective bargaining and the fortunes of the product markets within which it is conducted. Over our quarter century, collective bargaining has retreated fastest in those work-places that, relative to others, were in product markets with particular competitive characteristics. Their workplaces faced more geographically local competition. They confronted more competitors. Their industries had lower profit levels. And their industries faced a relative worsening of profitability. The growth of collective bargaining in the twentieth century had been nurtured by imperfect competition. Tightening product market competition suffocated it.

Privatisation – a 'natural experiment'

A final way of looking at the question of how far product market change accounts for the retreat of collective bargaining is to take a very timely 'natural experiment'. This was the privatisation of many industries, almost all of them highly unionised industries, over the period under consideration. Between the mid-1980s and the late 1990s, at different times but with similar briskness, whole industries were exposed to the rigours of private sector competition. What happened to collective bargaining?

We got a glimpse of the diversity of response from the broad sectoral divisions in Table 2.2. For the energy and water sector, the bulk of privatisations took place in 1986 in gas, in 1989 in water, and between 1990 and 1998 in electricity. But the coverage of all workplaces by collective bargaining remained between 94 and 96% throughout. Another major sector affected was transport and communication. Here privatisation was a more extended process. For air transport it started in 1987, with ports following around 1992, buses around 1994 and rail around 1996. Telecommunications privatisations were spread from 1984 to 1993. Table 2.2 shows that the coverage of collective bargaining fell, but less than proportionately, from 73% of workplaces in 1984 to 60% in 1998, rising slightly to 63% in 2004. The third of the table's broad sectors affected by privatisation was 'other services'. Dominated by government, this sector saw a large number of relatively small privatisations of research laboratories, regulatory agencies, leasing, property, broadcasting and fringe defence operations between 1990 and 2003. And here, by contrast, Table 2.2 shows the fall in coverage in collective bargaining to have been disproportionately large, from 86% in 1984 to 53% in 2004. This diversity calls for further investigation. Does it undermine our argument concerning the role of product market competition in the decline of collective bargaining?

Crucial to answering this question is the fact that privatisation has not been, by any means, the royal road to perfectly competitive product markets. There is no necessary relationship between private ownership and free markets. Many of the industries sold off to the private sector had unavoidable elements of natural monopolies – railways, water, gas, electricity, communications, for example. Their product markets are to some extent inherently uncompetitive. Indeed, in acknowledgement of this, all these have official regulatory bodies – Ofrail, Ofwat, Ofgem and Ofcom – committed to minimising their abuse of this position.

Providing trade unions could maintain their organisational strength – as they could, for example, with the railways, but not with many out-sourced civil service operations – they could maintain collective bargaining coverage. A private sector natural monopoly is potentially at least as vulnerable as a public sector one to being affected by a well-organised union. There are, consequently, many privatised firms where collective bargaining flourishes. Their aircraft pilots, train drivers, dockers, power station workers, refinery technicians, filter-bed staff, telephone engineers and so on remain highly unionised. Their pay and working conditions continue to be fixed by collective bargaining, although mostly by a form of collective bargaining less all-embracing than when their predecessors were nationalised. In summary, the uneven fortunes of collective bargaining in the wake of privatisation reflects the uneven success of privatisation in eliminating natural monopolies.

Let us now explore the impact of privatisation in greater detail. To identify which WERS workplaces belonged to privatised industries we looked at the percentage of workplaces that were privately owned in each highly disaggregated industry over time. Those moving from pre-dominantly public ownership to largely private ownership were classified as 'privatised' industries. This was the case even though not all of the workplaces in those industries were privately owned by the end of the period. However, in nearly all cases the industry was predominantly publicly owned pre-privatisation, and was largely privately owned post-privatisation.[7] From this information we derived two measures of pri-vatisation. The first was a dummy variable identifying whether a WERS workplace belonged to an industry that was privatised over the period. The second variable distinguished between industries that were priva-tised early in the period (1980–84), those privatised in the middle period (1984–1990) and those privatised late on (1990–2004).[8]

---

[7] The exceptions were construction, road haulage and property which were predominantly privately owned at the outset but became almost exclusively privately owned.

[8] We coded our data at four-digit SIC level. The time series data contains SIC 1980 codes for all years except 1998 when we conducted the same exercise using SIC 1992 codes. The industries identified as privatised were: electricity generation; gas supply; water supply; chemicals manufacture; shipbuilding; train manufacture; aerospace; construc-tion; railways; bus and coach services; road haulage; supporting services to sea trans-port (including docks); supporting services to air transport (including British Airports

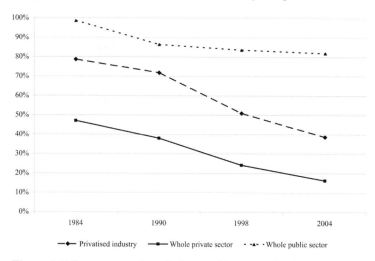

Figure 2.5 Percentage of workplaces with any collective bargaining (Source: WERS 1984–2004)

We start with the overall picture. How did privatisation affect collective bargaining in the industries affected? Figure 2.5 presents the incidence of collective bargaining at workplace level for the whole private sector, the whole public sector and for workplaces in industries that were privatised over the period. At the outset, workplaces belonging to industries that were eventually privatised looked more like public sector workplaces than they did private sector workplaces in terms of their use of collective bargaining. During the course of the next two decades, collective bargaining incidence declined more rapidly in these workplaces in privatised industries than it did in the private sector in general. The decline in the public sector was modest by comparison.

This clearly suggests that privatisation increased the rate of decline in collective bargaining. To test it more formally, we introduced the privatisation indicator into the regression analysis reported in Model 1 in Table 2.3. The coefficient was negative but statistically non-significant. But when we allowed the privatisation effect to vary by year, the analysis revealed a clear time trend in the privatisation effect. Allowing for other workplace characteristics, workplaces in privatised industries had a

Authority and Civil Aviation Authority); telecommunications; real estate; refuse collection and street cleaning; higher education; hospitals; social/residential homes; community services (including tourist offices). WERS does not contain some industries that were privatised, such as coal mining. The timing of privatisations corresponds with other sources, such as the privatisation barometer (www.privatizationbarometer.net/database/php).

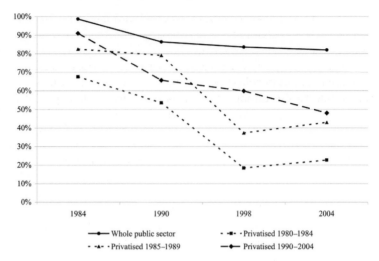

Figure 2.6 Percentage of workplaces with any collective bargaining, public sector versus privatised sector (Source: WERS 1984–2004)

higher pre-privatisation incidence of collective bargaining coverage than other comparable workplaces. But the subsequent decline in collective bargaining, after privatisation happened, was greater than it was for other, unaffected workplaces between 1990 and 2004, as is suggested by Figure 2.5. The impact of privatisation on collective bargaining was relatively slow to emerge, coming through after 1990. This reflected the fact that many privatisations were occurring around that time, while some still had to take effect, and it is to be expected that there was a lag between privatisation and changes in the new owner's collective bargaining policy.

Analyses for single years tell the same story. In 1990, workplaces belonging to those industries targeted for privatisation were about 10 per cent more likely to have collective bargaining than otherwise comparable workplaces. By 1998, there was no statistical difference between workplaces in privatised industries and other workplaces. However, by 2004 the full effect had come through. Workplaces in privatised industries had a 10 per cent lower probability of collective bargaining than unaffected workplaces when controlled for other observable differences. Far from the public sector traditions of collectivism living on after privatisation, there seems to have been an adverse reaction against them by management.

We address the timing of industry privatisations more directly in Figure 2.6, which compares the incidence of collective bargaining in the whole public sector with its incidence in privatised industries, distinguishing between early, mid-period and late privatisations. We see again that the percentage of workplaces using collective bargaining for at least some of their employees has remained high in the public sector throughout the period. In contrast, privatised industries have seen substantial declines in collective bargaining coverage. But the patterns differ according to the timing of privatisation. First, it is apparent that early privatisations up to 1984 were targeted on industries with relatively low collective bargaining incidence.[9] Examples would be British Petroleum, Associated British Ports and Cable and Wireless. As privatisation progressed, so the government shifted its focus to politically tougher industries with higher levels of collective bargaining. For example, British Aerospace, British Gas, British Airways, Rolls-Royce, British Airports Authority, British Steel and the water boards followed in the years to 1989. After 1990, major privatisations included the electricity industry, British Telecommunications, the coal industry and the railways. Privatisation was pushed deeper and deeper into the traditional heartlands of collective bargaining.

It is notable that coverage of collective bargaining among workplaces located in industries that were privatised in the 1980s continued to fall throughout the 1990s. It is also apparent from Figure 2.6 that collective bargaining incidence was already in decline in late-privatised industries prior to their privatisation. It is possible that this reflects employers' anticipation of privatisation. The post-privatisation decline in the coverage of collective bargaining in the later privatised industries has been less steep than the decline that occurred shortly after privatisation in the earlier privatised industries. But the incidence of collective bargaining in industries privatised in the 1980s appears to have stabilised since New Labour came to power in 1997. Employers' treatment of trade unions has always been sensitive to their perceptions of government attitudes. New Labour may have sought to avoid looking too friendly towards unions, but their 'arms length' approach was undeniably more tolerant than that of their Conservative predecessors. This evidence suggests that New Labour's arrival reduced the destructive effect of privatisation on collective bargaining.

How robust are these findings about the adverse effect of privatisation on collective bargaining? We carried out additional regression analyses in which we replaced the dummy variable for privatisation with a variable distinguishing between the three phases of privatisation identified in Figure 2.6. Those workplaces in sectors that remained in the

---

[9] Because Figure 2.5 suggests some delay in the impact of privatisation, we take the 1984 level as indicative of the extent of bargaining before privatisations began for the 1980–4 group.

Table 2.5 *Incidence of collective bargaining coverage, comparing workplaces in privatised industries with those in the public sector, OLS*

	Pooled	1984	1990	1998	2004
When privatised (ref: always public)					
1980–84	−0.230	0.035	−0.073	−0.429	−0.406
	(4.20)**	(0.46)	(0.46)	(4.99)**	(3.42)**
1984–90	−0.127	−0.099	0.143	−0.204	−0.233
	(4.25)**	(2.72)**	(2.42)*	(2.09)*	(4.18)**
1990–2004	−0.058	−0.098	0.208	−0.099	−0.403
	(1.37)	(1.69)	(2.65)**	(1.84)	(2.71)**
WIRS 1990	−0.107				
	(3.64)**				
WIRS 1998	−0.170				
	(6.12)**				
WIRS 2004	−0.196				
	(6.80)**				
Constant	0.813	0.811	0.583	0.705	0.763
	(13.57)**	(9.18)**	(4.01)**	(5.75)**	(6.68)**
Observations	2932	788	675	786	683
R-squared	0.36	0.43	0.36	0.42	0.42

Note: Models include controls for region (10 dummies), industry (9 dummies), foreign ownership, proportion of part-time employees.
Source: WIRS/WERS data. Workplaces with 25 or more employees.
*p < 0.1, **p < 0.05.

private sector throughout the period were dropped from the analysis. The results are presented in Table 2.5. It confirms that, throughout the period, workplaces in privatised industries were less likely to have used collective bargaining compared with 'like' workplaces in industries that remained publicly owned throughout. More importantly, Table 2.5 sheds some light on the timing of privatisation effects. The effects of early privatisation (1980–4) were not significant in the 1990 survey, but became statistically significant by 1998 and persisted into 2004. There is a negative association between mid-period privatisation (1984–90) and collective bargaining incidence in 1984, consistent either with a rapid privatisation effect or else a pre-existing lower coverage differential in these workplaces relative to their public sector counterparts. In any event, the negative effect had doubled by the late 1990s and persisted into 2004. In the case of late privatisations (1990–2004), despite having a fairly high probability of collective bargaining at the outset in 1990, their probabilities of collective bargaining incidence were 40 per cent lower than those of comparable public sector workplaces by 2004.

In summary, there can be no doubting that privatisation has been a major contributor to the decline of collective bargaining. It has done this by exposing hitherto sheltered industries to increased product market competition. It is true that collective bargaining does live on in some privatised sectors, but the main reason for that is that those sectors enjoy natural monopolies. The experience of privatisation reinforces our over-riding argument, that collective bargaining in Britain has been eroded by increasing product market competition.

Conclusion

This has been the story of the decline of the principal means of protecting labour standards in Britain. Collective bargaining developed over the twentieth century as a result of employers being able to compromise with organised labour. They could do this so long as the markets in which they traded were sufficiently imperfect in their competition. In this study we have used the unique data of the WERS to demonstrate that tougher competition has undermined this tacit settlement between employers and their employees' trade unions. Labour standards in the modern workplace have become more vulnerable as a result.

3 Trade union decline and the economics of the workplace

David G. Blanchflower and Alex Bryson

Introduction

The past quarter century has been extraordinarily bad for trade unions. Falling union membership has been a feature for most developed countries in the last quarter century (Ebbinghaus and Visser, 1999; Visser, 2003). Although unionisation generally remains an important feature in public sector employment, trade union decline in the private sector has been rapid. Britain is no exception. It has seen a substantial fall in the propensity of workers to join unions. Accompanying this has been a fall in the incidence of workplace-level union recognition by employers for pay bargaining.

It is often assumed that union decline is an inevitable consequence of structural change in the economy and, in particular, of the demise of large-scale manufacturing plants. But, while the departure of once strong union bastions has indeed deprived them of members, employer engagement with unions depends on more than their industrial location. In Britain's voluntarist climate, engagement has always been an employer choice, albeit one constrained by worker bargaining power. Nor are unions necessarily incapable of colonising new workplaces and new occupations.

It is also often assumed that union decline must, inevitably, entail a diminution in the effects that unions have on workers and on firms. But, while the effects of unions on workers and firms across the economy as a whole will inevitably diminish with their coverage, it is unclear, a priori, what effect unions will have on those workplaces that remain unionised. Their impact will depend on their ability to do what they have traditionally done, namely to bargain on behalf of their members using their ability to control labour, and to act as the representative voice of workers to management (Freeman and Medoff, 1984). Whether they are able to do so depends, in part, on what sort of union organisations remain at the local level, and how strong they are. It also depends upon firms'

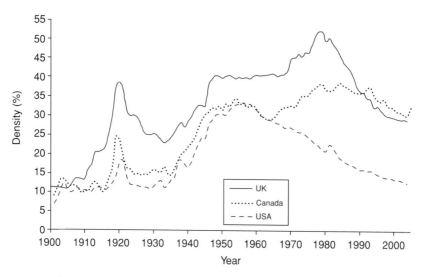

Figure 3.1 Union density, Canada, the United States and the United Kingdom, 1900–2004

preparedness and ability to either resist their demands or accommodate them.

Figure 3.1 shows the history of overall union membership density rates in Britain, the USA and Canada over the past century. It is apparent that all three countries saw a rising trend with a peak at the end of the First World War, and another at the end of the Second World War. Britain and Canada saw further increases during the 1960s and 1970s. Both Britain and the United States have experienced dramatic declines in density since the late 1970s. The US decline started in the 1950s and predates that of Britain that started around 1980, the year in which the first Workplace Industrial Relations Survey was conducted.

There have, however, been substantially different trends in union membership density in the public and the private sectors in all three countries. Table 3.1 provides details of changes in overall density rates as well as in the public and private sector by year since 1993 for Great Britain. The Labour Force Surveys and WIRS/WERS broadly agree on the picture of declining union density, and also on the substantially different experience in the private and the public sectors. The distinctive story of the public sector will be discussed in Chapter 13, and we shall not touch it further here.

In this chapter, we examine the decline in unionisation in the private sector. In asking first why it has happened, we consider the role played

Table 3.1 *Union decline in Great Britain*

Union membership	Private	Public
1993	24.0	64.4
1994	22.8	63.6
1995	21.5	61.4
1996	20.7	60.9
1997	19.8	60.8
1998	19.5	61.0
1999	19.3	59.9
2000	18.7	60.0
2001	18.5	59.0
2002	18.1	59.3
2003	18.1	58.8
2004	17.1	58.4
2005	17.1	58.2
2006	16.5	58.5
Union recognition	Private	Public
1980	50	94
1984	48	99
1990	38	87
1998	24	87
2004	22	87
Union density – employee weighted	Private	Public
1980	57	84
1984	45	81
1990	36	72
1998	25	58
2004	20	58

Sources: Union membership: Grainger and Crowther (2007) using individual data from the autumn Labour Force Surveys, 1993–2006 (quarter 4 in 2006); union recognition and union density: Blanchflower and Bryson (2008) using WIRS/WERS data.

by the changing composition of workplaces in terms of industry, region, size and so on. We then turn to the consequences of the decline for the economic life of the workplace. We look at changes in the impact of unions on four sorts of outcome. What has happened to their effect on wages? Has there been any change in their impact on employment growth? Has their decline affected the firms' financial performance? And what have been the consequences for a more elusive contextual aspect of the economic performance of the firm, the climate of relations between managers and workers? Our primary data source is the five surveys in the WIRS/WERS series conducted in 1980, 1984, 1990, 1998 and

2004. These cover workplaces that employ at least twenty-five employees, either full or part-time. Because this size-threshold was lowered in the more recent surveys, for some investigations we include workers in workplaces with five or more employees. The twenty-five-employee selection rule means that the survey covers roughly two-thirds of employees each year. These surveys exclude the self-employed, whose numbers rose to approximately 13 per cent of workers over the period (Blanchflower and Shadforth, 2007).

The decline in private sector union recognition

The simplest method of dividing workplaces into those that are unionised and those that are not is to establish whether the employer recognises unions for pay bargaining. In WIRS/WERS union recognition relates to whether one or more unions are recognised for purposes of bargaining over pay and/or conditions for one or more groups of workers at that workplace. This coverage may arise from an agreement at workplace, organisation or industry level.

Table 3.2 reports union recognition rates in the private sector in 1980 and 2004 by workplace characteristics. The most striking finding is that union recognition has fallen precipitously across every workplace characteristic – no sector or group has been immune. The decline in recognition rates has been greatest in the energy and water sector, the East and West Midlands, and the biggest workplaces, all of which experienced declines of over 40 percentage points. Declines were smallest in 'other services' (−5 percentage points) and in East Anglia (−7 percentage points), where unionisation rates have traditionally been very low. In both 1980 and 2004, the workplaces with the lowest union recognition rates were single independent establishments. Workplaces in the energy and water sector were the most heavily unionised at the beginning and the end of the period, despite experiencing rapid de-unionisation.

We earlier saw that 1980 was a watershed in union membership; it appears also to have been one in terms of workplace union recognition. The recognition rate among workplaces set up prior to 1980 is double that for workplaces set up in the 1980s onwards. Millward *et al.*, commenting on this cohort effect, speculated that the move away from union recognition may, in fact, have started much earlier, perhaps as early as the early post-war period (2000: 101–3). Chapter 2's analysis of collective bargaining is consistent with this. But Table 3.2 points to another interesting phenomenon: the decline in union recognition among workplaces set up before 1980. Their union recognition rate fell from 50 per cent in 1980 to 32 per cent in 2004 – a decline of just over one-third.

Table 3.2 *Private sector union recognition rates by workplace characteristics, 1980 and 2004*

	% with recognition		% point fall
	1980	2004	1980–2004
Industry:			
Energy/water	99	58	41
Mineral/chemicals	67	55	12
Metal/engineering	65	27	38
Other manufacturing	65	27	38
Construction	52	19	33
Distribution/hotels & catering	36	12	24
Transport/communications	59	39	20
Banking, etc.	54	26	28
Other services	26	19	7
Region			
East Anglia	42	37	5
East Midlands	59	18	41
North	55	16	39
North-West	60	19	41
Scotland	62	41	21
South-West	54	21	33
Wales	71	36	35
West Midlands	65	21	44
Yorkshire and Humberside	54	37	17
South-East	38	15	23
Establishment size			
25–49	41	20	21
50–99	50	13	37
100–199	65	36	29
200–499	75	48	27
500+	92	48	44
Single independent	30	6	24
Belongs to multi-site firm	58	29	29
Foreign owned	49	27	22
Domestically owned	50	22	28
Establishment age			
<5 years old	38	18	20
5–9 years old	46	13	33
≥10 years old	51	25	26
Decade workplace was born			
Birth <1980	50	32	18
Birth 1980s	–	16	–
Birth 1990s	–	15	–
Birth 2000s	–	18	–

Source: WIRS/WERS data. Workplaces with 25 or more employees.

There has also been a decline in union recognition rates among those set up in the 1990s: in 1998, their recognition rate was 20 per cent, but this had fallen to 15 per cent by 2004.[1] This is surprising. It is often argued that union derecognition is a relatively rare occurrence in Britain, and that the demise of unions is largely accounted for by new workplaces choosing not to recognise trade unions (Willman *et al.*, 2007). The evidence here suggests that this is not the whole story by any means. Workplace closure rates are largely unaffected by unionisation (Machin, 1995; Bryson, 2004a; Bryson and Dale-Olsen, 2008), so that much of the decline in the unionisation rate among older workplaces may be due to union derecognition.[2] More important, however, is that new workplaces are being born that are primarily non-union.

What are the circumstances under which union recognition has persisted? To establish the independent effect of workplace characteristics on union recognition we ran linear probability models of union recognition using Ordinary Least Squares (OLS) estimation for each of the five years of data pooled together (Table 3.3, column 1), and then separately for each year in the remaining columns. These equations estimate the probability of a randomly selected workplace being unionised, conditional on its characteristics. The models account for roughly one-fifth of the variance in union recognition in Britain. The results are broadly consistent with those reported earlier that were based on the descriptive means. There has been a decline in the probability of union recognition with time, primarily between 1980 and 1998. But since 1998 there has been little change; indeed, the difference in coefficients between 1998 and 2004 is not statistically significant.

There are substantial and persistent industry differences: the distribution, hotels and catering sector has by far the lowest probability of unionisation, while the energy and water sector has the highest. There are also sizeable region effects in all years, with the probability of unionisation being the lowest in the South-East of England. Throughout the period the probability of recognition tends to rise with workplace size, but this effect has weakened a little over time. The negative effect of being a single independent establishment, on the other hand, has remained strong and persistent over time, reducing the probability of recognition by around one-quarter. The table also includes three variables capturing the workforce composition at the workplace, namely the proportion of females,

---

[1] Substantial declines are also apparent among workplaces set up in the 1980s. The union recognition rate was 47 percent among this group in 1980–4, but this had fallen to 16 percent by 2004.

[2] Bryson (2004a) finds some evidence of a positive union effect on workplace closure, but the effect is sensitive to the closure measure used.

Table 3.3 *Union recognition, private sector, 1980–2004*

	(1) Pooled	(2) 1980	(3) 1984	(4) 1990	(5) 1998	(6) 2004
Industry (ref: other services)						
Energy and water	0.395	0.387	0.237	0.490	0.592	0.206
	(6.21)**	(3.93)**	(1.54)	(4.32)**	(9.77)**	(0.94)
Minerals, chemicals	0.108	0.079	0.030	0.181	0.005	0.308
	(1.99)*	(0.78)	(0.28)	(1.59)	(0.06)	(2.07)*
Metal, engineering	0.034	0.147	0.030	−0.017	0.006	0.026
	(0.91)	(1.67)	(0.31)	(0.18)	(0.09)	(0.31)
Other manufacturing	0.108	0.148	0.138	0.069	0.146	0.106
	(3.07)**	(1.69)	(1.49)	(0.79)	(2.25)*	(1.27)
Construction	0.041	0.020	0.006	0.075	0.115	−0.009
	(0.87)	(0.20)	(0.05)	(0.59)	(1.11)	(0.11)
Distribution and hotels	−0.093	−0.061	0.038	−0.098	−0.136	−0.131
	(3.28)**	(0.85)	(0.49)	(1.41)	(2.58)**	(2.68)**
Transport and communication	0.167	0.115	0.312	0.206	0.142	0.161
	(3.59)**	(1.05)	(2.46)*	(1.93)	(1.88)	(1.87)
Banking and finance	0.063	0.051	0.220	0.072	0.034	0.004
	(1.87)	(0.52)	(2.24)*	(0.85)	(0.62)	(0.06)
Region (ref: South-East)						
East Anglia	0.033	0.046	−0.113	−0.041	0.009	0.141
	(0.75)	(0.55)	(1.27)	(0.46)	(0.13)	(1.53)
East Midlands	0.083	0.159	−0.003	0.100	0.091	0.055
	(2.80)**	(2.33)*	(0.04)	(1.27)	(1.79)	(1.02)
North	0.110	0.180	0.188	0.083	0.061	0.009
	(2.90)**	(1.98)*	(1.73)	(0.92)	(1.23)	(0.16)
North-West	0.158	0.157	0.219	0.103	0.198	0.102
	(5.58)**	(2.65)**	(3.11)**	(1.49)	(3.19)**	(2.25)*
Scotland	0.154	0.232	0.032	0.079	0.098	0.280
	(4.72)**	(3.49)**	(0.39)	(1.28)	(1.71)	(3.80)**
South-West	0.078	−0.104	0.162	−0.006	0.110	0.114
	(2.24)*	(1.58)	(1.96)	(0.08)	(1.66)	(2.10)*
Wales	0.192	0.241	0.294	0.091	0.106	0.204
	(4.11)**	(2.04)*	(2.23)*	(0.81)	(1.32)	(2.35)*
West Midlands	0.123	0.236	0.153	0.013	0.098	0.096
	(4.04)**	(3.40)**	(2.05)*	(0.16)	(1.45)	(1.84)
Yorkshire and Humberside	0.112	0.165	0.245	0.027	−0.042	0.205
	(3.26)**	(2.58)**	(3.33)**	(0.40)	(0.89)	(2.75)**
Establishment size (ref: 25–49 employees)						
50–99	0.034	0.082	0.099	0.041	0.039	−0.088
	(1.79)	(1.85)	(2.04)*	(0.91)	(1.11)	(2.51)*
100–199	0.144	0.132	0.240	0.069	0.195	0.096
	(6.56)**	(2.96)**	(4.58)**	(1.45)	(4.73)**	(2.02)*
200–499	0.253	0.209	0.246	0.262	0.330	0.198
	(10.91)**	(4.32)**	(4.50)**	(4.87)**	(7.63)**	(4.09)**
500+	0.325	0.298	0.399	0.303	0.410	0.200
	(13.79)**	(6.75)**	(7.73)**	(5.71)**	(7.98)**	(3.72)**

Table 3.3 (*cont.*)

	(1) Pooled	(2) 1980	(3) 1984	(4) 1990	(5) 1998	(6) 2004
Foreign	−0.093	−0.154	0.005	−0.024	−0.204	−0.068
	(3.57)**	(2.23)*	(0.07)	(0.37)	(5.34)**	(1.60)
Single	−0.230	−0.301	−0.167	−0.227	−0.186	−0.259
	(12.51)**	(8.01)**	(3.38)**	(5.41)**	(5.54)**	(7.52)**
Workplace age (ref: 10+ years)						
<5 years	−0.049	−0.118	−0.021	−0.106	−0.048	−0.011
	(1.87)	(1.80)	(0.25)	(1.98)*	(1.14)	(0.21)
5–9 years	−0.105	−0.063	−0.089	−0.243	−0.055	−0.095
	(4.56)**	(1.25)	(1.42)	(5.39)**	(1.14)	(2.70)**
Proportion female	−0.078	−0.122	−0.225	−0.083	0.011	−0.035
	(1.85)	(1.47)	(2.00)*	(0.93)	(0.12)	(0.39)
Proportion part-time	0.020	−0.170	−0.022	−0.043	0.125	0.016
	(0.45)	(1.53)	(0.15)	(0.39)	(1.35)	(0.23)
Proportion non-manual	−0.070	−0.202	−0.234	−0.069	0.006	0.024
	(2.54)*	(2.79)**	(3.04)**	(1.03)	(0.13)	(0.56)
Survey year (ref: 1980)						
WIRS 1984	−0.012					
	(0.44)					
WIRS 1990	−0.116					
	(4.41)**					
WIRS 1998	−0.213					
	(8.35)**					
WIRS 2004	−0.241					
	(9.30)**					
Constant	0.496	0.572	0.490	0.472	0.188	0.239
	(11.73)**	(5.86)**	(5.14)**	(4.87)**	(2.79)**	(3.06)**
Observations	5840	1273	1081	1189	1241	1056
R^2	0.22	0.27	0.19	0.19	0.21	0.23

Source: WIRS/WERS data, t-statistics in parentheses. Workplaces with 25 or more employees.
*p < 0.1, **p < 0.05.

the proportion of part-timers and the percentage of non-manual workers. In the early period, the probability of union recognition was lower in workplaces with a high proportion of non-manual workers and those with a high proportion of female employees. However, these effects have disappeared over time, mirroring the disappearance in the union membership gap between males and females and manual and non-manual workers (Bryson and Gomez, 2003).

It is sometimes argued that union decline is largely due to death of old industries and of large workplaces, which were once strongholds of unionism. Table 3.2 showed that this is far from being the whole story,

Table 3.4 *Effects of compositional and within-group change on union recognition, private sector 1980–2004*

Year	1980	2004
Actual union recognition rate	49.5	22.3
Percentage point decline	–	−27.2
Rate with compositional change only	–	40.8
Percentage point decline due to compositional change	–	−8.7(32%)
Percentage point decline due to within-group change	–	−18.5(68%)

Note: to obtain these figures we generate the predicted probability of union recognition using the 1980 and 2004 models in Table 3.3. The change in union recognition due solely to compositional change is obtained by applying the predictions under the 1980 model to the 2004 sample. The resulting union recognition rate is the rate that would have obtained in 1980 with 2004 workplace characteristics, that is, with compositional change alone. The difference between this rate and the overall change in union recognition is due to within-group change.

Source: WIRS/WERS data. Workplaces with 25 or more employees.

since union recognition declined across all sectors and types of workplace. To establish how much of the decline is accounted for by compositional change, we use the models in Table 3.3 to predict what the recognition rate would have been if the composition of workplaces had remained constant since 1980. The results are presented in Table 3.4. Roughly one-third of the 28 percentage-point decline in private sector union recognition is attributable to changes in workplace characteristics that are contained in the model. The remaining two-thirds of the decline is not related to the structure of workplaces or their workforce composition, but to 'within-group change', which might be interpreted as the choices employers make, conditional on their observable characteristics. This finding is consistent with studies which suggest that a large part of the decline in unionisation is due to employers turning their back on trade unions – preferring to 'go' or 'remain' non-union, or reduce the range of issues for which recognition is effective (Bryson *et al.*, 2004; Brown *et al.*, 1998). It is also consistent with the analysis of the decline of collective bargaining discussed in Chapter 2. A strong reason for employers turning their backs on trade unions is probably the costs that they impose at the workplace, an issue to which we now turn.

How have union effects on workplaces changed?

What are the implications of this massive decline in unionisation for economic outcomes at the workplace? What have been the consequences for wages, employment, financial performance and, a more amorphous notion with implications for effective management, the climate of employment relations? We need to distinguish between trade unions' impacts on unionised workplaces, on the one hand, and on the non-union sector, on the other.

The impact that unions have on unionised workplaces arises in part from the direct impact they have on pay determination and as a 'voice' mechanism, although their impacts on less tangible issues such as innovation and the organisation of work will also be important (Freeman and Medoff, 1984). A priori, it is unclear what the impacts of shrinkage in the unionised sector will be on those workplaces that remain unionised. Are the unions that remain the stronger ones in terms of their local and national organisation, as might be the case if the weaker had gone to the wall? Alternatively, are the unions that remain the weaker organisations that have such a minimal impact that employers are happy to tolerate them or let them simply 'wither on the vine? Even if the stronger union organisations are among the survivors, at a time when union influence has been diminishing generally at the workplace (as evidenced by the fading away of industrial action in most of the private sector), their bargaining strength is likely to have diminished. The impacts of union decline will depend in large part on the bargaining strength of the unions that remain, compared to their strength back in 1980.

There are two schools of thought regarding the bargaining power of unions at workplace level. The first is that most of that power has gone, primarily because of increased competition from the growing domestic non-unionised sector and lower labour cost competitors elsewhere in the world. The result is that any union success in bargaining wages and conditions above market-determined levels will erode the firm's competitive advantage, unless those additional costs can be recouped with improved productivity. In this narrative, the only reason unions remain in place at all is because employers do not need to take account of them and may, in some instances, find them useful in effecting workplace changes. They are, to some extent, hollow shells.

The second school of thought is that, whilst the first story is often true, there are many instances in which unions continue to monopolise the supply of labour to firms that are less dependent on labour cost-based comparative advantage for their profits. These firms include those in highly regulated sectors and those in product markets facing little or no domestic or foreign competition. Indeed, it is arguable that it is only those unions that are in such relatively strong positions that have been able to survive the wider decline. Chapter 2 has developed this argument in its investigation of the decline of collective bargaining. WIRS/WERS data for the period through to 1998 suggested that there was a bifurcation of union strength in British workplaces. Some union organisations continued to show signs of organisational strength in terms of high membership and high collective bargaining coverage, but there was a long tail of weaker organisations (Millward *et al.*, 2000).

When Freeman and Medoff addressed the question 'what do unions do?', they concluded that they 'compressed things' – not just wages, but other things too. However, the influence of union behaviour may spill over into the non-union sector through two countervailing forces. First, it may produce employment spillover from the union to the non-union sector by setting above-market terms and conditions which lead to union job loss. This results in a queue for jobs in the non-union sector that employers can use to their advantage to keep terms and conditions lower than they might otherwise be. This depresses conditions in the non-union sector. On the other hand, the risk that workers might join unions in order to obtain union-like conditions means non-union employers may pay higher wages than they might otherwise have paid in the absence of unions. The threat of unionisation thus encourages them to improve on market-clearing rates (Rosen, 1969). The massive decline in unionisation has important implications for employment-related outcomes in the non-union sector, because it may affect the size and extent of both employment spillover and threat effects. When unions are pervasive and strong – as they were in the early 1980s – these impacts can be expected to be very marked. However, when unions are largely absent, as is now the case in much of the private sector, one would expect these union spillover and threat impacts to be muted.[3]

How are union impacts estimated? Let us take the example of wage effects. Usually union effects are estimated as $(W_u - W_n)/W_n$ where W_u is wages in the union sector and W_n is wages in the non-union sector. However, the overall union effect can only be estimated relative to a scenario in which unions are wholly absent. This scenario can be written as $(W_u - W_a)/W_a$ where W_u is wages in the union sector and W_a is wages in the same economy absent unions. It is coming closer in the private sector in Britain, especially when one considers the tail of small firms that are invariably non-union which do not appear in WIRS/WERS. Nevertheless, a union sector still exists, so union activity may still affect the non-union sector. These effects on the non-union

---

[3] We can gauge the decline in the union threat effect from the predicted probability of union recognition among non-union workplaces using the models reported in Table 3.3. Under these models, the mean predicted probability of union recognition among non-union workplaces fell from 37 per cent in 1980 to 18 per cent in 2004. This halving of the threat effect is of a similar magnitude to the actual fall in workplace union recognition over the period.

sector can be thought of as $(W_n - W_a)/W_a$ where W_n is the wage in the non-union sector. Such impacts on the non-union sector may, as has been discussed, be either positive or negative: it is an empirical question.

This framework can be extended using the same formulation to estimate the impact of unions on outcomes other than wages. The literature on this is extensive (Bennett and Kaufman, 2007). With these thoughts in mind, we consider the impacts of unions at the workplace, in turn, on wages, employment growth, financial performance and the climate of employment relations. We do not seek to distinguish between unions' direct effects on the union sector and their spillover and threat effects in the non-union sector. Our estimates can be interpreted as the net impact of these effects combined.

Wages and salaries

Early studies examined the impact of union recognition on wages using the 1980 and 1984 WIRS (Blanchflower, 1984; Blanchflower, 1986; Stewart, 1987; Blanchflower et al., 1990). These indicated that the impact of unions on wages differed across types of worker, with manual workers tending to receive a higher union premium, driven in part by the closed shop. Since then, the closed shop has been legislated against and has effectively disappeared; workplace-level union density has declined, and it has become increasingly difficult for unions to monopolise the supply of labour to firms (Millward et al., 2000). The demise of the union sector and the attenuation in union bargaining power might have resulted in a lower threat effect on wage setting in the non-union sector. In spite of these developments, union threat effects appeared to have continued to raise the wages of workers in the non-union sector in the 1998 WIRS (Belfield and Heywood, 2001). What is more, union members continued to earn higher wages than non-members, controlling for other factors. Although the premium has diminished in recent years, it seems that the decline is, at least in part, a counter-cyclical rather than a secular decline (Blanchflower and Bryson, 2007).[4]

Estimates of the union wage premium in the first three WIRS relied on managers' responses to questions on wages and unionisation relating to 'typical' workers from a variety of skill groups such as semi-skilled and skilled manuals, clerical workers and middle managers. Since 1998, the surveys have provided linked employer/employee data that allows us to estimate the impact of union membership and union recognition on employees' wages at the level of the individual. Table 3.5 reports

[4] Blanchflower and Bryson (2003) find evidence for a counter-cyclical union wage premium in Britain and the United States in the last three decades of the twentieth century.

Table 3.5 *Union membership (UM) hourly wage premium, WERS 2004, private sector workplaces*

	25+ employee workplaces			5–24 employee workplaces		
	UM dummy only	UM + controls	UM + controls + recognition	UM dummy only	UM + controls	UM + controls + recognition
Union member	0.082	0.058	0.064	0.198	0.090	0.079
	(7.83)**	(6.84)**	(6.94)**	(7.13)**	(3.66)**	(2.95)**
Union recognition			−0.011			0.031
			(1.24)			(1.13)
DK if union recognition			0.032			−0.168
			(1.93)*			(3.96)**
Observations	11,894	11,838	11,838	2,746	2,742	2,742

Notes: (1) UM = union membership; (2) interval regression for hourly wages, unweighted, robust estimator. T-stats in parentheses; (3) Controls are: male, age (10 dummies), academic qualifications (9 dummies), vocational qualifications (4 dummies), health problems, non-white, full-time employment, occupation (10 dummies), firm size (3 dummies), single establishment organisation, industry (10 dummies), workplace aged 25+ years, foreign owned, largest occupational group (8 dummies).
Source: WIRS/WERS data.
*p < 0.1, **p < 0.05.

estimates of the union membership and union recognition wage premia in the private sector using WIRS 2004. The first three columns estimate union effects on the traditional WIRS population in workplaces with at least twenty-five employees. The remaining columns run the same estimates for the population in smaller workplaces with five to twenty-four employees, traditionally omitted from WIRS.

If we take workplaces with at least twenty-five employees, the union membership premium in 2004 was around 8 per cent, dropping to 5–6 per cent with the inclusion of detailed individual job and workplace controls. There appeared, however, to be no premium associated with union recognition. This finding is robust to the exclusion of the union membership variable. If one compares the wages of union members with non-members in the same workplaces (by replacing the workplace controls with workplace fixed effects) the premium attached to membership is 4 per cent.[5] These findings suggest that the union wage premium attached to workplace union recognition that had been identified in analyses of early WIRS has disappeared. However, there remains a small but statistically significant premium associated with union membership. The picture is rather different among the smallest workplaces with five to twenty-four employees. Here the raw union membership premium is 20 per cent but falls by half when controls are added. It remains 8 per cent when union recognition is added. Although there is no premium attached to union recognition in models incorporating union membership, if union membership is removed, much of the premium attached to it transfers to the union recognition variable.[6] If one replaces the workplace-level variables with workplace fixed effects, the membership premium in workplaces with five to twenty-four employees is 8 per cent.

There are three striking conclusions. First, the exclusion of the smallest workplaces from the traditional WIRS/WERS sample has resulted in an underestimate of union effects on wages. Second, the union recognition wage premium is confined to the smallest workplaces. Third, union membership continues to generate a wage premium.[7]

Table 3.6 gives equivalent evidence from the autumn Labour Force Surveys (LFS), which provide information on both wages and union membership status since 1993. The premium has fallen a little from around 6% in 1993–9 to 3% in 2000–6. Among the traditional

[5] The membership coefficient is 0.040 (t = 4.13).

[6] In the small workplace model with controls, but excluding membership, the union recognition coefficient is 0.061 (t = 2.45).

[7] To establish whether there was any union threat effect we ran estimates for workers in non-unionised workplaces incorporating the predicted probability of workplace union recognition as an explanatory variable. It was not statistically significant.

Table 3.6 *Private sector union/non-union hourly wage differentials, 1993–2006*

	(1) 1993–9 all	(2) 1993–9 <25 employees	(3) 1993–9 ≥25 employees	(4) 2000–6 all	(5) 2000–6 <25 employees	(6) 2000–6 ≥25 employees
Union	.0566	.1144	.0452	.0277	.0933	.0121
	(11.67)	(9.86)	(8.62)	(6.23)	(9.29)	(2.45)
Age	.0656	.0592	.0706	.0635	.0561	.0697
	(75.72)	(43.89)	(62.06)	(82.77)	(48.39)	(67.79)
Age2	.0007	.0006	.0008	.0007	.0006	.0008
	(65.65)	(38.35)	(53.70)	(73.05)	(43.00)	(59.74)
Male	.2011	.1852	.2096	.1718	.1576	.1817
	(47.87)	(25.29)	(41.21)	(46.38)	(25.07)	(39.82)
Black	.1538	.1003	.1746	.1649	.1396	.1727
	(8.28)	(2.94)	(8.02)	(11.13)	(5.28)	(9.76)
Asian	.1682	.1698	.1670	.1315	.1432	.1206
	(12.41)	(6.93)	(10.41)	(12.54)	(7.72)	(9.58)
Chinese	.0202	.0602	.0620	.1459	.1534	.1161
	(0.49)	(1.07)	(0.96)	(4.43)	(3.16)	(2.58)
Other races	.0312	.0133	.0388	.1105	.1115	.1040
	(1.55)	(0.38)	(1.58)	(7.23)	(4.24)	(5.59)
Constant	.3263	.3057	.3457	.8946	.8941	.8633
Size dummies	6	3	3	6	3	3
Schooling dummies	40	40	40	47	47	47
Adjusted R^2	.4549	.3487	.4722	.4624	.3686	.4867
N	63,295	23,942	39,353	74,323	28,626	45,697

Notes: All equations also include 6 year dummies, 21 region of work dummies and 61 industry dummies; Excluded category is white. Employees only. T-statistics in parentheses.
Source: LFS 1993–2006 autumn quarters.

WIRS/WERS population of employees in workplaces with twenty-five or more employees, the premium has fallen from 4–5% to a mere 1%. As in the case of the WERS 2004 analysis, the premium is bigger among those employees in smaller workplaces. In the LFS, the membership premium among those in workplaces with fewer than twenty-five employees is 11% in 1993–9 and 9% in 2000–6. Thus the decline in the premium since the early 1990s is largely confined to those in the population of workplaces of twenty-five employees and over. It is unclear why the membership wage premium should be much larger in smaller workplaces throughout the period.

It appears that the wage effect of trade unions has diminished over the course of our quarter century, whether one considers union membership or union recognition. For workplaces of twenty-five or more employees, a small premium continues to be associated with union membership, but no longer with union recognition. What is of particular note concerns smaller workplaces, with five to twenty-four employees, where individual employees have always been more dependent, for better or worse, upon their employer. Our findings imply that workers in these small workplaces enjoy a disproportionately large wage premium from both union membership and union recognition.

Employment growth

What has been happening to the influence of unions on employment at the workplace? The WIRS/WERS literature has focused on changes in workplace employment levels in the private sector. Early studies used retrospective data from managers on employment levels in earlier years to estimate union effects on employment change. More recent studies have begun to use the WIRS/WERS panel data to obtain more accurate information. A priori, union effects on employment growth are ambiguous. The higher wage costs associated with trade unions might induce employers to substitute capital for labour, such that employment levels are lower in both the union and the non-union sector. On the other hand, if unions' ability to bargain a greater share of the employers' profits (or 'capture rents', as economists might say) discourages capital investment, this may limit capital substitution. If unions improve productivity by, for example, enabling effective workplace partnership, thus enhancing the firms' competitiveness, it is conceivable that employment levels and growth will be higher in the union than the non-union sector. In spite of these conflicting theoretical propositions, studies tend to find that the average effect of union recognition is to lower employment growth by 2.5–4 per cent per annum relative to non-union workplaces, ceteris paribus (Blanchflower et al., 1991; Machin and Wadhwani, 1991; Bryson, 2004b; Addison and Belfield, 2004). This has led some analysts to refer to the employment impact of unions as the 'one constant' in studies of unions' economic effects (Addison and Belfield, 2004).

In all years except 1980, mean workplace-level employment growth was positive (Table 3.7, row 1). In every year employment growth was faster in non-union than union workplaces (rows 2 and 3). Following the WIRS/WERS tradition, Table 3.7 presents unweighted estimates of union effects on employment levels at the time of the survey. The raw unadjusted gap is statistically significant in three of the five years (row 4).

Table 3.7 *Union effects on employment growth among private sector workplaces with 25 or more employees*

	Pooled	1980	1984	1990	1998	2004	1990–2004
All	.032	–.003	.013	.024	.075	.043	.049
Union	.003	–.016	–.007	.014	.022	.024	.003
Non-union	.048	.001	.033	.029	.092	.048	.048
Raw gap	–.029(5.24)**	–.030(2.64)**	–.033(2.44)**	–.015(1.15)	–.029(2.38)**	–.014(1.05)	–.020(2.63)**
Regression-adjusted gap	–.018(2.88)**	–.018(1.41)	–.037(2.59)**	–.006(0.41)	–.014(1.05)	–.008(0.53)	–.009(1.07)

Notes: (1) Rows 1, 2 and 3 are unconditional weighted means for log employment growth which is log ((employment in t minus employment in previous year)/employment in previous year) having removed 12 outliers; (2) Row 4's 'raw gap' is the union recognition coefficient (t-statistics in parentheses) for unweighted OLS estimates of log employment in time t. Log employment in t-1 is one of the explanatory variables; (3) Row 5's regression adjusted gap in log employment controls for log employment in t-1; single-digit SIC; region; single; foreign; % female; % non-manual; workplace age.

Source: WIRS/WERS data.

*p < 0.1, **p < 0.05.

The regression analysis, in row 5, conditions on the same workplace features as those used in the analyses of financial performance below, but replaces establishment-size dummy variables with continuous lagged employment one year previously (see the table footnote for details). This regression-adjusted gap (which controls for other workplace characteristics) is only significant in 1984. This is a surprising result since it runs counter to the general view that there is a robust negative association between unions and employment growth. However, we formally tested for a trend in union effects over time by interacting union recognition with year dummies in the pooled analysis. They were not jointly significant; nor were the interactions significantly different from the 1980 base year. Thus we are unable to reject the hypothesis that there has been no significant change in the underlying negative union effect apparent in the pooled regression.

The conclusion we draw from this is that there is evidence from the whole period 1980–2004 that unions have lowered employment growth, but that this is driven primarily by effects in the early 1980s. The evidence from the later period suggests that there are no effects. But we do not find significant year/union interactions, mostly because of the large standard errors of the estimates from the later years.[8] The final column pools the three later years and, even though there is a significant raw union gap, this disappears when controls are included. It appears that there are no union employment effects in the data since 1990. The result was the same when we experimented using union density rather than recognition. While unions may have had an adverse association with employment growth at the workplace during the 1980s, this has disappeared more recently.

Financial performance

Past evidence suggests that unions enhance productivity where management are supportive of the union (Freeman and Medoff, 1984; Bryson et al., 2006), and where they are associated with high-performance management practices (Bryson et al., 2005). Unions also appear to have closed the productivity gap with the non-union sector in the 1980s (Bryson et al., 2005). Nevertheless, the broad consensus is that British unions have either a negative or neutral impact on labour productivity (Metcalf, 2003a; Pencavel, 2003). If unions are unable to compensate for the union wage premium with better productivity than the non-union

---

[8] The 95 per cent confidence intervals for the union recognition point estimates were as follows: 1990 −.03 to +.02; 1998 −.04 to +.01; 2004 −.04 to +.02.

sector, this implies that they hit company profits. Their actions may adversely affect profits in other ways too. For instance, their ability to capture rents might reduce firms' incentives to invest, while industrial action can damage the reputation of a firm with customers or directly affect its ability to sell goods or services (Metcalf, 2003a). For these reasons, one might expect unions to have an adverse impact on firms' financial performance.

Since 1980, WIRS/WERS has asked managers: 'Compared with other establishments in the same industry, how would you assess your workplace's financial performance?' Respondents choose an answer on a five-point ordinal scale from 'a lot above' to 'a lot below' average. This subjective measure reflecting the impressions of employment relations managers is not ideal. In practice, however, it appears to provide a reasonable measure of performance in that it has been shown to be predictive of subsequent closure probabilities and does not appear to be systematically biased with respect to union measures (Machin and Stewart, 1996). It is this measure that has been exhaustively analysed over the last quarter century (Metcalf, 2003a; Bryson et al., 2005). Early studies found unions were negatively associated with workplace financial performance in the 1980s (Blanchflower and Oswald, 1988). By WIRS 1990, the relationship between unions and financial performance was highly contingent on unions' interaction with other factors such as market conditions, workplace practices, firm size and union strength, which led to speculation that unions' ability to extract rents from firms had diminished over the 1980s (McNabb and Whitfield, 1997; Bryson, 1999; Addison and Belfield, 2001; Machin and Stewart, 1996). By 1998, most studies were finding no significant relationship (Bryson and Wilkinson, 2002; Addison and Belfield, 2001).

Differences in methodologies across studies make it difficult to be sure about trends in the association between unionisation and workplace financial performance. We overcome this problem in Table 3.8, which compares union/non-union differences in financial performance for each WIRS using an identical approach (see footnotes to the table for details). Row 1 shows the score for all workplaces in each WIRS; every year, on average, managers score their own workplaces slightly 'above average'. Rows 2 and 3 present the means for union and non-union workplaces. Managers in unionised workplaces tend to score their workplaces more poorly than managers in non-union workplaces, but the raw gap is not significant after 1984 (row 4). This gap may be due to differences between union and non-union workplaces rather than to unionisation itself, so in the final row we present regression-adjusted estimates of the gap. The pooled analysis for all years shows a strong negative union effect,

Table 3.8 *Union effects on workplace financial performance relative to industry average among private sector workplaces with 25 or more employees*

	Pooled	1980	1984	1990	1998	2004	1990–2004
All	2.45	2.41	2.40	2.48	2.53	2.49	2.51
Union	2.40	2.37	2.32	2.50	2.51	2.37	2.47
Non-union	2.50	2.46	2.48	2.47	2.53	2.52	2.52
Raw gap	−.319(5.71)**	−.425(3.27)**	−.580(4.23)**	−.161(1.25)	−.001(0.01)	−.155(1.19)	−.122(1.68)*
Regression-adjusted gap	−.219(3.23)**	−.474(2.94)**	−.630(3.83)**	.050(0.31)	−.073(0.49)	−.148(0.96)	−.055(0.63)

Notes: (1) Rows 1 and 2 are unconditional survey-weighted means for financial performance relative to industry average where 1 = below/a lot below average, 2 = average, 3 = above/a lot above average; (2) Row 3's 'raw gap' is the coefficient with z-statistics in parentheses for unweighted ordered logit estimates of the (1, 3) financial performance measure; (3) Row 4's regression adjusted gap controls for single-digit SIC; region; establishment size; single; foreign, % female; % part-time; % non-manual; workplace age.
Source: WIRS/WERS data.
* p < 0.1, ** p < 0.05.

having controlled for the observable features of workplaces detailed in the footnote to the table. However, there has been considerable change over time in the relative performance of union and non-union workplaces. The final column, which pools the last three years, confirms the view that there is no union effect on financial performance once controls are included, and only weak evidence of any effect when they are not. This story broadly reflects the one emerging from the literature to date. Unions were associated with poorer financial performance in the early 1980s. But this difference has since disappeared, and it has been due to an improvement in the relative position of unionised workplaces rather than any deterioration among non-unionised workplaces.[9]

Employment relations climate

The climate of employment relations is an unavoidably subjective notion, but no-one with experience of the world of work would deny its importance for effective working relationships. The higher the level of mutual trust, for example, the easier it is to innovate and adapt to changing economic circumstances. Unions may have an adverse effect on managerial perceptions of the climate of employment relations where the bargaining process creates a polarised, 'them and us' mentality. On the other hand, some employers value a more independent role played by unions, and they view the dialogue it offers as a means of achieving more harmonious employment relations. In the strike-prone years in which the WIRS/WERS series was launched, unions were popularly associated with industrial action. WIRS played an important role in furnishing policy makers and academics with a range of climate-type measures to aid understanding of what engendered better employment relations in the workplace. Among these measures was a question, asked of managers, that has been asked in every WIRS: 'How would you rate the relationship between management and employees generally at this workplace?' Respondents are asked to rate relations on a five-point scale from 'very good' to 'very poor'. This measure turns out to be associated with other 'climate' measures (industrial action, the number of employment tribunal cases, sanctions against employees, days lost through sickness and absence) in the way one would imagine (Bryson, 2005; Kersley et al., 2006).

---

[9] We formally test for a trend in union effects over time by interacting union recognition with year dummies in the pooled analysis. The interaction effects for later years are statistically significant relative to 1984 (for 1990, .396, $z = 2.08$; for 1998 .500, $z = 2.67$; and for 2004 .366, $z = 1.91$). This is confirmed in analyses for the period 1984–2004 which use the five-point financial performance scale available only in those years.

Table 3.9 *Managerial perceptions of the employment relations climate among private sector workplaces with 25 or more employees*

	1980			1984			1990			1998			2004		
	All	U	NU	All	U	NU	All	U	NU	All	U	NU	All	U	NU
Average	3	3	3	4	4	4	7	12	4	9	8	9	7	10	6
Good	45	49	41	54	61	46	59	60	59	52	53	52	55	58	54
Very good	52	48	56	42	35	50	34	28	37	39	39	39	38	32	40

Notes: U = workplace with recognised union(s). NU = workplace without recognised union(s). Table shows column percentages, survey weighted data; Unweighted N for whole series is 5,805. Union workplaces N = 3,146. Non-union workplaces N = 2,659; 5-point climate scale collapsed into three points: average/poor; good; and very good.
Source: WIRS/WERS data.

Management perceptions indicate an improvement in employment relations climate since 1990, but relations in 2004 were still perceived to be poorer than they were in the early 1980s. In both the union and non-union sectors, the percentage of managers characterising employment relations as 'very good' fell by 16 percentage points between 1980 and 2004 (Table 3.9). Of course, it is possible that the norms and expectations governing what constitutes a 'good' climate have shifted. A relatively harmonious workplace in an era when industrial disputes dominated the press might appear less remarkable in a subsequent period of national industrial peace. If so, it would be difficult to infer change in the real world based on these perceptions. The table also shows that, whereas managerial perceptions of climate were poorer in union workplaces than in non-union workplaces in 1980–90, the gap disappeared in 1998, only to open again in 2004. This demands further investigation.

Table 3.10 takes this descriptive analysis a stage further by isolating the independent effect of union recognition having controlled for other workplace characteristics. The five-point scale is collapsed into a three-point scale, where higher scores indicate better relations (see the footnotes to the table for details).[10] The descriptive means in row 3 show that in the non-union sector managerial perceptions of climate deteriorated markedly between 1980 and 1990, levelling out thereafter. The means in row 2 show that, in the union sector, perceptions of climate fell between 1980 and 1990, but then improved somewhat in 1998 before deteriorating once again by 2004. The raw gaps in perceived climate are sizeable

---

[10] The results reported here are replicated when we use a four-way climate variable that distinguishes between 'poor', 'average', 'good' and 'very good'.

Table 3.10 *Union effects on employment relations climate among private sector workplaces with 25 or more employees*

	Pooled	1980	1984	1990	1998	2004	1990–2004
All	2.35	2.49	2.38	2.26	2.30	2.31	2.29
Union	2.31	2.46	2.31	2.16	2.31	2.22	2.23
Non-union	2.37	2.53	2.46	2.32	2.29	2.34	2.32
Raw gap	$-.371(7.11)^{**}$	$-.556(4.63)^{**}$	$-.815(6.32)^{**}$	$-.525(4.39)^{**}$	$-.233(2.06)^{**}$	$-.585(4.58)^{**}$	$-.442(6.46)^{**}$
Regression-adjusted gap	$-.259(4.08)^{**}$	$-.398(2.70)^{**}$	$-.582(3.87)^{**}$	$-.271(1.87)^{*}$	$-.005(0.04)$	$-.157(1.05)$	$-.142(1.76)^{*}$

Notes: (1) Rows 1, 2 and 3 are unconditional means for employment relations climate where 1 = poor/average 2 = good 3 = very good; (2) Row 4's 'raw gap' is the union coefficient with z-statistics in parentheses for unweighted ordered logit estimates of the (1,3) climate measure; (3) Row 5's regression adjusted gap controls for single-digit SIC; region; establishment size; single; foreign, % female; % part-time; % non-manual; workplace age.

Source: WIRS/WERS data.

* p < 0.1, ** p < 0.05.

and statistically significant in all five years. However, some of the union–non-union difference is accounted for by differences in the characteristics of workplaces in the two sectors. When these differences are taken into account, the regression-adjusted gap was only statistically significant at conventional levels for the three years 1980, 1984 and 1990. The gap was not statistically significant in 1998 and 2004.

This suggests that, while unions may have been detrimental to the climate of employment relations earlier in the period, such an impact disappeared from the later 1990s. However, one has to be cautious when drawing such a conclusion. We formally tested for a trend in union impacts over time by interacting union recognition with year dummies in the pooled analysis. They were not jointly significant at conventional levels. Nor were the interactions significantly different from the 1980 base year.[11] Thus we are unable to reject the hypothesis that there has been no significant change in the underlying negative union effect apparent in the pooled regression. Indeed, even in the final column, which pools the last three years, there is statistically weak evidence of a negative, although smaller, union impact than was observed pre-1990. What is clear is that, if managers thought that union decline would bring about a general improvement in the climate of employment relations, they were wrong. Their responses suggest that managerial perceptions of climate have deteriorated considerably since the early 1980s across the whole private sector, whether the workplace is unionised or not. This deterioration seems to have occurred in the 1980s, with perceptions recovering a little since then, but remaining well below the perceptions of good climate in the early 1980s.

To establish whether this finding was peculiar to the managerial perceptions of WIRS/WERS respondents, we ran regressions using the British Social Attitudes Surveys (BSAS) for all employees in employment working ten or more hours over the period 1983–2005. The means in the first row of Table 3.11 show employees' perceptions of the climate of worker/employee relations deteriorated over the period in the 1980s and 1990s, but have since recovered.[12] This pattern is apparent in both unionised and non-unionised workplaces, although, in the case of non-unionised workplaces, perceptions remain less positive than they were in the early 1980s. Throughout the period, perceptions of climate were poorer among employees in unionised workplaces than they were

---

[11] The 95 percent confidence intervals for the union recognition point estimates were as follows: 1998 −.27 to +.26; 2004 −.45 to +.14.

[12] Drinkwater and Ingram (2005) found a U-shaped trend in perceptions of climate using BSAS through to 2000.

Table 3.11 *Union effects on employment relations climate among private sector employees in British Social Attitudes Surveys, 1983–2005*

	Pooled, 1983–2005	1983–1989	1990–1995	1996–2000	2001–2005
All	3.12	3.17	3.06	3.10	3.17
Union	2.96	3.02	2.91	2.91	3.02
Non-union	3.23	3.32	3.20	3.19	3.24
Raw gap	−.724	−.855	−.727	−.700	−.604
	(25.40)**	(14.94)**	(13.78)**	(11.55)**	(10.36)**
Regression-adjusted	−.396	−.483	−.509	−.309	−.288
gap	(10.94)**	(6.36)**	(7.05)**	(4.11)**	(4.19)**

Notes: (1) Rows 1, 2 and 3 are unconditional means for employment relations climate where 1 = not at all good 2 = not very good 3 = good 4 = very good. Unweighted N for pooled regressions is 19,190; (2) Row 4's 'raw gap' is the union coefficient with z-statistics in parentheses for unweighted ordered logit estimates of the (1,4) climate measure; (3) Row 5's regression adjusted gap controls for union membership; female; age (6 dummies); ethnic dummy; region (6 dummies); sector (4 dummies); part-time dummy; social class (8 dummies); years.
Source: WIRS/WERS data.
*p < 0.1, **p < 0.05.

among those in non-unionised workplaces. The raw gap (row 4) is partly explained by observable differences in the characteristics of workers, their jobs and their workplaces, but the regression-adjusted difference remains significant (row 5). Thus, contrary to the WIRS/WERS analysis of managers' perceptions, these findings point to a persistent negative union impact on employees' climate perceptions although, as suggested in the earlier analysis, the gap between unionised and non-unionised workplaces appears to be closing. Once again, any conclusions need to be heavily qualified. Anyone's perceptions of the climate of employment relations within a workplace contains an unavoidable element of comparison, calibrated both by personal memory, which fades, and by perceptions of the employment relations climate in the wider society, which has altered so much over the period in question.

Conclusion

We have investigated the demise of unionisation in the private sector in Britain over the last quarter century, and the impact of this on the economics of the workplace. How far was the decline of unions the result of the closure of the big factories and embattled industries where they had once been so strong? The answer is that this sort of compositional change among workplaces only explains a minor part of union decline. Two-thirds of their decline is not related to changes in the structure of workplaces or their workforce composition, but to other processes, independent of these, influencing employer and employee behaviour. The economic consequences of union decline at the level of the workplace thus reflect much more than the changing fortunes of particular industries.

What have been the economic consequences at the workplace? We argued that theoretical predictions of the impacts of union decline on workplace outcomes are not clear-cut. But the broad picture emerging from our empirical analysis is clearer, and it is one of a widespread change in the economic effects of unions over the course of our period. Our main finding is that the relatively strong impacts of unions observed in the 1980s have diminished and even disappeared. Whether or not one considers a positive impact of unions on wages to be desirable or not depends very much upon whether one is paying wages or receiving them. But such an impact has diminished substantially in the private sector since the 1980s. There is evidence that unions still had a significant impact on wages in 2004, but the size of this is quite small, especially in larger workplaces. Indeed, a notable finding was that, by 2004, the relatively rare presence of union influence in small private sector workplaces of under twenty-five employees was particularly beneficial to the wages of the employees concerned.

In the 1980s, trade unions had a negative association with employment growth, financial performance and the climate of relations between employees and managers. But this apparent union relationship has diminished. There was a significant time trend in the case of financial performance, showing a relative improvement of unionised workplaces relative to non-unionised workplaces since 1984. In the case of employment growth and the climate of industrial relations, there was not a significant time trend, but there was clear evidence that union impacts were diminishing and, by 2004, were not adverse. The decline of trade unions has been associated with a diminution in their apparent impact upon the economics of the workplace.

4   Employee representation

Andy Charlwood and John Forth

Introduction

The stereotypical employee representative of the 1960s and 1970s was a middle-aged, male, trade union shop steward working in the manufacturing or extraction industries. Despite the popular notoriety that this figure enjoyed as portrayed, for example, in the 1959 comedy film *I'm All Right Jack*, the empirical evidence suggests that negative and politically motivated activists such as Fred Kite were relatively rare.[1] The Royal Commission on Trade Unions and Employers' Associations of 1965–8 (Donovan Commission) undertook a systematic investigation of the role of shop stewards in British industrial relations. Its research concluded that they more usually fulfilled the role of a 'lubricant' rather than an 'irritant' (McCarthy and Parker, 1968: 5). Shop stewards typically represented their members by negotiating with foremen in disputes arising, for example, from poorly controlled payment systems. They were more a sticking plaster for managerial failings.

The largely benign image put forward by the Donovan Commission was to be challenged during the 1970s, as high inflation, and government incomes policies to try to control that inflation, led to falling real wages for many workers. In the private sector, stiffer competition in product markets forced managers to challenge prevailing practices. Similarly, in the public sector, work reorganisation and the introduction of incentive pay systems had a marked effect on the tenor of industrial relations, as unions reacted to managerial attempts to challenge custom and practice. Where workers responded, shop stewards emerged as the non-commissioned officers of a militant and angry trade union movement, on the front line of industrial conflict. Spurred by an influx of new, more radical activists into the trade union movement in the years after 1968, the shop steward system spread to areas of the workforce where it had

---

[1] As the term 'shop steward' was that most commonly used in the literature, we use this term throughout this chapter; it could however be used interchangeably with the term 'union lay representative'.

not previously existed (Turner, 2003). It developed, for example, among white-collar employees in the public sector, and was adopted in a more militant, union-like form in industries, such as banking and insurance, where non-union staff associations with lower levels of workplace representation had once been the norm (Jenkins and Sherman, 1979; Hyman and Price, 1983). Union militancy provoked a political response with the election of Mrs Thatcher's Conservative government in May 1979. The broader changes that affected industrial relations in Britain following that election were to have profound effects for trade unions. Union membership fell by 40 per cent, collective bargaining coverage halved, and there was a loss of political influence.

How did these changes affect employee representation in the workplace? Did the numbers of shop stewards fall in line with union membership and coverage? How important was the decline of traditional manufacturing industries in explaining the pattern of change? Have the characteristics of shop stewards altered over time, and has their role changed as the collective power of unions has declined? Looking beyond shop stewards, did a declining preference for unionism combine with legislative support for employee consultation to breed more extensive systems of non-union employee representation? WIRS/WERS provides unrivalled empirical evidence that can be brought to bear upon these questions, which we seek to answer in this chapter. We focus primarily on workplace trade union representatives, which is where the evidence is most plentiful. But non-union representatives will also be discussed, as far as the data allow.

Shop steward organisation in the 1960s and 1970s

There were several attempts to estimate the number of shop stewards in the 1960s and 1970s. Together, they suggested that the network of lay union representatives in British workplaces expanded considerably over that time. McCarthy and Parker (1968: 15) arrived at an estimate of 175,000 stewards in the mid-1960s, with around two-thirds of these in manufacturing plants and the remainder in service sector workplaces. Clegg (1979: 51–2) went on to provide estimates of at least 200,000 for the early 1970s and as many as 300,000 for the end of that decade.[2]

---

[2] These rather rough estimates seemed justified when Brown's authoritative survey of manufacturing plants with fifty or more employees implied that, in 1978, there were 119,000 manual stewards and 37,000 non-manual stewards in these larger manufacturing plants alone (Brown, 1981: 62).

One of the striking things about this expansion in shop steward organisation was that it outstripped the substantial rise in union membership. The result was that the ratio of stewards to union members fell from around 1:50 in the late 1960s to around 1:40 at the end of the 1970s.[3] Shop stewards were also spending more time on union duties. The number of full-time shop stewards (lay representatives permitted by their employer to spend all of their time on union duties) was estimated to have quadrupled between the mid-1960s and mid-1970s (Brown *et al.*, 1978, 144; Brown, 1981: 66). Part of the reason lay in the growing importance of workplace-level collective bargaining (Brown *et al.*, 1978: 147; Clegg, 1979: 12–19; Terry, 1983: 73). This implied a considerable degree of autonomy for shop stewards from their national union organisation, because their primary engagement was with foremen and other lower-level managers.

The contemporary consensus was that this system of representation served the interests of union members reasonably well. However, some of its vulnerabilities were already apparent. Women were under-represented among shop stewards; for example, it was estimated that, in the mid-1970s, only 27 per cent of shop stewards in the National Union of Public Employees were women, compared with 63 per cent of the union's membership (Fryer *et al.*, 1978). There were also some infamous cases of shop stewards promoting racist exclusionary practices against black and minority ethnic workers (Virdee, 2000: 552). Shop steward effectiveness also depended on the attitudes of local managers, and the lack of a robust national union structure was to prove a weakness when managers sought to win back control of work on the shop floor during the 1980s and 1990s.

The incidence of shop stewards, 1980–2004

The Warwick Survey of 1978 had shown that shop stewards were ubiquitous in manufacturing wherever unions were recognised for pay bargaining (Brown, 1981). But apart from the tentative estimates of the overall numbers of stewards mentioned earlier, there was no systematic evidence of the extent of shop steward organisation outside the manufacturing sector. The first column of the upper panel of Table 4.1 uses the WIRS/WERS data set to show that, where unions were recognised for collective bargaining, the spread of shop steward

---

[3] Estimates derived by dividing the the estimated numbers of stewards discussed in the preceding paragraph into the numbers of union members cited by Waddington (2003: 220).

Table 4.1 *Percentage of workplaces with shop stewards of recognised trade unions*

	1980	1984	1990	1998	2004
Where unions recognised	79	83	72	69	62
Sector					
Private manufacturing	86	98	90	92	70
Private services	69	69	59	58	56
Public sector	82	85	73	71	63
All workplaces	50	55	38	26	23
Sector					
Private manufacturing	55	54	40	25	26
Private services	28	30	21	13	11
Public sector	77	84	64	59	55

Source: WIRS/WERS data. Workplaces with 25 or more employees.

organisation in the public sector in 1980 was on a par with the situation in manufacturing, and was only slightly less extensive in private services.[4] The proportion of all workplaces with shop stewards did show considerable variation at the time, as is evident from the first column of the lower panel of Table 4.1, but this was primarily due to differential rates of union recognition.

The ratio of members to stewards was also similar across the three sectors of the economy (Table 4.2), and the figures for manufacturing were broadly in line with those estimated a couple of years earlier by the Warwick Survey (Brown, 1981: 62). The principal difference across the three sectors that emerged from WIRS was that, in private services, a higher proportion of members were located in workplaces without stewards (Table 4.3).

Using the various items of data present in WIRS/WERS, it is possible to arrive at estimates of the total numbers of shop stewards of recognised unions in workplaces with twenty-five or more employees. In 1980, we arrive at an estimate of 328,000 stewards (Table 4.4), indicating that Clegg's estimates were, in fact, rather conservative. The estimates deriving from WIRS for manufacturing were similar to those produced by the Warwick Survey, but WIRS provided the first systematic estimates for private services, which were estimated to support some 42,000 shop

---

[4] The situations in manufacturing and the public sector were not directly equivalent, however, because manual employees had less extensive steward networks in the public sector than in the private sector, but non-manuals were equally well served (Millward and Stevens, 1986: 80).

Table 4.2 *Aggregate number of members per on-site shop steward of recognised unions*

	Number of members per steward				
	1980	1984	1990	1998	2004
All workplaces					
Where at least one steward	25	23	32	30	30
All workplaces	27	25	37	37	38
Private sector manufacturing					
Where at least one steward	26	23	34	32	30
All workplaces	28	24	36	34	33
Private sector services					
Where at least one steward	23	24	36	30	34
All workplaces	30	30	50	41	48
Public sector					
Where at least one steward	24	23	29	30	28
All workplaces	26	25	34	36	35

Note: union members only identified among full-time employees in 1980.
Source: WIRS/WERS data. Workplaces with 25 or more employees.

Table 4.3 *Percentage of union members working in workplaces with at least one on-site shop steward of a recognised union*

	1980	1984	1990	1998	2004
All workplaces	92	93	85	83	79
Private sector manufacturing	95	97	94	92	89
Private sector services	79	81	73	74	72
Public sector	92	94	85	82	81

Note: union members only identified among full-time employees in 1980.
Source: WIRS/WERS data. Workplaces with 25 or more employees.

stewards, and the public sector, which was estimated to have 153,000, and which therefore accounted for the greatest share overall.

The total number of stewards appears to have grown further in the first half of the 1980s to reach an estimated 335,000 stewards by 1984 (Table 4.4), although the increase is not statistically significant. There were important variations, however, with a decline of some 30 percentage points in the number of stewards in manufacturing being offset by considerable gains in private services and the public sector. Further detail

Table 4.4 *Numbers of shop stewards of recognised trade unions, 1980–2004*

	Assuming no change in the total number of workplaces in the population					Independent estimate for 2004
	1980	1984	1990	1998	2004	
All workplaces with 25+ employees						
On-site reps of recognised unions	328,000	335,000	178,000	137,000	102,000	128,000
As percentage of 1980 total		102%	54%	42%	31%	
Average change per annum		+1,800	−26,200	−5,100	−5,800	
Private sector manufacturing						
On-site reps of recognised unions	132,000	94,000	49,000	38,000	18,000	23,000
As percentage of 1980 total		71%	37%	29%	14%	
Average change per annum		−9,700	−7,400	−1,400	−3,300	
Private sector services						
On-site reps of recognised unions	42,000	48,000	29,000	25,000	26,000	33,000
As percentage of 1980 total		115%	70%	61%	63%	
Average change per annum		+1,600	−3,100	−400	+100	
Public sector						
On-site reps of recognised unions	153,000	193,000	99,000	73,000	58,000	72,000
As percentage of 1980 total		126%	65%	48%	38%	
Average change per annum		+10,000	−15,700	−3,200	−2,500	

Notes: On-site representatives of recognised unions in workplaces with 25 or more employees. Totals estimated by keeping the total number of workplaces with 25 or more employees constant at 1980 levels, as we are unable to identify that proportion of the increase (from 135,000 workplaces in 1980 to 169,000 in 2004) which might be attributable to improvements in the coverage of the official business register. We expect this to account for a substantial proportion of the apparent increase, since the total number of employee jobs (albeit in the UK rather than Britain) increased by only 8 per cent over the period (Office for National Statistics, 2008). The figures presented in the second column for 2004 do not fix the total number of workplaces at 1980 levels. Numbers of reps have been rounded to the nearest thousand; average changes per annum have been rounded to the nearest hundred. Average and percentage changes were computed before the rounding of totals. Excludes representatives who are exclusively concerned with health and safety. The standard errors of the 'all workplaces' estimates are in the region of 12,000 reps for 1980 and 1984, 7,000 reps for 1998 and 5,000 reps for 2004. Each of the year-on-year changes for 'all workplaces' are statistically significant, except for 1980–4.
Source: WIRS/WERS data. Workplaces with 25 or more employees.

from the 1984 WIRS showed that, summing across the whole economy, non-manual stewards were nearly as common as manual shop stewards by the mid-1980s (Millward and Stevens, 1986: 84–6). The prevailing stereotypes were clearly in need of some revision.

Despite some high profile incidents around this time in which managers of manufacturing plants had sought to wrestle back control from militant shop stewards, such as the sacking of Derek Robinson at British Leyland's Longbridge plant in 1979, the principal cause of the decline in the number of stewards in manufacturing was a decline in the number of workplaces in the sector that recognised unions. This was the result both of the closure of relatively large manufacturing plants, and the shrinkage of the sector as a whole.

In retrospect, the mid-1980s proved to be a historic turning point, when trade unions' hopes that their fortunes would recover with the economic cycle were dashed. There were defeats in a series of set-piece industrial battles, including the miners' dispute of 1984–5 and the Wapping dispute of 1986–7. At workplace level, the second half of the 1980s also saw a substantial fall in the overall rate of union recognition, from 66 to 53 per cent, and an even more precipitous decline in the number of shop stewards which, in 1990, stood at only 178,000 (see Table 4.4). The number of stewards of recognised unions had fallen by almost half in just six years. As in manufacturing in the early 1980s, the decline in the rate of recognition was one important factor behind the decline in shop steward numbers. But those workplaces that did recognise unions also became less likely to support stewards (Table 4.1), and the average number of stewards also dropped where they were present, causing a considerable rise in the ratio of members to representatives (Table 4.2).

Local union organisation faltered even when the formal structures of influence remained. Further shifts in employment away from manufacturing and the public sector and towards private services, where the steward network was weaker, served only to accentuate the decline. One result of the shrinkage in the steward network was that fewer union members now worked in an establishment that had an on-site lay representative: the proportion fell from 93 per cent in 1984 to 85 per cent in 1990 (Table 4.3). It was full-time officials who increasingly were called upon to fill the widening gaps in representation (Millward *et al.*, 1992: 111–14).

The decline in shop steward numbers continued during the 1990s, although the rate of decline did slow down considerably in each sector of the economy. The total number of stewards fell by a further 12 percentage points between 1990 and 1998. Further declines in rates of union recognition in the private sector were the dominant cause, followed by further shifts in employment away from manufacturing and the public sector. One countervailing factor in the private sector was an increase in the average number of stewards in workplaces where they were present – perhaps a 'batting average' effect indicating that stronger organisations endured longer. This served to bring about slight improvements in the member:steward ratio in manufacturing and private services. It was, however, insufficient to alter the overall trajectory.

The election of the Labour government in 1997 was expected to signal some reversal of fortunes for the union movement and, indeed, between 1998 and 2004, rates of union recognition stabilised among workplaces with twenty-five or more employees (Kersley *et al.*, 2006: 121). The number of stewards, however, continued to shrink, due to a further fall in the proportion of recognised workplaces with stewards, and a return of the decline in the number of stewards in workplaces where there were any. Stewards had broadly maintained their presence in recognised workplaces in the 1990s, but between 1998 and 2004 the pattern of union representation had returned to that seen in the late 1980s, when representation had thinned out even where unions remained recognised. One outcome was that lay representatives were increasingly called upon to represent members in workplaces other than their own (Kersley *et al.*, 2006: 124). The situation in 2004 was such that the total number of stewards stood at just 102,000, which was less than one-third of the total in 1984.[5] Moreover, only four-fifths (79 per cent) of all members now worked in an establishment with an on-site union rep. Shop steward organisation in manufacturing suffered in particular. Manufacturing workplaces with twenty-five or more employees supported only 18,000 stewards in 2004 – just 14 per cent of the 1980 figure. Manufacturing had accounted for two-fifths of all stewards at the beginning of the period, but by the end of the period it accounted for less than one-fifth.

The causes of decline

The preceding discussion has pointed to a number of factors that played a part in the substantial reduction in shop steward organisation in Britain over the period 1980–2004. First, there were falling rates of union recognition and, second, a declining propensity for recognised workplaces to support on-site lay union representatives. Third, there were fewer shop stewards in workplaces where on-site representation had been maintained. Finally, there was the shift in employment towards private

---

[5] See the source note of Table 4.4 for the basis of these time-consistent estimates, and see the final column of Table 4.4 for the best available estimates of the total number of stewards in 2004.

services, where unions were traditionally less well organised. Shift-share analysis confirms that these four factors each played roles of approximately equal importance over the course of the twenty-year period from the high point of 1984 to the low point of 2004.

What lay behind these profound changes? Sharp drops in manufacturing employment can be partly attributed to the impact of technological change, which led to employers replacing workers with capital equipment. However, the process of deindustrialisation was hastened dramatically by the length and depth of the recession of the early 1980s, which led to the closure of many large, highly unionised workplaces which had had elaborate shop steward networks embedded within them. The depth and length of recession can be attributed in large part to the monetarist policies pursued by the Thatcher government (Keegan, 1984). The appreciation in the value of the pound after the arrival of North Sea oil exacerbated the problems for manufacturing industry by adversely affecting exports and stimulating import competition. Similarly, the contraction of the employment share of the public sector can be attributed primarily to political decisions to privatise and contract out, while limiting employment growth in what was left by holding down public spending to allow for tax cuts.

The new workplaces that sprang up to replace the casualties of recession were considerably less likely to recognise unions than those that they replaced (Disney et al., 1995). This reflects a number of influences, including legislative changes which removed the limited statutory trade union recognition procedures introduced in the 1970s. Trade unions were also weakened by high unemployment and greater competition and deregulation in product markets, which increased both incentives and opportunities for employers to oppose union recognition, while reducing the benefits for employees that recognition conferred (Brown et al., 1997; Pencavel, 2003). Consequently, when unions attempted to organise new workplaces during the 1980s and 1990s, success rates were low and recognition did not spread sufficiently among established workplaces to compensate (Beaumont and Harris, 1990; Millward et al., 2000: 103, 106; Millward et al., 1992: 74–5). Unions began to enjoy more success in organising after 1996, once the election of a Labour government, committed to introducing a statutory recognition procedure, became a realistic prospect. But they were not able to organise enough new workplaces to mitigate the losses of the 1980s (Gall and McKay, 1999).

Shop steward incidence declined in workplaces where unions were recognised for a number of reasons. Regression analysis shows that stewards are more likely to be present in certain types of recognised workplaces. These are the larger workplaces, those with higher levels of union membership, those with higher proportions of male employees, those where managers engage in workplace bargaining, and those where managers support union organisation by deducting union subscriptions direct from the payroll (Table 4.5).

Certain of these features became less common over the past quarter century among workplaces with recognised unions. These workplaces became less male-dominated, their union density declined, and the incidence of workplace-level bargaining also fell. Comparing the coefficients on the year dummies in the two columns of Table 4.5, we can see that these changes accounted for some part of the overall decline in the percentage of recognised workplaces with a shop steward between 1984 and 2004. They nonetheless add up to only a minor part of the story.

Further insights come from qualitative research of that period. In the minority of new workplaces where unions were able to win recognition, they had more difficulty recruiting shop stewards than in workplaces with established unions. One reason for this failure is that recognition was often awarded by management following 'beauty contests' where unions competed to demonstrate the benefits to management that their union would confer, for example by signing 'no strike' agreements (Bassett, 1986).[6] It made it difficult to establish a social norm of membership and activism, which in older workplaces had developed over time through cycles of confrontation and accommodation with management. So it became harder to recruit shop stewards. For example, a study of Nissan's flagship Sunderland factory, established in 1986, pointed to the difficulty that unions had establishing effective shop steward organisation in new workplaces. Management selected a single union to represent the workforce before any worker had been hired. In these circumstances, the union struggled to recruit members and activists. Only around a third of the workforce joined the union, and there were few shop stewards (Garahan and Stewart, 1992).

The wider political and economic climate of the 1980s and early 1990s also contributed to union difficulties in recruiting and retaining shop stewards in workplaces where they continued to enjoy recognition. For example, recession and union defeat meant that workers in the 'sunrise' labour market of Swindon apparently lost faith in the efficacy of unions (Rose, 1996). In another contemporary case-study of a heating factory, shop steward organisation among white-collar workers collapsed during the 1980s in the face of persistent restructuring of the workforce and

---

[6] 'No strike' agreements are those in which both parties commit to abide by arbitration if there is a failure to agree.

Table 4.5 *Probit analysis of the determinants of a recognised workplace having a shop steward*

	Model 1	Model 2
Year (ref. 1984)		
1980	−0.131	−0.282***
1990	−0.385***	−0.417***
1998	−0.445***	−0.233*
2004	−0.653***	−0.445***
Industry sector (ref. private: metal goods and engineering)		
Extraction		0.037
Manufacturing		0.033
Energy and Water (private sector)		0.268
Construction (private sector)		−1.187***
Distribution, retail, hotels and catering (private sector)		−0.209
Transport and communication (private sector)		−0.222
Banking and financial services		−0.605***
Other private sector services		−0.351
Energy and water (public sector)		−0.040
Transport and communications (public sector)		−0.159
Central and local government		0.274
Education		−0.014
Health		−0.121
Other public sector		−0.177
Workplace size (ref. 25–49 emps)		
50–99		0.356***
100–199		0.727***
200–499		1.068***
500–999		1.338***
1000+		1.460***
UK owned		0.054
Single independent		−0.063
Decade established (ref. before 1980s)		
1980s		−0.202*
1990s		−0.320**
2000s		−0.494*
DK		−0.411*
% female		−0.007***
% female missing		−0.080
% union members		0.009***
% union members missing		−0.104
Any workplace bargaining (ref. = No)		
Yes		0.612***
DK		0.167*
Deducts union subs (ref. = No)		
Yes		0.261***
DK		0.198
Constant	0.947***	0.314
Number of observations	6,438	6,437

Note: Analyses were weighted to account for differential sampling probabilities of workplaces.
Source: WIRS/WERS data. Workplaces with 25 or more employees and recognised unions.
*p < 0.1, **p < 0.05, ***p < 0.01.

associated redundancies, which resulted in all of the union's key activists leaving the factory (Fairbrother, 2000).

Changing characteristics of shop stewards

Shop steward organisation was considerably smaller by the start of the twenty-first century than it had been some twenty years earlier. But did the characteristics and activities of shop stewards also change over that time?

Research into shop stewards conducted prior to 1980 was partly concerned with identifying the characteristics of shop stewards in terms of gender, age and ethnicity, to see the extent to which they reflected the wider workforce that they represent (Clegg *et al.*, 1961; McCarthy, 1967; Brown, 1981). As WIRS/WERS has always included a survey of shop stewards (and, latterly, of all employee representatives) it allows us to examine how the personal characteristics of shop steward respondents have changed over the past twenty-five years. Have unions succeeded in attracting shop stewards who are representative of an increasingly diverse membership? It should be noted that WERS focuses only on the senior shop steward of the largest recognised trade union at the establishment. Nevertheless, while these will not necessarily be representative of all shop stewards, they are likely to be the most influential group of stewards.

Table 4.6 compares the characteristics of senior shop stewards with the characteristics of union members. Compared with a quarter century earlier, senior lay trade unionists in 2004 were more likely to be female, older, less likely to work in manufacturing, and more likely to be found in the public sector. There has, however, been little change in their ethnic profile or in the proportion working in private sector services. Changes to the characteristics of senior shop stewards have partially mirrored changes in union members. They also, as a group, became more likely to be female, older and less likely to work in manufacturing. Nevertheless, the proportion of senior shop stewards who are white, male and over forty actually rose from 41 per cent to 47 per cent between 1980 and 2004, whereas the proportion of union members who shared these characteristics remained constant at 29 percent. The apparent increase among senior shop stewards is not statistically significant because of the relatively small samples, but it indicates that senior shop stewards may have became less representative of the wider union membership over the previous twenty-five years, rather than more so.

Why has the proportion of senior shop stewards who are over forty increased? It may be an issue of concentration. One key reason why the average age of union members has risen is that young workers tend

Table 4.6 *Characteristics of senior reps of the largest recognised union*

	Senior shop stewards		All union members	
	1980	2004	1983	2004
Demographic characteristics				
Male	77	63	64	49
White	97	97	96	94
Age (mean)	42	46	40	43
Aged 40+	52	78	49	60
White male aged 40+	41	47	29	29
Workplace characteristics				
Private manufacturing	31	13	28	12
Private services	25	27	18	33
Public sector	45	60	54	55
Observations	881	607	4,608	14,305

Sources: Senior shop stewards: WIRS/WERS data; Union members: 1983 General House-hold Survey and 2004 Labour Force Survey.

to work in young workplaces, and unions have not been able to get recognition in such workplaces (Machin, 2003a). Twenty-five years ago, new workplaces were being organised, so younger shop stewards may have been more likely to be elected to represent workforces composed predominantly of younger workers. It may also indicate that unions are finding it increasingly difficult to recruit their younger members into shop steward roles.

In 1980, there was some validity in the stereotypical shop steward as a middle-aged, male, manufacturing worker. What is surprising is how little this had changed by 2004. Unions have been partially successful in recruiting more female shop stewards. But women remain under-represented, and unions have not succeeded in recruiting more younger and ethnic minority workers into senior representative positions. It has been argued that there needs to be a generational change in activists for unions to renew themselves (Fairbrother, 2000). This is further evidence of their failure.

The changing activities of union representatives

Having considered the incidence and characteristics of stewards, we now move on to consider changes in the role and activities of shop stewards within the workplace. Research into workplace trade unionism in the 1970s made it clear that shop stewards of that time could be powerful figures within their own workplaces (Batstone *et al.*, 1977; Brown, 1973; Beynon, 1973). Although this research focused primarily on manufacturing, accounts of trade unionism in some service sectors during this period tell a similar story (Jenkins, 1990). Where shop stewards were powerful, this was partly a function of the ideological resources and orientation of the shop steward, and the social organisation of production (Batstone *et al.*, 1977).[7] It was also shaped by the intensity of product market competition, because firms in less competitive product markets were likely to cede more power and influence to shop stewards as they had less incentive to keep control of costs (Brown, 1973). High inflation, which eroded real wages, increased the sense of collective grievance among the workforce, and shop stewards emerged as spokespersons for this sense of grievance (Jenkins, 1990).

The environment that sustained shop steward power in the 1970s changed radically after 1980. How did the role and activities of shop stewards change in response? There is a limit to what WERS can say in this regard because, of necessity, its questions altered as behaviours changed. Some of the activities in which shop stewards were involved in 1980 steadily diminished in significance and consequently received less attention in the surveys – examples are stewards' activities to maintain the closed shop and to organise industrial action. Subtle changes in question wording also compromise comparability over the series on some issues. The WERS data set does have a small number of questions about the role and activities of senior shop stewards which were put in reasonably consistent ways to comparable individuals in 1980, 1998 and 2004. We explore what these indicate below, but, before we do, we will briefly consider the wider evidence on the changing role of shop stewards over the period.

The political and economic shock of the early 1980s did not have an immediate effect upon shop steward organisation. Case-studies suggested substantial resilience after 1980 (Batstone, 1985). But case-study evidence from later in the 1980s suggests that the period 1983/1984 was something of a turning point. For example, studies of workplace union organisation in a number of West Midlands workplaces reported some examples of resilience, but also evidence of decline. In one case, after 1990 shop steward organisation among manual unions came to be increasingly dominated by the management agenda. In another, the shop stewards became increasingly defensive in the face of management threats

---

[7] For example, the way in which production was organised often resulted in a steady stream of grievances and disputes about the intensity of work, linked to production-line speeds and the use of 'payment by results'.

about the future of the factory if the unions failed to co-operate with the management (Fairbrother, 2000). Another study of Merseyside factories found that two had closed and, in the case of Ford's Halewood plant, the shop steward organisation had been radically recast as a result of management efforts to reform industrial relations and improve productivity (Darlington, 1994). A further study identified similar processes at work among the shop stewards representing baggage handlers at Manchester Airport. Despite a successful strike in 1989, they became demoralised by the reshaping of industrial relations on management's own terms, driven by the compulsory competitive tendering of the service (Darlington, 1995).

A study of workplace union organisation in thirteen firms in different sectors in the mid-1990s also noted significant qualitative changes in the nature of workplace union organisation (Brown et al., 1998). Single-table bargaining, fear of derecognition and increasing competitive pressures, often coupled with threat of redundancies or workplace closure, resulted in union organisations that were increasingly cut off from the wider union movement. Union institutions that linked workplaces, such as combine committees, multi-workplace union branches and district committees declined rapidly. It became harder for unions, which were struggling financially, to support and sustain shop steward organisation, which became increasingly dependent on management (Willman and Bryson, 2006). At the same time as this loss of independence, there was a narrowing of the scope of collective bargaining. Such findings were common to the majority of workplaces studied by researchers undertaking qualitative studies in the later 1980s and 1990s.

Evidence from WIRS/WERS is generally consistent with the qualitative studies. The number of non-pay issues subject to collective bargaining declined between 1980 and 1984 (Millward et al., 2000: 167), but was stable over the period from 1984 to 1990. This suggests that the role and influence of shop stewards diminished in the early 1980s, even though their numbers were increasing at that time. WIRS/WERS also shows that the 1990s saw the growth of 'hollow shell' trade unionism, that is, workplaces where nominally union recognition agreements existed, but where pay was no longer determined through collective bargaining. By 1998, 14 percent of workplaces with union recognition did not use collective bargaining to determine pay and conditions (Millward et al., 2000: 164), and the number of issues negotiated over was small (Brown et al., 2000). Over the period from 1998 to 2004, there was further erosion of the collective bargaining role, as the number of issues subject to negotiation fell, with consultation becoming more common (Brown and Nash, 2008; Kersley et al., 2006).

Mobilisation of the membership in support of collective disputes also became less common in the 1980s and 1990s. In 1980, almost one-third (29 per cent) of senior stewards said that industrial action of some form had taken place at their establishment in the previous twelve months, but the equivalent proportion in 2004 was less than one-fifth (18 per cent). Indeed, the 2004 WERS suggests that individual casework – welfare work and dealing with grievances and disciplinary cases – had become a key part of what shop stewards do. Whilst around two-fifths of stewards in the 2004 WERS said that the most important issue they had spent time on in the previous twelve months involved some aspect of terms and conditions, such as rates of pay or hours of work, a further one in six chose disciplinary matters or grievances, and one in ten chose welfare issues, such as equal opportunities or health and safety (Kersley *et al.*, 2006: 150). Moreover, shop stewards involved in focus groups concerned with facilities for workplace representatives suggested that they spent the majority of their time on individual casework and, furthermore, that the amount of time spent on casework had increased over the last decade as a result of the increasing body of individual employment rights (BERR, 2007).

The picture that emerges from this quantitative and qualitative evidence on the activities of shop stewards suggests that there has been a substantial diminution of their role within the workplace. In some cases, workplace trade unionism has become a hollow shell, where shop stewards enjoy little substantive influence or a procedural role. In others, the procedural role for shop stewards has been preserved, but their influence has declined markedly as they spend less time on collective bargaining and more time on representing individual members.

What is interesting, in the light of this decline in procedural support, is that there appears to have been no substantial change in the degree of material support that stewards receive from employers, at least where they remain present. Trade union representatives have, since the 1970s, enjoyed a legal right to reasonable time off to undertake their representative duties. But many employers have also provided shop stewards with a level of clerical and administrative resources to help them undertake union work, and the degree to which they have done so does not appear to have declined substantially. The proportion of senior stewards with use of an office declined only from 68% in 1980 to 60% in 2004, and the proportion with use of a telephone declined only from 93% to 88%. But the proportion of workplaces with shop stewards in which management deducts union subscriptions direct from union members' pay using the 'check-off' system remained similar in both years, standing at around four-fifths. Steward organisation can indeed be caricatured as a shell of facilities from which their procedural role and substantive achievement have been hollowed out.

Another indicator of the support provided to shop stewards is the proportion of workplaces with one or more shop stewards in which at least one of these stewards is permitted to spend all of their working time on union activities. Questions in the WERS management questionnaires on the incidence of such 'full-time' lay stewards are different for the periods 1980 to 1990 and 1990 to 2004, so it is not possible to make direct comparisons across the whole of the period. But the data do point to stability in the proportion of workplaces with a full-time shop steward between 1980 and 1990 and, perhaps surprisingly, an increase in the proportion of workplaces with a full-time shop steward between 1998 and 2004. There is also evidence from WERS of worker representatives that shop stewards who only spent a proportion of their working hours on representative activities were spending more time on union duties in 2004 than they were in 1998 (Kersley et al., 2006: 148). It thus seems likely that, among workplaces that still have on-site shop stewards, there has been approximate stability in the degree of practical support for union representatives. What does appear to have changed, however, is the balance of stewards' activities, which are now tilted less towards the determination of the wage-effort bargain and more towards individual casework, with a subsequent diminution of their influence on the broad scope of workplace affairs.

What do workers think?

Given these wide-reaching changes, what did workers themselves think of these changes to the role and power of union organisations in their workplaces? The case-studies discussed above provide some anecdotal evidence on this. Resigned disillusionment in some of the cases described by Darlington and Fairbrother, indifference in the Swindon workplaces studied by Rose. The British Social Attitudes Survey (BSAS) allows us to get some quantitative insights. In 1989, 1998 and 2005 it asked respondents who were employees in workplaces with a trade union presence whether they thought that the union at their workplace had too much, about the right amount or not enough power. Table 4.7 summarises the results. We need to be cautious in inferring too much from this question. In-depth interviewing would probably suggest more nuanced and complex reactions to the declining power and influence of shop stewards. Nevertheless, the BSAS provides an interesting summary measure.

The BSAS data suggest that by 1989, a significant proportion of employees in union workplaces thought that the union at their workplace,

Table 4.7 *Workers' perceptions of changing union power at their own workplace*

	1989	1998	2005
All in union workplaces			
Unions have too much power	4	2	5
Unions have about the right amount of power	56	48	55
Unions have too little power	40	50	40
Union members			
Unions have too much power	1	2	4
Unions have about the right amount of power	44	49	51
Unions have too little power	55	49	46

Source: British Social Attitudes Survey.

personified by shop stewards, had too little power. Given the size of possible sampling errors in the BSAS, the proportion thinking that unions have too little power had not changed much since 1989, although there is evidence of a small downward trend among union members. In the light of the analysis presented in the previous section, it might suggest that union members have become habituated to union weakness, perhaps as a result of the arrival of younger workers, more indifferent to, and inexperienced in, trade unionism.

The 1998 and 2004 WERS also provide an interesting insight into the views of workers because their Surveys of Employees asked employees in workplaces with unions what they thought of the union in their workplace. In 2004, 55 per cent of union members thought that the union(s) at their workplace was/were taken seriously by management, while 46 per cent thought that unions make a difference to what it is like to work at the workplace. There was little change in these figures between 1998 and 2004. However, union members were more likely to think that the union 'makes a difference' if there was a shop steward on site (Table 4.8, column one). In workplaces where a union was recognised, the presence of an on-site union representative was associated with more widespread perceptions of union effectiveness than if no representative was present. Moreover, union members in workplaces with full-time or nearly full-time shop stewards were more likely to think that unions make a difference than members in workplaces with part-time stewards.[8]

---

[8] The differences shown in column 1 of Table 4.8 between employees' perceptions in the presence of full-time reps and those in the presence of part-time reps were statistically significant at the 1 per cent level, as were the differences between employees' perceptions in the presence of part-time reps and those in the absence of reps.

Table 4.8 *Union members' views on the effectiveness of trade unions in the workplace*

| | Trade union would best represent you in dealing with managers here about... | | | | |
	Unions make a difference to what it is like to work here	Getting increases in your pay	Getting training	Making a complaint	Facing discipline
No recognised union	37	39	8	27	49
At least one recognised union	46	73	12	48	75
At least one recognised union					
No on-site reps	35	62	8	36	64
No on-site reps, but largest recognised union has rep(s) at another site in the organisation	36	69	9	42	70
On-site reps but all part-time	45	75	12	48	75
At least one on-site rep who spends all, or nearly all, of their time on union duties	53	77	16	55	81

Source: WERS 2004. Union members in workplaces with 5 or more employees where the employee reports that a union or staff association is present.

Table 4.8 also hints at the areas in which unions are seen to be most effective. The WERS 2004 Survey of Employees asked employees who they think would best represent them in dealing with managers over certain issues, with 'trade union' being one of the possible response options.[9] Again, union recognition was a key factor informing union members' responses, but the presence of shop stewards again played a part. Union members in workplaces with part-time shop stewards were more likely than members in workplaces without on-site stewards to believe that the union would best represent them, and this was true across all four issues: pay, training, grievances and discipline. The presence of full-time reps further raised the likelihood that employees would choose 'the

[9] Other options were: myself; employee representative (non-union); another employee; somebody else.

union', although only in respect of training, grievances and disciplinary matters.[10]

This suggests that employees do recognise the value of having access to on-site shop stewards. There are, however, two cautions. First, it is apparent that substantial minorities of union members do not choose 'the union', even when the workplace has full-time union representatives. This may be because members will not necessarily have access to a representative of their particular union. However, some union representatives do represent members of other unions (Kersley *et al.*, 2006: 160). And so it is as plausible that it serves as an indication of the ineffectiveness of some shop stewards.[11] The second point is that, even though many employees do acknowledge the value of on-site lay representation, as the discussion earlier has shown, members are increasingly having to manage without it.

Non-union representation

Understanding changes in non-union forms of employee representation since 1980 is a more difficult task. Non-union forms of employee representation have attracted much less attention from researchers than union representation (Terry, 1999). Whilst successive WERS have contained questions about non-union employee representation, the questions have changed from survey to survey, with the result that it is difficult to build up a picture of what has changed. The best available estimates on the incidence of individual non-union representatives in the 1980s suggests that they were present in around one in ten workplaces at both the beginning and end of that decade (Millward *et al.*, 1992: 164). Figures from the more recent WERS indicate that this proportion rose to around one in seven by 1998, a level at which it has since stabilised. Non-union representatives may also sit separately on joint consultative committees (JCCs). WERS unfortunately cannot robustly indicate the changing proportion of JCCs with non-union representatives, but the survey series does show that JCCs became slightly less common overall between 1980 and 2004, having been present in around one-third of workplaces with twenty-five or more employees in 1980, but only one-quarter in 2004.

---

[10] The differences shown in columns 2 to 5 of Table 4.8 between employees' perceptions in the presence of part-time reps and those in the absence of reps were all statistically significant at the 1 per cent level, as were all of the differences between employees' perceptions in the presence of full-time reps and those in the presence of part-time reps, with the exception of 'getting increases in your pay'.

[11] It is not possible to discern whether union members identified in the WERS Survey of Employees belong to the same union that has on-site reps.

The available evidence does not point towards any substantial expansion of non-union representation, despite the considerable interest provoked in recent years by the transposition of the European Union's Information and Consultation Directive into UK law.

Development work for the 2004 Workplace Employment Relations Survey sought to revise the questions on employee representation so as to provide a more robust picture of the incidence of non-union forms of representation. We are thus now better able to chart the relative prevalence of union and non-union representatives and, because of the expanded scope of WERS 2004, can do so in the population of workplaces with five or more employees. In 2004, 7% of workplaces with five or more employees had non-union representatives on site, whilst 8% of workplaces had on-site shop stewards; around 2% of workplaces had both forms of on-site representation (Charlwood and Terry, 2007). This left 85% of workplaces without any on-site representatives. So, although non-union representation may not have expanded to any great degree over the past twenty-five years, the decline in on-site union representation has been such that the spread of the two phenomena is now similar. Union representation does cover a larger proportion of all employees than non-union representation (around 37% compared with around 17%) because union representatives tend to be more common in larger workplaces. But non-union representatives are as numerous as shop stewards – there are roughly 150,000 of each in workplaces with five or more employees – because non-union JCC representatives tend to exist in large numbers where there is a JCC (see Kersley et al., 2006: 159).

The characteristics of non-union representatives are, however, somewhat different from those of shop stewards They are younger, on average, and more likely to be female, and they are also likely to have been in post for a shorter period of time (Kersley et al., 2006: 146). They are also less likely to have been appointed through an election process.

How do the processes of representation differ for shop stewards and non-union representatives? On average, non-union representatives spend only half as much time on representative duties as union representatives. But there is evidence that non-union representatives are consulted more regularly than their shop steward counterparts, and that non-union representatives in dual-channel workplaces are consulted more than shop stewards in dual-channel workplaces (Charlwood and Terry, 2007). Whilst this may reflect the more collaborative relationship that is generally found to exist between non-union representatives and workplace managers, it is nevertheless important to acknowledge that cases where non-union representatives actually negotiate with management over terms and conditions in the way that some shop stewards do are extremely unusual (Kersley *et al.*, 2006: 168–75). Joint regulation of terms and conditions through bargaining remains the preserve of union representatives.

This final point is reinforced when one investigates employees' views on the efficacy of different forms of representation. We noted earlier that, when faced with a variety of options as to who would best represent them in certain matters, union members invariably chose the union as their preferred agent where shop stewards were present. But non-union representatives enjoy no such popularity among non-members. Instead, only a minority of non-members in workplaces with non-union representatives (between 15 and 20 per cent, depending on the issue) believe that a non-union representative would be the best person to represent them. In such workplaces, employees generally prefer to represent themselves.

Conclusions

How has workplace representation changed since 1980? The first key point is that there is much less of it than there was. In 1980, there were around 328,000 shop stewards, with shop stewards present in 50 per cent of workplaces. By 2004, equivalent estimates suggest that there were only around 102,000 shop stewards, while shop stewards were present in 23 per cent of workplaces. But in workplaces with shop stewards, there were important continuities between 1980 and 2004. In 1980, senior shop stewards were likely to be older, white men. By 2004, this had not changed. Those shop stewards remaining in 2004 continued to enjoy similar levels of management-provided facilities to their counterparts of 1980. There is also evidence that shop stewards were spending more time on representative duties in 2004 than they were in 1998. But, despite this institutional continuity, there is widespread evidence of a dramatic decline in the influence of shop stewards over the management of the workplace, and of a change in their role.

Shop stewards were still, in 2004, quite clearly perceived to make a difference to many employees' experience of work. But there was nonetheless a degree of scepticism among a substantial minority of union members as to the efficacy of their representatives, with some considering that unions lacked power, that they were not taken seriously by management, and that they made no difference to the workplace. Nevertheless, union shop stewards have not been replaced substantially by non-union employee representatives. In workplaces that have non-union representatives, employees are less likely to think that these non-union representatives would be effective in representing them than equivalent employees in workplaces with union shop stewards. Overall, then, changes in employee representation can be seen as part of a wider pattern of declining collectivism, and the shifting ideologies of workplace governance. There has been a shift from governance regimes predicated on pluralist assumptions, with shop stewards as powerful autonomous actors able to represent the interests of union members to management, to unitarist systems of governance under which shop stewards or non-union representatives, if they exist, are often relegated to the role of managerial assistant.

5 Voice at the workplace: where do we find it, why is it there and where is it going?

Paul Willman, Rafael Gomez and Alex Bryson

Introduction

What has been happening to communication in the modern workplace? The term 'voice' refers to the various forms of two-way communication available to employers and employees targeted at resolving problems and settling differences. Perhaps because of the impact of Freeman and Medoff's (1984) seminal contribution, which identified voice with trade unions, debate about workplace voice has focused on trends in unionisation. This is misleading in general and overlooks some important trends in Britain. In 1980, union presence at establishment level was much more common than in 2004. For example, back in 1980 two-thirds of workplaces recognised unions for pay bargaining, including half of all private sector workplaces. Over the quarter century we discuss here, unionisation has contracted but voice has not.

As many recent studies recognise, voice mechanisms may exist at establishment level where unions are not present. Unlike the United States, on which Freeman and Medoff focused, a mix of union and non-union voice mechanisms is not only possible in Britain but prevalent. In this chapter, we argue that the history of voice regimes in the last quarter century is very different from that of union organisation. Whereas union membership and recognition have contracted, the coverage of voice has not. But the type of voice in establishments in 2004 is very different from that of 1980. Above all, much voice in the modern British workplace is employer-initiated. We show why this is the case.

The structure of the chapter is as follows. First, we clarify concepts. Second, we present descriptive data from WIRS/WERS indicating the pattern of voice regimes and their change over time. We also indicate sources of variation at specific data-points. Third, we look at what kinds of voice are prevalent at the end of the period. The collapse of union voice has coincided with the expansion of employer-generated voice mechanisms. We examine what kinds of mechanisms are involved. Fourth, we relate voice types to workplace outcomes such as quits and industrial

97

climate. This comparison reveals, first, the importance of distinguishing union from non-union voice; second, the value in separately identifying what we term 'dual' voice regimes (that is, those where union and non-union voice co-exist); and, third, the resilience of voice, and likely future developments.

Concepts and approaches

The concept of voice has a longer history than its usage in employment relations. In Hirschman's (1970) approach, it is characterised in terms of the resolution of a particular collective action problem. Specifically, how do consumers of an organisation's output react to and remedy a quality decline? The classical economic reaction to an adverse price or quality movement would be to switch to another organisation's output and, when enough individuals had switched, the original organisation would react to market signals and remedy the decline. Hirschman noted that this separation of reaction and remedy might be inefficient for both organisation and consumer. He suggested that, in certain circumstances, collective voice pressuring the organisation directly towards a remedy might emerge. This would depend on the costs and benefits to the members of collective action versus individual exit, that is, their resignation. Voice could be more efficient for the organisation where individual exits do not yield remedial information quickly, and for the consumer where either switching costs (that is, the cost of moving to a new provider) or where sunk costs (that is, investment in the current product) are high.

This description is important in light of Freeman and Medoff's (1984) deployment of the concept in employment relations. First, the identification of voice with unionisation was an innovation. The original Hirschman conception does not have unionisation or even representation at its core, but rather two-way communication; the array of voice mechanisms is potentially broad. Second, voice mechanisms may be initiated by the organisation (employer) or the consumer (employee), depending on the costs and benefits of exit and voice for either party. Third, voice is unlikely to endure where only one party benefits; whatever the origination of voice, its persistence implies mutual benefit and co-operation.

Voice mechanisms may be seen as investments in governing the employment contract. These investments are likely to be greater where the sunk costs of both parties are higher. One would thus expect investment in voice to be positively related to other forms of investment in employment contracts. In particular, where employers wish to make investments in improving employee performance, they are likely also to invest in voice. This approach leads to predictions that are different from those associated with voice-as-unionisation. A substantial set of investments in employee performance are represented by human resource management techniques. Several authors (Kochan 1980; Guest 1989) view human resource management and union voice as substitutes. More recently, Machin and Wood (2005) have argued – using WIRS/WERS data – that there is no relationship between human resource management and unionisation in Britain. However, using the voice typology used in this chapter, Bryson *et al.* (2007) find that human resource management adoption does vary with the type of voice regime.

What does this broad approach to voice predict? First, since employment contracts typically do involve sunk and switching costs for both parties (Williamson, 1973), we would expect voice mechanisms to be both widespread and resilient over time. Second, we would expect the demand for voice to be independent of the specific institutions that provide it. In other words, the demand for voice is not simply the demand for unionisation or even representation. Third, we would expect voice to be in demand by both employers and employees, with the balance between the two being an empirical question dependent on the costs and benefits in specific circumstances. Fourth, we expect voice to be correlated with outcome measures at the workplace, such as lower quits. However, we suspect that not all voice types necessarily work in the same ways. For example, voice provision provided by employers may be better at eliciting information to make the job more 'enriching', but may do much less to advance equity concerns in the way that union voice might. Therefore, we expect that different forms of voice may be associated with different outcomes, and this may explain part of the pattern of voice change. To pursue this reasoning, we turn to the measures of voice and of workplace outcomes available in WIRS/WERS.

Data, measures and methods

We use every WIRS/WERS from 1980 to 2004. Our analysis is based on the data collected from managers responsible for workplace industrial relations which contain the voice-related and outcome variables needed for our analysis. All analyses are weighted by the inverse of the workplace's probability of selection for the survey.

By 'voice' we mean two-way forms of communication between management and employees. This takes the form of representation by a union or non-union intermediary, or direct communication that is not mediated by representatives. Direct communication is, by definition, non-union voice. Over the course of the survey series, WIRS/WERS has become more sophisticated in its attempts to capture voice mechanisms at the workplace. This chapter concentrates on voice measures present in the data since 1984, supplemented by some measures present since 1984 or 1990. In some cases, the data go right back to 1980. The following voice items are present throughout WIRS/WERS 1980–2004:

1 any union members at the workplace
2 union recognition
3 on-site union lay representation
4 on-site joint consultative committees (JCCs): we distinguish between those that meet at least once a month ('functioning JCCs') and those that do not, and between those with some union representatives and those with none.

The first three are forms of union voice. The fourth is treated as union voice if the JCC includes union representation, otherwise it is non-union representative voice.

The following direct voice items appear in WERS for 1984–2004:

5 regular meetings between senior management and all sections of the workforce
6 team briefings.

A further two non-union forms of direct voice are present between 1990 and 2004:

7 on-site non-union representatives
8 problem-solving groups.

Throughout most of the remainder of the chapter, we focus on a voice typology which relies on the data items available for 1984–2004, that is, items 1–6. We supplement this with a measure incorporating items 7 and 8 for the shorter period of 1990–2004. Our typology distinguishes workplaces with union-voice only (items 1–3 plus item 4 if the JCCs have union representation) from those with non-union voice only (item 4 if there are no unions involved, items 5 and 6 and, for the period since 1990, items 7 and 8). Our typology also identifies workplaces with a combination of union and non-union voice, which we term 'dual-channel' voice. The fourth category in our typology is 'no-voice' workplaces, which are defined by the absence of two-way forms of representative or direct communication between workers and management.

The incidence of voice over time is mapped and the results of multivariate analyses identifying independent associations between workplace features and voice mechanisms are discussed. Regression analyses are also used to demonstrate the links between outcome measures at the

Table 5.1 *Incidence of voice types in Britain, all workplaces (whole economy), 1984–2004*

	Year			
	1984	1990	1998	2004
Panel A: All workplaces				
1. No voice	16	19(14)	18(12)	14(12)
2. Voice (all types)	84	81(86)	82(88)	86(88)
Panel B: Voice workplaces only				
3. Union only	24	14(11)	9(6)	5(4)
4. Union and non-union	42	39(42)	32(35)	33(34)
5. Non-union-only	16	28(33)	41(47)	46(48)
6. Voice, but nature not reported	2	<1(<1)	<1(<1)	2(2)
All observations (unweighted N)	2,019	2,059	1,920	1,647

Notes: This voice typology is constructed using voice items 1–6 in the text. All values are column percentages. Panel B columns may not add up to total voice percentages in row 2 due to rounding. Numbers in parentheses present the incidence of a modified definition of voice which incorporates two additional voice items only available since 1990. The additional measure of voice captures 'any non-union on site representatives at the workplace' and the presence of 'problem solving groups at the workplace'.
Source: WIRS/WERS data.

workplace, and the presence of voice types.[1] The outcome measures for workplaces are: quits, industrial action, industrial climate, financial performance and labour productivity. Our aim is to see what links, if any, emerge between voice types and these outcomes.

The pattern of voice

We begin by describing the voice landscape in Britain. Table 5.1 Panel A shows aggregate statistics for voice in Britain across the period 1984–2004 for the whole economy.[2] Despite substantial change in the

---

[1] Full regression analyses are not presented in the chapter but are available from the authors on request.

[2] The voice typology in Table 5.1 is based on measures of voice available for the entire 1984–2004 period. A second measure of voice available only since 1990 (on-site non-union representatives and problem-solving groups) is presented in parentheses in Table 5.1. Voice incidence is not overly sensitive to the inclusion of these variables. However, one can see that the overall provision of voice increases as a result, and non-union voice does grow larger at the expense of union-only voice.

composition of workplaces across the period, at least four out of five establishments have voice in each year.

Union-only voice has all but disappeared in Britain. It declined by about four-fifths from 24 per cent of establishments in 1984 to 5 per cent in 2004. This was a period of steeply falling union membership and density overall (Metcalf and Charlwood, 2005). However, the fall in union-only voice contrasts with that of dual-voice regimes, which combine union with non-union voice: these declined by about one-quarter.

The endurance of dual voice regimes is interesting for several reasons. First, throughout the period, employers could mix union and non-union voice mechanisms in varying ways, an option unavailable to employers elsewhere, for example in the United States (LeRoy, 2006). We have characterised this elsewhere as a form of 'hedging' by unionised employers, since it entails both augmenting union voice and reducing dependence on it, thus mitigating counter-party risk (Bryson et al., 2004). Second, dual-channel voice is far more common than union-only voice throughout the period. Indeed, by the end of the period, one may say that the 'normal' condition of establishment-level unionism in Britain is as part of a dual-voice regime. This may have implications for the impacts of unionisation in the workplace research on voice, which usually overlooks the interaction between union voice and other forms of voice.

The dominance of dual-channel regimes may have prevailed for much longer than the time period covered by WERS. Using the question from WERS 1984 on establishment set-up date, we have shown that dual-channel voice regimes were more common than union-only regimes even in establishments set up before 1960 (Bryson et al., 2004). Of course, establishments may have switched voice regimes between set-up date and the survey in 1984, but there would have had to have been considerable switching to negate the conclusion that dual-channel voice has been the dominant form of unionised voice in post-war Britain.

We do not know from these data whether dual-voice regimes typically emerge when employers augment union-only voice with non-union mechanisms, or whether unions are successful in organising previously non-union only voice regimes.[3] Either way, in a period of declining union coverage, and where the contraction of union-only voice is far more pronounced, it may be that the ability that employers have had in Britain to blend voice in dual-channel regimes at establishment level reduces

---

[3] In earlier work (Willman et al., 2007) using a panel of workplace voice switchers in the 1990–98 WERS data, we found that switching was a rare occurrence, with most switching occurring in and out of non-union and no-voice regimes and almost none from union to non-union or no voice. Not surprisingly most of the union switching occurred from union only to dual voice.

Table 5.2 *Incidence of voice types in Britain, public versus private workplaces, 1984–2004*

	Year							
	1984		1990		1998		2004	
	Public	Private	Public	Private	Public	Private	Public	Private
Panel A: All workplaces								
1. No voice	<1	24	4	25	1	24	1	18
2. Voice (all types)	99	76	96	75	99	76	99	82
Panel B: Voice workplaces only								
3. Union only	34	18	21	11	18	6	10	4
4. Union and non-union	64	30	66	27	68	18	76	19
5. Non-union only	1	25	8	36	10	51	12	57
6. Voice, but nature not reported	1	3	<1	<1	<1	<1	2	2
All observations (unweighted *N*)	830	1189	632	1429	612	1317	500	1148

Notes: This voice typology is constructed using voice items 1–6 in the text. All values are column percentages. Panel B columns may not add up to total voice percentages in row 2 due to rounding.
Source: WIRS/WERS data.

the attractions of switching away from unions. This could explain the protracted nature of union voice decline in Britain. Union decline might have been faster had employers had to make stark choices (Willman and Bryson, 2007).

By 2004, non-union-only voice was the most common voice regime. It was found in 46 per cent of workplaces, a three-fold increase since 1984. Whatever the mix of union and non-union mechanisms within dual channel regimes, the inevitable implication to emerge from panel B in Table 5.1 is that, by 2004, voice at the workplace was predominantly an employer-generated phenomenon.

Voice patterns differ markedly across sectors (Table 5.2). Union-only voice has declined in both public and private sectors, but its incidence is roughly twice as high in the public sector throughout the period. Dual-channel voice is the dominant voice regime in the public sector, and has been rising, so that, by 2004, it accounted for three-quarters of all public sector workplaces. In the private sector, on the other hand, dual-channel voice has been in decline, and accounted for only one-fifth of private sector workplaces in 2004. Since 1990, the dominant regime in the private sector has been non-union-only voice. By 2004, it accounted for nearly six in ten private sector workplaces. Non-union-only voice has also been increasing in the public sector, but still only accounted for one in eight public sector workplaces at the end of the period.

The existence of 'no voice' at the workplace is almost exclusively a private sector phenomenon throughout the period. It was lowest in 2004. But what are the no-voice workplaces, and what does it mean to have no voice? Willman *et al.* (2006) found that it is more prevalent in small establishments and single-establishment organisations. It is also associated with lower investment in employees more generally. Utilising the very rich data available in the 1998 WERS, Willman *et al.* found that no-voice workplaces had a thinner set of employer–employee communication channels, that is, compared to voice workplaces they tended to do less communicating on every dimension.

Throughout most of the period, Britain had an essentially 'voluntarist' approach to voice generation, allowing parties to make cost-benefit decisions about voice mechanisms. This changed in 2000 with the introduction of a statutory route to recognition for trade unions (Ewing *et al.*, 2003). The direct impact of this appears to have been limited (Moore, 2004). The pattern of voice over this period is thus likely to reflect the choices made by the parties. Moreover, the enduring coverage of voice mechanisms in both the private and public sectors indicates that in this period of rapid contraction in union coverage the mechanisms of voice delivery changed, but the incidence of voice did not.

One may debate causality, but as union provision of voice at establishment level has contracted, employer provision has expanded to sustain aggregate voice incidence in the economy. Some (mostly US authors) have argued that non-union voice substitutes for and squeezes out union voice, either by reducing employee demand for unions or by offering employers an alternative to union-based voice (Bronfenbrenner and Juravich, 1995). In contrast to the United States, there is no evidence that employer-initiated voice has reduced desire for unionisation among non-members in Britain (Bryson and Freeman, 2006). Nevertheless, during the 1980s and 1990s, employees stopped joining unions even where they were present at establishment level, leading to a rise in 'never-membership' – that is, the number of employees who have never been in a union (Bryson and Gomez, 2005). Whether the collapse of union voice was, in part, precipitated by employer actions in the early 1980s or was largely endogenously driven (Willman, 2005), its demise has created space for the rapid expansion of employer voice provision.

Employer-made worker voice

In this section, we look at trends in non-union voice mechanisms across the period and address two questions. First, if employers are introducing voice in the absence of unions, what kinds of mechanisms are involved? And, second, is non-union voice different in the presence of unions?

To pursue the first question, we present in Table 5.3 the incidence of employer-provided voice for all workplaces in the economy across the period. The union voice figures are included for comparison purposes in panel B. Rows 1–3 present representative voice and rows 4–6 present direct voice.

Joint consultative committees (JCCs) are employer-provided in that, by definition, they are management-initiated. They may include union representatives, of course, in which case there is an element of union voice too (Millward et al., 2000: 121–6).[4] The incidence of on-site JCCs has dropped since 1984 (row 1). Since 1990, WERS has asked 'how influential do you think this committee is on management's decisions affecting the workforce?' In 1990, 32% of managers thought JCCs were 'very influential'. The figure was virtually unchanged in 1998 (33%), but it had fallen to 23% by 2004.

There has also been a considerable fall in the number of JCCs meeting at least once a month, from 31% in 1984 to 17% in 2004. With both the incidence and influence of JCCs on the wane, it is unclear how employers are planning to meet their new responsibilities to provide voice if these are necessary under the European Union Information and Consultation Directive. These trends also indicate that representative voice in general, not just union voice, is in decline. The exception appears to be the presence on site of non-union representatives. Their presence increased from 8% of establishments in 1990 to 14% in 2004 (row 3). This is, however, largely a private sector phenomenon: between 1990 and 2004 the percentage rose from 14% to 23% in private manufacturing, and from 8% to 15% in private services.

While representative voice has been in decline, direct voice items have been either constant or increasing in frequency since 1984. The incidence of team briefings has nearly doubled. Regular meetings with senior management became more prevalent over the period 1984–90 and have stabilised since. As the notes to the table point out, the time series on problem-solving groups is problematic because questions are not

---

[4] In workplaces with union members and a JCC, a little over half of JCCs had union representatives between 1980 and 1990, but this fell from 55% in 1990 to 24% in 1998 and 22% in 2004, clearly suggesting a diminishing role for trade unions in JCCs over time.

Table 5.3 *Incidence of representative and direct voice and their components in Britain for all workplaces, 1980–2004*

All workplaces		Year			
	1980	1984	1990	1998	2004
Panel A: Employer-provided voice					
Representative voice					
1. Any on-site joint consultative committee (JCC)	34	34	29	28	24
2. On-site JCC that meets at least once a month ('functioning' JCC)	30	31	26	22	17
3. Non-union on-site representatives (excluding health and safety)	NA	NA	8	15	14
Direct voice					
4. Regular meetings between senior management and all sections of the workforce	NA	34	41	37	40
5. Team briefings	NA	36	48	52	71
6. Problem-solving groups	NA	NA	35	42	30
Panel B: Union-provided voice					
7. Any union members	73	73	64	52	52
8. Any recognised union	64	66	53	41	38
9. Any on-site union lay representative	50	54	37	25	23

Notes: All values represent percentages. Figures are for all workplaces with 25 or more employees. 'NA' means 'not available'. Rows 1–3 characterise the representative voice mechanisms provided by employers. Rows 4–6 characterise the direct voice mechanisms provided by employers. Some items are not wholly comparable over time. Regular work-force meetings: the measure of regular meetings changed in 2004. For the first time the question asked how often meetings occurred, rather than whether they occurred 'regularly'. Throughout the chapter we say regular meetings occurred in 2004 if they took place at least once a month. If we use 'at least once a fortnight' the incidence drops to 21% in 2004. If we use 'at least once every three months' it rises to 64%. In 2004 the question is: 'Do you have meetings between senior managers and the whole workforce (either altogether or group by group)?' whereas the 1998 question refers to 'regular meetings with the entire workforce present'. Millward *et al.* (2000: 118–20) note concerns about comparability of the measure in earlier years too. They argue that the 1998 question is not comparable to 1984 and 1990 questions. They therefore present a figure for 1998 based on a combination of cross-section and panel data producing an estimate of 48% in 1998 instead of the 37% presented above. Team briefings: in 2004 managers are asked: 'Do you have meetings between line managers or supervisors and all the workers for whom they are responsible?' If asked, the interviewer explains, these are sometimes known as "briefing groups" or "team briefings".' The 1998 question is: 'Do you have a system of briefings for any section or sections of the workforce here?' Millward *et al.* (2000: 118–20) argue that the 1998 question is not comparable to 1984 and 1990. They therefore present a figure based on a combination of cross-section and panel data of 65% in 1998 as opposed to 52% presented above. Whichever measure one adopts, briefings rose substantially over the period but whether the 'spurt' occurred between 1990 and 1998 or between 1998 and 2004 is a moot point. Problem-solving groups: this time series is very problematic. Kersley *et al.* (2006: 94) say the 1998 and 2004 consistent over the years. Efforts to construct a more consistent series for the period 1998–2004 suggest modest growth in their use over the period (Kersley *et al.*, 2006: 93–4).

We can look at the difference between public and private sector workplaces; the data are presented in Table 5.4. Cursory inspection reveals that public sector workplaces are much more 'voice-filled' than private sector workplaces. Furthermore, the nature of voice differs markedly with public sector workplaces being generally much more likely to have representative forms of voice, and the private sector having relatively greater incidence of direct forms.

Trends in voice in the two sectors are also markedly different. If we consider direct voice, team briefings have become more common in both sectors, but the rise in regular meetings between senior management and the workforce is confined to the public sector. Although the time series is problematic, it also appears that problem-solving groups have become more common in the public sector, although their incidence has been higher in the private sector throughout the period. Turning to non-union forms of representative voice, there seems to be a small increase in the use of non-union representatives in both sectors and a decline in the use of JCCs. However, whereas the decline in JCCs has been gradual in the private sector, their incidence actually rose in the public sector until 1990, though it has declined since then. Finally, the decline in private sector union voice is well documented, but its decline in the public sector is often overlooked. Whereas nearly all public sector workplaces have had at least some union members throughout the period, union recognition dipped in the mid-to-late 1980s, and has remained constant since. On-site union lay representation has continued to decline in the public sector, suggesting a 'hollowing-out' of unions' ability to represent workers, even where unions continue to be recognised (Willman and Bryson, 2007).

measures are not comparable because a change in question wording in the 2004 Cross-section Survey restricted it to groups of solely non-managerial employees. They therefore present estimates combining the cross-section and panel data (the panel question didn't change). Footnote 11 of Kersley *et al.* (2006) Chapter 4 gives details of the method. Using the 2004 'restricted' definition the incidence of problem-solving groups was 16% in 1998 and 21% in 2004 for the 10+ employee population. Using the less restrictive definition the figures are 28% and 36% respectively. The time series presented above does not use panel data and thus clearly understates the incidence of problem-solving groups. The reliance on time-series data gives the impression that these groups have become less common between 1998 and 2004 whereas better data (combining cross-section and panel) suggests that they have grown a little. Non-union on-site representatives: the question wording is ambiguous in 1998 so that respondents may have included representatives of non-recognised trade unions.
Source: WIRS/WERS data.

Table 5.4 *Incidence of representative and direct voice types and their components in Britain, public versus private workplaces, 1980–2004*

All workplaces	Year									
	1980		1984		1990		1998		2004	
Panel A: Employer-provided voice										
	Pub	Priv	Pub	Priv	Pub	Priv	Pub	Priv	Pub	Priv
Representative voice										
1. Any on-site joint consultative committee (JCC)	43	30	48	26	49	20	39	24	33	21
2. On-site JCC that meets at least once a month ('Functioning' JCC)	39	26	42	24	45	18	31	19	22	15
3. Non-union on-site representatives (excluding health and safety)	NA	NA	NA	NA	3	10	22	12	8	16
Direct voice										
4. Regular meetings between senior management and all sections of the workforce	NA	NA	33	34	46	39	44	34	54	36
5. Team briefings	NA	NA	46	31	62	42	60	49	76	70
6. Problem-solving groups	NA	NA	NA	NA	54	70	51	61	64	72
Panel B: Union-provided voice										
7. Any union members	99	60	100	58	99	49	97	36	97	37
8. Any recognised union	94	50	99	48	87	38	87	24	87	22
9. Any on-site union lay representative	76	38	83	38	63	26	50	16	54	13

Notes: See Table 5.3.
Source: WIRS/WERS data.

Let us now turn to the second question posed at the beginning of this section, namely, whether the character of non-union voice differs in the presence of unions. Figures 5.1(a) and 5.1(b) distinguish between non-union-only establishments (in black columns) and dual-channel voice establishments (in grey columns). Figure 5.1(a) looks at the incidence of non-union forms of representative voice in these two types of workplace, while Figure 5.1(b) looks at the incidence of direct voice in these regimes. Figure 5.1(a) shows that, throughout the series, JCCs are more common in dual channel workplaces than they are in non-union-only workplaces. There is also a greater likelihood that, in the presence of a

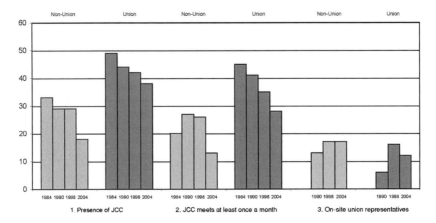

Figure 5.1(a) Incidence of non-union representative voice in non-union only and dual-channel workplaces, 1984–2004

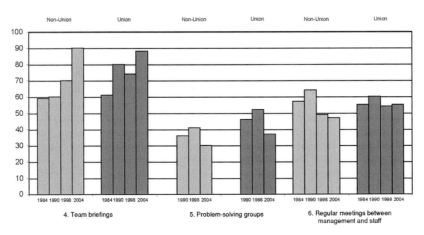

Figure 5.1(b) Incidence of direct voice in non-union only and dual-channel workplaces, 1984–2004

union, the JCC meets at least once a month. In 1990 and 1998, there was no difference in managerial perceptions of JCCs' influence over decision making in dual-channel and non-union-only workplaces. However, in 2004, 27 per cent of managers in dual-channel workplaces thought the JCC was 'very influential' compared with only 17 per cent in non-union-only workplaces. Taken together, these findings suggest that union voice may help bolster non-union representative voice. Figure 5.1(b) indicates that the incidence of direct forms of voice is broadly similar across non-union workplaces and dual-channel workplaces. Thus, unions do not appear to inhibit the use of direct voice.

Voice and workplace outcomes

Descriptions of shifting voice patterns across workplaces with and without union presence offer one way of exploring the evolution of voice provision in Britain over the past quarter century. Examining workplace outcomes such as quit rates provides another. Using WIRS/WERS we examine workplace 'health' indicators, and compare these to the nature of voice at the workplace. If some voice types are associated with 'better' outcomes, such as a better climate of industrial relations, then workplaces may, over time, substitute 'successful' for 'unsuccessful' voice. We make no attempt to provide a rigorous causal test of the associations uncovered in the data. Rather, we present empirical evidence of associations between voice regimes and outcomes and comment on whether the results are consistent with what we know about features of the British industrial relations landscape over the past twenty-five years. For the sake of brevity, we shall confine the analysis in this section to the private sector only. The results that we present are based on pooled and separate year regressions that control for single-digit industry, region, foreign ownership, age of establishment, single establishment, workforce composition (percentage of females, non-manuals and part-timers) and workplace size. Throughout, our voice typology is the one presented in Table 5.1.

Quit rates

The theory behind voice predicts a negative relationship between voice and exit (Hirschman, 1970). In the labour market, we can measure exit by voluntary turnover within the firm (Freeman and Medoff, 1984), and WIRS/WERS records such turnover –'quit rates' – since 1990. Turnover is measured as the percentage of employees who resigned or left in the previous year.

We begin in Figure 5.2(a) with a descriptive portrait of quit rates over time across the four voice regimes presented in Table 5.1.[5]

The presence of unions, whether in union-only or dual-channel regimes, is associated with lower quits than either non-union-voice and

---

[5] We have removed outliers with quit rates greater than 110% but their inclusion does not change the results appreciably.

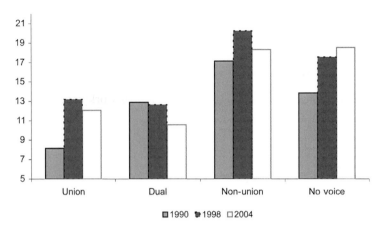

Figure 5.2(a) Percentage of employee quits by union versus non-union voice types in Britain, 1990–2004

no-voice workplaces. For example, the quit rate in 1990 for union-only workplaces was 8% versus 14% for no-voice workplaces – a gap of 6 percentage points. By 2004, quit rates in union-only workplaces had increased to 12%, but the no-voice workplace figure had increased to 18.5%, leaving an almost identical gap of 6.5 percentage points. Effectively, the relative quit rate between union-only and no-voice workplaces did not change in a decade and a half.

These observations are not surprising given the nature of union membership and its continued association with a wage premium, structured promotional opportunities, greater on-the-job training and seniority rules that encourage longer tenure (Blanchflower and Bryson, 2008). What is perhaps surprising is the minimal difference that exists between non-union-only voice and no-voice workplaces. In fact, based on the raw data, no-voice workplaces actually had lower quit rates than non-union-voice workplaces in 1990 and 1998.

We can contrast the impact on quits of representative versus direct voice, as in Figure 5.2(b). Representative forms of voice are associated with lower quits than the direct forms. Quits in the no-voice sector appear lower than quits in direct-voice-only workplaces.

It is possible that these differences in quit rates across voice regimes are, in fact, driven by other differences in workplace characteristics that happen to be correlated with the type of voice adopted, such as workplace size. To establish whether voice regimes had an independent association

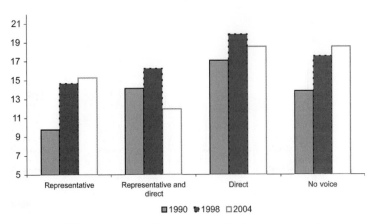

Figure 5.2(b) Percentage of employee quits by representative versus direct voice types in Britain, 1990–2004

with quit rates, we ran regression analyses controlling for the workplace characteristics noted earlier.[6]

Relative to non-union-only voice, both union-only and dual-channel voice regimes were associated with lower quit rates, other things being equal. This is true in the pooled years regression analysis and for separate year regressions in 1990 and 1998. In 2004, it is only true, however, for dual-channel versus non-union-only voice. The general pattern, despite some year-to-year variation, is that union voice variables are negatively related to quit rates in the British private sector. These results are consistent with individual worker-level analyses, which show union members are less likely to quit their jobs than otherwise similar non-members (Freeman and Medoff, 1984). The same pattern holds true with respect to representative versus direct forms of voice. The representative forms of voice have consistently significant negative signs as compared to direct voice forms. This is the case in the pooled and specific year regressions.

Industrial relations climate

In WIRS/WERS, managers are asked 'how would you rate the relationship between management and employees generally at this workplace?' Subjective ratings range from 'very poor' to 'very good'. Figure 5.3(a) reveals that the percentage of workplaces reporting 'very good' climate

---

[6] Quits were estimated using survey-weighted tobit regressions to account for the left-censoring of the data at zero. As with all the multivariate analyses presented in this section, full results are available from the authors on request.

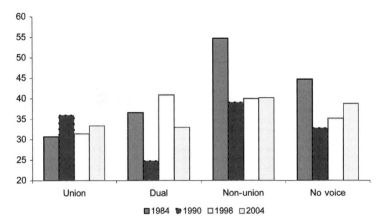

Figure 5.3(a) Percentage of workplaces reporting 'very good' industrial relations climate by union versus non-union voice types in Britain, 1984–2004

tends to be higher in the presence of non-union voice, and is poorest in union-only workplaces.

In the pooled regression results, the presence of non-union-only voice is associated with better climate. However, this is driven by associations in 1984 and 1990. These are absent in 1998 and 2004.[7]

If one considers direct and representative forms of voice, we find that the direct forms of voice are associated with the best climate responses amongst managers (Figure 5.3(b)).

In regression analyses, we find that, in pooled years, direct-only voice is associated with better climate than representative-only voice and no voice, but there are no significant differences between direct voice only and types that combine representative and direct voice. Thus climate is best when the voice combinations includes direct voice. These relations do change over time, however, as direct-only voice is not the 'best' regime from 1990 onwards. Indeed, in 1998, the combination of representative and direct voice is associated with better climate than all other voice types. By 2004, there are no significant differences across any types. When we split the voice types into their components and run the same regressions, the only statistically significant relationship is the positive one of having regular meetings between senior managers and all sections of the workforce.

---

[7] The climate regressions use survey weighted ordered probits distinguishing between 'poor/average', 'good' and 'very good' climate.

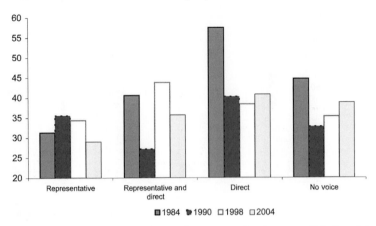

Figure 5.3(b) Percentage of workplaces reporting 'very good' industrial relations climate by representative versus direct voice types in Britain, 1984–2004

Financial performance

Managers have been asked in successive WIRS/WERS to assess their workplace's financial performance relative to the industry average. They respond on a scale running from 'a lot below average' to 'a lot above average'. There is evidence of a clear association between a workplace's financial performance relative to the industry average and its voice regime. Non-union voice is associated with better financial performance than union-only voice in all years, often by a wide margin (Figure 5.4(a)).

In the pooled regression non-union-only voice performs better than all other regimes.[8] The coefficients for the other three regimes are virtually identical. The effects are clear in the early 1980s, disappear in the 1990s, but return once again in 2004. Over the entire period, differences between the other three voice regimes are not statistically significant.

When distinguishing between direct and representative voice types, those with some direct voice appear to perform better than others (Figure 5.4(b)). In pooled regressions for all years we find that direct-only voice is positively associated with financial performance compared to no voice and union-only voice, but it is not significantly different from the combination of direct and representative voice. In the 1984 regression direct-only voice 'outperforms' all other types including the combination of direct and representative voice but, by 2004, the only significant

---

[8] The regressions are survey-weighted ordered probits distinguishing between 'below average', 'average' and 'above average' financial performance relative to the industry average.

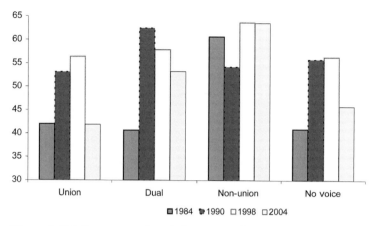

Figure 5.4(a) Percentage of workplaces reporting 'above average' financial performance by union versus non-union voice types in Britain, 1984–2004

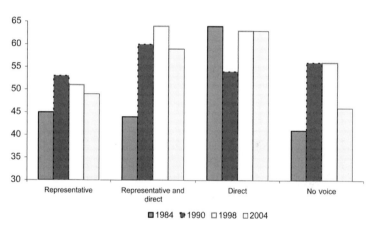

Figure 5.4(b) Percentage of workplaces reporting 'above average' financial performance by representative versus direct voice types in Britain, 1984–2004

difference is the significantly better performance of direct-only voice over no voice.

Labour productivity

Since 1990, WIRS/WERS has asked managers to rate labour productivity relative to the industry average in the same way as they were asked to

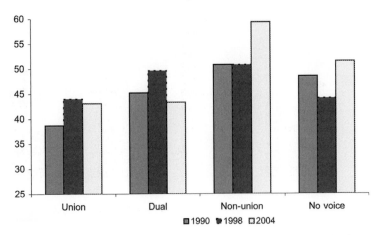

Figure 5.5(a) Percentage of workplaces reporting 'above average' labour productivity by union versus non-union voice types in Britain, 1990–2004

rate financial performance. Descriptive analyses in Figure 5.5(a) indicate that labour productivity is highest in non-union-only voice workplaces, and lowest in union-only regimes. The gap is most pronounced in 2004.

In the pooled regressions, union-only voice is associated with lower productivity than non-union-only voice.[9] Dual-channel voice is also associated with lower labour productivity than non-union-only voice, though the association is only on the margins of statistical significance. Separate year models are less clear-cut, as no statistically significant differences across voice regimes exist, and no obvious time trends emerge. Figure 5.5(b) suggests that regimes containing direct voice have higher labour productivity than others, though the differences are not large. Regression analyses suggest a negative association between labour productivity and representative-only voice relative to direct voice only, but the relationship is only statistically significant in the pooled years regression. There is no compelling case for implementing direct-only voice on productivity grounds, however, since it is not even significantly different from no voice.

Industrial action

Our final outcome variable is industrial action at the workplace in the previous year. Managers have been asked whether there has been any

[9] The regressions are survey-weighted ordered probits distinguishing between 'below average', 'average' and 'above average' labour productivity relative to the industry average.

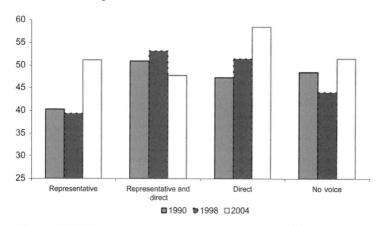

Figure 5.5(b) Percentage of workplaces reporting 'above average' labour productivity by representative versus direct voice types in Britain, 1990–2004

form of industrial action at the workplace in the last twelve months (excluding lockouts), with types of action presented on a show-card.

Our descriptive results in Figure 5.6 show that there has been an over-all reduction in industrial action across all workplaces. Not surprisingly, union-based regimes are associated with higher probability of indus-trial action than non-union-voice-only and no-voice workplaces. This is confirmed in regression analyses for the pooled years, and in separate regressions for 1984–98. However, by 2004, there were no significant differences across voice regimes. If one reruns the regression analyses separately, identifying constituents of the voice typology, workplaces with unions recognised for pay bargaining continue to have a higher probabil-ity of industrial action than otherwise 'like' non-unionised workplaces in 2004.

To summarise, it seems that over the last quarter century union voice – especially union-only voice – has been associated with poorer climate, more industrial action, poorer financial performance and poorer labour productivity than non-union voice and, in particular, direct voice. On the other hand, union-based voice regimes have experienced lower quit rates than non-union and no-voice regimes, as theory predicts. Over that time, while the workplace incidence of voice has remained constant, with roughly eight out of ten workplaces providing some form of voice, there has been a big shift from union to non-union voice, particularly direct employer-made voice. This raises an important question for future research: is there a link between the demise of union-only voice, and its association with poorer workplace outcomes?

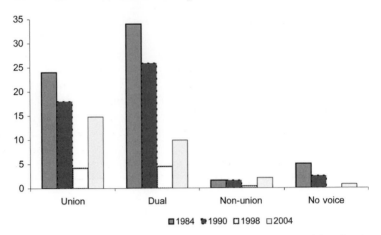

Figure 5.6 Percentage of workplaces reporting 'any industrial action in the last 12 months' by voice types in Britain, 1984–2004

Conclusion

Union decline in Britain over the past twenty-five years has not meant the end of employee voice. Voice is an enduring workplace phenomenon. Although there has been substantial shift in the origination of voice – from workers through unions to employers – throughout the period, around four in five workplaces had two-way communication mechanisms that provided for worker voice. Employers are prepared generally to bear the costs of voice provision, and manifest a reluctance to engage with their workforce without voice mechanisms in place. The association of voice mechanisms with desirable workplace outcomes suggests that voice costs may be lower than the benefits that voice generates.

Union-only voice has all but disappeared. Where union voice persists, it is nearly always found alongside non-union forms of voice, what we have termed 'dual-channel' voice regimes. These workplaces, which make up around one-third of workplaces in Britain with twenty-five or more employees, are voice-rich in the sense that they offer their workers the biggest array of voice options. For example, if a worker wishes to have some form of non-union joint problem-solving group at the workplace, they are more likely to find it in a firm with union presence.

There are a number of implications. First, although there is likely to be substantial change to voice provision in the future, we would argue that this is likely to be within the context of continued wide voice coverage. Much of the period we have studied was characterised by the absence of any statutory mechanisms to promote voice. If employers have a desire to dispense with voice in Britain, the period 1980–98 was one where they had freedom to do so. They are unlikely to do so in the near future if European directives on information and consultation have an impact. Second, if union presence does become more prevalent again, it is likely to be because it generates voice with outcomes beneficial to both employers and employees. The persistence of dual-voice regimes across this period is highly significant for the union revitalisation debate. One implication is that unions are more likely to survive where there is non-union voice. Another is that union voice provision might seek complementarities with non-union voice mechanisms in Britain, rather than seeing them simply as competitive. Most employment contracts seem to need voice mechanisms.

6 From industrial relations to human resource management: the changing role of the personnel function

David Guest and Alex Bryson

Introduction

In organisations of any size, someone has to take responsibility for managing employment relations. In small workplaces, this may be the manager of the enterprise, but as organisations get larger, it is increasingly a role for a specialist. Boxall and Purcell define this role as being concerned with 'all those activities associated with the management of the employment relationship in the firm' (2003: 1). The purpose of this chapter is to explore the changes over the five Workplace Employment Relations Surveys (WIRS/WERS) for evidence about who is responsible for this activity, what it entails and what impact it has in the workplace.

During the twentieth century, the personnel management function in organisations grew from a predominantly welfare activity in a few factories to a core activity in all organisations of any size (Niven, 1967; Watson, 1977). When the first WIRS was undertaken in 1980, personnel managers were faced with a range of challenges and pressures. Industrial relations and, in particular, industrial conflict had a high profile, with a continuing shift towards greater emphasis on the management of industrial relations at the company and workplace level rather than through national agreements. Legislation enacted by the Labour governments in the 1970s had extended workers' individual rights, and the implementation of that legislation had provided an increased role for personnel specialists. In many sectors, personnel managers faced chronic shortages of key labour, and had to give constant priority to attracting and retaining staff. Growing concerns about low productivity and poor quality in British industry placed pressure on personnel managers to ensure appropriately trained staff and to search for acceptable kinds of productivity deal. On top of this, although many of them would not be aware of it, Legge (1978) had argued persuasively that personnel managers were often not capable of bringing about the kind of employment relations innovations that seemed to be required.

In the intervening years, industrial relations has moved out of the headlines. Instead, contemporary debates focus more on human resource management. The resource-based view of the firm (Barney, 1991; Barney and Wright, 1998) has raised the stakes by arguing that human resource management is central to corporate success; but this same debate has also raised again the question of who should be responsible for this activity, and what part personnel specialists should play.

Personnel managers have always tended to be somewhat insecure about their role in organisations. This insecurity was effectively captured in Legge's (1978) outline of the ambiguities and contradictions in the role. It was further reinforced by the analysis in the United States of Wickham Skinner (1981) who used the memorable phrase 'big hat, no cattle' to describe a propensity of the personnel function to promise much and deliver little, implying at the same time that personnel issues were too important to be left to personnel specialists. At a more personal level, Ritzer and Trice (1969) presented evidence about how executives in the United States perceived the qualities of personnel managers, using terms such as passive, reactive, not business-oriented, and risk averse. The advent of human resource management helped to alter this perception to the extent that *Fortune* in the United States produced an article proclaiming human resource managers as the 'new corporate heroes' (Meyer, 1976). Given residual insecurities, it is also not surprising that Ulrich's (1997) guidance on how to become 'human resource champions' was welcomed with open arms by the personnel community. All this raises a number of questions that can be explored using the WERS series. Is the presence of a personnel specialist associated with the adoption of innovative practices and has the shift from 'personnel' to 'human resource management' made any difference to what these specialists do and the impact they have?

Another way of countering concerns about personnel specialists has been to professionalise the function. Within the lifetime of the WERS series, Britain's Institute of Personnel Management has expanded from a qualifying association to become the Chartered Institute of Personnel and Development (CIPD), reflecting its status as the representative body for the function. An underlying assumption of this status is that those with CIPD professional qualifications are likely to meet certain standards of competence and to be in the vanguard of the application of contemporary best practice. A further issue that can be explored within the WERS series is therefore whether the development of more professionally qualified managers has made any difference in terms of the activities they engage in and the impact they have.

The WERS series provides an opportunity to explore how far the employment relations function has changed over the past twenty-five years. The surveys include a number of relevant indicators. If employment relations has become increasingly important, we might expect to see a growth in the number of workplaces with a specialist role. Any shift in emphasis from industrial relations to human resource management might be reflected in the titles and the activities of those in specialist roles. If the status of the function is growing, we could expect to see an increase in its professionalisation, which might be indicated by the proportion of specialists who have relevant qualifications. The status of the function might be reflected in greater board-level representation. In the early days of people management, with a focus on welfare and human relations, it was quite likely that the specialist role would be filled by a woman. In the era when industrial relations dominated, it was sometimes perceived, rightly or wrongly, as more suitable for men. The advent of a focus on human resource management has shifted the balance again, raising the issue of whether the role is becoming increasingly the domain of women. As human resource management has achieved greater prominence, there has been growing interest in its impact on performance (Guest, 1997; Wall and Wood, 2005). Rather less attention has been paid to any association between features of the specialist function and performance. However, it is plausible to expect that any trend towards the employment of more professionally qualified specialists will be associated with the adoption of more contemporary human resource practices and therefore, directly or indirectly, with superior workplace performance. All these issues can be explored in the WERS series.

The chapter is divided into three main sections. The first explores the presence of the specialist personnel role and the kind of people in this role, and how far these have changed. The second considers what those responsible for personnel management do, and how this has changed. The third examines any evidence about their impact on outcomes, including performance. We are interested in whether the person responsible for the function (particularly so far as it is a professionalised specialist activity) has any independent impact on outcomes. We will use the generic terms 'personnel management' and 'personnel specialists' to describe the role and those who occupy the role. The actual titles used and their implications for practice are issues we address in the sections that follow.

One of the challenges in exploring changes over the twenty-five years and five WERS is that the questions have tended to change, and it is particularly tempting to focus on the two most recent surveys, which provide fuller accounts of personnel practices. However, in keeping with the spirit of a review of twenty-five years of WIRS/WERS, we will focus on items that are covered across at least three of the surveys, including the 1980s surveys wherever possible. This inevitably restricts the items that can be covered, but sufficient remain to provide a reasonably comprehensive picture of changes over the period.

The changing personnel management role

There are conflicting arguments about the trends in the growth of the specialist personnel manager role. On the one hand, the increased emphasis on the importance of human resource management, and the growth of professionalism in general, might lead to an increase in specialists; on the other, the personnel role might be particularly susceptible to the trend towards outsourcing of some non-core activities. The most influential view about how the personnel function should be structured has come in recent years from Ulrich (Ulrich, 1997; Ulrich and Brockbank, 2005). There is evidence that many organisations have followed, in full or in part, Ulrich's advocacy of a three-legged approach (CIPD, 2007). Under this the key roles are those of: first, business partner, offering strategic and policy advice; second, centres of specialist expertise, covering areas such as recruitment and selection, training and development, and pay and rewards; and third, shared service centres, providing an administrative input and advice, as well as dealing with queries from managers and staff, sometimes in a call centre. The CIPD survey evidence shows that where shared service centres have been adopted, they are usually in-house rather than externalised. Nevertheless, they may challenge the need for a personnel specialist at each site (CIPD, 2007). So what can we learn from the WERS series about changes in the presence of personnel specialists in the workplace?

The presence of a personnel specialist in the workplace

All five surveys collected information about the presence of a personnel specialist in the workplace. The results are shown in Table 6.1. It should be noted that personnel specialists are defined according to their formal job title. This differs from the definition used by Kersley *et al.* (2006: 39), which also takes account of the time spent on personnel/employment relations matters. Our definition is the same as that used by Millward *et al.* (2000: 52) and includes all those in the first two rows of Table 6.1.

There has been significant growth in the specialist personnel/human resource role since 1990 and more particularly between the 1998 and

Table 6.1 *Presence of a workplace personnel specialist*

	1980	1984	1990	1998	2004
Personnel/HR	14	14	16	22	30
Employee/staff/industrial relations	1	2	1	1	0.5
General manager	49	49	24	35	37
Branch/depot/establishment manager	21	11	22	10	10
Other (e.g., finance)	15	24	33	32	23

Note: Data based on title of the person responsible for employment relations at the workplace. The unweighted numbers range from 1856 in 1980 to 1380 in 2004.
Source: WIRS/WERS data.

2004 surveys. This trend remains significant after controlling for any changes in workplace composition, and counters any suggestion of a decline in the role as a result of the devolution of activities to line management, or the growth of shared services.[1] Given the presumed trend from industrial relations to human resource management, we might expect to see a decline in the proportions with titles containing the words 'industrial relations' or 'employee relations'. But what the surveys reveal is that these titles were very rarely used, even in the early 1980s. There is some evidence that those based in workplaces that belonged to multi-site organisations were able to draw on specialist employment relations expertise located elsewhere in the organisation.

The relatively marked increase in the presence of a workplace specialist between 1998 and 2004 might be explained by the growing influence of human resource management. Titles may be of predominantly symbolic significance, but they can serve as one indication of a growing recognition of the importance of human resource management. Systematic evidence on this is only available in WERS since 1990, but it confirms a clear trend. In 1990, less than 1% of those responsible for employment relations had adopted this title. In 1998, it had grown to just under a third, 7%, of the 22% who were personnel specialists. By 2004, it had grown to two-thirds, since 20% out of the 30% identified as specialists had adopted the 'human resource' title. The move towards the human resource title has been more marked in some workplaces than others. For example, it has been more prevalent in the private sector than the public sector, and particularly the private service sector. It is more common in larger workplaces and those belonging to multi-site organisations, in foreign-owned

[1] The multivariate analysis is available from the authors on request.

establishments, and in workplaces with higher percentages of non-manual workers and lower percentages of part-time workers.

Qualified personnel specialists

A second indication of a growing professionalism of the personnel function is the presence of specialists with relevant qualifications. Has there been a growth in the numbers with relevant specialist qualifications? The results are shown in Table 6.2.

In 2004, about two-fifths of those responsible for employment relations, and who spend at least one-quarter of their time dealing with employment relations matters, have a professional personnel qualification. This is an increase of around one-third since the early 1980s. Two-thirds of those in specialist roles, defined in terms of their job title, had a professional qualification by 2004. Although the proportion increased markedly between 1990 and 1998, this trend has not been sustained in 2004. It is notable that since 1990, a quarter of those in non-specialist roles also claim to have specialist qualifications in employment relations. This implies that the professionalisation of management, and more particularly personnel management, has been steadily advancing.

Regression analysis indicates that specialists with professional qualifications are more likely to be found in larger workplaces, in those that are less than five years old, and in those with a higher proportion of non-manual workers. They are also more likely to be found in foreign-owned workplaces. There is some indication when the data are pooled across the

Table 6.2 *Percentage of those with responsibility for employment relations at the workplace who have relevant specialist/professional qualifications*

	1980	1984	1990	1998	2004
Specialists	52	57	57	72	67
Other managers	16	19	24	26	24
All managers	31	30	35	45	41

Notes: Managers are asked to say if they have 'formal qualifications in personnel management or a closely related subject'. The table is confined to workplaces employing at least 25 people and where the respondents are located at the establishment and spend at least 25% of their time on employment relations matters (or 'a major part' in 1980). The numbers range from 933 in 1980 to 1227 in 1984.

Source: WIRS/WERS data.

Table 6.3 *Time spent in function and in present role among personnel specialists*

	1980	1984	1990	1998	2004	Total
Time in current job						
Less than 2 years	29	24	31	31	28	29
2 years to less than 5	30	28	33	40	41	36
5 years or more	41	48	36	30	32	36
Time in personnel management						
Less than 2 years	5	6	2	10	6	
2 years to less than 5	10	14	16	12	13	
5 years to less than 10	27	18	19	21	21	
10 years or more	59	62	63	58	60	

	1998		2004	
Time in personnel/HR	HR title	Other title	HR title	Other title
Less than 2 years	2	2	4	23
2 years to less than 5	18	15	10	15
5 years to less than 10	17	19	22	17
10 years or more	63	63	64	45

Source: WIRS/WERS data.

years that they are more likely to be found in the private manufacturing sector compared with the public sector, but this was heavily influenced by results from the earlier surveys, notably 1984, and had completely disappeared by 2004. Analysis across the surveys indicates that, controlling for other factors, the probability of having a qualified specialist running employment relations at the workplace rose by a statistically significant 14 percentage points between 1980 and 1998, and by 15 percentage points between 1980 and 2004.

There is some indication in the more recent surveys that those using the 'human resource' title are more likely to have specialist qualifications. Among those using this title, 72% in 1994 and 67% in 2004 claimed specialist qualifications, while among those using other specialist titles, such as 'personnel manager', the proportion had dropped from 71% in 1998 to 55% in 2004. This is a large and unexpected drop. It might be explained by those with qualifications seeking to get their post re-titled, although the more detailed analysis by Kersley *et al.* (2006) suggests that this is unlikely; or it may reflect an influx of unqualified specialists into workplaces where the more traditional title was preferred, a possibility supported by the data in Table 6.3 above.

Women in personnel management

Are more women now working in personnel management? Given the growing proportion of women among those gaining CIPD qualifications, we might expect to find an increase in the proportion of women in specialist personnel roles. The surveys did not collect data on the gender of the interviewee in 1984 and 1990, so we can only compare data from the 1980, 1998 and 2004 surveys. The proportion of female personnel specialists has risen from 19% in 1980 to 62% in 1998, and to 68% in 2004. A similar, if less marked, trend is apparent in the proportion of female non-specialists, which has risen from 11% in 1980, to 31% in 1998, and to 35% in 2004. Both sets of figures confirm the growing presence of women in managerial roles. Regression analysis confirms that the increase in female personnel managers since 1980 is statistically significant; controlling for other factors the probability of having a female personnel manager rose by 22 percentage points by 1998, and by 26 percentage points by 2004. This trend was apparent across the public sector, private services and private manufacturing.

Experience in personnel management

With the growth in specialist employment relations managers, it is possible that those in personnel management are less experienced than in the past. The propensity for frequent reorganisations may also limit experience in a specific role. Indeed, the CIPD survey of the human resource function reported that most had been reorganised in the past year (CIPD, 2007). Nevertheless, the relevant evidence, presented in Table 6.3, shows no change in the time spent in the current job since 1990, challenging the assumption of an increase in turbulence and job change. In contrast, figures reveal an increase in 2004 in the proportion who are new to personnel management. The bottom of the table reveals that this has occurred predominantly among specialists who are not using the HR title. It should be borne in mind that these are a declining proportion of personnel specialists.[2]

Board representation

What has happened to board-level representation of the personnel function? Representation on the main board of an organisation is generally

---

[2] There has been a sudden decline in the employment relations experience of non-specialist managers since 1998: the percentage with at least ten years' experience fell from 67 per cent in 1998 to 46 per cent in 2004.

viewed as a desirable goal by the personnel profession since it can be interpreted as an indication of status, importance and centrality to the organisation. Indeed, there is evidence that employment relations issues are more likely to be viewed strategically where there is board level representation (Marginson *et al.*, 1993), and that the personnel function as a whole is likely to be more influential (Guest and Peccei, 1994). This assumption has not gone undisputed. Kelly and Gennard (2007) argue that the development and implementation of strategy is more likely to occur in an executive group or executive board.

When exploring this issue in the WERS series, the most valid comparison is based on a restricted set of organisations consisting of multi-establishment workplaces in the private sector which are at least 50 per cent British-owned. The surveys asked whether there was someone on the board or top governing body with particular responsibility for employment relations. This person may not always be someone with a specialist title. The evidence shows that there has been remarkably little change over the years. In 1980, 73 per cent of respondents indicated that the function was represented on the main board, and in 2004 this figure was 72 per cent. In the intervening years, the figures changed only slightly, although there was some indication of a dip in 1998.[3]

Summary

The analysis has highlighted and confirmed a number of trends. First, there has been some growth, notably since 1990, in the proportion of those with specialist titles who acted as workplace respondents with responsibility for employment relations. There has also been a marked growth over this period in the proportion of specialists who have adopted the 'human resource' title, to a point where it is much more common than 'personnel manager', 'people manager' or any other alternatives. At workplace level, in contrast to 1980, the specialist role is now dominated by women, and this trend appears to be continuing. Personnel specialists are also becoming better qualified, more particularly where they have adopted the 'human resource' title, so that a relevant specialist qualification is now the norm.

Some things have not changed. Time in the job and in the profession has remained fairly constant. Time in the job is especially noteworthy, given the assumption of continual organisational changes and claims about the reorganisation of the function. There has also been no change

---

[3] For a fuller discussion, see Millward *et al.* (2000: 76–7).

in the proportion of workplaces that have a board member, usually at a higher level, with responsibility for employment relations.

Finally, a theme of this chapter is the change from industrial relations to human resource management. There is strong evidence that personnel specialists have adopted the human resource management title in recent years, with foreign-owned workplaces leading the way. However, even in 1980, industrial relations was never reflected in the job titles of respondents. Such evidence as we can glean from those cases where respondents came from a higher level implies that where industrial or employment relations specialists existed, they operated at that higher level in the organisation. If any trend from industrial relations to human resource management is not readily apparent in job titles, it may be more apparent in the activities in the workplace. This is the focus of the next section.

Specialist roles and personnel practices

How far does the presence of a personnel specialist affect the kind of practices adopted in a workplace? Because of the greater focus they can give to the role and, in the case of those with specialist qualifications, the distinctive knowledge and training they have gained, we might expect that, where there is a specialist, the workplace will adopt more personnel practices. Furthermore, the workplace might be expected to have adopted more of those practices that might be construed as contemporary human resource practices, rather than the more traditional practices associated with an industrial relations focus.

In this section we will use two definitions of specialist. The first is based on the title of the workplace respondent. If the respondent has a title that refers to personnel, human resources, employment relations, industrial relations or other similar titles, then they are defined as having a specialist role. As noted in Table 6.1, the proportion of respondents with a specialist title grew from 15 per cent in 1980 to 30 per cent in 2004. The second criterion that we adopt is the possession of a professional qualification. This addresses the claims for the benefits of the professionalisation of the function, promoted in particular by the CIPD. There are restrictions on the comparisons that can be made using the WIRS/WERS data since, as noted earlier, questions about professional qualifications are only asked of those who spend 25 per cent or more of their time on employment relations matters. However, this has the advantage of providing a direct comparison among those spending a substantial amount of time on personnel activities (whether they are designated as a specialist or not), according to whether or not they are a specialist with a professional qualification.

A direct comparison of trends in practices could be misleading since the presence of practices is likely to be influenced by a range of factors such as workplace size, presence of trade unions and sector. We therefore undertook a series of regression analyses that enabled us to control for a range of background factors. Those we included were sector, number of employees in the establishment, foreign ownership, region, single or multiple site, age of establishment, the proportion of the workforce that were female, part-time and non-manual and, finally, survey date.

One theme of this chapter is to map any change in the focus of personnel management and, in particular, any trend from industrial relations to human resource practices. We wanted to focus on some practices that reflected each approach. Since we are also interested in trends over the twenty-five years of WERS, the number that can be included is strictly limited. Indeed, we had to relax this requirement and include some practices that have only been measured over three surveys. As a result, the practices that we monitor to explore the impact of the presence of specialists and professionals, with the dates of surveys in which they are covered shown in brackets, are:

Industrial relations:
• the presence of a trade union representative (1980–2004)
• establishment-level bargaining (1980–2004)
• a joint consultative committee (1980–2004).

Human resource management:
• employee share-ownership (1980–2004)
• profit-related pay (1984–2004)
• information provision (1984–2004)
• briefing groups (1984–2004)
• problem-solving groups (1990–2004).

We recognise that this is a limited list of practices and that recent surveys have included a larger number of human resource practices. However, our aim was to monitor trends over the years of WERS, and this list of practices should be sufficient to identify any significant influence of a personnel specialist and professionally qualified manager.

While accepting that these sets of what we have labelled 'industrial relations' and 'human resource' practices are incomplete, we undertook factor analyses to determine to what extent they combined in a coherent way. We found that there were two distinct factors. However, they did not work well as scales, having alpha values of 0.48 and 0.49 respectively. Nevertheless, we followed the practice in many studies of human resource management and performance, and obtained scores on the two sets of variables by measuring in each workplace the number that were present to provide a more global score on industrial relations practices and human resource practices.

The influence of a specialist on industrial relations practices

We look first at the influence of personnel specialists on the three industrial relations practices. The results are summarised in Table 6.4, which shows the pooled results across the five surveys. For each of the three practices, the first column shows the results for the presence of someone at the workplace with a specialist title, while the second shows the results when we compare specialists with a professional qualification with others who spend at least 25 per cent of their time on personnel issues.

The presence of a personnel specialist has no significant association with presence of a workplace union representative, but it is associated with bargaining at workplace level and with a workplace joint consultative committee. Separate year regressions (not shown but available on request) show that the association with workplace bargaining is significant in 1980, 1984 and 1998 but not the other survey years, and that there is no clear trend. The association between a personnel specialist and the presence of a joint consultative committee is significant in 1998 and 2004, and the coefficient has risen over time implying that the presence of a specialist has an increasingly important influence. Being a specialist with professional qualifications has less impact. Among those spending at least one-quarter of their time on employment relations matters, the only association with being a qualified specialist is with the greater likelihood of the presence of a joint consultative committee in the pooled data. However, this association is not significant in any specific year.

The analysis of the trend over the years shows that the presence of a union representative increased between 1980 and 1984, but has been declining steadily since then. Workplace bargaining has been following a similar trend, although the decline only became significant in 1998 and 2004. The presence of a joint consultative committee has tended to decline marginally over the years, but this decline has become more marked and reaches significance in 2004. This is somewhat surprising in the light of the impending legal requirement to institute consultative arrangements with employees. It is notable that the association between the presence of joint consultative committees and personnel specialists has strengthened over time, perhaps reflecting greater awareness in 2004 of the impending legislation in workplaces with in-house employment relations expertise.

Table 6.4 *The influence of a specialist on industrial relations practices*

	Presence of union representative		Workplace bargaining		Joint consultative committee		Combined measure of IR practices	
	Pooled (1)	Pooled (2)	Pooled (1)	Pooled (2)	Pooled (1)	Pooled (2)	Pooled (1)	Pooled (2)
Specialist title (1)	-0.01 (0.85)		0.04 (3.87)**		0.10 (4.44)**		0.13 (4.29)**	
Professional Qualification (2)		0.01 (0.34)		0.02 (1.64)		0.07 (2.36)*		0.09 (2.38)*
Union recognition	0.65 (39.14)**	0.65 (28.39)**	0.19 (16.43)**	0.20 (12.52)**	0.62 (3.53)**	0.03 (1.27)	0.90 (30.80)**	0.89 (20.77)**
Sector – manufacturing	-0.04 (2.05)*	-0.07 (2.82)**	0.25 (17.33)**	0.29 (14.15)**	-0.10 (3.65)**	-0.12 (3.19)**	0.11 (3.07)**	0.10 (2.03)*
Sector – private services	-0.08 (4.44)**	-0.08 (3.51)**	0.13 (13.07)**	0.13 (9.47)**	-0.13 (6.33)**	-0.14 (5.16)**	-0.09 (2.75)**	-0.09 (2.24)*
Size of establishment 50–99	0.05 (4.47)**	0.06 (3.24)**	-0.00 (0.17)	-0.01 (0.56)	0.09 (5.07)**	0.10 (3.51)**	0.15 (6.09)**	0.15 (4.11)**
100–199	0.12 (8.40)**	0.13 (6.37)**	0.02 (2.44)*	0.02 (1.33)	0.18 (8.53)**	0.22 (7.34)**	0.32 (11.37)**	0.37 (8.88)**
200–499	0.21 (12.61)**	0.21 (9.72)**	0.07 (5.07)**	0.08 (4.60)**	0.29 (11.51)**	0.33 (10.55)**	0.57 (16.55)**	0.63 (14.16)**
500+	0.23 (12.00)**	0.23 (9.30)**	0.11 (7.19)**	0.12 (6.09)**	0.35 (12.36)**	0.39 (11.90)**	0.70 (17.87)**z	0.74 (15.17)**
Foreign ownership	0.01 (0.89)	0.00 (0.07)	0.06 (4.30)**	0.05 (2.64)**	-0.04 (1.29)	-0.06 (1.47)	0.04 (1.06)	-0.01 (0.21)
Single establishment	0.00 (0.20)	0.01 (0.48)	0.04 (3.95)**	0.06 (3.52)**	-0.06 (3.54)**	-0.08 (3.17)**	-0.02 (0.80)	-0.02 (0.47)

Age of establishment	<5 years	−0.00	0.03	0.00	−0.00	−0.01	−0.05	−0.01	−0.02
		(0.29)	(1.56)	(0.34)	(0.18)	(0.43)	(1.63)	(0.37)	(0.43)
	5–9 years	−0.12	−0.01	−0.00	0.01	−0.00	0.02	−0.02	0.02
		(1.15)	(0.35)	(0.29)	(0.81)	(0.08)	(0.44)	(0.64)	(0.41)
Proportion of women		−0.10	−0.12	−0.01	−0.01	0.00	−0.07	−0.11	−0.20
		(4.06)**	(3.47)**	(0.93)	(0.64)	(0.01)	(1.24)	(2.38)*	(2.84)**
Proportion of part-time		−0.51	−0.05	0.01	−0.01	−0.02	−0.02	−0.07	−0.10
		(1.82)	(1.41)	(0.77)	(0.83)	(0.57)	(0.41)	(1.20)	(1.18)
Proportion of non-manual		0.01	−0.01	−0.00	−0.01	0.04	0.03	0.04	0.00
		(0.40)	(0.42)	(0.29)	(0.82)	(1.48)	(0.81)	(1.27)	(0.12)
WERS 1984		0.03	0.06	−0.01	−0.03	−0.00	−0.01	0.02	0.03
		(2.07)*	(2.46)*	(1.07)	(1.45)	(0.11)	(0.21)	(0.70)	(0.59)
WERS 1990		−0.03	−0.01	−0.01	−0.01	−0.03	−0.06	−0.07	−0.07
		(1.98)*	(0.37)	(0.54)	(0.47)	(1.35)	(1.68)	(2.15)*	(1.53)
WERS 1998		−0.08	−0.07	−0.03	−0.03	−0.02	−0.04	−0.12	−0.14
		(4.66)**	(2.95)**	(2.79)**	(1.69)	(0.86)	(1.11)	(3.98)**	(2.89)**
WERS 2004		−0.08	−0.07	−0.02	−0.02	−0.06	−0.05	−0.16	−0.14
		(4.09)**	(2.80)**	(2.49)*	(1.34)	(2.65)**	(1.26)	(4.94)**	(2.84)**
Constant		0.11	0.12	−0.17	−0.15	0.28	0.37	0.23	0.34
		(4.40)**	(3.43)**	(10.62)**	(6.69)**	(8.45)**	(7.12)**	(4.71)**	(4.77)**
Observations		7,676	4,867	7,676	4,867	7,665	4,863	7,676	4,867
Adjusted R²		0.62	0.65	0.24	0.28	0.13	0.15	0.50	0.52

Notes: Reference categories are public sector for sector; 25–49 employees for size; 10+ years for age; WERS 1980 for the surveys. Region was included in the regressions and is sometimes significant but is not included in the table. OLS regressions weighted with establishment survey weights.

Source: WERS data.

*p < 0.05, **p < 0.01.

Table 6.5 *The influence of a specialist on human resource practices*

		Briefing groups		Problem-solving groups		Information provision	
		Pooled (1)	Pooled (2)	Pooled (1)	Pooled (2)	Pooled (1)	Pooled (2)
Specialist title (1)		−0.01 (0.63)		−0.08 (3.17)**		−0.00 (0.05)	
Professional qualification (2)			−0.00 (0.00)		−0.04 (1.10)		0.06 (0.90)
Union recognition		0.07 (3.15)**	0.08 (2.54)*	0.02 (0.88)	0.06 (1.69)	0.34 (6.78)**	0.38 (6.00)**
Sector – manufacturing		−0.13 (3.74)**	−0.06 (1.46)	0.01 (0.32)	0.09 (1.59)	0.10 (1.28)	0.14 (1.52)
Sector – private services		−0.04 (1.60)	−0.00 (0.07)	−0.06 (1.97)*	−0.02 (0.53)	−0.02 (0.40)	0.05 (0.78)
Size of establishment	50–99	0.04 (1.80)	0.03 (1.06)	0.01 (0.33)	0.02 (0.56)	0.13 (2.72)**	0.07 (1.05)
	100–199	0.06 (2.67)**	0.05 (1.49)	0.09 (3.03)**	0.06 (1.46)	0.10 (1.79)	−0.03 (0.45)
	200–499	0.08 (2.92)**	0.04 (1.29)	0.14 (4.51)**	0.07 (1.82)	0.18 (3.01)**	0.09 (1.19)
	500+	0.10 (3.34)**	0.07 (1.98)*	0.22 (6.42)**	0.15 (3.60)**	0.38 (5.84)**	0.30 (4.19)**
Foreign ownership		−0.03 (0.79)	−0.04 (0.82)	0.03 (0.78)	0.06 (1.17)	−0.04 (0.44)	−0.13 (1.14)
Single establishment		−0.06 (2.48)*	−0.07 (1.90)	−0.08 (2.95)**	−0.07 (1.76)	−0.44 (7.76)**	−0.43 (5.55)**

	(1)	(2)	(3)	(4)	(5)	(6)
Age of establishment <5 years	0.04 (1.02)	0.07 (1.27)	−0.03 (0.75)	−0.05 (1.10)	0.03 (0.37)	0.10 (1.01)
5–9 years	0.05 (1.58)	0.05 (1.17)	−0.04 (1.22)	−0.07 (1.52)	−0.05 (0.77)	−0.11 (1.26)
Proportion of women	0.18 (3.86)**	0.11 (1.82)	0.17 (3.25)**	0.23 (3.46)**	−0.01 (0.07)	−0.15 (1.25)
Proportion of part-time	−0.04 (0.78)	−0.06 (0.87)	−0.13 (2.31)*	−0.11 (1.47)	0.28 (2.46)*	0.35 (2.46)*
Proportion of non-manual	0.02 (0.60)	0.02 (0.43)	0.09 (2.33)*	0.08 (1.72)	0.34 (4.91)**	0.29 (3.40)**
WERS 1990	0.11 (4.15)**	0.16 (4.36)**			0.18 (3.11)**	0.27 (3.72)**
WERS 1998	0.17 (6.26)**	0.12 (3.13)**	0.10 (3.62)**	0.02 (0.54)	0.47 (8.14)**	0.48 (6.51)**
WERS 2004	0.38 (14.37)**	0.38 (11.32)**	−0.00 (0.16)	−0.07 (1.91)	0.47 (8.05)**	0.51 (7.03)**
Constant	0.30 (6.43)**	0.31 (4.85)**	0.30 (5.68)**	0.27 (3.94)**	0.97 (9.95)**	1.09 (8.44)**
Observations	5,907	3,930	4,308	2,805	5,907	3,930
Adjusted R^2	0.13	0.11	0.06	0.07	0.14	0.12

Notes: Reference categories are public sector for sector; 25–49 employees for size; 10+ years for age; WERS 1984 for the surveys for briefing groups and information provision and WERS 1990 for problem-solving groups (because they are not present in 1984 data). Region was included in the regressions and is sometimes significant but is not included in the table. Information provision is based on management provision of information on investment plans, financial position of the workplace and staffing plans. OLS regressions weighted with establishment survey weights.

Source: WERS data.

*p < 0.05, **p < 0.01.

To gain a more coherent picture of the association between the presence of a personnel specialist and traditional industrial relations practices, we combined the three measures by simply counting how many were present in each workplace. This revealed that 50% had none of them, 31% had one, 17% had two and only 3% had all three. Using this measure, the pooled results, summarised in the right hand columns of Table 6.4, show a significant positive association between the presence of both a personnel specialist and a professionally qualified specialist and the greater use of these practices. In the case of a personnel specialist, this can be largely accounted for by the stronger and statistically significant association in the 1998 and 2004 surveys. For the professional specialists, the association is consistently positive in each year, but only statistically significant in the pooled years regression. These results should be viewed against a backdrop of a steady decline in the use of these practices in successive surveys. Relative to 1980, the probability of scoring an additional point on the (0,3) scale falls by 6 percentage points between 1980 and 1990, by 12 percentage points between 1980 and 1998 and by 16 percentage points between 1980 and 2004. The pattern noted above for the whole economy is closely mirrored when the analysis is restricted to the trading sector.

The influence of a specialist on human resource practices

The influence of a personnel specialist on the adoption of what we have defined as human resource practices is shown in two separate tables. Table 6.5 shows the results for practices that apply to the whole economy while Table 6.6 shows results restricted to the trading sector since they are concerned with aspects of profit-sharing and employee share-ownership that can only occur in this sector.

Table 6.5 addresses briefing groups, problem-solving groups and information sharing. Briefing groups are defined as regular meetings that occur at least monthly between line managers and the workers for whom they are responsible. Problem-solving groups are defined as groups that solve specific problems or discuss aspects of performance or quality. Information sharing occurs when management distributes information on investment plans, the financial position of the establishment and staffing plans. They are not particularly novel practices, but they are commonly found in lists of human resource practices (see, for example, Appelbaum et al., 2000) and serve to represent such practices. If specialists are more likely to adopt human resource practices in general, then we might expect them to do so in the case of these practices.

Table 6.5 implies almost no significant influence of personnel specialists or those with professional qualifications on the adoption of each of these practices. The only significant results show that personnel specialists are less likely to be associated with the adoption of problem-solving groups. Closer inspection reveals that the presence of a personnel specialist was negatively associated with the use of problem-solving groups in each of the three surveys where this question was included, and was significantly negative in 1998. For those specialists with professional qualifications, it was significantly negative in 1990, but had shifted to becoming a marginally positive association by 2004. However, neither set of results suggests that specialists are at the forefront of innovation in human resource practices. Separate year regressions for the use of briefing groups also show a small and statistically insignificant negative sign in each year for both measures of specialism, with the exception of 1990 when the sign becomes positive. Finally, with respect to information provision, the general pattern for both specialist roles and specialist qualifications reveals small positive associations in each year except 1998, when, in the case of personnel specialists it is significantly negative, and for those with specialist qualifications, it is marginally negative. In summary, there is no evidence that personnel specialists in general, or those with professional qualifications, set the trend with respect to human resource practices. If anything, in a context where use of these practices has been growing over the years – as indicated by the trends in the survey year coefficients in the pooled regressions – the workplaces in which specialists are present tend to lag behind in adopting them.

Practices associated with financial participation can only be considered in the context of the trading sector. The relevant findings for profit-related pay and employee share-ownership are shown in Table 6.6.

The results in Table 6.6 confirm the pattern noted for the other practices. There is no significant association between either indicator of personnel specialists and the uptake of either form of financial participation. This is despite a big growth in the use of employee share-ownership between 1980 and 1990, after which there was less change and a big growth in use of profit-related pay between 1984, when data about this were first collected and 1998, followed by a levelling off. Closer inspection of the results for separate years reveals that the association between profit-related pay and the two measures of personnel specialist is always negative but non-significant, except for the single case of qualified specialists in 1998, when the sign becomes positive before reverting to negative in 2004. In contrast, the signs for employee share-ownership are positive in each year, and are significantly positive in 1990 for both measures of personnel specialism. However, once again, the pattern is somewhat

Table 6.6 *The influence of a specialist on human resource practices (private trading sector only)*

		Profit-related pay		Employee share-ownership		Combined measure of HR practices	
		Pooled (1)	Pooled (2)	Pooled (1)	Pooled (2)	Pooled (1)	Pooled (2)
Specialist title (1)		−0.05 (1.52)		0.03 (1.17)		−0.00 (0.05)	
Professional qualification (2)			−0.01 (0.44)		0.05 (1.67)		0.05 (1.55)
Union recognition		0.00 (0.12)	−0.04 (1.43)	0.11 (5.95)**	0.11 (3.82)**	0.23 (5.39)**	0.16 (3.00)**
Sector – private manufacturing		−0.01 (0.34)	−0.04 (1.08)	−0.02 (1.05)	−0.08 (2.81)**	−0.08 (1.63)	−0.11 (1.59)
Size of establishment	50–99	0.04 (1.38)	0.04 (1.00)	0.02 (1.31)	0.01 (0.45)	0.16 (3.46)**	0.06 (0.95)
	100–199	0.07 (2.40)*	0.06 (1.64)	0.03 (1.55)	0.04 (1.23)	0.24 (4.58)*	0.13 (1.96)
	200–499	0.09 (2.57)*	0.11 (2.68)**	0.12 (4.35)**	0.13 (3.68)**	0.37 (6.15)**	0.26 (3.75)**
	500+	0.11 (2.86)**	0.12 (3.00)**	0.11 (3.47)**	0.13 (3.42)**	0.56 (8.10)**	0.47 (6.28)**
Foreign ownership		−0.04 (1.06)	−0.05 (1.17)	−0.11 (3.65)**	−0.09 (2.17)*	−0.17 (2.45)*	−0.20 (2.49)*
Single establishment		−0.18 (6.67)**	−0.20 (5.34)**	−0.25 (14.55)**	−0.24 (9.48)**	−0.44 (9.94)**	−0.52 (7.87)**
Age of establishment	<5 years	−0.02 (0.43)	0.02 (0.32)	−0.00 (0.01)	0.01 (0.29)	0.11 (1.78)	0.25 (2.69)**
	5–9 years	0.03 (0.79)	0.05 (1.08)	−0.01 (0.31)	−0.01 (0.44)	0.13 (2.20)*	0.13 (1.63)

	(1)	(2)	(3)	(4)	(5)	(6)
Proportion of women	−0.14	−0.24	−0.07	−0.15	0.02	−0.23
	(2.49)*	(3.35)**	(1.99)*	(2.84)**	(0.25)	(1.94)
Proportion of part-time	−0.04	0.07	0.15	0.21	−0.07	0.07
	(0.63)	(0.83)	(3.29)**	(3.15)**	(0.66)	(0.57)
Proportion of non-manual	0.22	0.16	0.19	0.19	0.38	0.27
	(5.61)**	(3.31)**	(6.72)**	(4.70)**	(5.65)**	(3.29)**
WERS 1984			0.07	0.08		
			(3.49)**	(2.37)*		
WERS 1990	0.25	0.27	0.15	0.21	0.39	0.50
	(8.97)**	(6.98)**	(6.92)**	(5.47)**	(7.22)**	(6.61)**
WERS 1998	0.30	0.31	0.13	0.14	0.54	0.50
	(10.08)**	(7.81)**	(5.29)**	(3.78)**	(10.38)**	(6.60)**
WERS 2004	0.28	0.29	0.16	0.17	0.83	0.84
	(8.83)**	(7.59)**	(5.95)**	(4.58)**	(14.69)**	(11.64)**
Constant	0.20	0.23	0.07	0.11	0.60	0.81
	(4.63)**	(3.82)**	(2.42)*	(2.10)*	(7.61)**	(7.16)**
Observations	4,070	2,639	5,273	3,280	4,070	2,369
Adjusted R^2	0.13	0.14	0.18	0.17	0.23	0.23

Notes: Reference categories are private services for sector; 25–49 employees for size; 10+ years for age; WERS 1980 for the surveys but note that the question about profit-related pay was not asked in 1980 so the reference category becomes 1984. Region was included in the regressions and is sometimes significant but is not included in the table. The measure of profit-related pay includes deferred schemes for 1984–1998 but not in 2004. OLS regressions weighted with establishment survey weights.

Source: WERS data.

*p < 0.05, **p < 0.01.

inconsistent with a small negative association for the specialist role in 1990 and for the qualified specialist in 1984.

To obtain a more general picture of the role of personnel specialists in the adoption of human resource practices, we combined the four human resource management practices available since 1984 (share-ownership, profit-sharing, information provision, and briefing groups) into a single measure for workplaces in the trading sector. The count variable runs from zero to three, with workplaces scoring each time they have: a briefing group, all three types of information provision, either profit-sharing or share-ownership. The results are shown in the right hand columns of Table 6.6. There is no statistically significant association between the human resource management count and the presence of a personnel specialist, except in 1998 when there is a negative association. In the case of the qualified specialists, there is no significant association, except in 1990 when it is positive. The very limited influence of personnel specialists should be viewed against a backdrop of the steadily increasing adoption of these practices over the years in which the surveys were conducted.

Our analysis so far has combined the various specialist titles. One possibility is that those with the 'human resource' title engage in different practices from those with more traditional titles. We have not undertaken an in-depth analysis of this because good evidence is only available in the two most recent surveys in the WERS series. However, this issue has been carefully examined by Kersley *et al.* (2006), building on an earlier study of the 1998 survey by Hoque and Noon (2001), and they found a number of differences. Those using the title of human resource manager tended to have more autonomy and to devolve more to line managers than those titled personnel managers. With respect to their duties and responsibilities, the differences were generally small with the exception of pay and, to some extent, pensions where those with the human resource title were more likely to have responsibility. Taking account of the different backgrounds and qualifications and the differences in autonomy and delegation, Kersley *et al.* (2006) conclude that there are differences of substance and not a mere re-titling of the role.

Summary: personnel specialists and personnel practices

The results outlined above are almost the opposite of those we expected to find. While the analysis of the trend over successive WERSs confirms the decline in the use of industrial relations practices, where a personnel specialist is present these practices are more likely to persist. Within the specialist personnel population, this tendency is slightly stronger where there is a qualified specialist. How are we to explain this? It is possible that organisation size plays a part, although we controlled for size of establishment and multi- versus single-site organisations in the regressions. It is also possible that personnel specialists are associated with the formalisation of policy and practice, and then help to maintain formal practices such as workplace bargaining and consultation.

The findings from this analysis of successive WERS confirm the decline in industrial relations practices and the growth of human resource practices. However, contrary to expectations, personnel specialists, including qualified specialists, are not in the vanguard of human resource innovations. If anything, they tend to lag slightly behind the general trend. Although those using the human resource title are more likely to engage in a number of activities that are a little closer to what authorities such as Ulrich (1997) have advocated, there is little basis in these results on which to claim that they are 'human resource champions'. Furthermore, they are much more likely to be associated with the maintenance of traditional industrial relations arrangements.

The rather traditional stance of personnel specialists is understandable if it is associated with higher performance. But much of the recent debate and research about human resource management and performance has confirmed an association between the adoption of more of what we have termed human resource practices and organisational performance (Boselie et al., 2005: Combs et al., 2006). However, the earlier analyses suggest that trade union recognition is associated with the adoption of human resource practices, and it is possible that maintenance of traditional industrial relations practices also contributes to this (Bryson et al., 2005). The next section therefore looks for any association between the presence of a personnel specialist or a professionally qualified specialist and workplace performance, taking into account the presence of various personnel practices.

Personnel specialists and workplace performance

Is the presence of a personnel specialist associated with better workplace performance? Given the evidence for an association between human resource practices and firm performance, it is plausible, despite some of the findings in the previous section, to assume that the presence of specialists who have some responsibility for these practices may also be associated with superior workplace performance. This section sets out to answer the question by analysing two sets of outcome measures. The first, which can be reasonably objectively assessed and which potentially applies to all workplaces, concerns levels of labour turnover and the incidence of industrial conflict. While there may be cases in which organisations seek a higher than normal level of labour turnover, we are assuming in the present context that a lower level of staff turnover is a positive outcome. We are making the same assumption in the case of industrial conflict.

The next three outcomes are based on ratings by the respondent of the employment relations climate and of comparative levels of productivity and financial performance. These are standard questions that have been asked in several surveys in the WERS series. They are subject to a positive skew and are also likely to suffer from common method variance, in so far as the same respondent is providing information about both the independent and dependent variables (Spector, 2006; Wright *et al.*, 2001). There is also an as yet not fully resolved debate about how closely these subjective ratings provide an accurate reflection of actual performance (See Wall *et al.*, 2004, and chapter 10 in Kersley *et al.*, 2006). However, if we assume that the error randomises out, and the skew is reasonably consistent, then these ratings still provide a potentially useful way of assessing any link between personnel specialists and workplace performance.

In what follows we restrict the analyses to workplaces in the private trading sector. It should be borne in mind that the first column in each of the tables explores the impact of a specialist personnel role using the full sample of workplaces while the second column, focusing on the impact of a qualified specialist, is restricted to workplaces that have a manager spending at least 25 per cent of their time on employment relations matters. We refer to these as samples 1 and 2 respectively.

Labour turnover and industrial conflict

The results for the first two items, covering labour turnover and industrial conflict, are presented in Table 6.7. Labour turnover is measured using a banded variable where 1 is low (5 per cent or less), 2 is middling (5 to 13 per cent) and 3 is high (more than 13 per cent). Industrial conflict is a (0,1) outcome with workplaces scoring 1 where they report some form of industrial action in the past twelve months. The survey date coefficients in the pooled regressions indicate no consistent trend in labour turnover over the period. In contrast, the incidence of industrial conflict has declined since 1984, although the main decline was between 1984 and 1990; since then the levels of conflict have remained fairly stable and very low. There is no significant association between either the presence of a personnel specialist or a qualified specialist and lower labour turnover or industrial conflict. We also ran the analysis using

Table 6.7 *The association between personnel specialists and workplace performance (private trading sector)*

		Labour turnover		Industrial conflict	
		Pooled (1)	Pooled (2)	Pooled (1)	Pooled (2)
Specialist title (1)		0.07		0.00	
		(1.25)		(0.28)	
Professional qualification (2)			0.08		0.01
			(1.24)		(1.21)
Industrial relations practices		−0.08	−0.08	0.03	0.03
		(1.81)	(1.77)	(3.45)**	(2.13)**
Human resource practices		−0.02	−0.09	0.01	0.02
		(1.00)	(2.83)**	(1.80)	(2.61)**
Union recognition		−0.26	−0.30	0.05	0.05
		(4.01)**	(3.83)**	(3.39)**	(2.41)*
Sector − manufacturing		−0.15	−0.13	0.02	0.02
		(2.31)*	(1.60)	(1.60)	(1.31)
Size of establishment	50–99	0.01	0.00	0.01	−0.00
		(0.12)	(0.05)	(1.12)	(0.35)
	100–199	0.21	0.23	0.02	0.03
		(3.83)**	(3.17)**	(1.85)	(1.84)
	200–499	0.12	0.13	0.03	0.03
		(1.68)	(1.62)	(2.24)*	(1.37)
	500+	0.08	0.15	0.11	0.10
		(0.99)	(1.80)	(5.63)**	(4.11)**
Foreign ownership		0.05	−0.01	−0.01	−0.01
		(0.81)	(0.17)	(0.78)	(0.67)
Single establishment		−0.07	−0.08	−0.01	−0.01
		(1.21)	(0.97)	(1.19)	(0.57)
Age of establishment	<5 years	0.14	0.21	0.00	0.01
		(1.70)	(2.57)*	(0.21)	(0.47)
	5–9 years	0.12	0.13	0.01	0.03
		(1.93)	(1.45)	(0.69)	(1.38)
Proportion of women		0.32	0.25	−0.02	−0.05
		(2.99)**	(1.77)	(1.42)	(2.09)*
Proportion of part-time		0.27	0.38	−0.02	0.00
		(2.47)*	(2.68)**	(1.78)	(0.02)
Proportion of non-manual		−0.13	−0.07	−0.01	−0.02
		(1.69)	(0.74)	(1.20)	(1.29)
WERS 1990				−0.04	−0.07
				(3.45)**	(3.46)**
WERS 1998		0.11	−0.01	−0.07	−0.12
		(1.96)*	(0.11)	(6.61)**	(7.15)**
WERS 2004		−0.01	−0.03	−0.06	−0.11
		(0.24)	(0.43)	(4.31)**	(5.71)**
Constant		2.21	2.36	0.05	0.82
		(23.55)**	(16.37)**	(3.35)**	(3.24)**
Observations		2,849	1,817	4,039	2,622
Adjusted R^2		0.12	0.16	0.12	0.16

Note: Reference categories are private services for sector; 25–49 employees for size; 10+ years for age; WERS 1980 for the surveys. Region was included in the regressions and is sometimes significant but is not included in the table. The reference category for survey years is 1984 for industrial conflict and 1990 for labour turnover reflecting the survey years in which relevant data were first collected. OLS regressions weighted with establishment survey weights were used.

Source: WERS data.

*p < 0.05, **p < 0.01.

a continuous measure of labour turnover, excluding those with annual turnover above 110 per cent, and again found no significant associations.[4]

For these analyses, we used the two combined measures of traditional industrial relations and more contemporary human resource practices to explore the more conventional analysis linking practices and performance. We also conducted a separate analysis looking at each individual practice. In general, greater use of traditional industrial relations practices is not significantly associated with levels of labour turnover. However, the presence of a union representative at the workplace is significantly associated with lower labour turnover in the pooled data, and specifically in 2004. This is over and above the negative association with union recognition, also shown in Table 6.7, which is a standard finding in the literature (Freeman and Medoff, 1984). The presence of more industrial relations practices is associated with higher levels of industrial conflict, but it is only significant when we examine the pooled data across the surveys and in 1998. Among the industrial relations practices, the presence of establishment bargaining is significantly associated with more industrial conflict, both in the pooled data and in 1990, even having accounted for the positive effect of union recognition.

In the private trading sector as a whole (sample 1), the greater use of human resource practices is not associated with labour turnover or industrial conflict. However, the results are different among the sub-sample of workplaces with managers spending at least one-quarter of their time on employment relations (sample 2). In this sub-sample, the greater use of human resource practices is associated with lower labour turnover and higher incidence of industrial conflict. The pattern of association between more human resource practices and lower labour turnover is consistent across the surveys and is strong and significant in 2004. The significant association between human resource practices and incidence of industrial conflict, while significant in the pooled analysis, is attributable mainly to the results for 1984 and 1990, and the association all but disappeared in the two more recent surveys. Among the specific practices, the provision of more information is associated both with lower labour turnover and with more industrial conflict in the pooled data in samples 1 and 2.

This initial analysis of outcomes indicates that practices are more strongly associated with turnover and conflict than the presence of a personnel specialist. The previous analysis showed that personnel specialists appeared to have had very little influence on the presence of human resource practices, but were associated with the continuing presence of traditional industrial relations practices. It is possible in the case of these

---

[4] The results were the same when we ran similar analyses for the whole economy.

practices that they mediate the influence of specialists with respect to higher industrial conflict. But we can conclude that there is no mediating process in operation with respect to human resource practices.

Personnel specialists and ratings of employment relations climate, productivity and financial performance

Neither the presence of a specialist personnel role nor the presence of a qualified personnel specialist is associated with the climate of employment relations at the workplace (Table 6.8). There is also no association between the traditional industrial relations and human resource sets of practices and employment relations climate, although the positive association between human resource practices and employment relations climate is close to significance in the pooled data and is significant for 1998 in sample 2. The only individual practice that is significant in the pooled data is the provision of information which is associated with a more positive employment relations climate.[5] It is notable that the ratings of the employment relations climate appear to have deteriorated since 1984, notably between 1984 and 1990, but have been stable since 1990.

The association between the two personnel specialism variables and labour productivity is generally negative, but not statistically significant at a 95 per cent confidence level.[6] There is a positive association between the combined measure of human resource practices and labour productivity. In sample 2, it is significant in the pooled regression and the separate regressions for 1990 and 1998, while in sample 1 it is close to significance in the pooled regression and significant in the 1990 regression.

The final outcome measure, financial performance, is again not significantly associated with either measure of personnel specialism in the pooled data. In the separate year regressions, the signs in both cases are negative, and in the case of the presence of a personnel specialist, the association is significantly negative in 1990. Industrial relations practices are not associated with financial performance (with the exception

---

[5] In the pooled years regressions information provision is associated with both more industrial conflict and a better employment relations climate. The link to industrial conflict is driven by positive associations in 1984 and 2004, both of which are statistically significant at a 90 per cent confidence level. The association with a better employment relations climate is driven by results in 1998. Thus these seemingly conflicting results are partly explained by different effects of information provision in different years. This is not wholly surprising since employers may be inclined to provide more information under two very different scenarios, namely as part of a partnership ethos, or else in response to problems at the workplace.

[6] In the pooled years regression the associations are significant at a 94 per cent confidence level (t = 1.89 in sample 1 and t = 1.95 in sample 2).

Table 6.8 The association between personnel specialists and workplace performance (private trading sector)

		Employment relations climate		Labour productivity		Financial performance	
		Pooled (1)	Pooled (2)	Pooled (1)	Pooled (2)	Pooled (1)	Pooled (2)
Specialist title (1)		−0.05 (1.27)		−0.09 (1.89)		−0.08 (1.75)	
Professional qualification (2)			−0.06 (1.17)		−0.12 (1.95)		−0.10 (1.67)
Industrial relations practices		−0.01 (0.44)	−0.04 (1.23)	0.00 (0.11)	−0.04 (1.06)	0.00 (0.13)	−0.02 (0.51)
Human resource practices		0.01 (0.69)	0.05 (1.91)	0.03 (1.84)	0.06 (2.64)**	0.04 (2.55)*	0.05 (2.28)*
Union recognition		−0.01 (0.29)	0.08 (1.49)	−0.08 (1.48)	0.02 (0.33)	−0.11 (2.36)*	−0.10 (1.67)
Sector – manufacturing		−0.05 (1.42)	0.03 (0.54)	−0.08 (1.55)	−0.14 (2.00)*	−0.06 (1.39)	−0.11 (2.00)*
Size of establishment	50–99	−0.04 (1.33)	−0.08 (1.53)	0.04 (0.95)	0.06 (1.05)	0.08 (2.14)*	0.09 (1.57)
	100–199	−0.12 (3.09)**	−0.16 (2.98)**	0.05 (1.06)	0.10 (1.44)	0.09 (1.98)*	0.13 (2.21)*
	200–499	−0.18 (3.78)**	−0.27 (4.55)**	0.06 (1.10)	0.09 (1.30)	0.13 (2.36)*	0.15 (2.22)*
	500+	−0.13 (2.35)*	−0.20 (3.15)**	0.11 (1.77)	0.17 (2.17)*	0.18 (2.91)**	0.19 (2.60)**
Foreign ownership		−0.00 (0.00)	−0.03 (0.52)	−0.03 (0.44)	−0.01 (0.12)	−0.02 (0.35)	−0.12 (1.68)
Single establishment		0.10 (3.06)**	0.10 (2.12)*	0.09 (2.16)*	0.10 (1.53)	0.01 (0.31)	−0.03 (0.56)

		(1)	(2)	(3)	(4)	(5)	(6)
Age of establishment	5 years	0.13	0.14	0.03	0.02	0.04	−0.03
		(2.81)**	(2.43)*	(0.39)	(0.21)	(0.68)	(0.40)
	5–9 years	−0.05	−0.08	0.07	0.08	0.05	0.04
		(1.18)	(1.25)	(1.44)	(1.30)	(1.11)	(0.64)
Proportion of women		0.17	0.15	0.01	0.08	−0.01	−0.02
		(2.62)**	(1.75)	(0.09)	(0.72)	(0.10)	(0.19)
Proportion of part-time		0.09	0.17	−0.10	−0.09	−0.08	−0.16
		(1.22)	(1.74)	(1.04)	(0.78)	(0.80)	(1.28)
Proportion of non-manual		−0.02	−0.05	0.08	−0.07	0.11	−0.00
		(0.52)	(0.84)	(1.38)	(1.04)	(2.12)*	(0.01)
WERS 1990		−0.13	−0.14			0.02	−0.06
		(3.36)**	(2.60)**			(0.58)	(1.00)
WERS 1998		−0.12	−0.13	0.02	0.08	0.07	−0.01
		(2.97)**	(2.13)*	(0.40)	(1.23)	(1.45)	(0.24)
WERS 2004		−0.11	−0.13	0.05	0.07	0.01	0.01
		(2.47)*	(2.29)*	(1.00)	(1.10)	(0.16)	(0.20)
Constant		2.32	2.28	2.32	2.22	2.36	2.53
		(43.24)**	(28.35)**	(30.41)**	(19.79)**	(36.14)**	(29.11)**
Observations		4,057	2,629	2,627	1,684	3,491	2,264
Adjusted R^2		0.06	0.09	0.03	0.05	0.04	0.05

Notes: Managers are asked to rate the relationship between management and employees on a five-point ordinal scale from 'very good' to 'very poor'. The analysis collapses this scale, distinguishing between workplaces with 'very good/good', 'neither good nor poor' and 'poor/very poor' relations.

Managers are asked to rate labour productivity and financial performance at their establishment 'compared with other establishments in the same industry' on a five-point ordinal scale running from 'a lot better than average' to 'a lot below average'. These scales are collapsed to distinguish between 'above average', 'average' and 'below average'.

Reference categories are private services for sector; 25–49 employees for size; 10+ years for age; For climate and performance WERS 1984 is the reference for the survey years but it is WERS 1990 for productivity due to the absence of productivity data in 1984. Region was included in the regressions and is sometimes significant but is not included in the table. OLS regressions weighted with establishment survey weights were used.

Source: WERS data.

*p < 0.05, **p < 0.01.

of the negative association with union recognition), but there is a significant positive association between the presence of more human resource practices and ratings of comparative financial performance for both samples. This is driven, in particular, by the use of briefing groups and the measure of financial participation which combines share-ownership and profit-related pay. The role of briefing groups is apparent in samples 1 and 2, whereas the significant effect of financial participation is confined to sample 1.

Summary

This set of results is consistent in revealing no positive association between various outcomes and the presence either of personnel specialists or qualified specialists as compared with those who lack such qualifications. Indeed, the general trend suggests that any association is more likely to be negative rather than positive. At the same time, the analysis provides reasonably consistent evidence of an association between the presence of more human resource practices and positive outcomes, while any link with the more traditional industrial relations practices is non-significant.

Discussion and conclusions

The evidence from a quarter century of the Workplace Employment Relations Surveys shows that a growing number of workplaces have a personnel specialist in place, and that an increasing proportion of these specialists have relevant qualifications. Personnel management is becoming more embedded and more professionalised. It is reasonable to assume that personnel specialists are hired to apply contemporary best practice and thereby, perhaps indirectly, to improve performance. Our analysis fails to support this assumption. Personnel specialists are more likely to be associated with traditional industrial relations practices rather than human resource practices. Yet, on the basis of assessments that they have provided, where more human resource practices are in place, performance is more highly rated. Moreover, where personnel specialists are present, including qualified specialists, performance tends, if anything, to be poorer. This raises challenging questions for the personnel profession. First, however, we need to consider how robust these findings are and to set them in a wider context.

The starting point for the analysis in this chapter was an assumption that personnel departments and those who work in them have shifted their main focus over a quarter century of WIRS/WERS from industrial relations to human resource management. The 1980s and 1990s were decades in which the importance of effective management of the workforce appeared to receive higher priority, spurred in part by the shift in focus towards human resource management. If, in the past, a key element in the role had been to 'manage' industrial relations, by the 1980s the focus switched to the need for a more effective management and utilisation of human resources. This coincided with the burgeoning of research on human resource management and performance and the up-beat call-to-arms for personnel specialists issued by Ulrich when he invited them to become 'human resource champions'. If this call was ever answered at the corporate level, and there is strong evidence that Ulrich's work has been highly influential (CIPD, 2007), it does not appear to have filtered down to the workplace. While we have seen a growth in the presence of personnel specialists, and while they have become more qualified, this does not seem to have been reflected in any pioneering of new human resource practices. Indeed, if anything, personnel specialists have been bringing up the rear, holding on to the well-established industrial relations practices, rather than championing the introduction of human resource management.

The possibility that the main innovations in human resource management have occurred at the corporate level rather than in the workplace is one that needs to be considered. A potential source of evidence about this is the comparison between single-site establishments and those that are part of a larger organisation. Tables 6.5 and 6.6 confirm that single establishments are less likely to have put in place each of the human resource practices examined in this study, and are also less likely to operate joint consultative committees. This suggests that being part of a larger organisation does have a positive influence on the use of these practices, and the corporate level may be the source of human resource innovations. Nevertheless, even in workplaces that are part of larger organisations, the application of human resource practices does not appear to be enhanced by the presence of workplace personnel specialists.

Although this chapter has focused on personnel managers, it has also provided some further evidence about the association between human resource management and various outcomes. Even using the limited set of human resource practices that were collected over a number of the surveys, the analysis supports the general findings of the major reviews (Boselie *et al.*, 2005; Combs *et al.*, 2006) in revealing an association between the adoption of more human resource practices and measures of comparative labour productivity and financial performance. While this is an encouraging finding, we need to bear in mind the limitations of subjective ratings of workplace performance (Forth and McNabb, 2008).

On a more salutary note, there is also an association between more use of human resource practices and incidence of industrial conflict, echoing the findings of Fernie *et al.* (1994), who analysed some of the earlier WERS. This finding could be interpreted as lending support to the argument of Ramsay *et al.* (2000) that human resource management is associated with labour intensification. To explore this more fully would require an analysis of the data on employee attitudes and perceptions which is beyond the scope of this chapter.

Those with an interest in employment relations might find something positive in the persisting association between the presence of personnel specialists and some of the features of more traditional industrial relations. On the other hand, these findings do not fit the image promulgated by the CIPD of a profession at the forefront of innovations in human resource management. Despite Ulrich's encouragement, personnel specialists cannot lay claim to be workplace human resource champions. Many years ago, Karen Legge (1978) suggested that if personnel managers were to establish themselves as credible players in organisations, they needed to engage in either deviant or conformist innovation. This analysis provides little evidence of either. Instead, workplace personnel specialists are traditionalists, who are not to be found in the vanguard of human resource innovation. If anything, the evidence suggests that they are bringing up the rear, their presence associated with traditional employment relations, and their time presumably engaged in a range of operational activities. There are indications in the analysis reported by Kersley *et al.* (2006) that some of those adopting the human resource title may be beginning to break out of this mould by devolving certain activities to line managers and by exercising greater autonomy.

Finally, while there is evidence of a positive association between the greater adoption of even a limited number of human resource practices and various indicators of performance, this must be set alongside the failure to find any association between the presence of a specialist personnel role or a qualified specialist and indicators of either human resources practices or performance. The evidence from a quarter century of WIRS/WERS suggests that those interested in innovations in human resource management and contemporary management practice in the workplace should not look to workplace human resource specialists to provide them.

7   High involvement management

Stephen Wood and Alex Bryson

Introduction

High involvement management (HIM) came to the fore in the early 1980s. Heralded by the American organisational psychologist Lawler, it was akin to what Walton and Beer called high commitment management (Lawler, 1986; Walton, 1985; Beer *et al.*, 1984). These authors were describing an innovative approach to management that would – and that they felt should – supersede the Taylorist model, or what Walton called the control approach, which was characterised by its tight division of labour, narrowly defined specialist jobs, limited opportunities for employee involvement and consequently low levels of worker commitment and trust.

Lawler and Walton believed that HIM was increasingly relevant to all organisations as they faced intensifying competition and uncertainty. But past approaches to employment relations that were associated with the Taylorist control model might have to change. HIM implied a more co-operative approach between management and workers or their representatives than the adversarial relationships that had developed on the bedrock of narrow job specifications, payment systems based on rigid job structures or piecework, and oligopolistic product markets.

While some of the early adopters of HIM in the United States were non-union, and some commentators saw HIM as a strategy to undermine unionism, Walton viewed the two as potentially compatible and Lawler implied that union engagement in HIM could be beneficial for its implementation (Lawler *et al.*, 1995: 124). Changes in the role and attitudes of both management and trade unionists might, however, be necessary. Employee participation in decision making on a wider range of issues might be required, perhaps centred on information sharing and consultation rather than bargaining. Kochan and Osterman (1994) went further, envisaging that, through these activities and the greater mutual understanding that they engendered, positive gains from HIM might be even greater when trade unions were involved in their introduction and operation.

The bottom line, it was argued, was that organisations that adopted HIM would achieve superior performance to those that continued with traditional methods. HIM enabled managements to confront increasing global competition whilst providing opportunities to workers for greater rewards and security, as well as the intrinsic satisfaction that employee involvement offered. Indeed, by the early 1990s the performance effects were so taken for granted by some that they labelled HIM 'high performance work systems' (US Department of Labor, 1993; Huselid, 1995).

It is thus timely, a quarter century on from the emergence of the high involvement concept, to examine three aspects of its impact. First, the nature and extent of the use of high involvement practices in Britain, and whether a unified HIM has emerged. Second, whether there is a relationship between HIM and trade unionism and what form it takes. Third, whether HIM is associated with improved organisational performance and, if so, whether this reflects greater levels of job satisfaction and well-being. In this chapter, we offer an overview of its development in Britain, to the extent that WIRS/WERS and other data allow, from the 1980s to the present, focusing on these three questions. Before we address them, we discuss the concept of HIM.

High involvement management

Lawler's concept of HIM and Walton's high commitment approach, which can be treated as synonymous, grew out of their earlier concern with work enrichment, the central feature of which is the development of distinctive job design principles that would reverse the narrow job specifications and rigid divisions of labour associated with Taylorism. Such jobs would increase worker wellbeing through greater autonomy and more challenging work. According to Walton, such principles should apply, so 'jobs are designed to be broader than before, to combine planning and implementation' (Walton, 1985: 79).

HIM, in contrast, meant involving workers in changing not only their roles, but also what Lawler calls 'the business as a whole' (Lawler and Benson, 2003: 156). This 'organisational involvement' extends beyond the role of involvement associated with work enrichment (Wall et al., 2004). We thus use the term HIM to refer to practices offering workers opportunities for organisational involvement, either directly or indirectly through the use of information dissemination and skill acquisition. HIM thus involves, firstly, work organisation practices such as teamworking, flexible job descriptions, and idea-capturing schemes which are means of encouraging greater flexibility, proactivity and collaboration; and, second, practices that give workers the opportunities for skills and knowledge acquisition that are needed to ensure that they have the capacities to work in an involved way. These include intensive training geared towards teamworking, functional flexibility and idea generation, and information sharing, particularly about the economics and market of the organisation.

An emphasis on increasing proactivity and idea generation at all levels of the organisation increasingly became a distinguishing characteristic of HIM, especially in the wake of the effective adoption of quality circles and other idea-capturing schemes in Japanese firms, which were seen as successful innovators, particularly in manufacturing (Wood, 1989, 1993; Jürgens, 1989). The thrust of the HIM model is towards the development of broader horizons amongst all workers, so that they will think of better ways of doing their jobs, connect what they do with what others do and take initiative in the face of novel problems. The purpose of HIM is to encourage workers to participate in what modern management theory calls a continuous improvement culture, the aim being to induce higher performance through the adaptation and proactivity that are thought to characterise modern work requirements (Griffin et al., 2007).

A number of motivational or supporting practices are also associated with HIM (Appelbaum et al., 2000; Forth and Millward, 2004: 100; de Menezes and Wood, 2006). These include incentives for individuals to make use of opportunities for participation, and to gain the skills required in a high involvement regime, and help the organisation to attract and retain suitable employees in order to secure the stable and committed workforce that underpins an effective high involvement regime. They include minimal status differentials, group compensation schemes, internal recruitment and job security guarantees.

The nature and extent of the use of HIM in Britain

The literature emphasises the importance of using HIM as a coherent set of practices if performance is to be optimised (e.g. Appelbaum et al., 2000: 34; Huselid, 1995). This raises the question of the extent to which management has, in practice, adopted HIM in a holistic fashion to achieve what has been termed 'internal fit' (Baird and Meshoulam, 1988). It was, however, commonplace in the 1990s to doubt whether British management was capable of the necessary degree of systemic thinking, the contention being that managers were orientated towards short-term profits and were inclined to eschew a long-term strategic approach to human and organisational issues (Edwards, 1995; Storey and Sisson, 1993: 68–79; Hutton, 1996). It was also believed that management was unduly susceptible to the latest ideas in management circles (Protherough and Pick, 2002: 61). The implication was that initial enthusiasm for particular practices with high visibility would wane as new competing ideas emerged (Marchington *et al.*, 1992). Since certain HIM practices are given more prominence than others at a particular time, one might expect management to adopt them in a rather piecemeal way, and not as a total package.

Organisations may also match their human resource system to its context, which can be either the organisation's core strategy or aspects of its environment (Baird and Meshoulam, 1988; Wood, 1999). According to contingency theory, we might expect HIM's effect on performance to vary with the extent to which it is consistent with relevant external factors. It may even be that there are contexts in which HIM will have no effect or even be counter-productive, which contrasts with the claim of Walton and Lawler that HIM is appropriate to all contexts. Some maintain that HIM's benefits are highest where organisations face a turbulent and uncertain environment, or that HIM is best suited to organisations adopting a high quality as opposed to cost minimisation strategy (Porter, 1985). If organisations are performance maximisers they will match their human resource management to the environmental or strategic context (Wood and Albanese, 1995: 5). If this theory relating fit to performance holds, then external or strategic factors would be associated, at least in the medium to long term, with the extent of HIM usage. Alternatively, if the theory is universally relevant, we would expect HIM not to be limited to certain situations. We would expect it to be more evenly spread across the economy, and its determinants largely to be factors internal to the organisation. It is also possible that the adoption of individual HIM practices has been more idiosyncratic to particular workplaces, or concentrated in certain industries, perhaps because followers of management fashion have mimicked their competitors.

The rise of HIM

Initial accounts of HIM in Britain were based on case-studies. Some of the first reported examples of its intensive use in the 1980s were from the new Japanese-owned manufacturing plants. The first personnel director of the Nissan car factory in the North-East of England, for example, chronicled how he and his colleagues introduced many of the practices associated with HIM (Wickens, 1988). The significant innovations for assembly-line car production included teamworking, complete functional flexibility, intensive selection, daily morning team briefing, intensive training and development, continuous improvement groups akin to quality circles, single status and merit pay for all workers, coupled with an enhanced role and status for the supervisor. Not only were all workers formally appraised, but the criteria used in the appraisal included creativity.

An investigation of fifteen large British organisations in both the private and public sector showed that some of the practices that were used in the Nissan site were being introduced elsewhere (Storey, 1992). These included direct communication methods, such as team briefing and teamworking; increasing functional flexibility; and quality circles and problem-solving teams, typically allied to other quality initiatives. The adoption of performance-related pay was often confined to managers. These initiatives were increasingly related to each other, and viewed as linked. Managers were not merely being opportunistic; the process of change appeared to be becoming more strategic. It was often part of a broader business change agenda that was led significantly by general or operational managers rather than by the personnel function (Storey, 1992: 266–7). Nevertheless, single status or harmonisation – where common terms and conditions are applied for production and white-collar workers – was confined to a small minority of organisations.

One of the first attempts to chart the rise of HIM in Britain was conducted in manufacturing. A survey of 135 plants in 1990, drawn from a sample of workplaces representative of British manufacturing industry in terms of size, region and sector distribution, showed that the use of practices characteristic of the Walton model had increased between 1986 and 1990 (Wood and Albanese, 1995). Work organisation practices such as functional flexibility, teamworking and workers being responsible for their own quality had all increased significantly in the period 1986 to 1990, as Table 7.1 shows. Quality circles, a type of idea-capturing scheme, were less popular, but their use had doubled from 8 per cent in 1986 to 16 per cent in 1990. Skill and information-acquisition practices such as team briefing, training budgets and performance appraisal for workers had also increased.

Motivational supports, such as career ladders and progression, no compulsory redundancy and single status provisions, were only used in a minority of workplaces. But half of them used motivation as a selection criterion in 1986, with this figure rising to nearly three-quarters (72 per cent) in 1990. Work enrichment, which was measured by whether the workplace had 'an explicit policy of designing jobs for ensuring the full use of workers' skills and abilities', was confined to 38 per cent of workplaces and was less common than the high involvement practices. But there had been a rise of 17 percentage points in its use since 1986.

Table 7.1 *Early evidence on the use of high involvement practices in UK manufacturing plants*

	1986	1990
High involvement practices		
Work organisation practices		
Flexible job descriptions	38	69
Teamworking	41	62
Quality circles	8	16
Production workers are responsible for their own quality	51	76
Skill and knowledge acquisition practices		
Team briefing	15	49
Training budgets	17	29
Formal assessment	23	39
Work enrichment practice		
Explicit policy of designing fulfilling jobs	21	38
Motivational practices		
Trainability as a major selection criteria	50	76
Motivation as a major selection criteria	53	72
Career ladders and progression	20	35
No compulsory redundancy	12	19
Single status	13	15
N	135	

Source: Wood and Albanese (1995: 234).

A similar survey was carried out of Japanese manufacturing plants in Britain. Considerable publicity was being given to inward investment from this source and it appeared from this that key plants were being established, like Nissan, with an emphasis on HIM. Moreover, HIM was widely associated with Japanese production methods such as just-in-time production and total quality management, which were beginning to be referred to as 'lean production' (Womack *et al.*, 1990). The comparison of results from 73 Japanese-owned manufacturing plants in Britain with those from the earlier study of 135 manufacturing workplaces showed that all practices, with the exception of teamworking, were more common in the Japanese workplaces (Wood, 1996a).

Evidence of the increasing use of HIM practices between 1996 and 2000 is available from a survey of 126 manufacturing companies with more than 150 employees conducted at the Institute of Work Psychology (IWP) (Wood *et al.*, 2004). This uncovered three trends. First, there had been growth in 'empowerment', a measure that combined both job and organisational involvement of workers. It was defined as 'passing considerable responsibility for operational management to individuals or

Table 7.2 *High involvement practice-use: a comparison of Japanese and non-Japanese plants*

	Non-Japanese plants Percentage use	Japanese plants Percentage use	X^2
High involvement practices			
Work organisation practices			
Flexible job descriptions	68	91	13.8***
Teamworking	67	72	1.4
Quality circles	16	39	13.2***
Production workers are responsible for their own quality	70	94	12.0***
Skill and knowledge acquisition practices			
Team briefing	52	86	26.9***
Training budgets	30	29	0
Formal assessment	29	80	28.4***
Work enrichment practice			
Explicit policy of designing fulfilling jobs	38	56	5.1**
Motivational practices			
Trainability as a major selection criterion	77	86	3.2*
Commitment as a major selection criterion	74.	90	9.2***
Career ladders and progression	35	77	33.3**
No compulsory redundancy	15	58	36.4***
Single status	23	77	57.7***
Merit pay of production workers	50	76	12.0***
Profit-sharing for production workers	25	23	0.6
N	134	73	

Source: Wood (1996a: 515).
*p < 0.1, **p <0.05, ***p < 0.01.

teams (rather than keeping all decision-making at the managerial level)'. Second, there had been an increase in the intensive development of workers, defined as 'providing a range of development opportunities for all employees (rather than training people occasionally to meet specific job needs)'. Third, there had been a growth in the use of teamwork, defined as 'placing operators into teams with their own responsibilities and giving them the freedom to allocate work between team members (rather than having everyone work as individuals)'. This increase in HIM practices was largely attributable to a more comprehensive deployment of existing practices within firms. But there was also a small number of new users, who were as likely to have commenced HIM by using all three practices together as to have introduced practices gradually.

The early WIRS contained few questions on HIM, but, to reflect the growing interest in it, some questions were added to the 1998 survey. They included questions about task flexibility, teamwork and performance appraisal systems, as well as about total quality management, the operational management method authors most commonly associated with HIM (Marginson and Wood, 2000: 490–2). This meant that, for the first time, it was possible to establish more fully the incidence of HIM practices – empowerment, intensive training and teamwork – track trends over time and explore where they might be used across the whole economy. Table 7.3(a) presents the data on practices for the years that it is available in the WERS series for the whole economy, while Tables 7.3(b) and 7.3(c) present data for the private and public sectors respectively.

The two high involvement work-organisation measures for which the WIRS/WERS series provides data since 1990 are suggestion schemes and quality circles. Suggestion schemes were used in a quarter of workplaces in 1984, and over one-third in 2004, a growth wholly accounted for by change in the private sector. The use of quality circles has fluctuated since 1990, but at no time did a majority of workplaces use them.

Information on two skill-acquisition practices is available from 1984, namely team briefing and information disclosure. The incidence of team briefing doubled between 1984 and 2004 from its use in 36 per cent of workplaces to 72 per cent. Three areas of information disclosure are measured. Disclosure about investment plans of the workplace rose significantly between 1984 and 2004, whereas disclosure of information about staffing plans remained at a fairly constant, high level. The use of disclosure of information about the financial position of the workplace was constant in the private sector, but rose significantly in the public sector. By 2004, it was more common in the public than the private sector. The only other data going back to the 1980s relate to financial participation schemes. The percentage of private sector workplaces with share-ownership schemes has doubled from 14 per cent in 1980 to 28 per cent in 2004 (Table 7.3(b)), but its peak use was in 1990, when it was used in 31 per cent of workplaces. Chapter 11 investigates in depth the trends in financial participation.

For 1998 and 2004, we have data on a fuller range of HIM practices. Since 1998, there has been a small but statistically non-significant increase in the two additional measures of flexible work organisation: team working and functional flexibility. The use of skill acquisition practices – team briefing, induction training, off-the-job training, training in human relations skills, and employee appraisal – grew significantly in both the private and public sectors.

Table 7.3(a) *Incidence of high involvement practices in workplaces with 25 or more employees for the whole economy*

	1980	1984	1990	1998	2004	p value for change from first year with data to 2004
High involvement practices						
Work organisation practices						
Teamworking				55	60	0.08
Functional flexibility				70	74	0.23
Quality circles			35	42	30	0.05
Suggestion schemes		25	28	32	35	0.00
Skill and knowledge acquisition practices						
Team briefings		36	48	52	72	0.00
Induction training				77	90	0.00
Training in human relations skills				53	62	0.00
Information disclosure about investment plans		27	41	53	49	0.00
Information disclosure about financial position		55	60	65	63	0.00
Information disclosure about staffing plans		67	60	60	66	0.58
Appraisals				47	66	0.00
Work enrichment practices						
Job variety				41	44	0.39
Method discretion				22	21	0.70
Time discretion				20	20	0.90
Motivational practices						
Motivation a major selection criterion				85	81	0.05
Internal recruitment				29	22	0.02
Job security guarantees				13	15	0.21
Single status				66	64	0.35
Profit-related pay			41	46	44	0.22
Share-ownership scheme	13	22	30	24	28	0.00
Total quality management						
Self-inspection				54	47	0.03
Records on faults and complaints				64	63	0.59
Customer surveys				49	55	0.03
Quality targets				42	57	0.00
Training in problem solving				24	25	0.54
Just-in-time production				29	27	0.52

Notes: The following variables relate to practices as they pertain to core workers: teamworking (equals 1 if 80%+ core employees in teams); functional flexibility; appraisals (equals 1 if all core employees appraised); work enrichment. Single status is if core workers are treated the same as managers in terms of benefits such as pensions.
Source: WIRS/WERS data.

Table 7.3(b) *Incidence of high involvement practices in workplaces with 25 or more employees for private sector*

	1980	1984	1990	1998	2004	p value for change
High involvement practices						
Work organisation practices						
Teamworking				49	54	0.11
Functional flexibility				71	75	0.21
Quality circles			30	39	28	0.45
Suggestion schemes		22	26	30	36	0.00
Skill and knowledge acquisition practices						
Team briefings		31	42	49	70	0.00
Induction training				76	90	0.00
Training in human relations skills				38	52	0.00
Information disclosure about investment plans		32	44	49	46	0.00
Information disclosure about financial position		56	56	60	58	0.47
Information disclosure about staffing plans		57	52	52	61	0.01
Appraisals				49	67	0.00
Work enrichment practices						
Job variety				40	39	0.65
Method discretion				21	19	0.59
Time control				20	21	0.77
Motivational practices						
Motivation a major selection criterion				84	80	0.11
Internal recruitment				32	26	0.04
Job security guarantees				6	10	0.01
Single status				63	61	0.57
Profit-related pay			42	46	45	0.31
Share-ownership scheme	14	23	31	24	28	0.00
Total quality management						
Self-inspection				53	44	0.01
Records on faults and complaints				64	62	0.52
Customer surveys				47	53	0.05
Quality targets				39	55	0.00
Training in problem solving				23	23	0.90
Just-in-time production				35	32	0.47

Notes: The following variables relate to practices as they pertain to the core non-managerial occupation at the workplace: teamworking (equals 1 if 80%+ core employees in teams); functional flexibility; appraisals (equals 1 if all core employees appraised); work enrichment. Single status is if core workers are treated the same as managers in terms of benefits such as pensions.
Source: WIRS/WERS data.

Table 7.3(c) *Incidence of high involvement practices in workplaces with 25 or more employees for the public sector*

	1980	1984	1990	1998	2004	p value for change
High involvement practices						
Work organisation practices						
Teamworking				72	77	0.29
Functional flexibility				32	32	0.96
Quality circles			45	49	36	0.04
Suggestion schemes		31	31	38	33	0.34
Skill and knowledge acquisition practices						
Team briefings		46	62	60	76	0.00
Induction training				80	87	0.11
Training in human relations skills				51	65	0.00
Information disclosure about investment plans		18	33	62	58	0.00
Information disclosure about financial position		52	70	79	80	0.00
Information disclosure about staffing plans		85	79	82	83	0.33
Appraisals				41	64	0.00
Work enrichment practices						
Job variety				45	61	0.00
Method discretion				27	28	0.70
Time discretion				19	16	0.31
Motivational practices						
Motivation a major selection criterion				89	86	0.20
Internal recruitment				18	12	0.07
Job security guarantees				33	33	0.92
Single status				74	71	0.44
Total quality management						
Self-inspection				56	59	0.57
Records on faults and complaints				64	65	0.91
Customer surveys				55	61	0.23
Quality targets				52	63	0.03
Training in problem solving				24	31	0.10
Just-in-time production				12	10	0.55

Notes: See notes to Table 7.3(b).
Source: WIRS/WERS data.

Evidence on work enrichment is also only available between 1998 and 2004. It shows that in four in ten workplaces core employees had 'a lot of variety' in their jobs (job variety), but with only one-fifth of workplaces providing core workers with 'a lot of discretion' over their working methods (method discretion) and 'a lot of control' over their time (time discretion). It is notable that there was no overall change in this pattern between 1998 and 2004, although job variety rose significantly in public sector workplaces. The extent of enriched work, however, remained fairly static in the private sector.

Apart from information on financial incentives and participation, that on other motivational supports is only available since 1998. It shows that employee motivation as a selection criterion was used in around four-fifths of workplaces in both 1998 and 2004. The provision of single status was used in around two-thirds of workplaces. In contrast, the use of internal recruitment and the provision of job security guarantees were much less popular. Use of internal recruitment had actually fallen, from 29 per cent of workplaces in 1998 to 22 per cent in 2004. Job security guarantees had remained constant in the public sector, and had risen a little in the private sector.

Reflecting these developments, the total use of high involvement practices rose over the period, the rise being statistically significant in the private sector (see Table 7.4). But this is largely attributable to a rise in the use of the skill-acquisition practices. The uptake of high involvement work-organisation practices has not changed: the modal score is 2 on a scale where 4 is maximum flexibility. The rise of total skill and acquisition practices reflected a big increase in the percentage of workplaces scoring the maximum, rising from 7 per cent to 23 per cent over the period.

Comparison of the later surveys, set out in Table 7.4, suggests that the total use of work enrichment remained static between 1998 and 2004 in both sectors, and is somewhat higher in the public than the private sector throughout. The modal score across the economy is 6 on a scale where 9 is maximum work enrichment, with no significant difference between the private and public sectors. The total use of motivational support scores declined a little, but not significantly so.

We may conclude, from both case studies and surveys, that there has been some growth in HIM practices in the 1980s and 1990s, but the WIRS/WERS series suggests that this has been uneven across the private and public sectors. Overall, the picture is of high use of some practices, particularly those geared towards teamworking and functional flexibility. However, this is within a context in which jobs may have relatively low levels of discretion and in which internal promotion and guarantees of job security remain scarce. The sustained increase in practices such as teamworking and team briefing suggests that their use does not reflect ephemeral initiatives on the part of most organisations that have used them. Moreover, what limited information we have suggests that it was very rare for firms to drop HIM practices.

Table 7.4 *Mean use of practices in workplaces with 25 or more employees, by sector, 1998–2004*

	Whole economy	Private sector	Public sector
High involvement practices			
1998	5.37	5.26	5.65
2004	5.86	5.79	6.05
Significantly different over time	Yes	Yes	No
High involvement work organisation practices			
1998	1.99	1.90	2.25
2004	1.99	1.93	2.16
Significantly different over time	No	No	No
High involvement skill and knowledge acquisition practices			
1998	3.26	3.23	3.34
2004	3.81	3.78	3.92
Significantly different over time	Yes	Yes	Yes
Work enrichment practices			
1998	5.75	5.59	6.18
2004	5.79	5.62	6.31
Significantly different over time	No	No	No
Motivational practices			
1998	1.94	1.86	2.15
2004	1.83	1.76	2.03
Significantly different over time	No	No	No

Notes: The total high involvement practices is the sum of the use of nine work organisation (functional flexibility, quality circles and suggestion schemes, teamworking) and skill/knowledge acquisition practices (team briefing), induction training, training in human relations skills, disclosure of information, appraisals. Significance tests report whether mean differences between 1998 and 2004 are statistically different. The total HIM work organisations practices index is the sum of the use of teamworking, functional flexibility, quality circles and suggestion schemes; the total high involvement skill and knowledge acquisition practices is the sum of the use of team briefing, induction training, training in human relations skills, disclosure of information and appraisals; work enrichment practices is the total score on three scales measuring job variety, method discretion and time discretion for core employees; the total motivational support practices is the sum of the use of motivation as a major selection criterion, preference for internal recruitment, job security guarantees for non-managerial staff and harmonised fringe benefits for managers and core employees.
Source: WERS 1998 and WERS 2004.

The connected use of HIM practices

Is it the case that the organisations which use one type of high involvement tend to use the other types? That is, are the correlations between the use of individual HIM practices strong? If so, does this reflect an underlying management belief that 'eliciting employee commitment will lead to enhanced performance' (Walton, 1985: 80)? It has been shown that the HIM practices used in British manufacturing plants in 1990 were correlated, and that this correlation between most practices could be explained by an underlying high involvement orientation on the part of management (Wood and Albanese, 1995). However, merit pay and profit-sharing and a 'permanent employment policy' were statistically unconnected to HIM, and piecework and individual bonuses were negatively associated (Wood, 1996b).

Analysts of the early, rather sparse, WIRS/WERS HIM data had concluded that a new high involvement style was not readily identifiable (Millward, 1994; Sisson, 1993; Sisson and Marginson, 1995). When the WIRS/WERS data were supplemented with data on a broader array of practices from a sister survey, the Employers' Manpower Skills Practices Survey, however, it was found that practices such as multiskilling, human relations skills as a selection criterion and training needs analysis were evident in a majority, and in most cases a sizeable majority, of workplaces (Wood and de Menezes, 1998). There were correlations between the practices, and a pattern was evident in their use that was not consistent with piecemeal adoption. The integrated use of HIM in the early 1990s might not have been as uncommon as contemporary commentators were suggesting.

Examination of the correlations between the practices in WERS 1998 and WERS 2004 shows that the practices within each of the three groupings of practices – high involvement, work enrichment and motivational practices – are, on average, more highly correlated with each other than they are with practices in one or other of the other groups. The correlations between the motivational practices are, however, considerably higher in the private sector than they are in the public, where they are in most cases not significantly related.

Analyses of the practices in WERS 1998 by de Menezes and Wood (2006) showed that the correlation between the high involvement practices was explained by a common factor, and thus they tended to be used as a single coherent system, which reflected an underlying involvement orientation. The work enrichment practices also formed a coherent system, but this was discrete from the high involvement orientation. The motivational practices were neither part of the high involvement orientation nor formed a unified set. This again suggests that HIM is an identifiable phenomenon, the use of which is not limited to contexts where jobs have high levels of autonomy or variety. It also suggests that the use of the motivational supports may be quite common without HIM.

These results are reflected in the correlations between the total use of practices. But the results using both 1998 and 2004 WERS data reveal differences between the private and public sectors, and over time. The total use of high involvement practices was unrelated to work enrichment in the private sector in 1998, but it was significantly positively related in 2004. The reverse was the case in the public sector, where the two were significantly related in 1998, but not in 2004. The count of high involvement practices was significantly related to the total use of motivational supports in the private sector in both years, but in the public sector there is no relationship in either year.

Where HIM is likely to be found

Assessments of where HIM is to be found have to be cautious because sources differ in sample and definition. Extending the Institute of Work Psychology survey series to services showed that HIM practices were just as likely to be used in public and private services as they were in manufacturing, although work enrichment was slightly more prevalent in services than manufacturing (Wood et al., 2004: 425). This is broadly consistent with our analysis of WIRS/WERS series thus far, which suggests some small differences in the extent of use between private (regardless of sector) and public organisations.

Data from manufacturing also suggest that links between HIM and the market or strategic context are weak (Wood and Albanese, 1995). The one external factor of importance, identified in analysis of the whole economy using WERS 1998, is membership of an employers' association or Chamber of Commerce. These networks appear to propagate or diffuse HIM (Bryson et al., 2007).

Various internal factors appear to play a role in where HIM is to be found. Two factors were identified as crucial in Wood and Albanese's (1995) manufacturing survey: whether the organisation was a profit centre, and the degree to which personnel management was integrated into the business. Ownership is also important. An analysis of WERS 1998 found that family-owned firms were significantly less likely to adopt HIM. It also found that HIM practice adoption was higher in workplaces belonging to multi-site organisations than it was in single-site organisations (Bryson et al., 2007).

Perhaps most significant is the positive association between HIM and the use of total quality management or lean production methods. The IWP study showed that HIM is used in conjunction with four distinct practices (Wood et al., 2004). First, it is associated with total quality management, which makes all staff responsible for quality and continuous improvement. Second, it is associated with just-in-time production, because of the need to make products in direct response to internal and external customer demands and not for stock. Third, it is associated with integrated computer-based technology, the linking together of computerised equipment to enable enhanced integration. Finally, HIM is associated with supply-chain partnering, which is concerned to develop strategic alliances and long-term relationships with suppliers and customers. The use of these practices has also been shown to have increased between 1996 and 2000, as has their correlation with HIM. This suggested an increased integration of lean operational methods with HIM. The association between HIM as measured by de Menezes and Wood's scale, and total quality management was confirmed for the whole economy by an analysis of WERS 1998 (de Menezes and Wood, 2006).

This picture is further supported by our analysis of the total use of high involvement practices in 2004. Concentrating on the private sector, where external competitive and strategic factors are likely to have the most effect, we found that external factors were less important than internal ones. The number of competitors a workplace faced was not important. By far the most important factor was total quality management, as the total use of total quality practices was positively associated with high involvement management. Second, workplace size plays a role, as the smallest workplaces (with ten to twenty-four employees) were the least likely to use HIM, although they were the most likely to use work enrichment practices. Third, the percentage of non-manual workers was positively correlated with total use of high involvement practices.

Nonetheless, industrial factors are important, since, controlling for other factors, we found significant variance across industries. 'Other services' was the biggest user of HIM practices, but this association was driven by greater use of skill-acquisition practices, rather than work-organisation ones. The industry making the most use of HIM work-organisation practices was energy and water. 'Other services' also, on average, had a higher level of work enrichment. There was little industry variance in the use of motivational supports, apart from their low incidence in the construction sector.

Overall, the evidence suggests that external or strategic product market factors are less significant than internal factors in determining the use of HIM. The fact that it is used where work enrichment is not, and that it is used alongside lean production, suggests that HIM is being driven by the priorities of production rather than by any humanistic values on the part of management (Sabel, 1982: 213).

HIM and trade unionism

When HIM came to the fore in the 1980s it was widely associated with non-unionism. Well-known non-union firms in the United States, such as IBM and Hewlett Packard, were seen as HIM pioneers. It was presented, particularly in the prescriptive management literature (e.g., Beer *et al.*, 1984), as providing the basis for a new win-win relationship between workers and managers, offering management the prospect of improved performance while improving workers' job satisfaction, security and perhaps also pay and benefits. This, it was suggested, would make redundant unions' role in voicing workers' grievances. Given this, managements might use HIM as a means of reducing worker demand for unionism. In Kochan's terms, HIM would be used as a union substitution tactic (Kochan, 1980: 183). Even if managements did not directly use HIM as an industrial relations weapon, some thought that managements who were pursuing it would prefer to deal directly with individuals, either independently or as members of teams, rather than with unions (Guest, 1989: 48). In a similar vein, one overview of HIM concluded that 'although there are formulations which give an important place to trade unions . . . most are silent on the issues or assume a non-union environment'. Unions were generally regarded as 'at best unnecessary and at worst to be avoided' (Sisson, 1994: 12).

The initial tendency to associate HIM with non-unionism was, however, never as strong in Britain as it was in the United States, except when the practices were associated with US multinationals. In the early 1970s, Fox saw the greater use of employee involvement methods as a potential way of addressing the ills of the British industrial relations system (Fox, 1974). He saw low levels of employee involvement as a major problem contributing to the low-trust dynamics between managers and workers. He maintained that job redesign could reverse this. In so doing, it could strengthen collective bargaining by transforming relations between managers and workers and their representatives into co-operative relationships based on high trust. According to this, we might expect job redesign, or HIM more generally, to be used in unionised organisations not as a way of undermining support for them, but to maintain, if not reinforce, their role.

The decades following Fox's book witnessed unprecedented union decline coupled with the increasing use of HIM practices. But, as this increase by the early 1990s appeared to be limited, some speculated that the non-union, low involvement workplace might be more prototypical of the future than was high involvement management. Reflecting on the findings of WIRS 1990, Sisson referred to this as the 'bleak house' model, involving austerity characterised by management dictat and high dismissal rates. It was even suggested that what little HIM there was might be more likely in unionised than in non-unionised workplaces (Sisson, 1993: 207; 1994). Though underestimating the rise in the use of high involvement practices and their integrated nature, this argument served to suggest that we should not take any link between the decline of unionism and the rise of HIM for granted.

The coincidence of a decline in trade union recognition with an increase in HIM begs the question of whether union substitution has taken place by design or default. Most cross-sectional analyses of the relationship between HIM practices have revealed no strong association between HIM and trade union recognition per se. Wood's analysis of his sample of manufacturing plants found no relationship between unionisation and HIM. Union recognition was, however, associated with a lower rate of HIM adoption from 1986 to 1990. Two individual practices – merit pay and appraisal – were exceptional in that they were significantly less likely to be used in union plants (Wood, 1996c).

Analysis of WIRS 1990 and WERS 1998 found that both HIM and work enrichment were unrelated to unionism, when controlling for employment size (Wood and de Menezes, 1998: 500–1; de Menezes and Wood, 2006). Union recognition was, however, strongly positively associated with the use of motivational supports in both 1998 and 2004. This is perhaps to be expected, since three of these four motivational supports are long-standing goals of trade union bargaining – preference for internal recruitment, job security guarantees and single status.

The most thorough investigation of the HIM–union substitution hypothesis over time used the WIRS/WERS series up to 1998 (Machin and Wood, 2005). Those practices directly associated with HIM that were included in the three surveys from 1984 to 1998 – quality circles, suggestion schemes, team briefing and other direct communication methods – had all increased over time. But the rate of change did not differ between the union and non-union sectors. The one practice where the rate of increase was greater in the non-union sector than the union sector was flexible pay, reflecting the possibility that the practice that is most antithetical to traditional unionism. When the practices were looked at jointly, there was again no significant difference in the rate of change between the union and non–union sectors.

Further analysis, including the additional practices that were first added in the 1998 survey, reveals a similar story. The use of HIM practices in union workplaces is either higher than, or on a par with, that in the non-union sector. Table 7.5 presents the incidence of individual HIM practices for the first and last time-point where the data on them are available in WERS. It does so for union and non-union workplaces separately. The figures relate to the whole economy, with the exception of the share-ownership and profit-related pay figures, which are for the private sector only.

The rate of change in the use of HIM does not differ markedly across the union and non-union sectors, although there are some exceptions (see the last column of Table 7.5). For instance, the increase in the use of suggestion schemes was greater in the non-union sector, though the incidence of suggestion schemes has always been higher in the union sector. Also, share-ownership grew more quickly in the union sector. But the biggest differences relate to skill and knowledge acquisition practices. The increase in the disclosure of information on investment plans and the workplace's financial position has been more marked in the union sector than the non-union sector. On the other hand, the growth in the disclosure of information about staffing plans has been greater in the non-union sector.

The lack of an HIM–union substitution effect is, perhaps, less surprising given that a major driver of increased HIM is the introduction of innovative approaches to production, which implies that HIM's role as a tool of industrial relations is at best secondary. Nor is it surprising, given that, at least in Britain, some of these HIM practices are viewed positively by unions and their members. Moreover, there is evidence that the average total use of high involvement practices is higher in workplaces that have joint consultative committees, which suggests that managements practising HIM are far from antithetical to providing formal mechanisms for employee voice. There are, of course, other underlying factors, far more influential than HIM, that explain the decline of trade unions in Britain, as discussed in Chapters 2, 3 and 5.

HIM, organisational performance and wellbeing

In the wake of the claims being made for HIM, a line of research developed that sought to test its association with organisational performance. HIM may directly enhance worker productivity by, for example, improving working methods, achieving high quality without reworking (right-first-time) and prompting greater knowledge sharing, including knowledge passed from workers to managers. Indirect effects may arise through HIM's purported effects on employees' wellbeing. If HIM improves job satisfaction or organisational commitment, this may spill

Table 7.5 *Incidence of high involvement management over time in union and non-union workplaces with 25 or more employees for the whole economy*

	Start year	End year	Union workplaces			Non-union workplaces			Difference (non-union–union)	p value for non-union–union difference between first and last year
			% in start year	% in end year	Absolute change	% in start year	% in end year	Absolute change		
High involvement practices										
Work organisation practices										
Teamworking	1998	2004	62	71	9.3	50	53	2.8	−6.6	0.23
Functional flexibility	1990	2004	45	74	28.9	40	73	33.4	4.5	0.39
Quality circles	1990	2004	39	36	−3.3	30	27	−3.5	−0.2	0.97
Suggestion schemes	1984	2004	31	39	8.4	15	32	17.9	9.5	0.04
Skill and knowledge acquisition practices										
Team briefings	1984	2004	39	76	37.0	31	69	38.1	1.1	0.81
Induction training	1998	2004	83	89	5.6	73	90	17.0	11.4	0.02
Training in human relations skills	1998	2004	59	61	2.1	47	62	14.8	12.8	0.03
Information disclosure about investment plans	1984	2004	28	60	32.3	25	42	16.9	−15.4	0.00
Information disclosure about financial position	1984	2004	60	79	19.1	45	54	9.3	−9.8	0.05
Information disclosure about staffing plans	1984	2004	78	74	−4.3	47	61	14.7	19.1	0.00
Appraisals	1990	2004	55	64	9.6	61	67	6.3	−3.3	0.53
Work enrichment practices										
Job variety	1998	2004	40	44	3.9	42	44	1.4	−2.5	0.65
Method discretion	1998	2004	22	21	−1.6	22	22	−0.5	1.1	0.81
Time discretion	1998	2004	20	16	−4.0	20	22	2.0	6.0	0.16

Motivational practices

Motivation a major selection criterion	1998	2004	89	84	-4.5	83	79	-3.9	0.6	0.89
Preference for internal recruitment	1998	2004	28	23	-5.5	29	22	-6.4	-0.8	0.87
Job security guarantees for any non-managerial employees	1998	2004	26	25	-0.9	4	10	5.3	6.1	0.12
Single status	1998	2004	76	75	-0.8	59	56	-2.6	-1.8	0.72
Profit-related pay	1990	2004	38	42	4.4	42	45	2.5	-2.0	0.76
Share-ownership scheme	1980	2004	16	46	29.4	10	23	12.8	-16.5	0.00

Note: The following variables relate to practices as they pertain to the core non-managerial occupation at the workplace: teamworking (equals 1 if 80%+ core employees in teams); functional flexibility; appraisals (equals 1 if all core employees appraised); work enrichment. Single status is if core workers are treated the same as managers in terms of benefits such as pensions.

Source: WIRS/WERS data.

over into higher productivity through greater discretionary effort, lower turnover and lower absenteeism. On the other hand, HIM may be costly to adopt and maintain, thus depressing the impact of productivity gains on the financial performance of the organisation.

As well as being of potential value to the employers' objectives, HIM's association with workers' wellbeing is important for Kochan and Osterman's (1994) mutual gains thesis, according to which HIM can create organisations that marry high organisational performance with high worker satisfaction – the 'win-win' model, as it is sometimes called. In contrast, other analysts have associated HIM with labour intensification and have suggested that it may increase stress levels, with the implication that it will reduce satisfaction (Ramsay et al., 2000). Thus, whether either the employer or the employee gains from HIM, and whether there are links between the two, are a priori uncertain.

HIM and organisational performance

The majority of studies of the connection between HIM and organisational performance have been undertaken in the United States, and the early studies suggested that there were significant positive links (Arthur, 1994; MacDuffie, 1995; Huselid, 1995). Subsequently, however, reviews of the research that followed these studies indicate considerable unevenness in the results, both across studies and across the performance measures used within individual studies (Wood, 1999; Godard, 2004; Wall and Wood, 2005). One review of twenty-five studies concluded that there is sufficient variability between the results, and of the practices included in the studies, to make any positive generalisation impossible (Wall and Wood, 2005). Moreover, the major study in the United States that used longitudinal data found no HIM effects on performance (Cappelli and Neumark, 2000). Four British studies tested the universal HIM–performance model prediction that positive performance effects would be associated with HIM equally throughout the economy; three out of four (Guest and Hoque, 1994; Guest et al., 2003; Wood and de Menezes, 1998) of these found no connection between HIM and performance, the exception being confined to the hotel industry (Hoque, 1999).

A subsequent study using WERS 1998 found stronger relationships between HIM and performance. Using measures based on core HIM practices, it found HIM was associated with higher productivity in the private sector, but only in unionised workplaces (Bryson et al., 2005). The authors showed that there was no evident relationship between

HIM and financial performance, and thus the productivity gains might be partly being offset by higher wages associated with HIM (Forth and Millward, 2004). They thus speculated that the combination of results might reflect union success in bargaining for concessions, rather than mutual gains arising from more co-operative relationships between employers and unions. Another analysis of WERS 1998 found that both HIM and work enrichment were significantly related to higher productivity (Wood and de Menezes, 2008a). Furthermore, the positive association of HIM with productivity is greater when total quality management is used, a result that may help explain why they tend to coexist. The studies that use WERS 2004 to analyse HIM's association with productivity and performance found that some HIM practices were positively associated with labour productivity, but that many were not, and there was little association with financial performance (Kersley et al., 2006: 293; Wood et al., 2008). This may reflect the costs of HIM as well as the fact that labour productivity is not necessarily the dominant influence on financial performance.

HIM and employee wellbeing

When considering the implications of HIM for workers themselves, it is useful to identify three dimensions of job-related wellbeing: between job dissatisfaction and satisfaction; between anxiety and contentment, and between depression and enthusiasm (Warr, 2002: 2–4; 2007: 19–60). The job satisfaction–dissatisfaction dimension is concerned with the pleasure a person gains from their job and their affective attachment to it. The anxiety–contentment and depression–enthusiasm dimensions are identified on the basis of their relationship to arousal in terms of mental alertness and energy. Anxiety is associated with low affect and high arousal, while contentment is associated with high affect and low arousal. Enthusiasm is associated with high affect and high arousal, while depression is associated with low affect and low arousal. Job strain is often taken to be a combination of anxiety and depression.

The employee survey of WERS 2004 included measures of job satisfaction and anxiety–contentment, but not depression–enthusiasm. Using data from both the management and employee surveys in 2004, it has been shown that HIM was unrelated to job satisfaction, and negatively related to anxiety–contentment. HIM increased anxiety, which is not consistent with a mutual gains model (Wood and de Menezes, 2008b). A core measure of work enrichment – the employee's job autonomy – was, in contrast, positively related to both job satisfaction and anxiety–contentment. Also, the more supportive or informative management was in the workplace, as gauged by the individual employee, the greater the level of job satisfaction and anxiety–contentment. Thus, while job characteristics, information sharing and consultation are important determinants of job satisfaction, HIM tends to increase anxiety and is unrelated to job satisfaction.

There would thus appear to be more support for the view that stress is increased by HIM, rather than the mutual gains view. However, work enrichment was related to wellbeing. It has also been found that some, but not all, of the relationship between work enrichment and higher productivity was accounted for by its association with job satisfaction (Wood et al., 2008). Similar relationships were found for other outcomes: quality of output, financial performance and absenteeism. These results for enriched jobs support the mutual gains model of employment relations.

The findings for HIM suggest that there may be a conflict between its impacts on employers' outcomes and those on employees, as their anxiety may increase with its use. This may arise if HIM entails labour intensification, as some argue. But there is not a strong link between HIM and job demands in WERS 2004. This suggests that the lowering of the wellbeing of workers is more likely to arise because the encouragement of workers to be proactive and flexible creates anxieties through the implied pressure to improve their overall contribution to the organisation. These may, in turn, raise concerns in the workers' minds both about their competencies and their job security, since the high involvement management may be seen as threatening their jobs if they do not raise their performance.

Conclusion

This chapter started with a specification of the nature of HIM, differentiating it from the associated notion of work enrichment or job-level involvement. It has shown that the use of HIM has risen in Britain over the quarter century, albeit to some extent unevenly between the public and private sector. There are signs of the systematic use of HIM and an underlying managerial philosophy of high involvement management. But it is still the case that only a minority of managements have a strong high involvement orientation. Furthermore, HIM is no more likely to be adopted in a context of enriched jobs than where jobs are more routinised. It is, however, strongly associated with total quality management and other lean production methods.

HIM usage was also found to be linked with the characteristics of the organisation itself, such as whether the organisation is family-owned, and the size and the composition of the workforce. There was no evidence that external factors are important. There was little evidence that HIM was driving trade unionism out, as suggested by the union substitution hypothesis.

The benefits of HIM are not clear-cut. But it is associated with higher productivity according to the most recent WERS. There was, however, no evidence from WERS 2004 to suggest that HIM improves worker wellbeing. If anything, it is associated with higher levels of anxiety. Work enrichment, on the other hand, is correlated with positive outcomes for workers and employees alike.

It may be argued that HIM is less widespread than early advocates might have anticipated. However, it has been an important influence on management thinking, and on the evolution of the modern workplace, particularly through its connection with operational management philosophies such as total quality management. The consequences have been mixed in Britain, with the evidence so far of positive consequences for productivity and negative ones for workers' contentment. An emphasis on the negative consequences for trade unions appears misplaced, as its role in the decline in trade unions appears to have been minimal. It is incorrect in the British context to view HIM as an alternative to management with trade unions. HIM appears to be as important to the organisation of work in unionised workplaces as it is elsewhere.

8 Conflict at work: the changing pattern of disputes

Gill Dix, Keith Sisson and John Forth

Introduction

Notions of conflict at work conjure up strong images in the popular imagination. The more familiar images are of large-scale, disruptive industrial disputes; the less common are of individual grievances, most dramatically illustrated by high profile tribunal cases. The past quarter-century has seen a concurrent decline in collective expressions of conflict and growth in the individualised expression of conflict, most transparently manifest in a dramatic fall in the incidence of strikes and a rising tide of claims to the employment tribunal. What was the scale of the changes, and what were the causes? This chapter draws upon a variety of indicators and sources to investigate the changing pattern of workplace conflict over the twenty-five year period.

Irrespective of how it is manifested and how it is measured, conflict is an inherent feature of the employment relationship. This is because the employment relationship is a special type of exchange, with the distinguishing feature being that it involves both market and managerial relations (Edwards, 2003: 8). Employees receive tangible and intangible rewards in return for selling their labour and/or knowledge power to be used largely at the employer's discretion. The contract cannot fully specify the rights and responsibilities of either party and is thus 'incomplete by design' (Collins, 1999: 161). This means that there is great uncertainty, fuelling the prospect of divergent goals and interpretation. The relationship is also on-going, which means that there are more or less constant pressures on – and opportunities for – both parties to seek to adjust the exchange in their favour. And it is contradictory, in so far as employees cannot be 'commodified', and employers have to pursue the potentially mutually exclusive strategies of control and commitment. It also involves a complex 'governance' regime of institutions or rules, with scope for differences over both substance and process. Alongside a hierarchically based structure dealing with work organisation and 'performance management' will be found statutory employment rights and collective agreement provisions (where trade unions are recognised), along with a raft of local informal norms ('custom and practice') and expectations of behaviour imported from the wider society. Encompassing such divergent paradigms, the relationship is, by its very nature, given to conflict as well as co-operation.

Notwithstanding these points, conflict – which might be defined as the discontent arising from a perceived clash of interests – can only be measured when it results in a transparent and overt manifestation. In practice, it may not always be measurable since some discontent may be hidden or suppressed. The most manifest expressions are disputes, which may be collective or individual, involving action such as a strike, raising a grievance or taking disciplinary measures. Other expressions embrace 'organisational misbehaviour' (Ackroyd and Thompson, 1999). Examples are theft and sabotage, absence and resignation, which can viewed as forms of 'exit' from unsatisfactorily regarded relationships.

Any attempt to obtain a valid indication of the overall extent or nature of conflict at work must therefore explore as comprehensive a set of indicators as possible. This chapter adopts that broad framework. It considers both collective and individual disputes. Other expressions of conflict are considered in as far as the data allow. As indicated, the overall pattern is well established. Although collective disputes have declined, individual ones have, on some measures, increased. Less clear is the pattern's composition; whether there have been changes in the types of workplaces and issues involved. Also of interest is the association between different forms of conflict – whether, for example, lower levels of collective disputes are accompanied by higher levels of absenteeism. And a further concern is the role of workplace institutions, including procedures for dealing with disputes, as well as arrangements for employee representation and involvement.

The pattern of disputes

Discussions of conflict have traditionally focused on the incidence of disputes (and principally on strikes) and on the rate of applications to the employment tribunal (ET). There is a lot to be said for this approach. Official statistics on strikes and employment tribunal claims have been collated and published throughout the twenty-five year period that is the focus of this volume. Indeed, strike data in the United Kingdom extend back to 1893. Nevertheless, official strike statistics tell us nothing about the incidence of either very short strikes that fall below the threshold for inclusion in official statistics or other forms of industrial action such as 'working to rule'. Similarly, numbers of ET claims tell us nothing about the overall extent to which employees raise formal grievances at work. In the sections which follow, we examine the pattern of disputes using this broader set of indicators. First, the pattern of collective and individual disputes is mapped, drawing variously upon data from the official series, WERS and other sources. Thereafter, some reflections on the changing patterns of disputes and the interrelationships between different types of dispute are provided.

There is a further concern, however, that statistics on such phenomena provide only a partial insight into the quality of workplace relations. This is because strikes, formal grievances and ET applications are each 'institutional expressions' of discontent, with the incidence of each being determined, in turn, by the strength of trade union organisation, the presence of workplace grievance procedures and the legislative framework of the tribunal system. Accordingly, a further section then goes on to present evidence on the broader incidence of conflict, drawing upon a number of direct and indirect measures of the state of workplace relations. The overall aim is to develop a multidimensional picture of the changing nature and extent of workplace conflict over the period from the late 1970s to the present. We return to the issue of institutional impacts on manifestations of conflict later in the chapter.

Collective disputes

Even the most casual observer of employment relations would be aware of the substantial decline in strike action since the early 1980s. Figure 8.1 shows a longer time series extending back to 1960 to demonstrate that the decline in the number of stoppages was part of a longer trend which began in the 1970s. However, that is not to suggest that industrial action was a declining problem in that decade. Large disputes kept the number of days lost high, and these increased at the end of the 1970s, culminating in the so-called winter of discontent.[1] This shifted the public focus from small unofficial strikes – the major concern of the 1960s – to large official stoppages. The average number of days lost per year in the late 1970s and early 1980s stood at around 7 million working days in official records, or 300 days per thousand employees (Figure 8.1). Contrast this with the latter half of the 1990s and early years of the twenty-first century, when

---

[1] The widespread stoppages in the winter of 1978/9 in response to government attempts to enforce limits on pay rises to curb inflation. In the period 1977–9 there were 21 stoppages that each accounted for at least 200,000 working days lost.

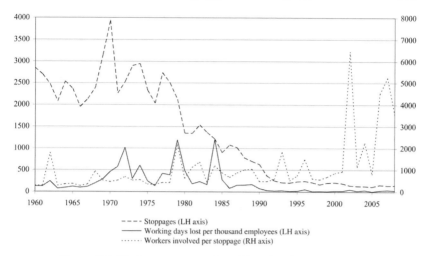

Figure 8.1 Work stoppages and working days lost, 1960–2006

days lost to officially recorded stoppages stood at around 0.5 million per annum – just twenty days per thousand employees.

To examine the trend in collective disputes in more detail, we can divide the twenty-five years into two broadly distinct periods that are characterised by changes in the level of activity, focusing first on the experience of the late 1970s and the 1980s and then on the more recent period. Official statistics showed a decline in strike activity through the late 1970s and the 1980s, with this being seen most obviously in the falling number of stoppages. The number of working days lost also shows a decline, albeit with a shallower gradient, if one excludes the spikes in the series on working days lost caused by the 'winter of discontent' and the miners' dispute (which alone accounted for over 80 per cent of days lost in 1984).

The first two surveys in the WIRS/WERS series added to this body of evidence in the 1980s by showing the extent to which strikes were either concentrated or dispersed across workplaces in the economy. Surveys undertaken in the late 1960s and 1970s had already provided some insight (Government Social Survey, 1968; Parker, 1974, 1975; Daniel, 1976; Brown, 1981), but their coverage was typically limited to large manufacturing workplaces.[2] WIRS, by contrast, covered

---

[2] Brown's survey had the most extensive coverage, extending to all manufacturing workplaces with fifty or more employees. Brown used his survey data to estimate that, in 1977/8, the official statistics captured only one-quarter of all strikes in manufacturing.

Table 8.1 *Industrial action within workplaces, 1980–2004*

	1980	1984	1990	1998	2004
Strike action	11	15	11	1	3
Non-strike action	11	13	5	1	3
Either strike or non-strike action	17	21	13	2	5
Strike action lasting					
Less than one day	4	10	4	*	1
At least one day	7	8	7	1	2
One day but less than one week	–	8	7	1	2
One week or more	–	1	1	*	*
Non-strike action					
Overtime ban/restriction	7	7	3	1	2
Work-to-rule	4	6	2	*	2
Blacking of work	3	2	1	*	*
Go-slow	1	*	*	*	*
Work-in/sit-in	*	*	*	*	*
Other action	*	1	1	*	*
Picketing	8	4	6	1	2
Employer action					
Lockout	1	*	0	0	0
Weighted	2,000	2,000	1,892	2,000	1,999
Unweighted	2,040	2,019	1,977	1,929	1,646

Notes: Relies solely on reports from management respondents – see footnote 3;
* less than 0.5 per cent but not zero.
Source: WIRS/WERS data.

manufacturing, private services and the public sector, and included workplaces with at least twenty-five employees – thereby accounting for roughly two-thirds of all employees in the economy. The first survey showed that one in ten workplaces (11 per cent) had experienced some strike action in the year 1979–80 (Table 8.1).[3] The proportions experiencing strike action were one in five

However, the official statistics' coverage of large strikes meant that they captured an estimated 94 per cent of all days lost (Brown, 1981: 100).

[3] Estimates reported here differ from those in early WIRS sourcebooks, since the latter used a combined measure of industrial action based on management and worker representative respondents. Sampling strategies for worker representatives differed across the WERS series and so their responses are not included in this discussion. Estimates in Millward *et al.* (1992) on the incidence of strike or non-strike action for 1980 (22%), 1984 (25%) and 1990 (12%) use the combined measure; these indicate that we may be understating the scale of decline in industrial action, but we are certainly not mistaking the direction of change.

Table 8.2 *Industrial action within workplaces, 1980–2004, by sector of ownership*

	1980	1984	1990	1998	2004
Private manufacturing					
Strike action	19	9	4	0	*
Non-strike action	16	12	7	1	2
Either strike or non-strike action	26	17	10	1	2
Private services					
Strike action	3	5	2	1	1
Non-strike action	3	3	2	*	2
Either strike or non-strike action	6	7	3	1	2
Public sector					
Strike action	15	31	31	3	9
Non-strike action	19	24	8	2	7
Either strike or non-strike action	26	38	34	5	14

Notes: Relies solely on reports from management respondents – see footnote 3;
* less than 0.5 per cent but not zero.
Source: WIRS/WERS data. Workplaces with 25 or more employees

in private manufacturing and one in seven in the public sector, but fewer than one in twenty in private services (Table 8.2). The survey data also allowed a better understanding of the types of workplaces that experienced strikes. Blanchflower and Cubbin's (1986) analysis, for example, challenged the views of those who saw strikes as 'accidents' (Siebert and Addison, 1981) or 'random processes' (Prais, 1978), showing instead that their occurrence could typically be explained by the presence of certain organisational characteristics, procedural arrangements and incentives.

The early data also provided interesting insights into the distribution of strikes across different sectors of the economy. The decline in employment in the manufacturing industry (Millward *et al.*, 2000: 19–20), along with a reduction in the incidence of industrial action in that sector in the first half of the 1980s (Table 8.2), meant that manufacturing establishments accounted for almost two-fifths of all workplaces experiencing strike or non-strike action in 1980, but less than one-fifth in 1984. Public sector workplaces, in contrast, had become both more numerous and more prone to industrial action. Having accounted for one half of all workplaces experiencing strike or non-strike action in 1980, they accounted for over two-thirds in 1984 – a dominance that they retain to the present day. This pattern prompted Dickerson and Stewart (1993) to investigate the possible reasons as to why the public sector appeared 'strike prone'. They concluded that the lack of product market competition was an important factor, along with the higher rates of unionisation and the larger average size of establishments.

A third contribution of WIRS in the 1980s was to highlight the incidence of non-strike action. Official statistics were silent on this issue and statistics available elsewhere only covered manufacturing (Milner, 1993). However, the early WIRS showed that, in the early 1980s, non-strike action occurred in as many workplaces as strike action. The two forms of action were also shown to be independent to some degree. There were many strongly unionised workplaces where workers resorted only to one of the two forms of collective expression. Non-strike action, for its part, was most common in the public sector, where around one-quarter of all workplaces were affected in 1984, compared with one in eight in private manufacturing and only 3 per cent in private services. The most common forms of non-strike action were overtime bans or instances of employees working to rule. Non-strike action was to see a sharp decline in the latter half of the 1980s, particularly in the public sector, where less than one in ten workplaces were affected in 1990. This combined with the decline in strike action to bring the overall incidence of industrial action – as indicated by WIRS – back to the level seen in 1980. A more dramatic change was to occur in the next period.

The late 1980s and early 1990s saw a dramatic fall in the number of officially recorded stoppages. Each successive year between 1986 and 1994 registered the lowest number of stoppages since the Second World War, and since 1994 the numbers of stoppages and working days lost have stabilised at these historically low levels. Comparisons between the third WIRS in 1990 and the fourth survey in 1998 showed a precipitous decline in strike action that combined with a further decline in non-strike action to bring the overall proportion of workplaces experiencing any form of industrial action down from one in eight to just one in fifty. The receding power of trade unions in the private sector was one part of the story, but not obviously to any greater extent than in previous periods. More notable in the 1990s, it seemed, was the changing experience of the public sector. Here, 34 per cent of workplaces reported some form of industrial action in 1990, but in 1998 that figure stood at just 5 per cent, a change which might be attributed in part to the increasing fragmentation and marketisation of the sector (as discussed in Chapter 13), along with the more generalised threats of legislation and unemployment.

The period since 1998 has seen stability in the official statistics on stoppages. There has also been stability in the survey estimates of the incidence of strike and non-strike action among private sector workplaces, with the percentages experiencing either form of action standing at or below 2 per cent in both private manufacturing and private services. There was, however, a rise in industrial action in the public sector between 1998 and 2004. This reflected the reactions of public sector trade unions and their members to government or government-inspired attempts to impose limits on the pay increases of particular public sector groups, and/or efforts to implement the change programmes that became an increasingly prominent feature throughout the period (for further details, see Prowse and Prowse, 2007). One in seven public sector workplaces experienced industrial action in the year preceding the 2004 survey, commonly a strike or employees working to rule, compared with one in twenty in 1998 (Table 8.2). This helps to explain the most notable trend in official statistics in recent years, which has been the rise in the number of workers involved per stoppage (Figure 8.1). This has arisen as the result of the decline in private sector stoppages, with national public sector disputes now dominating the statistics to a greater degree than ever before.

The pattern since 2004 can be observed only from official strike statistics, but these show that 2005 recorded the lowest number of stoppages and working days lost in the post-war period, with only six days lost per thousand employees. Stoppages and days lost both rose again in 2006, but both series are now fluctuating around very low averages by historical standards. The same cannot be said of claims to employment tribunals.

Individual disputes

Mindful of the particular nature of matters of dispute that had a foundation in statutory or contractual rights, the Donovan Commission (reporting in June 1968) addressed the need for new arrangements for dealing with disputes between individual employees and employers. The commission proposed that the industrial tribunals that already handled disputes arising under the Redundancy Payments Act 1965 be given an enhanced role in the administration of labour law to address 'all disputes between individual workers and his employer', and so provide an 'easily accessible, speedy, informal and inexpensive procedure' for achieving an amicable settlement of disputes (Donovan, 1968: para. 577). The same commission proposed the right not to be unfairly dismissed. The Industrial Relations Act 1971, which enacted this right, broadened the role of the industrial tribunals (renamed employment tribunals by the Employment Rights (Dispute Resolution) Act in 1998) to include unfair dismissal claims.[4]

---

[4] A new conciliation service was also created within government to assist parties towards voluntary settlement of cases, and as a less costly alternative to tribunal adjudication. This

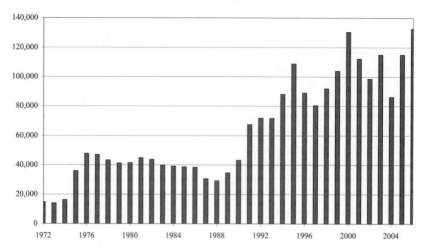

Figure 8.2 Total number of employment tribunal applications registered, 1972–2006

The introduction of unfair dismissal legislation was followed by a growth in the case-load, with the volume of cases increasing further with the reduction in the qualifying period for bringing unfair dismissal claims (from two years to one year in 1974 and to six months in 1975), as well as an increase in time limits for claiming (from four to thirteen weeks in 1974) from the dismissal. By 1980, the total volume of applications to industrial tribunals had grown four-fold to just over 41,000 (Figure 8.2). These were located largely under unfair dismissal and redundancy pay jurisdictions, though claims relating to equal pay and to sex and race discrimination were also within the scope of the tribunals.

The 1980s saw a small downward trend with applications falling to 29,000 in 1988. The steady growth in cases relating to equality issues, plus a new right to claim against infringement of wages payments, was offset by a small decline in unfair dismissal cases following a further change to the qualifying period (from one to two years, though in 1999 it again returned to one year). The picture changed again in 1989, when in excess of 34,000 applications were submitted and the 1990s heralded

role was later adopted by the Conciliation and Arbitration Service (established in 1974), later renamed the Advisory Conciliation and Arbitration Service (Acas) and established as an independent, tripartite statutory body under the Employment Protection Act 1975. To this date Acas has continued to hold a statutory duty to conciliate and promote a voluntary settlement in cases submitted to the now-named employment tribunals in order to avoid more costly, formal hearings.

a new era of considerable growth, with tribunal cases soaring to in excess of 100,000 by 1999 and reaching 130,000 cases in 2000/2001. Since the 1990s, employees have been given new rights to bring cases relating to breach of contract (transferred from the courts in 1994), and discrimination on grounds of disability (1995) and age, sexual orientation and religion or belief (2006). Applications have remained high, but fluctuated, falling below 100,000 in two separate years, but peaking again in 2006/7 (the most recent published figures), when 132,500 applications were registered.

Alongside a growth in overall volumes has been change in the configuration of applications. The growth in jurisdictions has inevitably led to some change in the composition of case-loads. Whilst in 1986 unfair dismissal represented three-quarters of claims, they now represent 40 per cent. Discrimination cases have formed a small, but significant, corner of the total case-load, today representing jointly around 15 per cent of all applications.

There has also been a change in the nature of cases, most significantly in the volume of applications involving more than one jurisdiction. This is where, for example, a dismissed employee alleges infringement of rights in relation to both unfair dismissal and sex discrimination. The issue first came to prominence in the 1998 Acas Annual Report, which noted that just under half of all applications in the preceding year had two or more jurisdictions, compared with only around one-third of applications in the year before that. In 2006/7, 132,500 registered claims covered a mix of 238,500 jurisdictions (an average of 1.8 per claim). This has been interpreted as an indicator of the increasing complexity of cases.

Another indicator of complexity is the level of representation which, irrespective of the absence of legal aid, has grown over the years, though it has now stabilised. In spite of Donovan's vision of informality, the vast majority of parties today seek advice during the course of their case, and more than half have a formal representative acting on their behalf. According to the 2004 Survey of Employment Tribunal Applications (SETA), 55 per cent of applicants and 59 per cent of employers had a representative handling their case, whilst most others had sought active professional support (Hayward et al., 2004). The figures demonstrate a small increase in the proportion of applicants receiving support since the 1998 survey, but a more significant change when compared with earlier research from the mid-1980s which indicated that around four in every ten applicants were represented at that time (Dickens et al., 1985).

A further significant feature of the current case-load is the incidence of multiple claims, i.e., those involving more than one applicant bringing the same case against the same employer, and usually involving the same representative. Sporadic instances are cited through the history of the tribunal service of sizeable multiples having an impact on the overall volume of cases.[5] However, recent years have seen a magnification of this. Between 2001 and 2005, a distinctive pattern emerged in which the number of single cases fell; it has since fluctuated, whilst there has also been an increase in the volume of multiple claims, heavily influenced by a relatively small number of large multiple cases (Gibbons, 2007). In 2005/6, 55 per cent of the total claims received were multiple claimant cases. This is an important point. A sizeable proportion of recent multiple claims relate to equal pay claims brought against local authorities in relation to the 1997 national agreement to seek the 'single status' of pay across employees.[6] These public sector claims are brought by unionised workers, and can thus be taken to represent an overt collective action, but one channelled through the tribunal system. The pattern of increased pursuance of individualised employment rights has been identified by some as an indicator of the 'individualisation phenomenon' (Latreille et al., 2007). For others, it reflects a strategic decision on the part of unions to enforce legally based rights in the context of reduced coverage and depth of collective bargaining (Dickens, 2000).

The periodic nature of the WERS series means that no light can be thrown on the considerable volatility in the annual rate of ET applications. Its design, nonetheless, provides a unique insight into how pervasive this rising volume of tribunal cases has been across British workplaces. Overall, it shows that, in spite of the significant growth in cases, in practice, they impact upon a minority of workplaces. Between 1980 and 1990, around 10% of workplaces (with twenty-five or more employees) had experienced an employment tribunal case in the year preceding the survey, the figure rising slightly to 13% and 15% in subsequent WERS. When workplaces with ten or more employees are taken into account, the equivalent figures are 6% in 1998 and 8% in 2004.[7]

---

[5] Notable examples have been in 1986, 5000 claims brought by News International workers, and in 1995, 25,000 claims from part-time employees claiming retrospective membership of their employer pension schemes.

[6] In its 2006/7 annual report, Acas reported that 10,000 claims relating to equal pay had been lodged in the tribunal against local authorities and 15,000 had been presented against NHS employers. In addition, using its statutory duty, during 2006/7 Acas brokered settlements in 56,000 potential claims against local authorities. Setting aside these very large multiples, in 2007, 1,580 multiple cases were submitted representing just under 17,000 claims (mean rate of 10 claims per case; 66 cases contained in excess of 50 claims) (Acas statistics).

[7] In 2004, the figure among the wider population of workplaces with five or more employees was five per cent.

WERS data also accord with other sources in suggesting that, while many claims arise in small businesses, it is medium-sized businesses, in particular, that generate a disproportionate share of claims. The 2004 SETA showed that 21 per cent of tribunal applications were brought by employees in organisations with 50 to 249 employees, although these organisations accounted for only 4 per cent of aggregate employment (Hayward *et al.*, 2004; for further discussion see Gibbons, 2007: 16). It may be that medium-sized organisations are effectively caught between two posts, being disadvantaged by the absence of the close working relationships that characterise small firms, yet at the same time not benefiting from the full formality of the larger organisation.

Reflections on the changing pattern of disputes

An initial question that is begged by the preceding discussion is whether the different forms of dispute are substitutes for one another. Indeed, some commentators see the rise in individualised conflict as the flipside of the decline in union power and with it, collective action (Shackleton, 2002); a reaction to the 'cathartic aspect of collective disputes', as unions find it more difficult to organise (Drinkwater and Ingram, 2005). One question is whether employment tribunal claims represent a new manifestation of the same conflict, previously voiced through collective action. Certainly, Figures 8.1 and 8.2 appear to suggest that the growth in ET applications is the mirror image of the decline in collective disputes. Moreover, these trends, taken together, bolster prevailing arguments that the fall in trade union membership and coverage of collective bargaining has refracted in the wider individualisation of the employment relationship (see, for example, Kelly, 1998; Brown *et al.*, 1998; Hawes, 2000).

Yet closer inspection of the data suggests that this pastiche may be oversimplistic. It is not just a case of the actors being different, but also the issues. Except in rare cases, such as a walkout in support of sacked colleagues, collective action has typically been prompted by concerns about pay levels, other general terms and conditions, and redundancies. In contrast, ET claims have typically been concerned with underpayment (rather than levels) of wages, unfair selection for dismissal or discriminatory behaviour. Furthermore, ET claims are rarely brought in the context of a continuing employment relationship. In the case of unfair dismissal claims, for example, re-employment has long been regarded as the 'lost remedy' (Dickens, 1981). Looking back across the period, it is therefore difficult on a number of counts to perceive ET claims in the same framework as Batstone's take on strikes as a 'tactical extension' to collective organised opposition through which the frontier of control in a workplace is either changed or maintained (Batstone *et al.*, 1977: 218).

It remains to be seen whether this pattern is changing. The recent growth in multiple ET cases involving a single issue (or set of issues) affecting a number of people in the same workplace or organisation suggests it might be. Indeed, Gibbons (2007) attributes the growth in multiple cases directly to collective issues, commenting that the rate of such cases 'fluctuates substantially because it is heavily influenced by large scale disputes'. The equal pay 'multiples' described earlier, many of which are union-led, are the most notable example.[8] Acas, which is responsible for handling such claims, expects the figure to rise higher in future years, particularly as the NHS tackles the pay anomalies emerging from its 'Agenda for Change' review (Acas, 2007).

The more challenging question that the discussion raises is why the trends in disputes have taken the pattern they have and why, in particular, there has been such a significant decline in collective disputes from the early 1990s. Undoubtedly, successive governments had a role to play through the programme of legislative change to restrict the activities of trade unions, instituted in Britain under Margaret Thatcher. As Metcalf (2003a: 175) reminds us, 'the strike threat . . . was weakened by a succession of laws which permitted a union to be sued, introduced ballots prior to a strike, and outlawed both secondary and unofficial action.' Post 1997, New Labour's White Paper *Fairness at Work* elected to maintain such a position, declaring that 'There will be no going back. The days of strikes without ballots, mass picketing, closed shops and secondary action are over' (DTI, 1998). However, whilst legislative change may have played some part, the fact that most countries experienced similar falls in collective disputes over this period (Scheuer, 2006; Gall and Hebdon, 2008) suggests that other factors were also at work. Recent overviews by Waddington (2003: 250) and Scheuer (2006) summarise a more complex set of explanations focusing on factors which, together, brought about considerable changes in the way employment relations was run. These include: the cyclical pattern of economic activity (the so-called long wave theory); shifts in the distribution of employment between sectors and occupations; a weakening in the structure for collective organisation, seen in reduced union density and bargaining coverage; an increase in human resource professionalism and proceduralisation; and increasing trade liberalisation and globalisation.

---

[8] The cost of such 'semi-collective action' (Gall and Hebdon, 2008) is significant – estimated at around £3 billion – and predicted to escalate potentially to £5 billion in back-pay liabilities and future wage bills (Fuller, 2007).

In the case of the United Kingdom, trade liberalisation and globalisation would appear to have been especially important in accounting for the decline of collective disputes in manufacturing. Intensifying competitive pressures in an increasingly global market place not only helps to explain the demise of many of the larger workplaces where collective action took place (for example, in the automotive sector), but also a decline in such action in the workplaces that remain. A similar argument concerning the decline of collective bargaining has been discussed in Chapter 2. Put simply, survival has become the name of the game, raising the cost of collective disputes to both employers and employees.

Overall, however, it was arguably fundamental changes in macroeconomic policy regimes that made the difference. That these were common in most industrialised economies gives them added force. In the light of the failure of Keynesian policies to deal with the external shocks of the 1970s and the relative success of the German Bundesbank's example, most countries, including the United Kingdom, moved towards a monetary regime in the 1980s that involved central bank targeting of relatively low rates of inflation with corresponding borrowing rates. The intention and effect was not only to help bring down the rate of inflation – a major consideration in the pay bargaining that figured so prominently among the causes of disputes – but also to make pay bargainers recognise that attempts to reach above-inflation settlements would now result in unemployment. In the light of so-called 'non-accommodating' monetary regimes, trade unions adjusted the point of resistance to the prevailing level of inflation in an attempt to maintain living standards, while employers did everything they could to minimise the impact on unit costs by insisting on major changes in working practices. The result was a convergence of pay settlements around the level of inflation (a 'European going rate' in the words of Hassel (2002)), increases in productivity, lower unit labour costs and, most obviously, reductions in manufacturing employment (see Marginson and Sisson, 2004: 252–61).[9]

A 'non-accommodating' monetary regime also affects the public sector, whose disputes now dominate the statistics to a greater degree than ever before. But the political considerations which encircle the public sector mean that the ability to pay is less constrained than in the private sector. Moreover, the implications of the withdrawal of essential

---

[9] Despite starting with one of the lowest proportions of employment in manufacturing, the United Kingdom experienced the largest rate of decline of major EU countries. As a percentage of total UK employment, manufacturing employment declined from 20.7% to 15.6% between 1993 and 2002. In Germany, it declined from 27.8% to 23.5%. France saw a decline of 1.5%, while Italy experienced a small increase. (Sisson, 2005: 59)

public services, coupled with their widespread coverage when disputes take place, raises the stakes considerably – life and death can be involved in some situations. This gives trade unions and their public sector members considerable bargaining power.

Turning to individual disputes, the starting point has to be what Dickens (2000) has termed the 'explosion' in individual employment rights, with the effect of legality gradually extending into areas of the employment relationships which had previously been a matter of voluntary determination (Dickens and Neal, 2006: 7). The expansion, which reflects developments in the European Union's social dimension as well as British governments' domestic agendas, means that more areas of working life are covered by the law, as are more employees. At the beginning of the period, there were around twenty individual employment rights under which an employee might bring a claim. By 2008, there were in excess of sixty (Employment Tribunal Service, 2008). Shackleton (2002) has also argued that it is not just the growth in rights, but frequent changes in the law that has contributed to the rise in claims as a result of the 'uncertainty' experienced by employees and employers about their respective rights and obligations. Moreover, those rights which have been introduced also rarely involved a collective representation role in their enforcement, thereby contributing to the individualisation of the employment relationship (Dickens, 2002).[10]

In the short run, widening the coverage of protection as well as changes in qualification periods has clearly had some impact. Earlier analysis showed the impact of reducing the qualifying period and increasing the time limits for unfair dismissal claims. But underlying considerations were almost certainly also of relevance. These include a greater awareness of the system, encouraged by landmark cases attracting considerable press attention.[11] Telling here is that the rise in applications does not just reflect an increase in the number of employment rights. The incidence of those claims against underpayment of wages, breach of contract and unfair dismissal (though the latter is subject to greater fluctuation) which continue to be the main issues of contention, has risen even if their overall proportion has fallen. As Burgess et al. (2000) suggest, it is difficult to escape the conclusion that a key factor has been an increase in the average value of awards over the period – in part due to the raising of the ceiling of awards and, in the case of discrimination, the lifting of any ceiling

---

[10] Arguably, statutory recognition and legal rights to information and consultation offered an opportunity to incorporate the handling of individual complaints and so reduce the reliance on ETs. The idea was not accepted at the policy level, however.

[11] See, for instance, Sinclair and Botten (1995) on the effects of claims relating to pregnancy discrimination in the Ministry of Defence.

in order to comply with European law (1993 for sex and 1994 for race cases).[12]

Evidence on the broader incidence of discontent

One clear conclusion from the foregoing discussion is that the level of disputes – whether collective or individual – can be heavily affected by factors other than the underlying degree of conflict at work. This raises a further question as to how levels of discontent – as opposed to levels of overt disputes – have changed over time.

First, it is clear that only a minority of employees experiencing a problem at work choose any kind of formal approach to addressing their complaint. For instance, Casebourne *et al.* (2006) report that only a quarter (24 per cent) of those who had experienced a problem at work had put their concern in writing to their employer, and just 3 per cent had brought a tribunal case as a result of their complaints. There are no data available that allow us to chart directly the changing incidence of problems at work among employees across our twenty-five year period. The closest objective indicator is perhaps provided by Citizens Advice, who record the number of employment-related problems raised with Citizens Advice Bureaux each year. This series shows an increase in the number of such problems reported through the 1980s and early 1990s, from 312,000 in 1980 to a peak of 882,000 in 1993 (Figure 8.3). The number has fallen back since that time, albeit with some fluctuations; the most recent available figure (for 2007) stood at 505,000. However, one must treat this series with some degree of caution, since it is plausible that the increase in volumes in the 1980s could partly be explained by some expansion of the network of Citizens Advice Bureaux following the introduction of government funding in the mid-1970s, whilst the broad downward trend since 2000 may be partly determined by the introduction of a web-based enquiry service in 1999. As an alternative, one can express the total number of employment-related problems as a percentage of all problems reported to the bureaux, and this series is also shown in Figure 8.3. It has its own limitations, since fluctuations in the series may be prompted by the changing incidence of problems in areas other

---

[12] In 2006/7, the median award for unfair dismissal cases was £3,800; for race discrimination cases it was £7,000 and it was £6,724 for sex discrimination. Analysis across a fourteen-year period, 1993–2006, shows considerable fluctuation in median awards, particularly in the area of race and sex discrimination. Across the period, adjusting for inflation, there was a 10 per cent rise in median awards for unfair dismissal, 61 per cent rise in race discrimination cases, and an 80 per cent rise in sex discrimination median awards.

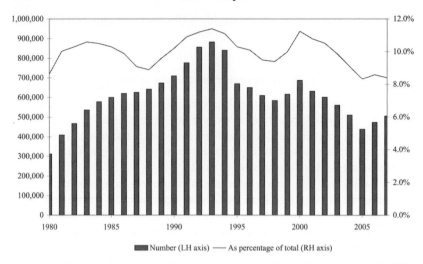

Figure 8.3 Number of employment-related problems raised with Citizens Advice Bureaux, 1980–2007

than employment (e.g., social security or housing). However, whilst the mid-1990s peak in the number of problems stands out less in this alternative series, one nonetheless retains the impression of reductions since 2000.

If we cast the net more widely, there are other indicators which provide some further insight into the changing quality of management–employee relations over the period since the early 1980s. Since 1983, the British Social Attitudes Survey (BSAS) has asked employees working ten or more hours per week to rate relations between management and other employees at their workplace. WIRS/WERS has asked a similar question of workplace managers in each of its five surveys. The proportions of respondents giving negative ratings in each case are charted in Figure 8.4.[13] Whilst there are some fluctuations in the BSAS series from year to year, the prevalence of poor relations seemed to have risen in both BSAS and WERS through the 1980s and early 1990s, to reach a high point in the mid-to-late 1990s. Relations appear to have improved

[13] The BSAS series in Figure 8.4 charts the proportion of employees that rated management–employee relations as 'not very good' or 'not at all good'; other possible responses were 'very good' and 'quite good'. BSAS did not take place in 1988 or 1992. The WERS series in Figure 8.4 charts the proportion of managers that rated management–employee relations as 'very poor', 'poor' or 'neither good nor poor'; other possible responses were 'good' or 'very good'. We treat the central category as a negative rating since very few managers (no more than 2 per cent in any one year) admit to relations being poor.

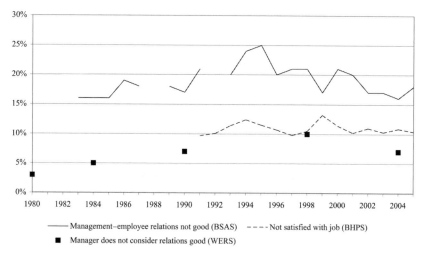

Figure 8.4 Levels of discontent at work, 1980–2005

somewhat since that time. Indeed, Drinkwater and Ingram (2005) show that the broad time trend in the BSAS series remains after controlling for a number of individual and job-related characteristics.

One can, of course, argue about the validity of tracking such attitudinal ratings of the employment relations climate over time. Respondents must use a reference point to make their comparison and, since that reference point is not fixed, one cannot expect them necessarily to evaluate the climate of employee relations in their workplace using the same reference point some twenty years apart. The broader context within which their evaluation is made is patently not the same. Nonetheless, comparisons across shorter time periods may be considered less contentious. It is also striking that the trends in perceptions of the employment relations climate from the BSAS and WERS series have echoes in the ratings associated with other work environment measures. For instance, a measure of overall job satisfaction, available from the British Household Panel Survey each year since 1991, also shows a peak in dissatisfaction in the mid-1990s, with another following in the late 1990s (Figure 8.4). Levels of satisfaction have improved since the late 1990s, in tandem with employees' ratings of climate.

It is difficult to find objective measures to corroborate this story. A measure of the incidence of employee grievances is available only in the 1998 and 2004 WERS, although the estimates do suggest a small decline in the incidence of workplace grievances over that period. The percentage of workplaces reporting that employees had raised grievances (formal or informal) in the previous year fell from 56% in 1998 to 47% in 2004 (Kersley *et al.*, 2006: 255). Measures of the incidence of dismissals are available over a longer time period, but changes in question wording mean that they are generally not comparable over the series. Indicators of the incidence of other disciplinary sanctions (available since 1990) show a mixed picture, comprising a slight fall in the proportion of workplaces issuing formal written warnings (from 59% in 1990 to 54% in 2004), stability in the proportion making deductions from pay (around 6%), and a rise in those suspending employees from work (from 20% in 1990 to 30% in 2004).

Labour turnover can be expected to correlate positively with employee discontent, but its value in contributing to the debate is compromised, since it represents the sum of various push and pull factors, and is also strongly associated with the economic cycle. In addition, whilst Gregg *et al.*(1999) show an increase in involuntary quits over the period 1990 to 1996, consistent estimates do not appear to be readily available for other periods. Rates of absenteeism, for their part, showed a small rise from around 3.0 per cent in the late 1980s to around 3.2 per cent in the mid-1990s, since which time they have returned to previous levels (Barmby *et al.*, 2004). However, non-genuine absenteeism – which should signal discontent – is estimated to account for only a small proportion of all absence (CBI, 2004), and so it is impossible to make any firm conclusions from the aggregate series. Accordingly, one is left to rely primarily on the CAB series and the subjective perceptions of employees and managers. The story emerging from these measures is that relations appear to have reached a low point in the mid-to-late 1990s, but may since have experienced something of a recovery.

The reasons for this trend have not been firmly established. Careful analysis by Green and Tsitsianis (2005) leads them to attribute the decline in job satisfaction in the mid-to-late 1990s to a decrease in task discretion and an increase in work intensification, an issue discussed in Chapter 9. However, similar in-depth analysis of the other measures of discontent discussed here is lacking. Data from BSAS point towards improvements in management style since the mid-1990s, which may well have contributed to better relations. A question which asks employees whether 'management always try to get the better of employees if they get the chance' is available only intermittently since 1984 but follows a broadly similar pattern to ratings of climate, showing a peak of discontent in the mid-to-late 1990s. Responses to a question asking whether 'the workplace is well managed' follow the same broad pattern, with ratings falling between 1983 and 1993/4 and rising thereafter. There is also some evidence to suggest that the material features of people's jobs – and thus some potential sources of discontent – improved after the mid-1990s. Fitzner (2006), for example, presents evidence of a decline in the risk of redundancy, a reduction in average working hours, and widespread gains in real wages between 1995 and 2005. But whether – and to what extent – these material factors may have contributed to changes in levels of discontent remains to be shown.

The role of institutions

Finally, attention turns to the role of different institutional arrangements in either promoting or resolving underlying feelings of discontent. Conflict can be ignored, suppressed or resolved as well as lead to disputes (Lipsky et al., 2003). Other things being equal, though, it is more likely to evolve into a dispute when there is a recognised vehicle for articulating concerns that employees believe offers the prospect of resolving the issue at stake. As Kersley et al. (2006: 211) point out, 'The formalising of procedures to manage disputes between employees and managers has been a feature of workplace change in the past twenty-five years, with a growth in arrangements to respond to individual and collective conflict.' By 2004, 78 per cent of workplaces recognising a trade union had a formal procedure for handling collective disputes. Even greater proportions of workplaces had formal procedures for dealing with individual grievances (88 per cent) and disciplinary matters (91 per cent). Furthermore, both types of procedure were universal in workplaces with one or more recognised union.

In the case of collective disputes, there is little evidence to suggest that the increased availability of institutional procedures has been a major factor in determining either the level or the form that conflict has taken. Most workplaces exhibiting high levels of collective action in the earlier part of our period, above all in the metalworking sectors, were well known for their disputes procedures. The same is true of the public sector organisations that have made the major contribution to the pattern of disputes in recent years. Formal procedures may not prevent strikes occurring, though they may well be a necessary feature in resolving disputes once they occur (Blanchflower and Cubbin, 1986: 37).

Similarly, the presence of individual disputes procedures does not appear to help in the avoidance of disputes, but instead provides a means through which discontent can be articulated and the resulting conflict addressed. Knight and Latreille, for instance, found that the presence of a formal disciplinary procedure had little bearing on whether or not a workplace had been subject to an employment tribunal (ET) claim (2000: 549). Accordingly, sectors with a high incidence of grievance and

Table 8.3 *Expressions of conflict, by type of voice*

	Any industrial action	Any grievances	Employment tribunal claims	Disciplinary sanctions	Absenteeism	Voluntary resignations	Relations between managers and employees
	% of workplaces	% of workplaces	Claims per 1,000 employees	Sanctions per 100 employees	% of working days lost per workplace	Resignations per 100 employees	% of employees rating 'poor' or 'very poor'
Union voice only	9	45	1.3	2.5	5.5	9.0	17
Union and non-union voice	7	44	2.1	4.2	6.9	8.8	19
Non-union voice only	1	40	2.7	7.8	4.3	17.2	11
No voice	*	31	2.9	6.1	3.2	18.3	11
All workplaces	2	38	2.4	5.9	4.5	13.8	15
Number of observations	2,223	2,191	2,115	2,020	1,838	2,055	21,295

Notes: Workplaces with 5 or more employees (columns 1, 2, 5); all employees in workplaces with 5 or more (columns 3, 4, 6); * less than 0.5 per cent but not zero.
Source: WERS 2004.

disciplinary procedures will not necessarily have low levels of individual disputes.

Nevertheless, procedures are an important, if not sufficient, condition for the formal expression and resolution of conflict by employees. If there are no collective disputes or grievance procedures, workers are less likely to be able to raise their concerns within the workplace, and so are more likely to 'resolve' the conflictual situation by quitting. The evidence from sectors such as 'hotels and restaurants' and 'other business services' supports this point. Workplaces here not only register the lowest levels of grievances and ET claims, along with the lowest levels of grievance procedures, but also report above average rates of voluntary resignations (Kersley *et al.*, 2006). In Head and Lucas' (2004: 249) words, the absence of dispute resolution procedures may in practice 'constrain the ability of aggrieved workers from taking action' in such sectors.

Institutions comprise far more than procedures for handling disputes. There are institutions that deal with the organisation of work, recruitment and selection, training and development and performance management – that is, the type of payment system and the level of wages, the working time arrangements, the disciplinary arrangements and so on. Links with such diverse arrangements are difficult to establish. However, authors have particularly stressed the importance of institutions that provide a 'voice' for employees (Freeman, 1980) or which serve as their agents in bargaining over change (Martin, 2003).

Institutions such as trade unions or joint consultative committees clearly provide a means of articulating the varied concerns of those they represent. They also perform an agency function which can lead directly to improvements in terms and conditions, working arrangements or even strategic direction, thus – at least in theory – reducing the areas for conflict. In principle, direct forms of voice (such as face-to-face meetings, two-way communication and problem-solving groups) can also bring about change, although the outcome may be less transparent to the workforce as a whole. These issues are explored in Chapter 5.

In their examination of the variations in the nature of conflict across industries, Kersley *et al.*(2006: 233) noted that industries with high levels of industrial action generally also experienced a high level of grievances, but also tended to experience comparatively low rates of disciplinary sanctions and resignations, and vice versa. It was suggested that the presence or absence of institutional arrangements for employee voice was one common thread linking these patterns. In common with Kersley *et al.*, Table 8.3 also draws on data from WERS 2004, but uses the typology proposed in Chapter 5 in an attempt to shed further light on any connections. It suggests, not surprisingly, that workplaces with representative voice arrangements involving trade unions report much higher levels of collective disputes and grievances than those that do not.[14] By contrast, the average rate of ET claims per 1000 employees is much lower in unionised workplaces than in non-unionised ones.[15] The evidence supports the idea that workplace representation encourages the internal resolution of disputes. The notion that collective representatives serve as 'the custodians of individual rights' (Brown *et al.*, 2000: 627) thus appears to have strong support.

As for the association between voice/agency mechanisms and other expressions of conflict, Table 8.3 shows that representative voice arrangements are associated with comparatively low rates of disciplinary sanctions and resignations (following Edwards, 1995, and Knight and Latreille, 2000), whereas the opposite is true of workplaces with no voice or non-union voice. On the other hand, perhaps more surprisingly, workplaces with no voice or non-union voice report lower levels of absenteeism. Arguably, it is the greater exposure to the dynamics of workplace debates, together with their awareness of the possibility of conflict and disputes, that also helps to explain the higher proportion of employees in these voice workplaces reporting 'poor' or 'very poor' relations between managers and employees.[16] Overall, it seems that, in keeping with the proposals of Freeman (1980), workplaces with no voice mechanism are characterised by strong disciplinary regimes in which the main expression of conflict takes the form of employees exiting from the organisation.

Conclusions

Collective disputes in Britain have declined massively over the last twenty-five years, as they have in other OECD countries. By contrast, individual disputes remain a prominent feature, with measures such as ET claims increasing substantially, though still affecting a relatively small percentage of workplaces. Meanwhile, other possible expressions of conflict, such as absenteeism and resignations, have shown no signs of reducing. Yet,

---

[14] Controlling for workplace size in the analysis of strikes and grievances (since one can naturally expect either to be more prevalent in larger workplaces, simply by weight of numbers of staff) means that the union / no union distinction remains in both cases, but becomes less clear cut in respect of grievances.

[15] Burgess and colleagues (2000) also found that declining union membership is associated with rise in claims.

[16] On the basis of his analysis of the 1998 WERS data, Bryson (2005) suggests that 'The only union effect common across employers and employees is poorer perceptions of employment relations where union coverage is at the level known to generate a union wage premium'.

contrary to the relationship that this suggests, the different forms of conflict are not, in the most part, substitutes to one another, with the issues as well as the parties being different. The more opportunities that employees have to air their grievances, especially through employee voice mechanisms, the more they are likely to do so. In the absence of these opportunities and mechanisms, conflict is likely to manifest itself in much higher levels of employee turnover.

This means that the question of whether or not relations have become better over the period cannot be answered with any confidence using the measures of disputes discussed in this chapter. Fewer strikes or ET claims do not necessarily mean that employment relations are better. At best, on the basis of the indicators of climate, it can be said that the early-to-mid 1990s were a low point on a number of measures, with some improvement since that time. As for future trends, much depends on the immediate context, as the 'spikes' in public sector strikes clearly demonstrate. If, more generally, there was to be a return to the job insecurity and extensive downsizing of the mid-1990s, the climate (along with the indicators of conflict) is likely to change again.

The chapter has been able to arrive at such conclusions because of the distinction that it draws between disputes and other expressions of conflict. Such a framework not only means that it is possible to put disputes into the wider context of conflict, but also offers opportunities to map the connections with the various institutions involved in managing the employment relationship. At the same time, it forces us to recognise that there are no 'pure' indicators of the extent of conflict at work that can be captured on the basis of survey evidence alone. A framework for understanding the nature and the extent of such conflict requires an appreciation of context, in this chapter explored through aspects such as procedural arrangements and voice mechanisms.

Focusing on WIRS/WERS, the value of collecting data on a number of indicators of conflict, and not just strikes, has also been demonstrated. The ability to analyse such data by size, sector and institutions, which is not available in most other surveys dealing with the issue, is a very particular strength. Lacking in WIRS/WERS is depth of evidence on the processes and negotiations that underlie disputes, and on both broader indicators of both employee discontent and whether or not there is an environment in which employees may express their concerns. Moreover the limitations imposed by the periodic nature of the survey – and the focus on a single year in question – is perhaps most keenly felt in relation to the measurement of conflict, which can be subject to year-on-year volatility.

Finally, the analysis touches on several policy matters. One is the reform of the institutional arrangements of the ET system. Such changes clearly have a considerable impact on the ET claim rate, and so need to be thought through with great care. The second is in reducing the number of disputes that result in strikes in the public sector. Here further consideration might be given to the Local Government Pay Commission proposal for 'assisted negotiation' as a means of helping the parties to resolve the issues between them.

More generally, the analysis suggests the value of thinking in terms of conflict management rather than dispute resolution. That is, it encourages the view that disputes are a warning of underlying issues that need to be addressed through a wider, strategic approach to management–employee relations. Here the proposed abolition of legislation relating to the so-called three-step statutory discipline and grievance procedures reinforces this perspective. Procedures alone provide neither the deterrent nor the solution to conflictual relations in the workplace. Instead a range of opportunities for employees to voice their grievances merit consideration. These range from training line managers to handle conflict better, to internal mediation arrangements, as well as revisiting the adequacy of representational arrangements. Outside the workplace, solutions may be found in the establishment of an agency dedicated to the enforcement of the full range of employment rights, such as a fair employment commission, which was most recently recommended by the Commission on Vulnerable Employment (Trades Union Congress, 2008: 160–1). The form of conflict at the workplace may have altered radically over the past quarter century, but the challenge involved in managing it is undiminished.

9   Employees' experience of work

Francis Green and Keith Whitfield

Introduction

The people of Britain were more than 70 per cent richer in 2004 than they were in 1980, as conventionally measured by gross domestic product per head. But did Britain's employees feel any better off at work after this substantial period of economic growth? How have they experienced the many changes in the employment relationship that are being explored in this volume? And, while there were 3.7 million more people in employment in 2005 than there were in 1980, was the expansion in the quantity of jobs at the expense of any losses in job quality? Is it possible to attain both more and better jobs, and if so, what would this entail?

Such questions are at the heart of a proper understanding of how work is affecting workers' lives in the modern era, and have been addressed in a number of ways. In this chapter, we consider what is known about a number of central aspects of job quality, and then bring to bear the evidence offered by WERS. Since WERS only began surveying employees (other than worker representatives) in 1998, the contributed evidence about changes in job quality pertains mainly to the 1998 to 2004 period. We also examine what WERS has to say about the links between worker, job and employer characteristics and some of the key elements of job quality.

The broader origins of changing job quality over the last quarter century lie in the complex interaction between the evolution of the competitive environment and the politically driven changes in the regulatory regime surrounding work. In this period, the economy has become more open, and many establishments have had to face increasingly competitive product markets. Multinational ownership has burgeoned, potentially bringing new ideas about the management of labour, and the privatisation movement has added to the competitive exposure faced by workers in those industries. Meanwhile, protection for labour has been lessened by the decline in union density. The decline was reinforced during the 1980s by the removal of low wage support in the Wages Council industries, and still further by the declines in social benefits that underpin the wage floor.

Nevertheless, the trend in this aspect of protection was reversed from the late 1990s by the introduction of the National Minimum Wage in 1999, and subsequently the enactment of laws mandated by European Community directives, from which the new Labour government no longer wished (or was not able) to claim exemption. Key legal enactments with a direct bearing on job quality were the Working Time Regulations 1998, the Part-Time Workers (Prevention of Less Favourable Treatment) Regulations 2000 and the Fixed Term Employees (Prevention of Less Favourable Treatment) Regulations 2002. Job quality is also influenced by the state through its broader macroeconomic policies (through their control of job security), through its education and training policies (by inducing and enabling employers to design more fulfilling jobs) and through other micro policies such as health and safety legislation. That said, unlike in Scandinavia, the government in Britain is not a major direct player in the determination of job quality, this normally being seen as an arena for employers to make decisions, in an exchange with workers. This makes an understanding of the range of policies and practices of employers all the more relevant to explanations of how job quality evolves in Britain's neo-liberal workplaces.

The story so far

Beginning with the material side of work, there is no doubt that workers in Britain in all categories are substantially better off for wages than they were a quarter of a century ago. Between 1985 and 2002, real wages rose by 37 per cent in private businesses (Green, 2006: 117). The advance has been sustained and even increased in the last decade, with real private (public) sector wages rising by an average of 2.75 per cent (2.25 per cent) per year over 1995 to 2005 (Fitzner, 2006: 10). Thus, taken on average, workers in Britain were at least gaining a portion of the increased affluence generated by rising productivity.

The wage rises were not, however, uniform across all workers. Changes in wage inequality meant that different groups experienced differential improvements in job quality as far as wages were concerned. For some, increased inequality may have been manifested as a reduction in the fairness of rewards. For most of the 1980s and 1990s, those on higher wages were also the relative gainers (Goos and Manning, 2007; Atkinson, 2007a, 2007b). Indeed, a continual theme of this period is the 'fanning-out' of top earnings. Among those in the top half of the distribution, the higher the wages, the greater was the wage growth. In the latter part of the 1990s, the pattern was altered in the lower half of the distribution. Between 1996 and 2003 wages for those in the lowest 10th percentile of the wage distribution were growing faster than median wages (Atkinson, 2007a; Fitzner, 2006). This reversal is linked to, but not entirely explained by, the introduction of the National Minimum Wage, which was introduced in 1999, and ratcheted up in real terms every October, especially in 2001, and again in 2003 and 2004.

Another significant feature of the changing distribution of job quality in Britain was the increasing proportion of low paid jobs, such as care work and hospital ward assistance. Between 1976 and 1995, although highly skilled and better-paid jobs increased the most, substantial positive employment growth also occurred for those in the lowest-wage (and arguably lowest-skilled) jobs – the so-called McJobs – while middle-wage jobs were declining. This 'hour-glass' economy describes a process of job polarisation, hypothesised to be a consequence of high productivity improvements in middle-level routine jobs derived from automation, while low-skilled, non-routine jobs continued to resist transformation by computers (Goos and Manning, 2007; Autor et al., 2003). However, job polarisation in Britain also appears to have reached a plateau by the mid-1990s. Since then, the pattern of jobs growth has become more complex. The very lowest paid jobs have gone into decline, while those in the second poorest decile and those in the richest decile grew rapidly; there was no further indication of a declining middle (Fitzner, 2006: 15).

Through the quarter century, changing wages and jobs growth interlinked to generate a pattern of, at first, substantially increasing wage inequality during the 1980s, followed by a mixed picture of either stable or slowly rising wage inequality during the 1990s. According to data from the Family Expenditure Survey, the Gini coefficient for men's wage inequality rose from 0.262 in 1980 to 0.324 in 1990, and more slowly to 0.350 by 1998 at the time of the fourth WIRS/WERS (Machin, 2003b). For women, the Gini coefficient also rose in the 1980s (from 0.359 in 1980 to 0.401 in 1990), but was virtually unchanged at 0.403 in 1998. Since its introduction, the National Minimum Wage, by raising the wages of low-paid workers a little faster than median-paid workers, has kept overall inequality in check. But there have been continued increases at the top end of the pay scale: the ratio of the top decile to median earnings increased steadily between 1980 and 2004 (Atkinson, 2007b). In recent years, high-level managers and performers in the United Kingdom appeared to reap especially large rises in earnings: the differential between the 95th and 90th percentile of the pay distribution was rising by 0.5 percentage points a year during 2000 to 2004 (Machin and Van Reenen, 2007).[1]

It is frequently argued that wages are, on their own and in themselves, a very good proxy for overall job quality. The evidence cited in support of this view is supposed to be that those earning high wages tend also to have good working conditions, enjoy more autonomy and experience less insecurity. Yet there are grounds for going beyond wages. For example, the correlation between wages and workplace autonomy is far from perfect, with many workers in lower-status occupations enjoying considerable task autonomy. Moreover, even if wages are overall positively associated with beneficial working conditions, it does not follow that changes over time in the one imply changes in the other in the same direction, since the association can easily strengthen or weaken over time.

The subjective evidence also indicates that workers often see other factors as important. When British respondents to the International Social Survey Programme (ISSP) survey of 2005 were asked to say what factors were important to them personally in a job, 74 per cent responded that high pay was important or very important, suggesting that pay is an essential aspect of job quality. However, the equivalent figures for job security, or a job that is 'useful to society' were 96 per cent and 68 per cent respectively.[2] Other aspects of job quality were also fairly highly rated, suggesting that high pay is only one among several constituents of the employees' experience, by no means standing out subjectively as the single most important one.

An understanding of changing job quality therefore necessitates a multifaceted perspective. Other key extrinsic aspects of the workers' experience are security and risk, work hours and work intensity, and the fit between work-life and the other parts of workers' lives ('work–life balance'). Just as important are the intrinsic features of jobs, among which autonomy and skill-use are central.

The problem of job insecurity – the risk of job loss or of other uncertainties within the job – is a perennial issue which could hardly be removed altogether in a capitalist society. Nevertheless, over the last quarter century, the progress on wages has been matched by a very significant improvement in workers' security, albeit after enduring a period of sustained mass unemployment. Thus, the aggregate unemployment rate, which at its peak reached nearly 12% in 1984 and which topped 10% for six consecutive years in the 1980s, hovered at around 5% since

---

[1] See Lemieux (2008) for a discussion of possible explanations of increasing inequality among those at the top.
[2] Authors' analysis, using ISSP data.

2001. The proportion of employment separations that were involuntary fell from 37% in 1995 to 28% in 2005, and the annual rate of redundancy fell from 8% to under 6% in the same period (Fitzner, 2006).

The reduction in these objective indicators of insecurity was followed eventually by reductions in subjective indicators. The perception of insecurity can be measured by workers' expectations of job loss. In 1986, some 15 per cent of workers reported that there was at least an even chance they would lose their job involuntarily within a year. Approximately the same proportion took this view in 1997, reflecting the persistence of the climate of fear that had been induced by mass redundancies in manufacturing during the 1980s, and in important service sectors during the early 1990s. However, by the end of the decade, the fear of unemployment was unsurprisingly wearing off, since this was the reality. The proportion expecting at least an even chance of job loss fell to 12 per cent by 2001 (Green, 2006). Should they in fact lose their jobs, employees became increasingly confident of finding equally good jobs elsewhere. In short, despite a less regulated employment system than that found in many European countries, the success of macroeconomic management, at least up until the time of WERS 2004, resulted in a more secure external work environment for many millions of workers.

Improvement is also to be seen over this quarter century in respect of another aspect of risk: the chances of being involved in work-based accidents have fallen. The Health and Safety Executive reports, for example, that the rate of fatal injuries was cut by a factor of two-thirds between 1981 and the present decade.[3] To some extent, this improvement is attributable to the decline in manufacturing industries over this period, but there were also big declines in injury rates within each industry. Working on a construction site, for example, is now far less risky than it used to be.

The main health and safety domain in which there is no consistent picture of improvement is self-reported stress. Though self-reports are not always reliable in this sphere, both these and other data indicate that stress became more of a problem through the 1990s; but the incidence of stress since 2000 has fluctuated, with no clear upward or downward trend.[4] In 2006–7 some 13.5 million working days were reported lost owing to stress, depression or anxiety, about 0.60 work days per worker year.

Stress and anxiety may be the overt symptoms of excess work effort. Increasing work effort in the last quarter century became an apparently

[3] See www.hse.gov.uk/statistics/history/fatal.htm.
[4] See www.hse.gov.uk/statistics/causdis/stress/index.htm.

paradoxical accompaniment to increasing affluence (Green, 2006; Fagan and Burchell, 2006). Up to the late 1970s, Britain's workplaces had been steadily reducing working time requirements for workers, which is interpretable as part of a very long term fall in work time, allowing more leisure and family time. The decline was halted, however, and followed by a small rise in average working time up to the middle of the 1990s. Extra pressure on time followed from an increasing concentration of work within households, while other households found themselves with no work at all for any member. Two-adult households added six hours to their joint weekly workload between 1981 and 1998. There was also a palpable increase in work intensity over this period, with workers being required to work harder during the hours they were at work. New technologies and associated forms of work organisation were facilitating the closing of the gaps in the working day, and hence this process is referred to as 'effort-biased technological change'. The increased work intensity, while hard to confirm and measure objectively, shows up in successive surveys that measure the proportion of workers who perceive their job 'requires (them) to work very hard' and assesses their attitude to other similar statements. The responses show substantive increases, on average, for all Britain between 1992 and 1997; and there are strong reasons to suspect that this intensification had begun some time earlier during the 1980s.

After 1997, however, average work effort remained on its already high plane, without showing signs of growing still more (Green, 2006; Green, 2008; Fagan and Burchell, 2006; Gallie, 2006). Employees' working hours had also peaked in the middle part of the 1990s at 33.5 hours per week (39.3 hours for full-timers), thereafter tracking downwards to around 32 (37.3) hours in 2004. There was a concomitant decline in the number of employees working especially long hours; for example, the proportion working over 45 hours fell by nearly 8 per cent between 1997 and 2003[5]. The declines in long-hours working and in average working hours are potentially attributable in part to the Working Time Regulations 1998, which decreed that employees could not be asked to work more than a forty-eight-hour week, when averaged over seventeen weeks. Nevertheless, the decline in hours began before the regulations were introduced, and can be found even in industries for which there are exemptions. Moreover, there remained after 1998 the possibility for employers to opt out of compliance with the regulations as long as they had their employees' consent.

---

[5] A total of 21 per cent of workers worked over forty-five hours a week in 2005.

The Working Time Regulation was, however, most definitely successful in one key aspect of time, namely the establishment of rights to paid holidays, which prior to 1998 had been denied to something like one in ten workers, the majority of whom were women (Green, 2003). As the regulation was phased in, four weeks' (or pro rata) holiday rights were granted to a large number of people in certain industries, particularly in areas of hotels and catering. The regulation was amended in 2007, preventing employers from including public holidays within the granted four weeks.

In the 1980s, the question of fitting their work into their general lives was less important for many than securing employment in the first place. Driven by the rise in and increasing concentration of work hours, and the emergence of workplace stress as a serious problem, work–life balance became a pressing issue during the 1990s. The eventual response, from both government and employers, was a policy emphasis promoting work–life balance features for workplaces – including 'family-friendly' practices. Over and above the working-time regulations, the government introduced a paternity leave right in 1999 (from 2003, paid for two weeks), and the right for parents to request flexible working patterns with a duty for employers to duly consider such requests. Chapter 10 discusses these issues.

Turning next to the intrinsic features of work during the last quarter century, what does prior research tell us about how workers have experienced the changes they have encountered over this period? As with the extrinsic features, the picture here is also mixed. An important aspect of job quality lies in the skills used in jobs, and there is clear evidence that, on average, workers are being called on to exercise higher levels of skills in several domains. Jobs are requiring higher entry-level qualifications, and taking longer to learn to do well, and have longer training times. Computer skills requirements have risen steadily since the mid-1980s, and the needs for other generic skills, such as problem-solving skills and communications skills, are all found to have been increasing over the 1997 to 2006 period (Felstead *et al.*, 2007). Educational achievement levels have been increasing rapidly over this period with, for example, increasing proportions of graduates in the workforce. Despite some evidence of increasing overqualification, the levels of perceived overskilling in the workforce did not substantially increase between 1992 and 2006 (Green and Zhu, 2008). Thus, modest though some of the increases are, as far as skill use is concerned, the workers' experience improved over the period.

However, against this improvement must be set the decline in workplace autonomy (Gallie *et al.*, 2004). Task discretion, the ability to determine aspects of the tasks that individuals do in their jobs, fell steadily between 1992 and 2001. Perceived choice over tasks appeared to have declined since at least 1986. The declines in discretion were found in all sectors of the economy, but were most pronounced among professional workers, many of whom found that their traditional presumptions of autonomy were being eroded.

Thus, while higher wages, greater use of skill, and reduced insecurity and accident risks all point in the direction of a better experience for workers, these pluses have been balanced by intensifications of work effort and declines in worker autonomy. One searches in vain for any single index of job quality, and so the normative verdict about the change in the experience of employees during our period of investigation must be summed up as 'mixed'. Can one, however, make use of psychological constructs to gauge the wellbeing of people that is associated with their work? During this period psychological research has advanced thinking about ways to characterise states of personal wellbeing. Instruments have been devised and tested, usually in small-scale settings, for measuring wellbeing at work. One indication of change in wellbeing is shown in responses to Warr's three-item index of work strain. This shows a rise in average work strain between 1992 and 2001 (Green, 2006). Unfortunately, more comprehensive instruments for worker wellbeing are not available on a consistent, population-wide basis over time, making it hard to measure change over the quarter century.

As second best, analysts have focused on job satisfaction, either in a range of work domains or with work overall. Job satisfaction is a useful concept, because it is shown to be correlated with worker turnover, and many employers make use of job satisfaction questionnaires as part of their overall human resource strategy. Nevertheless, the extent to which workers are satisfied depends on what they are expecting or hoping for from the job. Job satisfaction is not a measure of wellbeing. In general, most workers express high levels of job satisfaction, while there is some variation across occupations (Rose, 2005). Looking at how jobs have changed over time, using individual-based surveys, it is found that workers in 2001 were somewhat less satisfied overall than their counterparts in 1992 (Green and Tsitsianis, 2005). The decline in satisfaction was most evident with respect to the intrinsic domains of work. Thus, workers became less satisfied with 'the work itself'. Intrinsic domains often tend to dominate extrinsic domains in the determination of overall job satisfaction. Satisfaction with extrinsic domains, especially with pay and security, increased somewhat, especially at the turn of the millennium. Green and Tsitsianis (2005) show that the decline in overall job satisfaction can be attributed mainly to increasing work effort and declining autonomy.

Recent trends in job quality and job satisfaction: the view from WERS

The WIRS/WERS series contributes to our knowledge of changing worker wellbeing mainly in its more recent years, with the information gleaned from the employees' self-completion questionnaire (Brown *et al.*, 2006). With an eye on the policy background, our focus in this chapter will be on the prevalence and determinants of poor job quality, since it is arguably more pressing to find remedies for bad jobs than to make good jobs even better. We compare employees in 2004 working in establishments with at least ten workers with their counterparts in 1998. In this section we first report findings about changes in the major dimensions of job quality other than earnings (and associated conditions such as pensions), that is, security, effort and autonomy.[6]

The greatest improvement lies in the decline in feelings of insecurity. In Table 9.1 workers were asked how strongly they agreed with the statement 'I feel my job is secure in this workplace.' Most respondents would probably have interpreted this phrase to refer to the chances of losing their job, though, since it is imprecisely worded, it may for some people also capture other insecurities concerning the nature of the job. We assume that the interpretation remains unchanged between surveys. Since the proportions disagreeing or strongly disagreeing with the statement decreased by a significant 3 percentage points, we conclude that job insecurity decreased. Moreover, the breakdown by gender indicates that insecurity decreased for both sexes. This decline in subjective insecurity is consistent with the drop in the aggregate unemployment rate between 1998 and 2004, and the falling redundancies and reduced usage of temporary workers noted above.[7]

The reported level of work autonomy, assessed in terms of the workers' perceived lack of influence over work pace, shows a smaller but still significant change for the better. Men experienced some improvement, with a 3 percentage point drop in those with little or no influence. As measured by a lack of influence over how to do the work, however, there was virtually no change. Although based on just two variables,

[6] For a detailed breakdown of the changes reported here according to sector and income group, see Brown *et al.* (2006).
[7] See also Green (2008b), which contains similar findings for the UK, arising from a different data source.

Table 9.1 *Negative indicators of job quality: change between 1998 and 2004*

	1998	2004
Job insecurity		
'I feel my job is secure in this workplace'		
% who disagree or strongly disagree		
All	19.1	15.7***
Females	16.5	14.2***
Males	21.6	17.2***
Effort and stress		
'My job requires that I work very hard'		
% who strongly agree		
All	26.0	27.4**
Females	28.6	29.5
Males	23.5	25.2**
I never seem to have enough time to get work done		
All	13.9	14.2
Females	14.5	15.1
Males	13.3	13.3
I worry a lot about work outside of work hours		
All	5.6	6.7***
Females	5.7	6.6**
Males	5.5	6.7***
Autonomy		
'In general how much influence do you have over the pace at which you work?'		
% replying 'none' or 'a little'		
All	29.5	27.3***
Females	28.8	27.3*
Males	30.1	27.1***
'In general how much influence do you have over how you do your work?'		
All	16.8	15.9
Females	17.6	16.4*
Males	16.0	15.4

Source: WERS data.
$^*p < 0.1$, $^{**}p < 0.05$, $^{***}p < 0.01$.

these findings add to evidence that there has been a halt in the decline in workplace autonomy in British workplaces that had been previously noted during the 1990s (Felstead *et al.*, 2007). Our results show no sign of any radical reversal or improvement.

These modest rises in job quality were not matched by the evidence about work intensity and stress. Work intensity can, as has been mentioned, be seen as a negative indicator of job quality when it is reported to be at a high level. This can be interpreted as amounting to work overload. Accordingly, we focus here on the incidence of responses indicating the

Table 9.2 *Job dissatisfaction*

% either 'dissatisfied' or 'very dissatisfied'	1998	2004
Pay		
All	40.7	40.9
Females	36.4	40.1***
Males	44.8	41.6***
Sense of achievement		
All	14.6	10.5***
Females	12.2	9.5***
Males	17.0	11.4***
Amount of influence		
All	15.0	14.3
Females	12.5	13.4
Males	17.3	15.1***

Source: WERS data.
$*p < 0.1$, $**p < 0.05$, $***p < 0.01$.

highest workloads. After the period of intensification during the 1990s, have these rises been reversed? Unfortunately, the answer is 'no'. As Table 9.1 shows, there is a small but significant increase of 1.7 percentage points between 1998 and 2004 in the proportion of men who report that their 'job requires (them) to work very hard'. For women there was no change.

In parallel with these findings, there was also little change in perceptions of stress between 1998 and 2004. There were no changes for either sex in the proportion who strongly agreed with the statement 'I never seem to have enough time to get work done', taken as an indicator of time stress. And for both sexes, there were only small rises in the proportions strongly agreeing that they 'worry a lot about work outside of work hours', another subjective indicator of stress.

In short, the evidence here suggests that, if anything, work effort intensified further over the 1998 to 2004 period. The changes are nothing like as substantial as the intensification that occurred during the main part of the 1990s, and indeed are not greatly different from estimates from other sources referred to, which indicate that both effort and workplace stress reached a plateau in the first part of the current decade.

If these key elements of job quality other than wages have altered rather little, what has happened to job satisfaction, which might be expected to reflect these elements of job quality? Table 9.2 presents the proportions reporting job dissatisfaction in 1998 and 2004. Let us start with pay. Despite the fact that pay itself has increased over the period, there has been no overall rise in satisfaction with pay. This fact in itself suggests that satisfaction does not follow directly from job quality; rather, it depends on how the job measures up to expectations. More women were dissatisfied with their pay in 2004 than in 1998; but, in the same interval, fewer men reported dissatisfaction with pay. By 2004, we observe a convergence between men and women over pay, with just over four in ten employees expressing dissatisfaction with their pay.

When it comes to intrinsic domains of work, however, there are signs of improved job satisfaction for both men and women. The proportion of employees reporting they were dissatisfied or very dissatisfied with the sense of achievement they got from work decreased by 4 percentage points. For men, there is also a small reduction in dissatisfaction with the amount of influence that they have in their job, consistent with the small rise in the subjective autonomy for men reported above.

In sum, while previous studies have indicated that poor job quality in certain dimensions became a cause for concern in the 1990s, the analysis here presents an overall picture of relative stability in job quality and in job satisfaction over the 1998 to 2004 period, with some small improvements and some equally modest setbacks. It seems likely that ideas for improving job quality, or at least for redressing poor job quality, will be on the policy agenda for some time to come.

Correlates of worker discontent

Part of the problem facing policy advisers is that there remains much that is unknown about the determinants or even associates of good and bad job quality. This is despite the efforts of a wide range of researchers, not least psychologists, over recent decades. One issue is that most studies of job quality are focused on the small scale – on particular firms or jobs, or on tightly defined industries. The contribution that surveys like WERS can make is to provide evidence of economy-wide variation in quality and its correlates. The objective of this section, therefore, is to examine the correlates of poor employee experiences. We use measures of job insecurity, stress, work intensity, low job influence and dissatisfaction as dependent variables in multivariate analyses that include a wide variety of proxies for relevant organisational, establishment and individual factors. Given the cross-sectional nature of the data set, it is not possible to undertake a causal analysis, though some inferences can tentatively be made. Rather, the idea is to see which factors are most strongly associated with the employees' experience of work, as a potential basis for further research or policy-related work that can attempt to disentangle the underlying causal relationships. The results of these preliminary analyses using WERS 2004 are shown in Tables 9.3–9.10.

Table 9.3 *Probit analysis of insecurity perceptions*

Respondents strongly disagreeing or disagreeing with statement	'I feel my job is secure in this workplace'
	Coefficient
Employee variables	
Male	0.008
Contract type (omitted: permanent)	
Temporary	0.212***
Fixed	0.206***
Workload: have worked more than 48 hours in a week	−0.016***
Age (omitted: age 40–49):	
16 to 19 years	−0.099***
20 to 29 years	−0.063***
30 to 39 years	−0.025***
50 to 59 years	−0.004
60 years plus	−0.078***
Qualifications (omitted: no qualification)	
Degree	0.057***
A level	0.046***
O level/GCSE	0.041***
Vocational qualification	0.001
Ethnicity (omitted: white)	
Mixed	0.021
Black	−0.003
Asian	−0.023
Other	−0.039
Health problems/disability	0.037***
Marital status (omitted: single)	
Married	−0.011
Widowed	−0.070***
Divorced	0.013
Children (omitted: children age 0–4 years)	
No children	−0.006
Has children aged 5–11	−0.018*
Has children aged 12–18	−0.020*
Workplace variables	
Workplace size: log of number of employees	0.005*
Organisation size (omitted: less than 250 employees)	
250 to 10,000 employees	0.026***
10,000 plus employees	0.065***
Workforce composition:	
Proportion of workers 20 or under	−0.163***
Proportion of workers 51 or over	0.019
Proportion of workers with a disability	0.007
Proportion of workers from non-white ethnic group	0.010
Proportion of workers female	−0.043***
Proportion of workers unskilled	−0.055***

(cont.)

Table 9.3 (*cont.*)

Respondents strongly disagreeing or disagreeing with statement	'I feel my job is secure in this workplace'
Work organisation	
Quality circles	−0.011*
Joint consultative committees	−0.001
Briefing committees	0.035***
Team appoints its own leader	−0.023*
Team is responsible for quality	0.006
Recognised union	−0.011
Foreign ownership	0.024***
Establishment age (omitted: aged 10 to 14 years)	
less than 5 years	−0.046
5 to 9 years	0.191
15 to 24 years	0.123***
25 years plus	−0.037*
Industry and sector variables	
Private sector	0.021*
Industry (omitted: other community services)	
Manufacturing	0.058***
Utilities	0.124***
Construction	−0.044***
Wholesale and retail	−0.063***
Hotels and restaurants	−0.042*
Transport and communication	0.036**
Financial services	0.050***
Other business services	0.011
Public administration	0.047***
Education	−0.045***
Health	−0.049***
N	19,450
Pseudo R^2	0.0731

Source: WERS data.
*$p < 0.1$, **$p < 0.05$, ***$p < 0.01$.

The factors that might be expected to be associated with the employee experience are wide-ranging. Among the characteristics relating to the employee him or herself are gender, age, education, marital situation, family characteristics, ethnic background and whether the individual is disabled. Of particular interest here is whether women experience greater stress in their work-related activities because of the greater non-work, family-related responsibilities that they typically carry. This is likely to be more problematic for women with children, especially young children.

Table 9.4 *Insecurity perception interactions*

	Insecurity Coefficient
Male	0.010
Female × young children	0.020
Male	0.010
Female × children	0.006
Male	0.015
Female × married	0.011
N	19,450
Pseudo R^2	0.073

Source: WERS data.

Therefore, there are likely to be strong interactions between the gender variable and the family characteristics variables.

The job characteristics that could impact on the employee experience are the nature of the employment contract held (especially the degree to which it is permanent or not), and the number of hours that the individual works. The characteristics of the workplace that might influence the employment experience clearly include its size, and the size of its parent organisation if it is part of a multi-establishment group. They also include the composition of its workforce, the organisation of the work process, whether it is unionised, whether it is foreign-owned and its age. The industry and sector in which the workplace is sited might also be expected to affect the experience of its employees.

Job insecurity

There is no significant difference between men and women in terms of their perceptions of job insecurity evident in Table 9.3.[8] Adding the terms 'interacting gender' and 'family characteristics', as shown in Table 9.4, does not change this conclusion greatly.[9] There is weak evidence that

[8] Although the coefficient estimate is positive, indicating that men think that, other things being equal, they have higher insecurity, it is small relative to the other coefficients, and the difference between men and women is not significantly different from zero at the 10 per cent level.

[9] While both the size of the coefficient and the associated t-statistic on the male/female dummy variable increase after the interactions are added, the former is still low in all specifications, and the latter does not indicate significance at even the 10 per cent level.

married, single and childless women all perceive themselves to have less security, but it is significant only for married women.

Being on a non-permanent contract (either fixed-term or temporary) has, unsurprisingly, a strong association with perceptions of job insecurity. Working very long hours has the reverse relationship, indicating that those working longer hours feel more secure, though the size of this association is small. Those reporting a health problem or disability were more likely to feel insecure. A hint of the complex way in which domestic and working life interact is that those who were divorced were much less likely to feel insecure relative to those who were single.

Feelings of insecurity are higher in both larger workplaces and larger organisations. But also the composition of the workforce is strongly associated with feelings of insecurity. Workers perceive themselves to be less insecure, all other things equal, in workplaces with high proportions of young workers in particular, but also with high proportions of women and unskilled workers.

Workplaces in the private sector have slightly higher levels of perceived insecurity than those in the public sector. Feelings of insecurity also vary substantially between industries. They are particularly strong in utilities, but also stand out in manufacturing, transport and communication, financial services and public administration. By contrast, construction, wholesale and retail, hotels and restaurants and education and health are apparently felt to be relatively more secure.

Stress and work intensity

The questions on intensity and stress tap different aspects of workers' perceptions of how hard they work, and of the time pressures and worry of work. The analysis appears in Tables 9.5 and 9.6.[10] Unsurprisingly, it suggests that whether the individual works long hours or not is the most important factor associated with the requirement to work hard and with a high level of stress. Educational level is also salient, for it is workers with degrees who are more likely to state that they work hard, have no time to finish tasks and worry a lot about work than those who do not. All other things equal, women are more likely than men to feel under all three of these pressures. Also important are the proportions of both female and young workers at the workplace. Workplaces with high proportions of females and young workers have high proportions of workers who feel that they work hard and have no time to finish tasks, but not of workers worried about their work. It is notable that workers on non-permanent contracts are less likely to report all three aspects of work stress than

---

[10] Examples of recent large-scale studies of the determinants of work effort are Gallie (2006), Gorman and Kmec (2007) and Green (2006).

Table 9.5 *Probit analysis of stress and work intensity*

Respondents strongly agreeing or agreeing with statement:	'My job requires that I work hard'	'I have no time to complete the tasks'	'I worry a great deal about my job outside of work'
	Coefficient	Coefficient	Coefficient
Employee variables			
Male	−0.039***	−0.013**	−0.007*
Contract type (omitted: permanent)			
Temporary	−0.101***	−0.062***	−0.019**
Fixed	−0.075***	−0.056***	−0.011
Workload: have worked more than 48 hours in a week	0.181***	0.113***	0.070***
Age (omitted: age 40–49)			
16 to 19 years	−0.009	−0.088***	−0.035***
20 to 29 years	−0.007	−0.058***	−0.016***
30 to 39 years	−0.006	−0.030***	−0.016***
50 to 59 years	0.019*	0.012	0.004
60 years plus	−0.048***	−0.033**	−0.029***
Qualifications (omitted: no qualification)			
Degree	0.018*	0.087***	0.035***
A level	−0.005	0.063***	0.024***
O level/GCSE	0.004	0.033***	0.008
Vocational qualification	0.031***	0.014**	−0.004
Ethnicity (omitted: white)			
Mixed	0.021	0.028	0.040**
Black	0.081***	−0.016	0.004
Asian	0.032	−0.058***	0.010
Other	0.001	−0.063**	−0.049**
Health problems/disability	0.028***	0.032***	0.038***
Marital status (omitted: single)			
Married	0.017*	0.007	0.009*
Widowed	−0.012	−0.046**	−0.017
Divorced	0.017	0.009	0.010
Children (omitted: children age 0–4 years):			
No children	0.002	−0.009	−0.012**
Has children aged 5–11	−0.003	0.003	−0.003
Has children aged 12–18	−0.002	−0.013	−0.017***
Workplace variables			
Workplace size			
Log of number of employees	0.000	−0.007***	−0.001
Organisation size (omitted: less than 250 employees)			
250 to 10,000 employees	−0.002	−0.002	−0.002
10,000 plus employees	0.021**	0.015*	−0.002
Workforce composition			
Proportion of workers 20 or under	0.105***	0.035	0.032**

(*cont.*)

Table 9.5 (*cont.*)

Respondents strongly agreeing or agreeing with statement:	'My job requires that I work hard'	'I have no time to complete the tasks'	'I worry a great deal about my job outside of work'
Proportion of workers 51 or over	−0.077***	−0.011	−0.011
Proportion of workers with a disability	0.032	0.052	0.015
Proportion of workers from non-white ethnic group	0.038	0.008	0.008
Proportion of workers female	0.120***	0.045***	0.010
Proportion of workers unskilled	0.065***	−0.005	−0.017*
Work organisation			
Quality circles	−0.018***	−0.003	−0.008**
Joint consultative committees	−0.003	0.007	0.001
Briefing committees	0.020**	0.021***	0.014**
Team appoints its own leader	0.009	−0.012	0.002
Team is responsible for quality	0.003	0.000	0.000
Recognised union	−0.002	0.020**	0.007
Foreign ownership	−0.005	−0.003	−0.014**
Establishment age (omitted: aged 10 to 14 years):			
Less than 5 years	0.076	−0.031	−0.016
5 to 9 years	−0.106	0.304**	0.005
15 to 24 years	−0.075*	−0.072**	−0.014
25 years plus	−0.007	0.040**	0.008
Industry and sector variables			
Private sector	−0.040***	−0.064***	−0.042***
Industry (omitted: other community services)			
Manufacturing	0.048***	0.027*	0.019*
Utilities	−0.043	0.036	0.020
Construction	0.032	0.009	0.012
Wholesale and retail	0.017	0.035**	0.013
Hotels and restaurants	0.028	0.016	0.062***
Transport and communication	−0.015	−0.006	0.005
Financial services	0.035*	0.079***	0.021*
Other business services	0.013	0.019	0.026***
Public administration	−0.017	−0.010	−0.010
Education	0.094***	0.070***	0.032***
Health	0.071***	0.040*	0.010
N	19,957	19,782	19,680
Pseudo R^2	0.0515	0.0854	0.0743

Source: WERS data.
*p < 0.1, **p < 0.05, ***p < 0.01.

Table 9.6 *Stress/intensity interactions*

	'My job requires that I work hard'	'I have no time to complete the tasks'	'I worry a great deal about my job outside of work'
	Coefficient	Coefficient	Coefficient
Male	−0.042***	−0.015**	−0.007*
Female × young children	−0.026	−0.023*	−0.001
Male	−0.047***	−0.014*	−0.009*
Female × children	−0.024*	−0.003	−0.005
Male	−0.044***	−0.016*	−0.006
Female × married	−0.008	−0.005	0.001
N	19,957	19,782	19,680
Pseudo R^2	0.0515	0.0854	0.0743

Source: WERS data.
*p < 0.1, **p < 0.05, ***p < 0.01.

their counterparts in permanent jobs. But there does not seem to be a strong set of relationships with firm size. There is a slight suggestion that workers in larger organisations report being more highly stressed, but the results are neither significant nor consistent. When we look at industrial differences, what is notable is that all three indicators of perceptions of stress and intensity are higher in the public sector than the private sector. Education, in particular, stands out as having the workplaces reporting most stress at work.

Lack of influence

Where do workers feel they have least influence over the pace of their work or how their job is done? The analysis of these two lack-of-influence variables is summarised in Table 9.7.[11] The results of the two analyses are similar, despite their tapping slightly differing dimensions of influence deficiency.

There is a suggestion that men feel that they have slightly less influence than do women, but the coefficients are small and not significant. Adding the interaction terms to the analyses, shown in Table 9.8, does not change this conclusion greatly, but suggests that, relative to others, women who have children and women who are married feel that they lack influence over both the pace of work and how it is done.

---

[11] Earlier studies of the determinants of task discretion include Gallie *et al.* (2004), Green (2008a), Harley (2001).

Table 9.7 *Probit analysis of lack of influence*

Respondents strongly disagreeing or disagreeing with the statement *I have influence over*	'Pace of work'	'How tasks are done'
	Coefficient	Coefficient
Employee variables		
Male	0.015*	0.009***
Contract type (omitted: permanent)		
Temporary	0.026	0.056
Fixed	0.013	0.007
Workload		
Have worked more than 48 hours in a week	−0.026***	−0.031***
Age (omitted: age 40–49)		
16 to 19 years	0.049	0.067***
20 to 29 years	0.045	0.033***
30 to 39 years	0.002	−0.003
50 to 59 years	−0.005	0.001
60 years plus	−0.047	−0.029**
Qualifications (omitted: no qualification)		
Degree	−0.015	−0.033***
A level	−0.005	−0.003
O level/GCSE	−0.008	−0.002
Vocational qualification	−0.015**	−0.036***
Ethnicity (omitted: white)		
Mixed	−0.044	0.015
Black	−0.028	0.032
Asian	−0.035*	−0.011
Other	−0.096**	−0.002
Health problems/disability	0.042***	0.042***
Marital status (omitted: single)		
Married	−0.025***	−0.019**
Widowed	0.054*	−0.006
Divorced	0.007	−0.001
Children (omitted: children age 0–4 years)		
No children	−0.007	0.000
Has children aged 5–11	0.014	0.007
Has children aged 12–18	0.000	0.001
Workplace variables		
Workplace size		
Log of number of employees	0.009***	0.004*
Organisation size (omitted: less than 250 employees)		
250 to 10,000 employees	0.019*	0.005
10,000 plus employees	0.046***	0.023***
Workforce composition		
Proportion of workers 20 or under	−0.009	0.082***
Proportion of workers 51 or over	−0.021	0.034*
Proportion of workers with a disability	−0.123	−0.151**
Proportion of workers from non-white ethnic group	0.017	0.025

Table 9.7 (*cont.*)

Respondents strongly disagreeing or disagreeing with the statement *I have influence over*	'Pace of work'	'How tasks are done'
Proportion of workers female	0.047**	0.053***
Proportion of workers unskilled	−0.014	0.007
Work organisation		
Quality circles	−0.009	0.000
Joint consultative committees	−0.003	0.001
Briefing committees	0.004	−0.003
Team appoints its own leader	0.010	0.011
Team is responsible for quality	0.004	0.004
Recognised union	0.029**	0.024***
Foreign ownership	0.004	0.013*
Establishment age (omitted: aged 10 to 14 years)		
Less than 5 years	−0.022	0.117
5 to 9 years	0.115	−0.021
15 to 24 years	0.048	0.045
25 years plus	0.047*	0.047**
Industry and sector variables		
Private sector	−0.024*	−0.014
Industry (omitted: other community services)		
Manufacturing	0.023	0.027*
Utilities	0.016	0.022
Construction	−0.033*	−0.053***
Wholesale and retail	−0.021	−0.003
Hotels and restaurants	−0.026	0.001
Transport and communication	0.066***	0.082***
Financial services	0.036*	0.052***
Other business services	−0.011	−0.008
Public administration	−0.023	−0.005
Education	0.001	−0.020
Health	−0.040**	−0.039***
N	19,903	19,949
Pseudo R^2	0.0140	0.0331

Source: WERS data.
*$p < 0.1$, **$p < 0.05$, ***$p < 0.01$.

The age of the worker is strongly associated with perceptions of a lack of influence at work. Workers under thirty are substantially more likely to report a lack of influence over their jobs, while those aged sixty or more are less likely to. Workers with health problems are associated with feelings of lack of influence. But those who work forty-eight hours or

Table 9.8 *Lack of influence interactions*

	Pace of work	How tasks are done
	Coefficient	Coefficient
Male	0.013	0.011*
Female × young children	−0.013	0.017
Male	0.021**	0.022***
Female × children	0.017	0.039***
Male	0.036***	0.023**
Female × married	0.034**	0.022**
N	19,903	19,949
Pseudo R^2	0.0140	0.0331

Source: WERS data.
*$p < 0.1$, **$p < 0.05$, ***$p < 0.01$.

more, and those with degrees and vocational qualifications, are less likely to report a lack of influence.

A perception of a lack of influence over the pace of their work, and, to a lesser extent, over how their tasks are done, is associated with workers in larger workplaces, and for larger organisations. The same is found when there is a recognised union at a workplace. Workers in workplaces with high proportions of women are also likely to feel a lack of influence. Perhaps surprisingly, those in workplaces with quality circles, joint consultation committees and briefing committees are no less likely to perceive a lack of influence than those in workplaces without. There is no significant difference between the private sector and the public sector, and only transport and communications stands out from other industrial categories in terms of its workers being more likely to report a lack of influence.

Dissatisfaction

We now turn to perceptions of satisfaction at work. How far are workers satisfied with their pay, their sense of achievement at work, and their influence at work? The analysis is summarised in Table 9.9. It is notable that the responses to the question on pay dissatisfaction are quite different from those for achievement and influence dissatisfaction.

The major difference between men and women relates to pay. Men are much more likely to state that they are dissatisfied with their pay, all

Table 9.9 *Probit analysis of dissatisfaction*

Respondents strongly agreeing or agreeing with statement *Satisfied with*	Pay	Achievement	Influence
	Coefficient	Coefficient	Coefficient
Employee variables			
Male	0.034***	0.008	0.008
Contract type (omitted: permanent)			
Temporary	−0.053***	0.008	0.011
Fixed	−0.055***	−0.006	0.015
Workload:			
Have worked more than 48 hours in a week	−0.013	−0.011*	−0.015***
Age (omitted: age 40–49)			
16 to 19 years	−0.082***	−0.001	−0.026*
20 to 29 years	0.048***	0.008	−0.011
30 to 39 years	−0.002	−0.009	−0.018***
50 to 59 years	0.012	−0.012*	−0.012
60 years plus	−0.059***	−0.052***	−0.061***
Qualifications (omitted: no qualification)			
Degree	−0.049***	0.044***	0.039***
A level	−0.028**	0.054***	0.056***
O level/GCSE	−0.008	0.022***	0.017**
Vocational qualification	0.000	−0.003	0.001
Ethnicity (omitted: white)			
Mixed	0.078**	0.038*	0.060**
Black	0.064**	0.000	−0.019
Asian	0.002	−0.014	−0.008
Other	−0.033	−0.054**	−0.046
Health problems/disability	0.054***	0.038***	0.056***
Marital status (omitted: single)			
Married	−0.023**	−0.010	−0.009
Widowed	−0.052	−0.007	−0.008
Divorced	0.024	−0.006	0.007
Children (omitted: children age 0–4 years)			
No children	0.020	0.003	−0.007
Has children aged 5–11	−0.002	−0.011	−0.029***
Has children aged 12–18	0.026*	−0.015*	0.010**
Workplace variables			
Workplace size			
Log of number of employees	0.006**	0.005***	0.008***
Organisation size (omitted: less than 250 employees)			
250 to 10,000 employees	0.059***	0.018***	0.023***
10,000 plus employees	0.095***	0.039***	0.046***
Workforce composition			
Proportion of workers 20 or under	0.082**	0.029*	0.053**
Proportion of workers 51 or over	0.082***	0.029	0.041**
Proportion of workers with a disability	−0.006	−0.068	−0.042
Proportion of workers from non-white ethnic group	0.036	0.022	0.005

(cont.)

Table 9.9 (*cont.*)

Respondents strongly agreeing or agreeing with statement *Satisfied with*	Pay	Achievement	Influence
Proportion of workers female	0.022	−0.029**	−0.027*
Proportion of workers unskilled	0.009	0.006	0.012
Work organisation			
Quality circles	−0.010	0.000	−0.008
Joint consultative committees	0.006	0.006	0.008
Briefing committees	0.000	0.012*	0.014*
Team appoints its own leader	0.020	−0.025**	−0.011
Team is responsible for quality	0.001	0.004	0.000
Recognised union	0.025**	0.012	0.017**
Foreign ownership	−0.012	0.004	0.002
Establishment age (omitted: aged 10 to 14 years)			
Less than 5 years	−0.142	0.150**	0.155*
5 to 9 years	−0.188	0.002	0.024
15 to 24 years	0.139***	−0.044*	0.039
25 years plus	−0.024	0.027	−0.011
Industry and sector variables			
Private sector	−0.012	−0.010	−0.024**
Industry (omitted: other community services)			
Manufacturing	0.011	0.036***	0.021
Utilities	−0.053*	0.036	0.020
Construction	−0.106***	−0.006	−0.046***
Wholesale and retail	−0.013	0.002	−0.011
Hotels and restaurants	−0.021	−0.001	−0.027
Transport and communication	−0.032	0.033**	0.056***
Financial services	−0.009	0.046***	0.047***
Other business services	−0.033*	0.016	0.000
Public administration	0.018	0.010	−0.016
Education	−0.055***	−0.031***	−0.029**
Health	0.012	−0.010	−0.024*
N	19,981	20,044	19,887
Pseudo R^2	0.0169	0.0382	0.0310

Source: WERS data.
*$p < 0.1$, **$p < 0.05$, ***$p < 0.01$.

other things equal. The gender difference in relation to the other two aspects of dissatisfaction analysed are lesser, and not significant at the 1 per cent level. Adding the interaction terms to the analyses does not alter this situation greatly, but suggests that female workers with young

Table 9.10 *Dissatisfaction interactions*

	Pay	Achievement	Influence
	Coefficient	Coefficient	Coefficient
Male	0.027***	0.008	0.007
Female × young children	−0.051**	0.001	−0.005
Male	0.028***	0.006	0.006
Female × children	−0.014	−0.005	−0.004
Male	0.022*	0.008	0.004
Female × married	−0.016	0.001	−0.005
N	19,981	20,044	19,887
Pseudo R^2	0.0169	0.0382	0.0310

Source: WERS data.
*p < 0.1, **p < 0.05, ***p < 0.01.

children are generally less dissatisfied with their pay than those who are either single or have older children.

Those characteristics most strongly associated with worker dissatisfaction are, first, the nature of the contract, with those on both temporary and fixed contracts less likely to be dissatisfied than those on permanent contracts. Having a low stake in a job appears to mitigate against discontent. On the other hand, the possession of a degree is also linked to a lower sense of dissatisfaction. Where dissatisfaction is more evident is among workers with health problems. Those from a mixed ethnic group are also more likely to be dissatisfied with their achievement in this respect than others. Workers in larger workplaces are generally more dissatisfied than those in small workplaces. Those in larger organisations are generally more dissatisfied than those in medium-sized organisations. There is no strong difference between the public and private sector in terms of dissatisfaction. At industrial sector level, only construction stands out as having relatively high dissatisfaction with regard to pay.

Discussion

We have considered some of the correlates of perceived job quality. What are the features of workers and of working life that appear to influence these perceptions?

Let us start with gender. Studies have generally found that women have higher job satisfaction than men. Sloane and Williams (2000) suggested that this represents their self-selection into jobs with highly valued attributes rather than any innate gender differences. Bender and

Heywood (2006), in a study of PhD-level scientists, found that the lower level of job satisfaction of female academics was due to the lower value that they placed on pay and tenure. Our analysis of WERS suggests that working women tend to perceive a greater degree of stress and work intensity than men. Whether this reflects differences in the type of work that they do, or in greater difficulties in balancing work and other life pressures is debatable. A similar finding has been obtained in the United States and for an earlier British study (Gorman and Kmec, 2007). The explanation advanced there was that the gender difference is an implicit form of discrimination in that women are subject to more exacting demands. In contrast, Gaunt and Benjamin (2007) suggested that men are generally more vulnerable to job-related stress, and that gender ideology has a crucial role in moderating this relationship. They also suggest that men experience greater job insecurity. The current study also finds that men report greater job insecurity, though it is not statistically significant. Men are much more dissatisfied with the level of their pay than women, despite a continuing and significant gender pay gap. A possible explanation is that men have higher expectations for their pay than women. On all of the other proxies for the experience of work, there is very little difference between men and women.

There are strong findings for workers with disability and health problems. Workers who report these have a much more negative experience of work. In every analysis, the coefficient on this variable is positive and significant. This is hardly surprising, as poor health and/or a disability typically has a detrimental impact on experiences in all walks of life.

What about the effect of working long hours? There has been very little work on the relationship between long working hours and the employee experience of work, though Bacon *et al.* (2005) have indicated that workers moving from an eight-hour to a twelve-hour shift system expressed an increase in satisfaction. The analysis summarised in this chapter indicates that those who work long hours are less likely to feel insecure, or to report a lack of influence over their work. They are less likely to feel dissatisfied about the achievement that they get from their work, or the influence that they have over their job. However, long-hours workers are more likely to feel stress and high work intensity. These associations should not be seen as indicating a particular direction of causation. It might, for example, be that some workers choose to work long hours precisely because they are satisfied with their work.

The experience of work is not associated with the life cycle in a simple way. Younger workers tend to feel less insecure and less stressed, but they are more likely to report a lack of influence over their jobs. Moreover, there is no clear relationship between age and the amount of dissatisfaction that is expressed in relation to any of the aspects of dissatisfaction that we have examined.

Educational qualifications appear to play a part. Workers with degrees are more likely to feel insecure and to experience a high level of work intensity. But they are less likely to report a lack of influence at work. They are less likely to be dissatisfied with the amount of pay that they receive. But they are more likely to be dissatisfied with the sense of achievement that they gain from their work and the amount of influence that they have over their jobs. This finding supports the conclusion reached by Belfield and Harris (2002) that job satisfaction is neutral across different education grades.

The size of firm also appears to matter. Workers in larger organisations report higher levels of insecurity, more stress and work intensity, higher levels of lack of influence and more dissatisfaction than those in smaller and medium-sized organisations. The clear implication is that the employee experience in smaller workplaces is significantly better than in larger workplaces and organisations. It supports those who assert that 'small is beautiful', relative to those who see smaller workplaces as 'bleak houses' (Dundon et al., 2001).

Just how the changing organisation of work affects employees is explored in Chapter 7's discussion of high involvement management. We can summarise the findings with regard to employe experiences of work in terms of two competing views of the impact of high performance work organisation practices on employee experience. The more positive suggests that such practices typically lead to increased levels of discretion, improved job security and enhanced job satisfaction (for example, Kalmi and Kauhanen, 2008). By contrast, the more critical view suggests that these practices are more commonly associated with increased job intensity and reduced security (for example, Delbridge et al., 1992; Brenner et al., 2004). Harley (2001), however, using the WERS 1998, found no statistically significant relationship between team membership and measures of employee wellbeing. Also deploying WERS 1998, Cox et al. (2006) found that the greater the breadth and depth of employee involvement and participation practices, the higher the levels of organisational commitment and job satisfaction of workers. Using WERS 2004, Wood (2008) concluded that employee wellbeing is negatively related to job demands and positively related to the control that a worker has over his/her job.

The analysis of this chapter is that the experience of workers in workplaces with quality circles is less negative than in those without, and that the reverse applies to those in workplaces with briefing committees. Why this is the case is a matter for conjecture. It is notable that workers in workplaces with briefing committees and quality circles do not feel that they have less sense of influence at work than those without. While the latter is compatible with the findings of Delbridge and Whitfield (2001), using WERS 1998 data, the former stands in stark contrast to their results. The impact of joint consultative committees and teamworking on the employee experience does not seem to be strong. By contrast, using the earlier WERS data set, Delbridge and Whitfield (2001) found strong negative associations between team responsibility for a product or service and influence, but strong positive associations in relation to influence when a team appoints their own leader.

What does the analysis tell us about trade union members' work experience? Analysis of WERS 1998 indicated that union members are generally less satisfied than non-members (Guest and Conway, 1999, 2004). The authors ascribe this to the lack of strong employee voice in workplaces where employers are anti-union. Bryson *et al.* (2004) found that allowing for endogenous selection processes in the sorting of workers into unionised jobs eliminated the job satisfaction difference between unionised and non-unionised workers, implying that the lower job satisfaction of the former is due to selection rather than causal processes. The analysis undertaken for this chapter indicates that workers in workplaces with recognised unions tend to have a more negative experience of work than elsewhere. In particular, they are more likely to state that they have no time to get their work done, to express a lack of influence over their pace of work, and be dissatisfied about various aspects of their jobs. Well might trade unions have been described by C. Wright Mills as 'managers of discontent'.

Conclusion

Employees' experience of work has changed substantially during the twenty-five years that WIRS/WERS has been in existence. Although the surveys only examined this issue directly from 1998 onwards, evidence from other sources has suggested that, taken as a whole, workers have, on the one hand, experienced higher wages, greater use of their skills and reduced insecurity and risk of accident. But, on the other hand, they have experienced the intensification of work effort and a decline in worker autonomy. The two most recent WERS suggest that there has been tendency for relative stability both in job quality and in job satisfaction over the 1998 to 2004 period, with some modest improvements and some equally modest setbacks.

The experience of lower job quality is disproportionately associated, according to our analysis of the most recent WERS, with particular characteristics of workers and of workplaces. Workplace and organisational size have a persistent association with adverse employee experience. Workers in smaller workplaces generally report better experience of work. A second robust (if unsurprising) finding is that those with health problems are worse off. Bearing in mind that poor working conditions often contribute to health problems, they experience greater work stress and are more insecure. With the exception that women are more likely than men to report greater stress and work intensity, a third notable finding is that the experiences of men and women differ relatively little. Finally, while those working long hours feel relatively high stress and work intensity, this appears to be counterbalanced by perceptions of their having more influence over their jobs. In general, their levels of dissatisfaction are lower than those working shorter hours.

From WERS and related surveys we know that there is great variation across the economy in employees' experience of the quality of their working lives. Yet there are no simple answers to questions as to whether the experience of work is getting better or worse. What is clear, however, is that the current high levels of work intensity that evolved during the 1990s are a potent source of worker strain. Policies to enable smarter, more efficient, but less intensive working are needed if there is to be an improvement in this dimension of workers' experience. Also at the forefront of policy concern should be the lower level of worker autonomy that appears to have evolved through the 1990s, not least because highly intensive work combined with low autonomy is known to be especially detrimental to health. One of the pressing issues for contemporary research on job quality is whether the sorts of practices being advocated in managerial and government circles to generate 'high performance' in companies are also conducive to generating better jobs for workers.

10   Equality and diversity at work

Shirley Dex and John Forth

Introduction

At the time of the first Workplace Industrial Relations Survey, legislation had recently been enacted which signalled that an on-going revolution was taking place in Britain, concerned with achieving gender and racial equality in the workplace. This new legal framework included anti-discrimination and equal pay legislation, as well as legislation entitling women to statutory maternity leave and pay. Large employers and work-places – along with trade unions – were only just soaking up the implications of the 1970s legislation, and many small employers were ignoring this new tide, as they were allowed to by the laws' coverage conditions.

Over the subsequent quarter of a century, the law has been reinforced in various ways, and its coverage extended to employees working for smaller employers. Many leading-edge employers, wanting to be the 'employer of choice', have embraced this agenda wholeheartedly and willingly, and often well ahead of legislation, but this has not been the case for all. Court case battles on sex discrimination in the UK and European courts and at industrial tribunals have all served to strengthen the point that society as a whole considers equality to be a serious business. But they also demonstrate that some employers need to be forced to act on equality since they will not willingly address the workplace issues. Furthermore, while progress on equality monitoring measures is evident, they are not yet the practice of the majority of employers, and we are not within reach of equal outcomes at present.

Reviewing the developments over the WIRS/WERS quarter century divides itself neatly into periods characterised by political party ethos and approach. The early 1980s were Mrs Thatcher's early years, when she first set out to take on the trade unions and change the law governing trade union activity in order to restrain their activities and power. But these years also saw the bedding down of an active period of equality legislation that had been enacted in the 1970s. The late Thatcher years, from the end of the 1980s into the 1990s, were a time during which

230

the United Kingdom resisted the growing European Union's equality and diversity directives. The late 1990s then saw the beginning of a new era, in which equality and diversity legislation and initiatives were brought in alongside changed relationships with trade unions, following the election of the Labour government in 1997. These political eras were thus associated with distinct legislation on equality issues. However, it is not the intention of this chapter to argue that the legal framework and changes in the law have been the main drivers of changes in equality over these different political periods. Clearly, the law does set up an important framework in which employment relations on equality issues have to be played out, and this framework undoubtedly influences the majority of employers, even if some remain in a state of denial. But it is an empirical question whether changes in the law lead to widespread changes in behaviour, and particularly in employment relations, that would not have occurred if the law had not been changed. An alternative view is that the law largely reflects societal changes which have already occurred.

This chapter is based on the view that the initial changes of the law on discrimination and equality were a result of prior societal changes. Successive attempts at strengthening equality laws in later periods were attempts to drag compliance out of reluctant and anti-equality employers. Trade unions were initially supportive of bringing in anti-discrimination law. But unions often had their own internal struggles about taking equality seriously as the old male-dominated leadership and agendas had to face the reality of the growth in women's trade union participation and demands. Some pioneer legal cases fought and led by women did, however, help to turn around union agendas. As for employers, the lead was often taken by larger firms and the public sector and, in this respect, the state's role as employer was arguably as influential as its role as legislator. Despite these developments, including a strengthening of anti-discrimination law and a widening of its scope, equal outcomes have not been achieved in British employment relations. But there have been many enormous changes.

To review these developments, the chapter takes a firmly chronological approach. The second section presents more of the detail of the situation as regards employment law, employment policies and practices and employment outcomes in 1980. The changes that occurred since 1980 in these same elements – namely legislation, policies, practices and outcomes – are reviewed in the third section. Finally, in the fourth section, an assessment is offered of the point Britain had reached in its equality profile twenty-five years later. The focus is often on gender, as this is where the historic evidence in particular is strongest. The issue of race or ethnicity is discussed where possible. Less attention is inevitably given to those other grounds for discrimination that are now established in law and practice, namely disability and age, because they were less salient in the early part of the period, and therefore less well served by statistical and research evidence.

The position in 1980

There had been a steady increase in the levels of women's labour market participation during the 1960s and a large increase in levels of part-time employment, predominantly filled by married women (Robertson and Briggs, 1979). By 1979, 18 per cent of all employees worked part-time and of these 94 per cent were women (OPCS, 1982). The greater availability of part-time work both facilitated and was encouraged by married women's return to employment after a period out of the labour market for child rearing. Periods of absence were becoming shorter as part-time jobs enabled women to combine paid work with their unpaid domestic and caring work. Although the impetus to encourage women into the labour market had come from government and some employers who could see the advantages of part-time working, the fact of women starting to participate in paid work to a greater extent brought with it its own momentum. As levels of women's labour market participation rose, the political demand for legislation to improve their pay and conditions increased. The demand for equal pay was a long-established one – it had first been passed as a TUC resolution in 1888 – but it was not until the mid-1960s that the pressure for political action combined with the existence of a Labour government was strong enough to lead to legislation (Snell *et al.*, 1981).

The 1970s were a period of considerable change for women, both in their economic and social roles and in terms of public recognition. This was reflected in popular writings generated frequently by the growth of feminism, the emergence of a women's movement, pressure for equality from women in trade unions and finally a legislative programme on equality. At the same time, declining fertility rates, smaller family size, rising divorce rates and growing numbers of lone-parent families, as much as women's increased labour market participation and a concern to achieve equal pay and improved treatment both at work and more generally, all contributed to making women the centre of much political, social and intellectual attention from a range of different perspectives.

The Equal Pay Act, enacted by a Labour government in 1970 and fully implemented from 1975, coupled with anti-inflationary incomes policies with flat-rate rises, had an immediate effect on women's pay. Hourly earnings began to rise: the ratio of women's median full-time hourly earnings to those of men increased from 63 per cent in 1970 to 70 per cent in

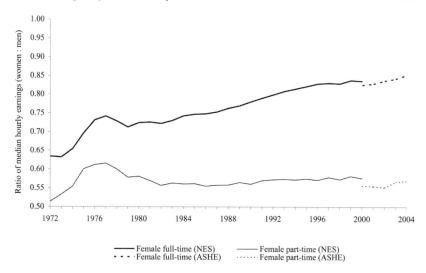

Figure 10.1 Ratio of women's median hourly earnings to those of male full-time employees 1972–2004, by hours worked. Base: Full-time employees in the UK on adult rates, whose pay for the survey period was not affected by absence. Full-time employees are those working more than 30 hours per week, excluding overtime and meal breaks. (Sources: NES = New Earnings Survey; ASHE = Annual Survey of Hours and Earnings. Figures supplied to authors by the Centre for Longitudinal Studies, Institute of Education).

1975, while for female part-time employees, median hourly earnings rose from 51 per cent to 60 per cent of male full-time earnings over the same period (Figure 10.1). These changes unleashed a momentum for wider change as legislation against sex discrimination more generally was seen as an essential complement to the Equal Pay Act. So the Sex Discrimination Act 1975 was passed and, for the first time, protection and pay were also given to qualifying pregnant women as statutory maternity pay and job reinstatement rights were enacted in the Employment Protection Act 1975.[1]

Studies had begun to document women's disadvantaged position and to explain the inequalities between men and women (DE, 1974a, 1974b, 1975a, 1975b; Hunt, 1975; Hakim, 1979). However, many of the studies were initially small-scale and unrepresentative of women as a whole. Official statistics were able to show that 43 per cent of employee jobs in 1980 were occupied by women, but the decision to run another

---

[1] Employers with five or fewer employees were excluded from the Sex Discrimination Act until 1984. Until 2007 they were also exempt from claims for unfair dismissal at the end of maternity leave if it was not reasonably practical for the worker to be reinstated.

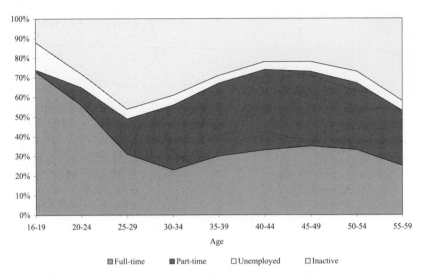

Figure 10.2 Women's economic activity in 1980, by age. Base: all women except full-time students. (Source: 1980 Women and Employment Survey. Figures compiled from table 2.3 in Martin and Roberts (1984: 11).)

major cross-sectional survey of women's employment (The Women and Employment Survey – WES) in 1980, and the initiation of the highly innovative, nationally representative 1980 Workplace Industrial Relations Survey (WIRS) by the same government department all started to offer greater opportunities for analysis and greater understanding of women's employment.[2] The move to focus on gender equality, as opposed to women's employment, came later. This increasing interest in, and use of, social science research and statistics within government also saw the launch of the Central Statistical Office (CSO) publication *Social Trends* in 1970, and the setting up of a Social Science (Research) Branch within the Department of Employment from the mid-1970s, staffed mainly by industrial sociologists and industrial relations experts.

The findings from 1980 WIRS and WES showed that women had now become permanent members of the labour force. Women still had breaks from employment for childbirth and child rearing, as shown in Figure 10.2 by the dip in women's economic activity in their twenties and thirties, but most returned to work after these breaks, even if the majority waited until their children reached school age (Martin and Roberts, 1984). Nevertheless, occupational segregation by gender was extensive.

[2] The Department of Employment had initiated a survey similar to the 1980 WES in 1968 (Hunt, 1975).

The Equal Pay Act stipulated that men and women doing the same work at the same place of work should be paid at the same rate. However, the 1980 WIRS showed that over one-fifth of all employees (22%) worked in establishments where at least 90% of the employees were all of the same gender (Table 10.1). The 1980 WES further showed that 63% of women worked in jobs which were only done by other women. Such occupational segregation was much higher for part-time workers (70%, compared with 58% for the full-time workers) and even higher for men; 81% of the husbands of the married women in WES said that they worked in jobs done only by other men (Martin and Roberts, 1984). Segregation was also extensive in senior posts: women comprised 38% of all employees in workplaces covered by the 1980 WIRS, but only 13% of employees in managerial occupations. The 1984 WIRS further showed that women were under-represented in managerial positions in 92% of workplaces (Table 10.1). The legislation on equal pay could not be expected to eradicate gender pay differentials if men and women were not doing the same kind of work at a specific workplace, which was found to be the most usual state of affairs.

The WES further showed that women who worked full-time hours in white-collar jobs which were also done by men enjoyed much better pay and conditions; they were clearly working in the primary sector. These women not only had better pay but were more likely to have training and promotion opportunities. But the majority of women were in secondary sector jobs, working mainly part-time hours, with poor pay and no pensions, and few opportunities for training or promotion (Martin and Roberts, 1984). These women also often had limited access to trade union representation. The proportion of women who were members of trade unions in 1980 was 51% of women employed full time and 28% of women employed part time (an average of 41%, compared with around 55% among men).[3] In part, this reflected the uneven coverage of the closed shop: in WIRS 1980, 26% of women worked in workplaces with a closed shop, compared with 42% of men (Table 10.1). Women were also less likely than men to work in an establishment with a recognised union (75%, compared with 82%).

Pay differentials between women's and men's hourly rates of pay were also still considerable in 1980, with average hourly earnings among women working full-time hours being only 71% of the average hourly earnings of male full-timers. This represented a considerable

---

[3] The figures for women derive from WES (Martin and Roberts, 1984: 55). WES provided no data on male employees, but the 1983 British Social Attitudes Survey placed union membership density among female employees at 42% – almost identical to the WES estimate – and membership density among male employees at 55%.

Table 10.1 *Gender in the workplace, 1980–2004, by sector of ownership*

	All					Private sector					Public sector				
	1980	1984	1990	1998	2004	1980	1984	1990	1998	2004	1980	1984	1990	1998	2004
Percentage of employees in workplaces where women comprise:															
Less than 10% of all employees	18	17	16	12	10	18	18	18	15	12	18	16	12	6	5
10–90% of all employees	78	78	78	82	84	79	79	78	81	84	77	78	78	83	83
More than 90% of all employees	3	4	6	6	6	3	3	5	4	4	5	5	10	11	12
Total %	100	100	100	100	100	100	100	100	100	100	100	100	100	100	100
Percentage of workplaces with mixed workforces in which female share of managerial positions is:															
Less than female share of all jobs	–	92	86	68	74	–	94	90	68	75	–	87	76	68	74
Equal to female share of all jobs	–	1	1	5	4	–	1	1	5	4	–	1	2	3	3
Greater than female share of all jobs	–	7	13	27	21	–	5	10	27	21	–	12	21	29	23
Total %		100	100	100	100		100	100	100	100		100	100	100	100
Percentage of employees in workplaces with a closed shop:															
Women	26	18	3	1	–	31	18	4	1	–	18	18	2	2	–
Men	42	31	6	1	–	43	29	6	1	–	40	36	5	1	–
Percentage of employees in workplaces with a recognised union:															
Women	75	78	63	58	54	62	58	45	39	32	96	99	91	90	92
Men	82	81	67	57	50	75	69	55	47	38	97	100	95	93	96
Percentage of employees in workplaces with an on-site union representative:															
Women	67	67	53	44	43	55	50	36	31	24	85	85	77	67	75
Men	76	74	59	50	44	69	63	48	42	33	92	93	89	81	85

Source: WIRS/WERS data. Workplaces with 25 or more employees.

improvement since 1972 when, as noted above, the ratio had stood at just 63%. A number of econometric studies concluded that there had been a directly beneficial increase in the ratio in favour of women as a result of the equal pay legislation (e.g., Zabalza and Tzannatos, 1986). But these improvements were primarily seen in the mid-1970s, and the turn of the decade saw a period of stability, if not retrenchment (Figure 10.1).

Considering the broader employment practices of employers, policies to address equal opportunities within workplaces were largely absent in 1980, although most large employers had personnel officers who were charged with making sure that there was compliance with the law on equality. WIRS/WERS did not see fit, until 1998, to ask questions about workplace policies on equality. Studies commissioned by the Department of Employment showed it was not uncommon by 1980 for employers to openly admit they flouted the law's equality requirements in their practices, probably more so in smaller workplaces (Snell et al., 1981).

This was also an era of increasing awareness about racial discrimination and the labour market position of ethnic minorities. Unemployment was significantly higher for ethnic minorities than for white workers despite high levels of self-employment among some groups, and studies showed that, once in employment, workers from ethnic minorities tended to occupy lower-status occupations and enjoy lower earnings (Brown, 1984). Black workers were also over-represented in manufacturing industries and so were particularly vulnerable to recession, even in the absence of the additional disadvantage that was caused by the use of discriminatory practices in choosing workers for redundancy (Smith, 1981). The situation-testing surveys by the Policy Studies Institute had shown clearly that racial discrimination in employment recruitment was a reality and extensive in Britain (see, for example, McIntosh and Smith, 1974). The 1976 Race Relations Act had been passed to prevent discrimination in employment on grounds of race; nevertheless, discrimination continued to be evident (Hubbuck and Carter, 1980; Brown and Gay, 1985). Organised labour served as a further brake on progress, as white workers resisted the access of ethnic minorities to higher-paid jobs and occupations in some instances, both informally and formally through their trade unions (Phizacklea and Miles, 1987; Wrench, 1987; Virdee, 2000). Union membership density was higher among ethnic minority employees than among white workers at the time but, as in the case of gender, it did not always prove easy to eliminate prejudice in workers' own organisations.[4]

---

[4] According to the British Social Attitudes Survey, union membership density was 61% among ethnic minority employees in 1983, compared with 49% among white employees.

Table 10.2 *Ethnicity in the workplace, 1980–2004, by sector of ownership*

	All					Private sector					Public sector				
	1980	1984	1990	1998	2004	1980	1984	1990	1998	2004	1980	1984	1990	1998	2004
Percentage of employees in workplaces where ethnic minorities comprise															
No employees	41	41	38	30	22	41	42	39	31	23	40	40	36	29	20
Less than 5% of all employees	41	41	41	43	38	38	38	40	42	37	45	46	44	45	41
At least 5% of all employees	18	18	21	27	40	21	20	21	27	40	15	15	21	26	39
Total %	100	100	100	100	100	100	100	100	100	100	100	100	100	100	100

Source: WIRS/WERS data. Employees in workplaces with 25 or more employees.

The 1980 WIRS asked employers about the proportion of their employees who were of 'African, Asian, West Indian or similar origin', allowing the incidence of ethnic minorities to be charted across workplaces for the first time. The survey showed, perhaps surprisingly, that three-fifths of all employees worked in an establishment with at least some ethnic minority workers (Table 10.2), a proportion that was to remain steady through the 1980s before climbing in the 1990s. However, the proportion of employees in workplaces in which ethnic minorities either met or exceeded their share of the total population was less than one-fifth. Until 1981, large-scale official surveys covering employment did not collect data on individual ethnic groups.[5] In fact, there was a vigorous debate leading up to the 1981 decennial Census about whether asking people to define their ethnicity was a good idea. This was based on a concern that focusing on employees' minority status might serve to reinforce them as a minority rather than help to integrate them into the mainstream. In fact, the discussion moved on to arguing about which categories should be used and, although such debates about which ethnic categories to use in data collection and monitoring have continued to have sporadic outbursts to this day, the value of collecting detailed information on an individual's ethnicity was clear once the varied experiences were more widely appreciated.

In looking back at this era and the starting point for this overview, we can therefore ask: what were the main drivers to the changes that were occurring in the labour market and in employment relations up to this point of 1980? Was it the law that brought about the new equality agenda? In brief, it is clear that changes in women's employment preceded the legislative changes on equality, building on the back of earlier increases in women's education and attitude changes. In addition, social change is never simply the result of a single driver. One might almost argue that the law changed in the 1970s to reflect the social changes that had become apparent. However, legal changes undoubtedly did have the effect of cementing the changes in the minds of employers, and helped to form the framework in which employment relations, employers' expectations and practices were played out.

From the early 1980s to the late 1990s

During the 1980s, equality was given further strengthening in law in the United Kingdom largely through case law rather than new statutes

---

[5] The Labour Force Survey introduced the category of white/non-white in 1979 but only introduced more detailed categories for ethnicity following their introduction in the 1981 Census.

(Dandridge and Clarke, 2005). A number of key cases started to make clear to employers that employees could successfully claim against indirect as well as direct discrimination, and that cases of women doing work of equal value to men could lead to successful court cases as well as cases in which men and women were in the same jobs but paid unequally. Amendments to the legislation also removed some exemptions for small firms which, Dickens argues, was necessary to 'keep pace with the progressive development of the European Community law' (Dickens, 2006a).

Clearly, the 1980s onwards was an era in which the United Kingdom's membership of the European Community was one of the driving forces to strengthen its equality legislation. The Conservative governments of 1979–97 even tried to prevent new European measures being enacted to improve the conditions of work of part-time employees, or to offer parental leave to parents. This approach culminated in the United Kingdom opting out of the Social Chapter of the Maastricht Treaty in 1992 which had, among other things, set equal opportunities as a focus for policy. There were also some further measures by the Conservative government in the late 1980s and early 1990s to weaken maternity rights and pay and to abolish wages councils, which regulated pay in the lowest paid sectors where many women were employed. And unions' rights were restricted and reined in, such that collective agreements to set minimum wage floors were removed (Dickens, 2006a).

The governments' priorities received little effective challenge. The trade unions, which had been active in supporting legislative change for equality in the 1970s and in championing women as workers, had few friends at court and larger problems to deal with, as they handled declining jobs, membership and popular support. The Equal Opportunities Commission, never a particularly strong organisation or independent of government, was not in a position to use the research findings to push for change in this new climate. The major exceptions to this were some spectacularly successful challenges to unequal pay and instances of sex discrimination throughout the 1980s and 1990s organised by women workers, usually through their trade union (see, for example, Jefferson, 1985). These were very much a minority activity, although they did set crucially important precedents for others.

However, alongside the lack of activity, even retrenchment, in the legal equality framework, employers were increasingly adapting to the changed environment. An increasing familiarity with maternity rights legislation, for example, resulted in a marked reduction in the proportion of employers reporting problems with the law, despite a considerable increase in the proportion of women exercising their right to return to work (McRae,

1991: 6). Some key large employers were also showing the initiative to expand policy options that would help women stay in the workforce. The 1980s witnessed much discussion about the expected demographic time bomb that was to hit the UK labour markets from the early 1990s onwards (see, for example, Institute for Employment Research, 1988). The decline in fertility was now going to begin to bite, with substantial falls in the numbers of 16-year-old school leavers expected. Employers saw women workers as the ones to fill the gap, and many forward-thinking employers began to adopt retention policies for women workers, by starting to offer enhanced maternity leave arrangements and career-break schemes (Metcalf, 1990). Some even went as far as investing in workplace crèche facilities or offering information or financial assistance with child care (Metcalf, 1990). It was a period when innovative employers started to take the initiative and the lead in addressing equality issues, with their own business case and recruitment and retention needs as the driver. These new developments started to be known under the heading of diversity, rather than equality, a term imported from the United States and operating in organisations in Britain. Banks were notable in these developments: the Midland Bank and Lloyds Bank, and companies such as British Telecom, led the field. Women champions in these organisations were often crucial to the developments.

The fact that, in the private sector in the late 1980s, such initiatives were commonly restricted to a few large employers meant that there were few signs of movement in that decade towards greater equality across the private sector as a whole (Table 10.1). For example, a comparison of WIRS 1984 and WIRS 1990 shows that the percentage of private sector workplaces in which women accounted for less than 10 per cent of all employees remained at 18 per cent, and that women remained under-represented in managerial positions in 90 per cent of private sector establishments. However, in the public sector, things were more encouraging. Studies at the time noted that practices to help women remain in the workforce were much more common in public sector organisations than in private sector businesses, and women working in the public sector were twice as likely to continue working as those working in private enterprises (Metcalf, 1990: 2; McRae, 1991: xi, 50–4). Indeed, a comparison of the situation in the public sector in 1984 and 1990 shows a reduction in the proportion of heavily male-dominated workplaces and a reduction in women's under-representation in management (Table 10.1).[6] The public sector also showed signs of an increase in the employment of ethnic

---

[6] Part of this change could also be attributed to the privatisation programme.

minorities in the second half of the 1980s, whereas the change in the private sector was more marginal (Table 10.2).

The early 1990s proved to be a period of recession in which the problems of the demographic time bomb never really materialised. Some organisations retrenched on the generosity of their policies over the early 1990s as they struggled with restructuring and downsizing in a harsh economic climate, and there was a concern that this marked the end of a focus on equality. However, after a temporary period of stagnation, employment rates began to improve again among mothers in the mid-1990s (Berthoud, 2006). They also improved among ethnic minorities, and it appeared that at least some groups were closing the pay gap with white workers (Clark and Drinkwater, 2007; Modood, 1997: 113–14). At workplace level, segregation by gender and race continued to decline in the public sector, and the first signs of a more widespread change were also seen in the private sector (Tables 10.1 and 10.2). There were also indications of more general declines in prejudice against working women and ethnic minorities (Crompton and Lyonette, 2007; Creegan and Robinson, 2007). The economic upturn in the mid-1990s brought equality issues back onto the agenda, and a more favourable political climate also emerged with the advent of New Labour, as described further in the next section.

Against this background of organisations taking the lead, debates started to emerge over whether equality would be compromised by the new diversity agenda. There was a concern in some quarters that a focus on diversity risked emphasising individual differences rather than group differences, and that it may thus lead to employers and policy makers overlooking the negative impact of some social-group characteristics (see Noon, 2007: 773–4 for a discussion).[7] In respect of working arrangements, for example, would workplaces that accepted the current male-dominated working practices remain the standard to which women had to aspire and respond if they wanted to be equal to men? Or was it possible to change working arrangements to be more favourable to women, and make these the new standards around which women (and men) would be judged? The debate was not won, but, as commonly occurs, things moved on. Women increasingly took up the diverse arrangements that were on offer, and indicated that they wanted more – not less – of such arrangements. Men have taken up the opportunities of such arrangements, on the whole, to a far lesser degree than women, but some movement has

---

[7] The EOC, among others, had a debate on this issue in the mid-1990s and published documents on the alternative viewpoints.

occurred, and men take up opportunities to work at or from home to a greater extent than many of the other flexible arrangements.

It was against the background of new initiatives led by organisations that large-scale survey investigations were conducted of the availability of extra-statutory maternity provisions and 'family-friendly' working arrangements (Callender et al., 1997; Forth et al., 1997). The study of maternity rights followed earlier studies that had been conducted in 1979 and 1988 (Daniel, 1980, 1981; McRae, 1991: xi, 50–4). It showed *inter alia* an increase since the late 1980s in the provision of extra-statutory maternity pay and widespread compliance with women's right to return to the same job, particularly in the public sector. The study of family-friendly working arrangements provided up-to-date, nationally representative evidence on the availability and use of practices such as flexitime, homeworking and child-care assistance. These arrangements had shown virtually no growth in popularity among employers in the 1980s, but each became more prevalent in the 1990s. Practical or financial assistance with child care remained limited, however, and this continued to restrict women's return to work (Forth et al., 1997: 183). The study also charted the incidence of certain practices that were to find legislative support a few years later, such as time off in emergencies, which was found at the time to be available to just over half of mothers who had returned to work after childbirth (Forth et al., 1997: 78).

The 1998 Workplace Employee Relations Survey (WERS 1998) added to this growing body of evidence by including new modules of questions on equality and fair treatment and family-friendly policies. The employees' questionnaire also gave a further insight into the employees' awareness of their employers' policies. Representative survey evidence on employers' equal opportunities policies and practices had been rare hitherto, and the findings showed that large- and medium-sized employers had been active in introducing such policies, but that the practices were not necessarily as widespread as the policy statements may have implied. Equal opportunities policies were present in 64 per cent of all workplaces with ten or more employees, according to the 1998 WERS (Table 10.3). The most commonly covered grounds were those already embedded in legislation up to 1998, namely sex, race and disability, each of which was explicitly referred to in around 80 per cent of workplace policies.[8] The 36 per cent of workplaces without any policies in 1998 were mainly small in size, part of private sector organisations, and non-union workplaces. Anderson et al. (2004) noted that the presence of an equal opportunities policy was positively associated with the presence

---

[8] The Disability Discrimination Act had been implemented in 1995.

Table 10.3 *Equal opportunities policies in 1998 and 2004, by sector of ownership*

	All		Private sector		Public sector	
	1998	2004	1998	2004	1998	2004
Equal opportunities policy	64	73	55	67	97	98
EO policy that explicitly refers to						
Gender	54	63	44	57	92	91
Ethnicity	54	63	44	57	91	91
Disability	52	61	43	55	88	88
Age	38	50	30	43	68	77
Religion or belief	45	59	36	53	82	88
Sexual orientation	35	51	27	46	67	76

Source: WERS data. Workplaces with 10 or more employees.

of other favourable employment practices, such as extra-statutory sick pay, job security guarantees and work-based pensions. It also made other fair treatment practices more common, namely workforce monitoring, reviewing procedures for discrimination, basing pay on job evaluation and encouraging job applications from disadvantaged and under-represented groups (Anderson *et al.*, 2004; Dickens, 2006b). But the presence of a policy was shown to be no guarantee that fair treatment practices would be present, with smaller workplaces, foreign-owned workplaces and those without a developed HR function all more likely than the average to have an equal opportunities policy which might be termed an 'empty shell' (Hoque and Noon, 2004).

WERS 1998 also charted the diversity elements of workplace policies and provisions. Substantial minorities of employers were now found to offer flexible working arrangements to employees. The proportions of workplaces making various types of working arrangement available to their employees in 1998 can be seen in the first three columns of Table 10.4. Analyses examined which WERS employers offered flexible working arrangements and found that provision was related to the type of product or service, the level of HR support, which would also be related to their size and structure, and the constraints of their business, but also to the nature of their workforce, its characteristics and skill level (Dex and Smith, 2002). The predictors of flexible working varied according to the precise nature of the arrangements, but as a general summary, flexible working arrangements were more common, after controlling for a range of other factors, in public sector workplaces, workplaces with a dedicated personnel function, those with a family-friendly ethos, workplaces with

Table 10.4 *Prevalence of entitlements to flexible working arrangements in 1998, by sector of ownership*

	Workplaces (whether any employees are entitled)			Employees (whether available to you personally)		
	All	Private sector	Public sector	All	Private sector	Public sector
Flexitime[a]	18	14	33	32	30	35
Term-time only[a]	13	8	32	–	–	–
Job share[a]	26	15	64	15	10	28
Working from or at home[a]	12	9	21	7	6	9
Ability to change from full to part-time hours[a]	42	37	64	–	–	–
Parental leave[a]	33	26	62	26	23	32
Paternity leave (paid or unpaid)	47	39	79	–	–	–
Special leave for emergencies	23	16	47	–	–	–
Unpaid leave for emergencies	19	22	6	–	–	–
Workplace nursery or help with cost of child care[a]	6	4	16	3	2	6

Note: [a] availability of arrangements to non-managerial employees.
Source: WERS 1998 survey. Workplaces with 10 or more employees.

high commitment management practices and those with a high share of female employees (but not a high share of part-time employees).

In addition, the extent of provision of flexible working to non-managerial employees was found to vary by industry sector (lower in manufacturing, utilities, construction and transport). Having a policy to recruit female workers was associated with higher levels of flexible working provision, although having recruitment difficulties was associated with lower levels. The nature of supervision and the dominant type of work in the workplace were also significantly correlated with the extent of flexible working: the provision of greater amounts of discretion, training and longer tenure to the dominant work group, as well as other fringe benefits, and a performance-related payment system were associated with greater extents of some types of flexibility. Many flexible working arrangements appeared less common in small workplaces, according to WERS 1998, but case-study work on flexibility in small businesses found that while formal policies were rare, informal, ad hoc and individualised arrangements were very common, but probably not picked up in survey questions that asked about formal entitlements (Dex and Scheibl, 2002).

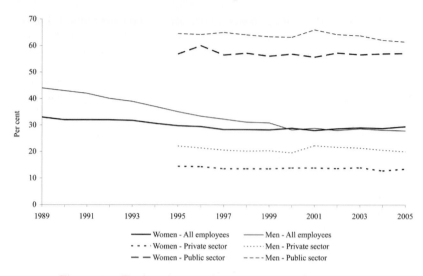

Figure 10.3 Trade union membership density in Britain 1989–2005, by sex and sector. (Source: Labour Force Survey. Figures compiled from Bird *et al.* (1993) and Grainger (2006).)

These UK findings were at variance with similar US studies in one major way. Earlier US studies found that organisations were either less likely to offer flexible arrangements where recognised unions were present, or that unions had a benign effect, but in Britain the relationship was generally found to be positive (Budd and Mumford, 2004). These findings tell us something about British employment relations in the 1990s, relevant to the issues of equality and diversity. Despite the historical struggles within some unions, noted earlier, unions in Britain have clearly been a mechanism for reflecting and implementing pressures for action on equality and diversity in recent years, in contrast to the situation in the United States. In addition, unions appear to have acted as more effective channels of communication to the workforce about the nature of employers' policies and practices. Union membership density has held steady among women in Britain over the past fifteen to twenty years, whilst density among men has declined (Figure 10.3). This has served to increase the female share of union membership, and their increased representation in official positions within those unions has undoubtedly played a part in pressing British unions to address equality and diversity agendas (see also Bewley and Fernie, 2003: 97–102). Nevertheless, Colgan and Ledwith (2002) suggest that women continue to experience unfavourable conditions in the workplace because of their position within trade unions; women are still a minority in the higher ranks of unions and are under-represented within posts of full-time officers and shop stewards. This, it has been argued, weakens their position in their call for equality.

The final three columns of Table 10.4 use the WERS 1998 employee data to show the extent to which employees personally had awareness of and access to flexible working arrangements. Earlier studies had indicated that employers afforded access only to certain groups of employees within their workforce (see, for example, Metcalf, 1990). Analyses thus took advantage of the linked employer–employee data in WERS to examine the factors associated with this access. Other case studies have also examined this issue. Access and awareness were found to be statistically associated with the employee's personal characteristics and circumstances, the constraints of the job and the value of the employee to their employer. Being female, a parent of young children, a union member, or having had recent training made employee awareness and possibly access to flexibility more likely (Dex and Smith, 2002; Bond et al., 2002). Higher qualified workers and those in higher grade or clerical jobs were also more likely than other workers to perceive they had access to flexible working arrangements (Dex and Smith, 2002; Yeandle et al., 2002; Dex and Scheibl, 2002). Those employer characteristics that had been shown to be positively associated with employer-level provision (larger size, belonging to the public sector, recognising trade unions, having more developed HR structures) were also confirmed in the employee-level analysis (Dex and Smith, 2002; Yeandle et al., 2002). Having active equal opportunities policies was also associated with an employee having an increased likelihood of being offered flexibility (Dex and Smith, 2002). This suggested that equality and diversity were being pursued side-by-side by the best employers. WERS 1998 data thus offered a rigorous analysis of employees' access to and awareness of flexible working arrangements, by controlling for other potential determinants of employee awareness and access at the same time. The fact that other case-study findings overlapped with the statistical analyses strengthened the conclusions.

One result of the expansion of maternity provisions and flexible working arrangements was to make it easier for women to return more quickly to the workforce after childbirth. In fact, there had been a remarkable rise in the proportion of women returning to work within nine months of having a baby: the figure stood at 67% in 1996, compared with 42% in 1988 and just 18% in 1979 (Callender et al.,1997: 152). As a consequence, the substantial dip that had been seen in women's employment rates during childbearing age in 1980 (Figure 10.1) had all but disappeared by the mid-to-late 1990s (Desai et al., 1999: 170). One cannot attribute such a dramatic change to the initiative of employers. The changing aspirations of women and economic necessities played a fundamentally important role, as did legislation giving women the right to return to the same employer, changes in the benefits system (particularly the introduction of the Working Families Tax Credit) and the expansion of child care. However, changing workplace practices helped to facilitate the changes that women wished to make to their working patterns. One further outcome was that women with children saw a notable increase in their average job tenure, which rose by over two-fifths, from two years, eight months in 1985 to three years, ten months in 1998 (Desai *et al.*, 1999: 173). This was despite job tenure falling among men and women without dependent children. Longer job tenure helps women to progress within the workplace and, indeed, the 1990s saw a further reduction in vertical segregation in both the private and public sectors of the economy (Table 10.1).

Other groups had done less well in the 1990s, however. Whilst the employment prospects of many ethnic minority groups improved – notably British-born Indian or black African men – the employment gap between British-born Bangladeshi men and white men widened over the decade (Wadsworth, 2003:120). The gap between the employment rates of disabled and non-disabled people also increased (Berthoud, 2006: 14). Employment rates among disabled people had been around 25 percentage points lower than those among non-disabled people in 1990, but this figure rose to over 30 per cent by the end of the decade. In fact, this widening gap was the continuation of a pattern that extended back into the 1970s and which, until 2000, showed no sign of a reversal.

The late 1990s onwards

The advent of the 1997 Labour government brought a new wave of employment rights and anti-discrimination legislation and an articulated focus on equal opportunities. As well as the existing focus on equal opportunities for gender, race and disability, additional rights were eventually added in respect of sexual orientation (2003), religion/belief (2003) and age (2006).

In 2001, an important milestone was passed in the 2000 Race Relations (Amendment) Act. For the first time – albeit only for the public sector – employers were given a statutory duty to promote race equality. A similar duty was placed on public sector employers in relation to disability in 2005 and gender in 2006. This was a partial move towards allowing the practice of positive discrimination which, while part of US equality legislation, had been definitely prohibited in the United Kingdom. This new legislative agenda followed substantial increases in women's employ-ment, and in the employment of minority ethnic groups (Tables 10.1 and 10.2). Mothers of young children had shown very large increases in employment over the 1980s and 1990s, as noted, and the populations of minority ethnic groups were growing from increases in immigration.

In addition, the Labour government signed up to enacting the EU legislation on parental leave (1999), paid paternity leave (1993), equal conditions for part-time as for full-time employees (2000) and employ-ees' rights to time off work for family reasons (1999). New Labour has brought an articulated family policy to the United Kingdom, a National Child Care Strategy (1998) to assist working parents, a National Carers Strategy (1998) and a recognition and concern about the voic-ing of concerns about employees' work–life balance. Labour governments since 1997 have also supplemented and extended maternity leave, mater-nity rights and maternity pay to cover the vast majority of women employ-ees, irrespective of their hours of work or length of employment tenure. They have also introduced a right to request flexible working conditions (2003) initially for parents with a child under six and then for all carers of adults (2006) with signals that it is to be extended to all workers later in the decade.

New Labour did not restrict its activity to legislation; it also offered inducements to employers, for example, as part of the Work–Life Balance Campaign (2000), and paid for consultants to help employers introduce new flexible working arrangements. This went alongside the Depart-ment for Education and Employment and later the Department of Trade and Industry (DTI) researching and publishing persuasive literature and findings emphasising the business case for having equality and flexibility in the workplace (Bevan et al., 1999; Dex and Scheibl, 1999; Metcalf and Forth, 2000). The government campaign around the business case for equality or flexibility has, nonetheless, been criticised as detracting from the social justice case, which many commentators feel should be the main, if not the sole basis, for arguing for equality and diversity (Dickens, 2006b; Noon, 2007).

The introduction in 1999 of the National Minimum Wage also reversed the wages councils' abolition, and put low pay regulation on a firmer foot-ing. This benefited many low-paid women employees (Dex et al., 2000). Despite the minimum wage being set at a low level at the outset, Rubery and Edwards (2003) estimated that it raised the pay of 1.7 million work-ers, two-thirds of whom were women. It had, therefore, a significant impact on the gender pay gap. In addition, equal pay claims through employment tribunals increased rapidly, a shift that partly reflects trade unions' increasing willingness to use the tribunal system as a means of

pursuing multiple claims. However, examining all of the employment tribunal cases from 1997 to 2002, Fox (2005) found that, with the exception
of discrimination claims, women were less likely than men to take a case.
In 2002, 5 men in every 1000 male employees made an application to an
employment tribunal, compared to 3.8 women per 1000 female employees. This is despite the fact that a DTI study found that women were
more likely than men to seek advice when they experienced a problem at
work that infringes legal rights (Meager et al., 2002).[9]

Building on women's greater activity to pursue their case for equal
pay, it is not surprising to see that the women/men's ratio of hourly earnings for full-timers reached 0.83 by 2000 and has carried on upwards
since. The picture for part-timers has not been a success story, however
(Figure 10.2). Why has the gender pay gap persisted after thirty years
of equal pay legislation? Occupational segregation is one reason. WERS
showed that, in 2004, one in ten women (11 per cent) and one in five men
(22 per cent) had jobs which, in their workplace, were done only by people of the same gender. This is a marked improvement from the situation
recorded by WES in 1980, but it indicates that the working patterns of
men and women remain to be fully integrated. In particular, women continue to be under-represented in the highest paid jobs, with there being
some suggestion that women may even have seen some retrenchment in
their share of managerial positions since 1998 (Table 10.1).[10] Analysis
of WERS also shows that both women (and men) continue to be paid
less in female-dominated jobs, all other things being equal (Forth and
Millward, 2004).

The government's new family policy and work–life agenda led to the
commissioning of many other new large-scale cross-sectional surveys of
employees and employers to provide an evidence base and evaluation of
its policies (Hogarth et al., 2000; Palmer, 2004). In addition, the 2004
WERS charted changes in the provision of equal opportunities policies
and practices since 1998. By 2004, 73% of workplaces had a formal
written equal opportunities policy, an increase over the 64% recorded in
1998 (Table 10.3). The 27% of workplaces without an equal opportunities policy were predominantly small private sector and non-union, as in
1998. However, the sizeable gap between the public and private sectors
closed to some degree over this period: indeed, the increase in the overall
prevalence of policies was almost wholly due to an increase in the percentage of private sector workplaces with a policy (from 55% in 1998 to

---

[9] Women also outnumber men among callers to the Acas telephone helpline (Fox, 2005).
[10] We are cautious because WERS 1998 used the 1990 Standard Occupational Classification, whilst WERS 2004 used the 2003 variant.

67% in 2004). Increases were also evident in the period since 1998 in the proportion of policies explicitly covering the newer grounds for equality, namely religion, sexual orientation and age, even well ahead of the legislation coming into force on age. This, in itself, points to employers being much more aware of equality concerns and legislative plans than in the past. This might suggest a greater willingness to co-operate to root out discriminatory practices, for at least some of these employers. It may also be a reflection of the fact that women were increasingly taking responsibility for the management of personnel issues: the proportion of women among workplace managers responsible for personnel or employment relations issues increased from 30% in 1998 to 43% in 2004 (Kersley et al., 2006: 44).

While there were some positive changes on equality in workplaces between 1998 and 2004, it was still the case that only a minority of workplaces had adopted good practices including essential monitoring. Under one quarter of workplaces in 2004 were undertaking monitoring for race, sex, disability or age discrimination and as few as 3% monitored for all four of these criteria (Kersley et al., 2006: 248). There was little reviewing of relative pay rates (7% of workplaces did this for gender differences in pay in 2004), although showing an increase on 1998. There was still widespread use of informal channels for recruitment: 71% of private sector workplaces had used this recruitment method in the past year in 2004 (Kersley et al., 2006: 73). Clearly, using informal channels for recruitment restricts the extent to which a more diverse workforce can be successfully recruited. Lastly, the proportion of public sector workplaces that used special procedures to try to attract more applicants from minority ethnic groups had gone down between 1998 and 2004 from 27% to 21%, despite the 2001 statutory duty on public sector employers to promote race equality (Kersley et al., 2006: 244).

As in 1998, the 2004 WERS found that recognised trade unions were involved in the development of forward-thinking and equality workplace policies and practices (e.g., Nadeem and Metcalf, 2007). Whether employers comply with their legal obligations has also been found to be related to the presence of active trade unions (Brown et al., 2000). Notably, the proportion of women working in an establishment with recognised unions (54%) is now higher than the equivalent proportion of men (50%), but this partly reflects the decline of private sector unionism and the prevalence of female employment in the public sector (see Table 10.1).

Comparisons between 1998 and 2004 on the prevalence of family-friendly and flexible working arrangements were compromised to some extent by changes in the WERS instruments, prompted by legislative changes (such as the introduction of rights to parental leave and time off work for family-related emergencies) and a concern to monitor practice in this area more comprehensively. However, the WERS cross-section and panel surveys were able, between them, to indicate increases in the prevalence of flexi-time arrangements, job sharing, homeworking and term-time only working (Kersley *et al.*, 2006: 252–4). There were also substantial numbers of employers in 2004 going beyond their new legal obligations by offering fully-paid paternity leave (55% of all workplaces), paid time-off for emergencies (49%) and paid parental leave (25%) (Kersley *et al.*, 2006: 258). Again, the public sector was taking the lead, as it had done in respect of other practices in earlier periods, but the private sector was closing the gap in provision when compared with the situation observed in the late 1990s.

From 1997/98 to 2005, equality legislation was strengthened and employers appeared to be more aware of this stronger and wider equality agenda, and be responding in some areas. However, much more marked was the greater spread of the diversity agenda to offer more flexibility to employees in their working arrangements. This aspect of working arrangements has caught on with a much larger proportion of employers. Employee awareness is notably much less than employer provision, however, and this low take-up may have helped to reassure employers to extend their provisions. It may also point to some employers paying lip service to more flexible arrangements, although it is also the case that employees become more aware of employers' provisions when their circumstances are such that they might need to benefit from them. What had started off, in the earlier era, as measures to help women with their dual roles as employers and carers, to address the demographic time bomb, was repackaged in this era to be about the work–life balance of all employees. While women still appear to be the major beneficiaries, increased participation and take-up of these provisions is visible among men by 2004, although not to a sufficient extent to set aside the worries that flexibility will become a female employee ghetto, with poorer working conditions, fewer benefits and restricted promotion prospects.

Conclusions: where are we now?

What we have seen over the past quarter century is a gradual extension of the role of the state into workplace employment relations – largely through legislation – to try to ensure equality and diversity become embedded into workplace employment policies and practices. The government has not always been a willing partner in equality, but the UK membership of the

EC and EU has undoubtedly meant that an equality agenda could not be ignored. The theory appears to have been that applying strict laws to the public sector will act as the government's flagship and gradually encourage private sector employers to embrace this agenda. Has this had the desired effects?

At one level, the constant need to strengthen the provisions in the light of less than full compliance might be seen as a failure of state intervention. However, the statistics also show that there has been a progressive increase in employers' compliance over time, in both the private sector and the public sector. The public sector still remains well ahead in its policies and equality procedures, partly reflecting the tradition of the 'model employer', but also the greater ability of the state to drive forward practice in this sector of the economy. However, another caveat against giving the enactment of laws all of the credit for the visible changes is that trade unions have in recent times actively promoted equality and diversity and many private sector employers have embraced the equality agenda well ahead of them becoming statutory duties. The evidence which points towards the patchy implementation of fair treatment practices, such as pay reviews, indicates however that we are still a long way off the EU hope that gender will be 'mainstreamed' into all policy and practices in the workplace, as well as in government policy.

In terms of labour market experiences, there have been some very encouraging developments over the past twenty-five years, but these are interspersed with significant failures. Employment rates have risen among women, particularly those with young children, and among some ethnic minority groups. However, in the absence of a substantial overall increase in total employment, these gains appear to have come at the expense of other ethnic minority groups and the disabled. Pay rates have also improved for some disadvantaged groups, with the gender pay gap among full-time employees having reduced from 28 per cent (ratio of 0.72) in 1980 to 14 per cent (ratio of 0.86) by 2004, although the pay gap between female part-time employees and male full-timers has seemed resistant to improvement. The headline figures on job segregation within the workplace also show reductions in segregation since the 1980s, but it remains extensive. In over half of workplaces (ten or more employees) three-quarters of employees are of the same gender; 56 per cent of workplaces have no ethnic minority employees; and 81 per cent of workplaces have no disabled employees. To be fair, minority ethnic groups are concentrated in a small number of urban conurbations, so it is unlikely that the figures on racial segregation could ever show the improvement that is possible for gender. More generally, however, the diverse workplace would appear to have some way to go.

As we approach the end of the first decade of the twenty-first century, we are at the beginning of a new era of administration of government concerns and monitoring of equality in society. Since May 2007, we now have a single commission to oversee equality issues, the Equality and Human Rights Commission (EHRC), brought into operation by the Single Equality Act of 2006. This encompasses the briefs of the earlier Equal Opportunities Commission (EOC), The Commission for Racial Equality (CRE), the Disability Rights Commission (DRC) as well as the newly legalised anti-discrimination criteria of sexual orientation, religious belief and age. This change is heralded by government as a 'step change in how we promote, enforce and deliver equality and human rights' (DTI, 2004b: 12). In addition, the 2006 Work and Families Act has introduced more rights for employees and duties for employers, especially for public sector employers. The Women and Work Commission report (2006), following on from earlier high profile reports (e.g., Kingsmill's Report, 2001), has also set out a wide and far-reaching agenda to promote gender equality, which includes the use of pay audits within companies.[11] A new Equality Bill has also been proposed which would require public authorities to publish statistics on the gender pay gap in their organisation, and which would allow companies to discriminate in favour of female and ethnic minority candidates when they have equal ability to male or white candidates (Government Equalities Office, 2008).

Trade unions, who were to be partners with government in the Women and Work Commission's new agenda for change, have already been playing a very important role in spreading and communicating the equality

---

[11] Kingsmill recommended that public and private sector organisations should make mandatory annual reports on women's employment and pay and conduct pay reviews. The Investor in People's standard should include these as criteria for awards; government should monitor compliance on the mandatory reporting, consider whether new legislation is required if compliance is low, require its contractors to show they undertake pay review and evaluation and pay its own senior staff according to job objectives, as well as investigate further the part-time pay gap. The Women and Work Commission listed forty recommendations (including more sub-sections) which built upon the Kingsmill recommendations for pay, but went much further and wider in their reach. This commission also tasked government to set goals and a new framework and materials and monitoring for vocational skills and work experience to promote gender equality, remove gender stereotypes and address all levels of teachers' training and practice, from early years, to school to careers guidance, as well as organisational managers' training; to have equality-led procurement; to have gender duties for tackling, for example, the gender pay gap and occupational segregation; to address the workforce issues and create opportunities for women to retrain and train to upgrade their skills; to implement the new thinking through all government programmes and agencies; and to encourage and promote change in ways of working in organisations which is more women friendly, and to set a target to change the nature of part-time work. This, clearly, is a very far-reaching set of aims.

and diversity agenda where they are present (see for example, the TUC's Changing Times website). The growing number of women in trade unions undoubtedly has helped to change union agendas from their earlier male dominated concerns. But union influence is limited by their absence in a large proportion of workplaces. It seems unlikely that trade union membership will grow sufficiently in the short-to-medium term to significantly increase their impact, except in the public sector.

A future WERS will be able to tell us how successful these additional legal and voluntary measures have been. Whether these will move us significantly forward in persuading employers to have a whole-hearted approach to equality practices and monitoring remains to be seen.

11 The changing use of contingent pay at the modern British workplace

Andrew Pendleton, Keith Whitfield and Alex Bryson

Introduction

Contingent pay schemes have become an important component of human resource policies throughout the world, and now play a prominent role in attempts to make organisations more effective in attaining their goals. While not new phenomena, such pay schemes have become more common in recent years, often as components of holistic performance management initiatives (variously named, inter alia, high performance work systems, high commitment and high involvement policies) aimed at improving organisational performance. Indeed, some commentators have suggested that many new human resource management practices are often only effective when allied to complementary gain-sharing mechanisms, such as contingent pay schemes – see, for example, Levine and Tyson (1990). How such schemes and other elements of the human resource architecture link together has therefore been subject to considerable debate in the HRM research literature (MacDuffie (1995), Huselid (1995)).

The nature and use of contingent pay systems in Britain has changed markedly over the quarter century that the Workplace Employment Relations Surveys have been conducted. Among other things, the widespread decline of collective industrial relations, the rise of human resource management and other approaches to the management process, the intensification of product market competition, the globalisation of production and changes in the political landscape over the last quarter century all seem to have promoted interest in the increased use of various forms of contingent pay. As a result of these and related changes, workplace managers have had both a greater opportunity, as well as an apparently greater need, to link workers' pay to measures of individual, collective, and/or organisational performance.

The analysis of the combined WIRS/WERS data set provides an excellent opportunity to examine what has happened in the area of performance-linked reward systems during the last twenty years or so.

In this chapter, we compare the use of contingent pay systems over the period 1984 to 2004 using this data set.[1] Five main groups of questions and propositions are addressed:

- Whether employers took advantage of the greater control that they acquired over the workplace following the decline in collective industrial relations to introduce more individual payments by results (IPBR) schemes.
- Whether employers increased their use of profit-sharing, employee share-ownership, and collective payment by results (where pay is linked to the performance of the work group, workplace or organisation), possibly as a consequence of the development of new production techniques involving multitasking and greater levels of teamworking.
- Whether the major structural and environmental changes of the WERS quarter century have changed the nature of the type of workplace that possesses contingent pay schemes.
- Whether there is a relationship between contingent pay and other high performance work practices, such as information disclosure and employee participation.
- Whether there has been an increase in the incidence and distribution of multiple types of contingent pay scheme at the same workplace.

Details of the incidence of each form of contingent pay are presented in the first part of the chapter. Then, multivariate analysis is used to examine the workplace characteristics associated with each. The final section of the chapter examines the use of multiple contingent pay systems, and the workplace characteristics associated with these.

Contingent pay in the modern British workplace: context and rationales

Contingent pay refers to those systems where some or all of employee remuneration is dependent (contingent) on some measure (objective or subjective) of output or performance. The unit of assessment might be the individual, work-group, workplace, or organisation. There are several reasons why employers use contingent pay of one sort or another:

- to elicit greater work effort (input) or output from workers
- to enhance employees' commitment to the employing organisation (Mitchell *et al.*, 1990)
- to attract better quality employees to the organisation (Lazear, 2000)
- to retain workers when labour markets are tight (Oyer, 2004)

---

[1] For the most part consistent data on payment systems is available only from 1984.

- to introduce a stronger element of fairness into remuneration by rewarding those who work hardest or most effectively
- to act as a substitute for the direct monitoring of worker performance and output, where such monitoring is most costly (Brown, 1990; Daniel and Millward, 1983; Drago and Heywood, 1995: Heywood *et al.*, 1997; Pendleton, 2006).

Contingent pay systems appear to vary in their power to bring about these outcomes (Prendergast, 1999). In general, the closer the performance unit to the employee, the more high powered the pay system is likely to be (Heywood and Jirjahn, 2006). An individual payment-by-results scheme is therefore likely to have the strongest incentive effects, as the linkage between individual performance and pay outcomes is the most direct. Any pay system linked to group performance will be vulnerable to free-rider effects: any individual in the group may free-ride on the efforts of their colleagues. Those pay systems linked to organisation-wide criteria are likely to have the weakest incentive effects, and some have doubted whether they have any incentive effects at all, especially in large organisations (Oyer, 2004; Prendergast, 1999).

Group incentive schemes are also likely to have more 'noise' than individual-based schemes (i.e., the extent to which external influences, not controllable by the worker, affect the level of contingent pay) (Baker, 2002). Typically, workers on these schemes will require higher insurance against risk (typically higher base pay), or a smaller fraction of total pay that is contingent on performance. Either can dilute incentives.

In contrast, those forms of contingent pay with the most direct incentive power are also most likely to give rise to a range of dysfunctional effects ('perverse incentives'). These include the restriction of output, conflict between workers and management and the pursuit of objectives that are harmful to broader organisational goals (Baker *et al.*, 1988; Gibbons, 1987; Gibbons, 1998; Holmstrom and Milgrom, 1994). These problems have been documented in the 'classic' literature on piecework in manufacturing workplaces (Roy, 1952; Lupton, 1963; Brown, 1973), in early WIRS discussions of payment by results (Daniel and Millward, 1983) and in recent literature on executive stock options (Core *et al.*, 2003).

Such long-standing problems with some forms of contingent pay led some in the 1970s to predict a long-term decline in the use of contingent pay, especially as the nature of work and technology changed to make tasks less 'discrete' and more interdependent (see Elliott and Murphy, 1986). However, the major changes in workplace environment and industrial relations that have occurred from the 1980s appear to have brought about precisely the opposite effect. Some of these changes may be seen as pressures, others as facilitators or opportunities. The foremost pressure can be traced to product market competition. An increase in competition may cause workplaces to use contingent pay to transfer risk to employees, and to provide incentives to workers to enhance their performance (Brown and Heywood, 2002; Drago and Heywood, 1995).[2] Increased opportunities for using contingent pay are related to reductions in the costs of using contingent pay, such as a decline in trade union power and the development of more sophisticated means of recording employee effort and output. Better quality management may have also increased the net benefits of using contingent pay, by ensuring that its effects on worker behaviour can be channelled into enhanced productivity. The emergence of high performance work systems (HPWS) amongst some firms may have encouraged the use of contingent pay, especially those forms which reward teamwork and quality as well as quantity of output (Ichniowski *et al.*, 1997). The provision of tax concessions for some forms of contingent pay may also have encouraged their usage. Equally, some of these factors may have discouraged the use of contingent pay, prime examples being the development of less costly and more sophisticated work monitoring systems, which, for example, might have obviated the need for pay incentives.

It is likely that different forms of contingent pay will have displayed different dynamics over the period. A shift to more complex and interdependent work-processes, and to the provision of services rather than material goods, may have favoured the use of collective PBR because it is better suited to rewarding worker co-operation and communication than individual forms (Holmstrom and Milgrom, 1994; Heywood and Jirjahn, 2006). Traditionally, individual PBR has been associated with conflict and manipulation of information, and has been thought to contribute to strike propensity (Blanchflower and Cubbin, 1986). An increase in the incidence of collective forms of contingent pay might also have resulted from workplaces increasingly using contingent pay to enhance employee identity with the firm or workplace rather than providing direct incentives to expend greater effort. Collective PBR is usually viewed as a 'lower-powered' incentive than individual PBR, and hence is likely to be less directly motivational in the sense of affecting work output. However, this form of PBR may be appreciated by employees, thereby possibly promoting favourable attitudes, particularly higher commitment to the firm, its goals and values.

There has also been increased recognition in parts of the literature that incentives that reward a range of behaviours (such as profit-sharing)

---

[2] Counter arguments are that competition acts in lieu of incentives because information on performance becomes more transparent, and pay premia can be costly in competitive environments.

may balance out the perverse incentives associated with more specifically focused incentives, especially the more high-powered types (Holmstrom and Milgrom, 1994). Also, an apparent growth in the range of tasks performed by many employees implies that contingent pay systems may need to incorporate a wider range of criteria if they are not to reward just one element of job behaviour at the expense of others (Baker, 1992). This increase in task range may have prompted firms to introduce multiple forms of contingent pay, on the grounds that any one type of scheme would be unlikely to provide the variety of incentives needed to encourage high levels of performance. Pay systems that take account of these factors are likely to have become increasingly prevalent over the period due to improvements in the quality of management, pressures to improve performance and greater opportunities for managers to innovate in human resource management (because of weaker unions, for instance).

WERS and contingent pay

The development of the combined WIRS/WERS data set covering the period 1980 to 2004 provides an excellent opportunity to explore changes in the incidence of various forms of contingent pay and the factors associated with them. There are four forms of contingent pay that are recorded in the data set for all or most years: individual payment by results (IPBR), collective payment by results (CPBR), profit-related payments (PRP), and employee share-ownership (ESO). The variables are as follows:

- IPBR – do any employees at the workplace receive individual-based payment by results?
- CPBR – do any employees at the workplace receive group, establishment or organisation-based payments by results?
- PRP– are there any profit-related payments or bonuses?
- ESO – are there any share-ownership schemes with eligible employees?

There are some differences in wording between each survey, and this must be borne in mind when considering results (detailed information on each variable is listed in Appendix 11.1 at the end of the chapter). Data on contingent pay from 1980 (apart from on employee share-ownership) could not be included because the questions used in that survey differ too much from subsequent WERS. In 1980, respondents were asked whether the *majority* of employees in various groups received PBR, whereas subsequent surveys have asked whether *any* employees receive it (there was also no question on profit-sharing in 1980). For this reason, 1984 is chosen as the start-point of the analysis. Even so, caution must be exercised. In 1984, the IPBR and CPBR questions were asked of specific occupational groups rather than the workplace as a whole, whereas subsequently questions were not so specific. The 1998 results also have to be considered with care as there was a substantial re-vamping of questions in that year. The data for that year show substantial falls in incidence, which are not confirmed by data from other sources. For this reason we do not include 1998 results in our analysis of IPBR. It is possible in some places, however, to draw on the WERS 1998/2004 Panel Survey to ascertain the change in the incidence of contingent pay in continuing workplaces, and thereby infer what the 1998 figure might have been.

Finding consistencies between different survey instruments, coupled with the limitations of secondary analysis, inevitably means some compromise in the richness of the data. It is not possible, for instance, to consider the coverage of contingent pay in each workplace, the proportion of pay linked to performance, or the specific form of performance to which pay is linked (except in the case of profit-related pay and, indirectly, employee share-ownership). It is also not possible to fully consider merit pay, where pay is linked to a subjective evaluation of employee behaviour or performance, because data are available in the unified data set only for 1990 and 2004.

The changing incidence of contingent pay 1984–2004

The first part of the analysis presents details of the incidence of each form of contingent reward at aggregate and broad sectoral level in 1984, 1990 and 2004. The results are presented in Figures 11.1 to 11.5.

The pattern of change for contingent pay as a whole is summarised in Figure 11.1. It indicates the proportion of workplaces that had any one of the four types of contingent pay scheme in place. The analysis suggests that the incidence of contingent pay grew considerably in the economy as a whole between 1984 and 1990, from 41% to 56%, but showed a slight fall (to 55%) up to 2004. There was a substantial decline in the public sector from 21% in 1984 to 11% in 1990, but a slight increase (to 14%) in 2004. The private sector change was similar to that for the economy as a whole, growing from 52% in 1984 to 72% in 1990, but then falling to 67% in 2004.

The findings for IPBR (summarised in Figure 11.2) indicate that, in both 1984 and 2004, approximately one-fifth of all workplaces had such a scheme in place, indicating little overall change over the twenty-year period. The overall incidence of IPBR grew between 1984 and 1990, but then declined.[3] Overall, incidence in 2004 was slightly higher than 1984. There is some evidence from the 1998/2004 WERS Panel Survey (not

---

[3] It is worth noting that the use of merit pay (not shown in the tables for the reason noted above) declined from 34 to 21 per cent between 1990 and 2004. This contrasts with a widely held view that the use of merit pay has been growing steadily in recent years.

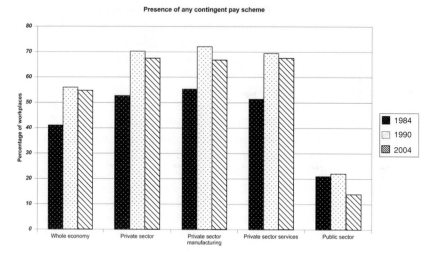

Figure 11.1 Presence of any contingent pay schemes

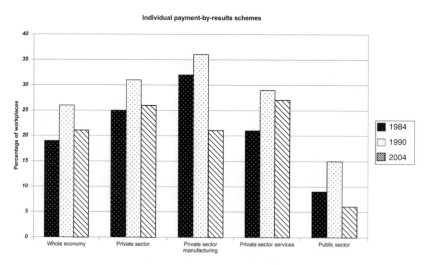

Figure 11.2 Individual payments-by-results schemes

shown in the figure) that the incidence of IPBR may, in fact, have risen in the years immediately leading up to 2004.

Behind the overall picture of little overall change between 1984 and 2004, there is evidence of substantial change within sub-sectors. IPBR has always been much less common in the public sector and, moreover, by

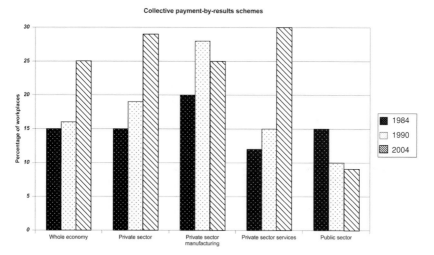

Figure 11.3 Collective payments-by-results schemes

2004 was even slightly below its low incidence in 1984, despite growth between 1984 and 1990. During this period, there is also a large fall (from 32% to 21%) in the percentage of private manufacturing workplaces using IPBR, whilst private services workplaces show an increased incidence (from 21% to 27%). In 1984, private manufacturing workplaces were the most common users of IPBR; by 2004, workplaces in private services had overtaken them. In 2004, one in four private sector services workplaces had IPBR schemes in place, compared to one in five private manufacturing workplaces.

The incidence of CPBR, and the pattern of changes therein, is rather different to that for IPBR – see Figure 11.3. Overall, there is substantial growth in the percentage of workplaces using CPBR between 1984 and 2004, such that its incidence increases from 15 to 25 per cent over the period. This appears to be the continuation of a trend towards the increased use of CPBR that had been observed prior to the WERS series in 1980, which was possibly a way of offering 'disguised' pay increases during periods of incomes policy in the 1970s (White 1981; Daniel and Millward 1983: 208). Although the incidence of its use declines between 1984 and 2004 in the public sector (from 15% to 9%), it doubles in the private sector (from 15% to 29%). By far the largest increase is in private services, where its incidence grows by two and a half times during this period, from 12% to 30%. By contrast, the growth in private manufacturing is more modest – by a quarter, to 25%.

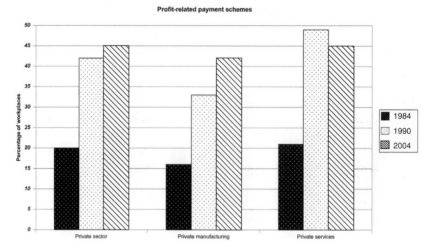

Figure 11.4 Profit-related payment schemes

The incidence of PRP in 2004 was more than double that in 1984, growing from 20% to 45% of private sector workplaces (see Figure 11.4).[4] The major increase in profit-based payments occurred between 1984 and 1990, and was likely to be the outcome of the introduction of the tax-advantageous profit-related pay scheme in 1987 (Blanchflower and Oswald, 1987). This scheme provided income tax concessions on that part of pay (up to 20 per cent) that was deemed to be flexibly linked to profits (Millward et al., 2000: 216). Although the tax relief was removed in 1997, the incidence of PRP stayed more or less unchanged, as confirmed by the 1998 Panel Survey.[5] PRP was slightly more common in private services than in private manufacturing in both 1984 and 2004. However, the gap between these sectors has been less in the case of PRP than for the PBR schemes. Moreover, the growth in the incidence of PRP during the period has been faster in private manufacturing than in private services, in contrast to the case for CPBR.

The incidence of employee share-ownership (ESO) schemes has also been highly responsive to the provision of tax concessions (Pendleton et al., 2003). In 1984, the proportion of private sector workplaces with a share-ownership scheme in place was 24 per cent, up 10 percentage

---

[4] Although WIRS asks publicly owned trading sector workplaces whether they have profit-related pay or share-ownership schemes, very few actually have them. We have therefore chosen to focus the analysis of profit-sharing and share-ownership on private sector workplaces only.

[5] Although the overall incidence has remained fairly stable after 1990, the Panel Surveys have indicated substantial switching in and out of PRP.

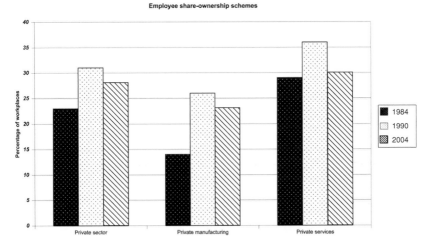

Figure 11.5 Employee share-ownership schemes

points on 1980. Earlier analysis of WIRS 1980 indicated that a substantial proportion of schemes observed in 1980 were new schemes introduced in the wake of the provision of tax breaks for the approved profit-sharing plan in 1978 (Daniel and Millward, 1983; see also Millward and Stevens, 1986: 289). The use of ESO then climbed through the 1980s (the widely-used Save As You Earn or Sharesave plan was introduced in 1980) to nearly one-third of private sector workplaces in 1990; see Figure 11.5. Between 1990 and 2004 the incidence of ESO declined slightly, though the 1998/2004 Panel indicates that incidence was more or less unchanged between 1998 and 2004. Moreover, although the overall incidence was unchanged between 1998 and 2004, there was considerable switching in and out of ESO in the period.

Over the period 1984 to 2004, share-ownership schemes were more common in private services than private manufacturing, though the gap did narrow during the period. Whereas the overall incidence was more or less stable in private services, there was an appreciable growth in the use of share schemes in private manufacturing.

Overall, the major change between 1984 and 2004 has been a relative shift from IPBR to more collective forms of contingent pay. In 2004, IPBR was more common than other forms of contingent pay; by 2004, it was the least common. Private sector workplaces experienced an increase in all forms of collective contingent rewards, but not in IPBR. However, the increase in profit-sharing and employee share-ownership occurred mainly in the 1980s. Since then, overall incidence has been broadly stable, though panel-based analysis indicates a fair degree of switching in and out of these. Meanwhile, public sector workplaces decreased their use of both IPBR and CPBR between 1984 and 2004. In private services, by contrast, all forms of contingent rewards, including IPBR, increased in incidence.

The correlates of contingent pay systems

Given that there has been much change in the relative incidence of contingent pay schemes in the period between 1984 and 2004, it might be asked whether the characteristics of workplaces using such schemes also changed over these years, and whether the various forms of contingent rewards share the same correlates. Any such analysis has to be limited to those variables for which there are consistent measures at the two points of time. In WERS, we have such information on the age, sector and geographical location of the workplace, the size of the workplace and (where relevant) the larger organisation, workforce composition, union presence, information disclosure and consultation and product market competition.

Previous analyses of the nature of contingent reward-using workplaces have typically drawn on a principal-agent framework for their motivation, wherein the rationale for incentives is viewed in the context of the costs and benefits of monitoring worker effort (Milgrom and Roberts, 1992; Brown, 1990). It is often suggested that larger workplaces will more likely use contingent pay because of the substantial cost of alternative forms of monitoring, whilst the costs of implementing contingent pay can be spread over a large group of workers (Brown, 1990; Heywood et al., 1997). Workforce composition is also frequently used as a proxy for monitoring costs. For instance, it has been predicted that contingent pay will more likely be used where there is a high proportion of part-time workers because these workers often have short job tenures, and hence benefit less from the incentive effects of rising earnings–tenure linkages (Heywood et al., 1997). In the same vein, the proportion of female employees has been predicted to be positively related to use of contingent pay (Brown, 1990). Union presence is widely seen as inimical to contingent pay on the grounds that unions typically seek a 'common rate for the job', but past evidence from WIRS/WERS tends to find positive associations between unions and some forms of contingent rewards (Gregg and Machin, 1988). Information disclosure and communication has been predicted to be positively associated with contingent pay (especially group-based forms), because the latter forms a pay-off for participating in information exchange, whilst those in receipt of variable pay may want to influence the conditions under which work is performed (Levine and Tyson, 1990). Employee involvement in decision making is also seen to help overcome the free-rider effects associated with group-based contingent rewards by facilitating peer pressure and co-operation (Kandel and Lazear, 1992; Weitzman and Kruse, 1990). Earlier WERS-based analysis has found linkages between some forms of employee participation and employee share-ownership plans (Pendleton, 1997a; Conyon and Freeman, 2004; McNabb and Whitfield, 1997). Finally, product market competition is usually predicted to increase the probability of using all forms of contingent reward because it forces managers to organise production more efficiently (Brown and Heywood, 2002).

The analysis of the correlates of contingent pay schemes undertaken in this chapter is based on workplaces with twenty-five or more employees. For each type of pay system, we undertake a series of probit analyses in which the presence of the given pay system at a workplace is the dependent variable. The general approach is as follows: results are presented for the whole economy (the private sector only for PRP and ESO), and then for the trading sector (private trading sector for PRP and ESO) with measures of information disclosure and product market competition. The product market competition variables are only asked of trading sector workplaces, so the samples for these models are smaller than the samples for the whole private sector. Marginal effects rather than coefficients are reported to ease the interpretation of results.

The following independent variables are also included in each regression. Dummies for region (reference category: London and the South-East) are included in the regressions, though to save space these are only reported where they are significant for either 1984 or 2004. Dummies are included for specific industrial sectors (*engineering*, etc; 'other services' is the reference category). There are a series of workplace-size dummies, with twenty-five to forty-nine employees being the reference category. Union presence is captured by a measure for whether a trade union is recognised for the purpose of pay bargaining (*union*). Other variables include dummies for foreign ownership (*foreign*), single-site operation (*single*), and the age of the workplace (though the latter is not reported in the tables as it is always insignificant). The composition of the workforce is recorded in the following way: *female* is the proportion of women in the workplace; *part-time* is the proportion of part-time employees; *non-manual* is the proportion of non-manual staff. *Briefing* is a dummy for the presence of briefing groups, whilst *information* records whether information is disclosed on the workplace's financial position, staffing plans, and investment plans. *No competition* records the absence of any competitor for the workplace whilst *low competition* records between one and five competitors (the reference category is six or more competitors).

Individual payment by results

The results presented in Table 11.1 show the factors associated with individual payment by results (IPBR) in 1984 and 2004 in the whole economy (columns 1 and 2) and the private trading sector (columns 3 and 4). In 1984, across the whole economy, the probability that a workplace used IPBR to pay at least some of its employees was higher if the workplace was unionised, middle-sized, consisted predominantly of manual workers, was located in the Midlands and operated in sectors other than 'other services' (the omitted category) and transport and communications. By 2004, much of this had changed. The probability of using IPBR was then higher in workplaces that did *not* recognise unions for pay bargaining, and rose with the percentage of full-time employees in the workforce. The significant difference between workplaces with differing proportions of manual workers no longer existed. The sectoral mix mattered much less. Use in chemicals, engineering and construction was no longer significantly different from 'other services', once the model accounted for other observable differences across workplaces. Other associations persisted: the probability of IPBR usage was still high in 'other manufacturing', distribution and finance.

If we confine the analysis to private sector trading workplaces (columns 3 and 4) we find similar patterns, the differences being ones of magnitude rather than direction. If we consider the association between IPBR and human resource management practices, these also reveal substantial change over time. Workplaces with IPBR in 1984 had a lower probability than non-IPBR workplaces of disclosing information and briefing employees. This is consistent with the view of PBR expressed at the start of the WIRS series that IPBR was used primarily as a means of direct control of worker effort (Daniel and Millward, 1983). By 2004, both associations were positive, though non-significant. If we consider the role of product market competition, we find a positive association emerges between exposure to a high level of competition – proxied by the number of competitors the manager says the workplace faces – and IPBR. In 1984, there had been no association between IPBR and product market competition.

The pattern of results therefore indicates substantial change between 1984 and 2004 in the character of workplaces using IPBR. In 1984, there is evidence to suggest that many workplaces using IPBR were unionised manufacturing sites, with a high proportion of manual workers.

Table 11.1 *Probit analysis of individual payment by results*

	All workplaces 1984	All workplaces 2004	Private sector trading workplaces 1984	Private sector trading workplaces 2004
Union	0.056	−0.102	0.094	−0.100
	(1.85)	(3.00)**	(1.76)	(2.19)*
Energy/water	0.144	0.082	See notes	−0.036
	(1.49)	(0.73)		(0.25)
Chemicals	0.223	−0.045	0.201	−0.131
	(2.37)*	(0.48)	(1.30)	(1.23)
Engineering	0.210	−0.054	0.077	−0.071
	(2.99)**	(0.81)	(0.62)	(0.73)
Other	0.236	0.283	0.144	0.265
manufacturing	(3.96)**	(3.00)**	(1.22)	(2.36)*
Construction	0.270	0.119	0.178	0.137
	(3.04)**	(1.29)	(1.09)	(1.10)
Distribution	0.202	0.209	0.147	0.203
	(3.85)**	(3.81)**	(1.39)	(2.76)**
Transport	0.002	0.171	0.118	0.269
	(0.02)	(1.78)	(0.66)	(1.87)
Finance	0.359	0.271	0.364	0.303
	(5.50)**	(4.25)**	(2.59)**	(3.29)**
East Midlands	0.209	0.006	0.259	0.029
	(3.35)**	(0.08)	(2.58)*	(0.31)
West Midlands	0.142	0.122	0.194	0.174
	(2.67)**	(2.01)*	(2.02)*	(2.13)*
Size 50–99	0.026	−0.040	0.066	−0.050
	(0.79)	(1.08)	(1.12)	(1.02)
Size 100–199	0.101	−0.002	0.100	0.005
	(2.80)**	(0.06)	(1.50)	(0.09)
Size 200–499	0.047	0.074	0.116	0.056
	(1.27)	(1.84)	(1.53)	(0.96)
Size 500+	0.072	0.076	0.132	0.063
	(1.76)	(1.69)	(1.66)	(0.96)
Foreign	−0.050	0.051	−0.124	0.065
	(0.99)	(1.09)	(1.90)	(1.05)
Single	0.035	0.008	−0.005	−0.023
	(0.91)	(0.17)	(0.08)	(0.41)
Female	0.061	0.123	0.204	0.173
	(0.77)	(1.43)	(1.43)	(1.39)
Part-time	−0.111	−0.206	−0.313	−0.284
	(1.05)	(2.67)**	(1.75)	(2.54)*
Non-manual	−0.167	0.041	−0.216	0.034
	(3.15)**	(0.85)	(1.92)	(0.49)
Briefing			−0.115	0.042
			(2.22)*	(0.88)

(*cont.*)

Table 11.1 (*cont.*)

	All workplaces 1984	All workplaces 2004	Private sector trading workplaces 1984	Private sector trading workplaces 2004
Information			−.108	0.077
			(2.00)*	(1.55)
No competition			0.008	−0.153
			(0.09)	(1.44)
Low competition			−0.081	−0.171
			(1.54)	(4.21)**
Observations	1,797	1,505	712	849
Pseudo R^2	0.123	0.119	0.119	0.148

Notes: Probit (marginal effects: robust Z statistics in parentheses); the energy/water industry dummy falls out of some specifications for 1984 because it predicts failure perfectly.
Source: WIRS/WERS data.
*$p < 0.05$, **$p < 0.01$.

These results are consistent with Daniel and Millward's contention that IPBR tended to be used as a substitute for direct managerial monitoring of manual workers in unionised, larger manufacturing establishments (1983: 202). This phenomenon appears to have dissipated by 2004, no doubt in large part because many of the very large manufacturing workplaces present in 1984 were no longer in existence twenty years later. By 2004, the more typical IPBR workplace was a non-unionised workplace in banking and finance facing high levels of competition. There is also some evidence that IPBR was no longer inimical to the high-commitment workplace. Workplaces with IPBR in 2004 were no less likely than non-IPBR workplaces to disclose information and brief employees in teams. However, the evidence is insufficiently strong to claim that that IPBR forms part of a 'bundle' of high commitment work and employment practices (cf. Wood, 1996b; Long and Shields, 2005).

Collective payment by results

As Figure 11.2 indicates, there was a sizeable increase in the incidence of collective payment by results (CPBR) between 1984 and 2004. Table 11.2 indicates that, across the whole economy, the workplaces with the highest probability of using CPBR in 1984 were larger workplaces, those belonging to larger organisations, and with high proportions of male, manual workers. Having accounted for these factors,

Table 11.2 *Probit analysis of CPBR schemes*

	All workplaces 1984	All workplaces 2004	Private sector trading workplaces 1984	Private sector trading workplaces 2004
Union	0.035	−0.081	0.075	−0.128
	(1.37)	(2.23)*	(2.55)*	(2.60)**
Energy/water	−0.072	0.210	See notes	0.144
	(1.93)	(1.46)		(0.78)
Chemicals	0.072	0.252	0.034	0.251
	(1.40)	(1.83)	(0.57)	(1.38)
Engineering	−0.038	0.147	−0.031	0.124
	(1.25)	(1.50)	(0.71)	(0.95)
Other manufacturing	−0.049	0.164	−0.054	0.106
	(1.70)	(1.82)	(1.41)	(0.96)
Construction	0.051	0.343	0.027	0.363
	(0.95)	(3.41)**	(0.38)	(2.65)**
Distribution	0.025	0.334	0.049	0.304
	(0.75)	(5.69)**	(0.96)	(3.76)**
Transport	−0.034	0.172	−0.002	0.021
	(0.93)	(2.03)*	(0.03)	(0.21)
Finance	−0.090	0.269	−0.109	0.266
	(3.37)**	(4.28)**	(2.71)**	(2.80)**
Size 50–99	0.083	−0.000	0.059	0.011
	(3.01)**	(0.01)	(1.69)	(0.21)
Size 100–199	0.152	0.027	0.099	0.044
	(4.53)**	(0.65)	(1.94)	(0.72)
Size 200–499	0.138	0.064	0.116	0.057
	(4.00)**	(1.51)	(2.32)*	(0.96)
Size 500+	0.342	0.060	0.115	0.051
	(7.44)**	(1.33)	(2.10)*	(0.74)
Foreign	−0.027	0.101	−0.050	0.136
	(0.68)	(1.91)	(1.93)	(2.13)*
Single	−0.065	−0.100	−0.068	−0.158
	(2.31)*	(2.30)*	(2.51)*	(2.78)**
Female	−0.163	0.092	−0.094	0.204
	(2.97)**	(1.05)	(1.16)	(1.58)
Part-time	−0.041	−0.152	−0.178	−0.233
	(0.53)	(1.78)	(1.65)	(1.94)
Non-manual	−0.149	0.031	−0.062	−0.001
	(4.23)**	(0.60)	(1.19)	(0.01)
Briefing			0.011	−0.019
			(0.40)	(0.38)
Information			0.007	0.103
			(0.24)	(1.93)
No competition			0.029	−0.121
			(0.54)	(1.20)
Low competition			−0.001	−0.027
			(0.04)	(0.58)
Observations	1,797	1,505	712	849
Pseudo R^2	0.195	0.123	0.243	0.133

Notes: Probit (marginal effects: robust Z statistics in parentheses); The energy/water industry dummy falls out of some specifications for 1984 because it predicts failure perfectly.
Source: WIRS/WERS data.
*$p < 0.05$, **$p < 0.01$.

only banking and finance had a significantly different (lower) probability of using CPBR from the 'other services' reference category (though the lower probabilities among energy and water and 'other manufacturing' were on the margins of statistical significance). These results are consistent with White's study (1981) which found that group and plant-level bonus systems were widely distributed across industries. Our results also suggest that CPBR tended to be found in similar workplaces to IPBR, though few workplaces operated both schemes. It is possible that CPBR was used in those workplaces where the costs of monitoring of individual performance or output tended to preclude IPBR.

By 2004, after substantial growth in CPBR's use, associations between it and workplace size and workforce composition were no longer significant. However, union absence had become a significant predictor of CPBR, while foreign ownership was on the margins of statistical significance. Industry effects also changed markedly: construction, distribution and hotels and transport and communications were all associated with a higher probability of CPBR usage than 'other services', having been statistically non-significant in 1984, while banking and finance had switched from being less likely to use CPBR in 1984 to more likely in 2004.

The pattern of results is roughly replicated in the analyses for the private trading sector (Models 3 and 4). It is clearer from this analysis that foreign ownership had switched from being negatively associated with CPBR in 1984 to positively associated in 2004, and that the association with union recognition had shifted in the reverse direction. There are no significant associations between information disclosure and team briefings and use of CPBR in either 1984 or 2004, though information disclosure became a stronger predictor of CPBR in 2004 (significant at a 90 per cent confidence level). Product market competition does not affect the probability of using CPBR in either year.

Overall, there is evidence of a distinct change in the pattern of usage of CPBR in the period between 1984 and 2004, with many of the strong associates of CPBR incidence becoming less important and sectoral factors becoming more important. In common with IPBR, the association with union recognition changed from positive to negative during the time period. In short, it is likely that the character of and role played by CPBR changed markedly in this time.

Profit-related payments

The proportion of private sector workplaces using profit-related payments (PRP) leapt between 1984 and 1990 due to the introduction of significant tax breaks, but then remained more or less constant. It might be expected that there was a change in the type of workplaces using PRP as a result of these tax concessions. There is some evidence that is compatible with such an explanation.

Models 1 and 2 in Table 11.3 relate to the whole private sector, while Models 3 and 4 are confined to trading workplaces. In addition to some changes in industry effects, there are four notable changes to the factors associated with PRP. The first is union recognition. Recall that the association between union recognition and both IPBR and CPBR had shifted from positive in 1984 to negative in 2004. In the case of PRP, there was also a positive association with unionisation in 1984. This association was no longer statistically significant by 2004, although it remained positive. Second, it is evident that foreign ownership, clearly inimical to PRP in 1984, had a benign effect by 2004. Third, the positive association with non-manual working in 1984 had disappeared. Fourth, there emerged a negative association with the percentage of part-time workers employed at the workplace. HR policies and product market competition played no role in either year.

Employee share-ownership

Employee share-ownership (ESO) schemes are often grouped together with PRP schemes under the generic heading of 'financial participation schemes'. A comparison of Tables 11.3 and 11.4 indicates just how misleading this can be, since their workplace-level correlates are different in a number of key respects. To begin with, the positive association with union recognition in 1984 – also found in previous studies (e.g., Gregg and Machin, 1988; Poole, 1988; Pendleton 1997a; Pendleton et al., 2001) – had strengthened for ESO by 2004, whereas it had become non-significant in the case of PRP. In the case of ESO, size effects are strong and persistent, whereas they were largely absent for PRP. Thus the probability of having ESO was between a quarter and a third higher in workplaces belonging to multi-site organisations compared with single-site organisations[6] and the probability of having ESO was around 12–13 per cent higher among workplaces with at least 500 employees compared with the smallest workplaces with fewer than 50 employees. Turning to workforce composition, the probability of having ESO rises with the percentage of employees who are non-manual workers, a relationship that persists over the period; whereas, in the case of PRP, the association becomes non-significant by 2004. The positive association between

---

[6] This is consistent with other studies of share-ownership (Pendleton, 1997a; Pendleton et al., 2001; Kersley et al., 2006; Bryson and Freeman, 2007).

Table 11.3 *Probit analysis of profit-related pay schemes*

	Private sector workplaces 1984	Private sector workplaces 2004	Private sector trading workplaces 1984	Private sector trading workplaces 2004
Union	0.117	0.068	0.098	0.074
	(3.40)*	(1.23)	(2.45)*	(1.17)
Energy/water		−0.053		−0.127
		(0.27)		(0.59)
Chemicals	0.478	0.248	0.619	0.150
	(3.54)**	(1.64)	(3.27)**	(0.76)
Engineering	0.141	0.127	0.143	0.056
	(1.32)	(1.06)	(1.01)	(0.43)
Other	0.204	−0.041	0.278	−0.127
	(1.96)*	(0.39)	(1.86)	(1.09)
Construction	0.280	0.082	0.429	0.014
	(2.01)	(0.67)	(2.13)*	(0.10)
Distribution	0.203	0.284	0.295	0.280
	(2.38)*	(3.68)**	(2.39)*	(3.28)**
Transport	0.121	−0.245	0.255	−0.281
	(0.87)	(2.23)*	(1.09)	(2.31)*
Finance	0.278	0.174	0.421	0.082
	(2.82)**	(1.98)*	(2.72)**	(0.79)
Size 50–99	0.028	−0.019	0.014	−0.066
	(0.74)	(0.34)	(0.32)	(1.07)
Size 100–199	0.085	−0.053	0.137	−0.055
	(1.79)	(0.91)	(2.30)*	(0.86)
Size 200–499	0.041	0.046	0.074	0.045
	(0.77)	(0.75)	(1.11)	(0.64)
Size 500+	0.057	0.093	0.041	0.101
	(1.19)	(1.38)	(0.69)	(1.35)
Foreign	−0.135	0.063	−0.136	0.125
	(4.73)**	(0.94)	(4.43)**	(1.67)
Single	−0.023	−0.095	−0.018	−0.085
	(0.63)	(1.61)	(0.42)	(1.29)
Female	0.023	−0.097	0.012	−0.023
	(0.25)	(0.67)	(0.12)	(0.14)
Part-time	−0.032	−0.195	0.007	−0.307
	(0.30)	(1.52)	(0.06)	(2.09)*
Non-manual	0.222	0.075	0.255	0.090
	(3.46)**	(0.97)	(3.27)**	(1.00)
Briefing			0.020	0.056
			(0.51)	(0.98)
Information			0.079	0.033
			(1.63)	(0.56)
No competition			0.011	−0.175
			(0.12)	(1.32)
Low competition			0.044	−0.041
			(0.04)	(0.06)
Observations	1,074	1,056	712	849
Pseudo R^2	0.161	0.113	0.234	0.131

Notes: Probit (marginal effects: robust Z scores in parentheses); The energy/water industry dummy falls out of some specifications for 1984 because it predicts failure perfectly.
Source: WIRS/WERS data.
*$p < 0.05$, **$p < 0.01$.

Table 11.4 *Probit analysis of employee share-ownership plans*

	Private sector workplaces 1984	Private sector workplaces 2004	Private sector trading workplaces 1984	Private sector trading workplaces 2004
Union	0.140	0.184	0.107	0.174
	(4.69)**	(3.94)**	(4.39)**	(3.16)**
Energy/water	0.193	0.663	0.202	0.634
	(0.78)	(2.62)**	(1.13)	(2.51)*
Chemicals	0.021	0.241	−0.012	0.149
	(0.28)	(1.56)	(0.24)	(0.85)
Engineering	−0.032	0.087	−0.034	0.045
	(0.54)	(0.76)	(0.82)	(0.38)
Other	−0.028	0.053	−0.030	0.003
	(0.50)	(0.50)	(0.75)	(0.02)
Construction	−0.014	0.290	0.051	0.241
	(0.20)	(2.31)*	(0.63)	(1.76)
Distribution	0.018	0.291	−0.018	0.243
	(0.33)	(3.90)**	(0.47)	(3.20)**
Transport	−0.075	0.217	−0.032	0.211
	(1.33)	(1.94)	(0.63)	(1.81)
Finance	0.133	0.311	0.134	0.363
	(1.74)	(3.62)**	(1.68)	(3.68)**
East Midlands	−0.077	−0.022	−0.046	0.012
	(2.09)*	(0.32)	(2.04)*	(0.16)
Size 50–99	0.060	−0.008	0.037	−0.014
	(1.73)	(0.17)	(1.32)	(0.28)
Size 100–199	0.054	0.040	0.020	0.022
	(1.37)	(0.83)	(0.64)	(0.43)
Size 200–499	0.159	0.131	0.135	0.073
	(3.28)**	(2.51)*	(2.84)**	(1.27)
Size 500+	0.206	0.120	0.132	0.129
	(3.98)**	(2.17)*	(2.64)**	(1.94)
Foreign	−0.111	0.046	−0.065	−0.002
	(3.34)**	(0.96)	(2.93)**	(0.04)
Single	−0.241	−0.272	−0.253	−0.319
	(5.18)**	(6.17)**	(7.97)**	(6.90)**
Female	−0.006	−0.002	0.005	−0.035
	(0.09)	(0.02)	(0.10)	(0.30)
Part-time	0.201	0.131	0.131	0.137
	(2.26)*	(1.56)	(2.01)*	(1.42)
Non-manual	0.125	0.121	0.118	0.115
	(2.32)*	(2.10)*	(2.66)**	(1.76)
Briefing			0.031	0.079
			(1.49)	(1.73)
Information			0.070	0.064
			(2.40)*	(1.42)
No competition			0.033	−0.072
			(0.66)	(0.61)
Low competition			0.010	0.006
			(0.51)	(0.15)
Observations	1081	1056	717	849
Pseudo R^2	0.285	0.251	0.392	0.310

Notes: Probit (marginal effects: robust Z statistics in parentheses).
Source: WIRS/WERS data.
*p < 0.05, **p < 0.01.

part-time working and ESO, apparent in 1984, becomes non-significant by 2004, whereas it is negatively associated with PRP by the end of the period. Finally, sectoral effects differ for ESO and PRP, although it seems that in 2004 both types of scheme were more likely to have been used in distribution and finance than in 'other services'. One point of similarity is the relationship of these two types of scheme to foreign ownership: as in the case of PRP, the negative association with foreign ownership that was apparent in 1984 had disappeared by 2004.

Summary

In 1984, individual and collective payment by results tended to be found in unionised manufacturing workplaces with a high proportion of manual workers. By contrast, share-ownership plans tended to be found in non-manual workplaces, albeit those with recognised unions. Profit-related payments were also associated with non-manual workplaces where there was union recognition. By 2004, the type of workplaces using payment by results had changed quite dramatically: PBR workplaces now tended to be non-union, whereas PRP and ESO workplaces continued to recognise unions. The overall pattern of results suggests that the various forms of contingent rewards tended to be found in distinctly different types of workplace in 1984 relative to 2004.

The relative importance of compositional and within-group change

A key question is whether the changes in the incidence of contingent pay schemes during this period reflect changes in the industrial structure of the British economy or changes in the behaviour of workplaces. Based on the results summarised in Tables 11.1 to 11.4, a shift-share analysis was undertaken to divide the changes in the incidence of various contingent pay schemes into those that reflect compositional change (change in the incidence of the types of workplace that were likely to have the contingent pay scheme in question), and within-group change (change in the propensity of differing types of workplace to have the contingent pay scheme in place); see Table 11.5.

There was a very small rise in the incidence of IPBR during the period. However, this would have fallen had there only been compositional change – that is, if there had been no change in the propensity of 'like' workplaces to have IPBR. In this scenario, the incidence of IPBR would have fallen to 15.9 per cent rather than risen to 21.5 per cent. This would have reflected the decline of manufacturing, a big user of IPBR in 1984. That it actually rose was due to a very strong within-group

Table 11.5 *Shift-share analysis of 1984–2004 changes*

Year	Actual rate	Difference	Rate with compositional change only	Impact of compositional change	Impact of within-group change
Individual PBR					
1984	19.3				
2004	21.5	+2.2	15.9	−3.4	+5.6
Collective PBR					
1984	15.1				
2004	24.9	+9.8	11.1	−4.0	+13.8
Profit-related pay					
1984	19.0				
2004	44.2	+25.2	14.6	−4.4	+30.6
Employee share-ownership schemes					
1984	22.2				
2004	27.9	+5.7	19.6	−2.6	+8.3

Note: Base: All workplaces (Individual and Collective PBR); private trading sector (profit-related pay and employee share-ownership schemes).
Source: WIRS/WERS data.

change of 5.6 percentage points. Private services developed an increased propensity to use IPBR over the period (offset somewhat by a reduced propensity in manufacturing and the public sector). Without the negative effects of compositional change, the use of IPBR would have risen to 24.9 per cent.

The same applies to CPBR, but even more starkly. The substantial rise in the incidence of CPBR of 9.8 percentage points reflects a 4.0 percentage point fall due to compositional change, and a 13.8 percentage point rise in within-group change. Had the impact of compositional change been zero, the actual incidence of CPBR would have been 28.9 percentage points. The substantial rise in CPBR therefore came despite a decline in the types of workplace that were more likely to have it in place in 1984.

The large increase in the incidence of PRP from 19.0 per cent to 44.2 per cent is the result of a negative impact from compositional change of 4.4 percentage points and a rise of 30.6 percentage points in within-group change. Had compositional change been zero, the incidence of profit-related pay would have increased to 49.0 per cent. The importance of within-group change undoubtedly reflects the introduction of tax breaks for profit-related pay in 1987.

The rise in the incidence of ESO resulted from a small negative impact of compositional change of 2.6 percentage points, and a larger positive impact of within-group change of 8.3 percentage points.

Overall, these results indicate that the changes observed in the incidence of each form of contingent pay primarily reflect changes in the behaviour of workplaces rather than changes in the sectoral composition of the economy.

Incentives: substitutes or complements?

A problem with contingent pay is that it can reward some desired behaviours but not others. One of the solutions is to use a variety of performance metrics and payment types so as to achieve a balanced set of incentives. Since managerial capacity to use schemes appears to have grown over the quarter century, we might expect growth in the use of more than one form of contingent pay. The results indicate considerable growth in multiple forms of contingent reward at the same workplace. The frequency of each combination of contingent pay scheme in 1984 and 2004 is shown in Table 11.6.

The results indicate that there has been a substantial increase in the proportion of workplaces with more than one form of contingent pay. In 1984, 23% of workplaces had more than one type of scheme in place; by 2004, this number had grown to 38%. The percentage of workplaces with just one type of scheme decreased slightly from 29% to 28%, and the percentage without any contingent pay fell from nearly half (47%) to a third (32%). The increase in contingent pay during this period was therefore wholly accounted for by those workplaces with more than one scheme. The percentage with more than a single contingent pay scheme included 5% of workplaces with all four schemes, something that was almost unheard of in 1984. The most common type of multiple combination in both years was profit-related pay and employee share-ownership.

A key question concerns the extent to which use of one particular scheme affects the probability of having other schemes. Table 11.7 provides a summary of the contribution of specific forms of contingent reward to the probability that various forms of contingent rewards will be used in the private sector. These results are obtained by inserting dummies for each payment scheme type in the probit regressions examining the correlates of each of the payment schemes reported earlier. For presentational ease, only the marginal effects of these dummies are shown: the models change little in other respects after the insertion of these dummies. In 1984, the relationships between pay schemes are positive in all

Table 11.6 *The use of several forms of contingent reward*

	1984	2004
No schemes	47.3	32.4
One scheme		
Individual PBR only	12.3	4.3
Collective PBR only	4.6	3.2
Profit-related pay only	4.7	14.4
Employee share-ownership only	7.7	6.5
Sub-total	29.3	28.4
Two schemes		
Individual PBR and collective PBR	3.7	4.1
Individual PBR and profit-related pay	2.2	1.8
Individual PBR and employee share-ownership	2.3	1.2
Collective PBR and profit-related pay	1.5	5.3
Collective PBR and employee share-ownership	1.9	1.2
Profit-related pay and employee share-ownership	6.0	7.9
Sub-total	17.6	21.5
Three schemes		
Individual PBR and collective PBR and profit-related pay	0.9	5.9
Individual PBR and collective PBR and employee share-ownership	0.6	1.9
Individual PBR and profit-related pay and employee share-ownership	2.6	1.6
Collective PBR and profit-related pay and employee share-ownership	1.1	2.6
Sub-total	5.2	12.0
Four schemes		
Individual PBR and collective PBR and profit-related pay and employee share-ownership	0.2	4.7

Note: Values shown are percentage of private sector workplaces.
Source: WIRS/WERS surveys.

instances, but the relationships are not significant in most (PRP and ESO being the exception). The situation is very different in 2004: for instance, both CPBR and ESO had a significant impact on the probability of IPBR being used. The use of CPBR increased the probability of using IPBR by 50 per cent (and 60 per cent vice versa). Overall, the results indicate that workplaces have been moving towards operating 'families' of contingent reward systems over the period.[7]

This evidence on the changing pattern of multiple-scheme incidence raises the further question of whether the workplace characteristics associated with the number of contingent reward systems in use have also

---

[7] In a separate analysis of WERS 2004, Bryson and Freeman (2007) find that contingent pay schemes have positive productivity effects only when there is more than one scheme in operation, a finding which may help to explain the move towards the use of multiple payment methods.

Table 11.7 *The impact of contingent pay systems on other contingent pay systems: summary of marginal effects*

	1984	2004
Individual PBR	Collective PBR+ Profit-related pay+ Employee share-ownership+	Collective PBR+50%** Profit-related pay+ Employee share-ownership+5%*
Collective PBR	Individual PBR+ Profit-related pay+ Employee share-ownership+	Individual PBR+60%** Profit-related pay+5%* Employee share-ownership–
Profit-related payments	Individual PBR+ Collective PBR+ Employee share-ownership+14%**	Individual PBR+ Collective PBR+19%** Employee share-ownership+15%**
Employee share-ownership	Individual PBR+ Collective PBR+ Profit-related pay+ 12%**	Individual PBR+12%* Collective PBR– Profit-related pay+11%*

Note: Base: private sector workplaces (except where profit-related pay and employee share-ownership: private trading sector).
Source: WIRS/WERS data.
$^{*}p < 0.05$, $^{**}p < 0.01$.

changed. Research in HRM has raised the possibility that some firms or workplaces use 'bundles' of organisational practices to achieve synergy (MacDuffie, 1995). Groupings of payment systems may be associated with other HR practices and workplace characteristics. Here we assess whether this is the case, and whether these relationships have changed over the quarter century. To do this, the dependent variable is a count for the number of contingent reward schemes that were in use at the workplace in the two years. Poisson analysis is used to estimate these equations. The results are presented in Table 11.8.

In 1984, union recognition was associated with using several schemes, but this association had dissipated by 2004. Several sectors (chemicals, construction, distribution and hotels, banking and finance) are notable for a greater likelihood of using several forms of contingent pay in both years: this might be related to a higher level of task complexity, the more widespread use of flow technologies and a perceived emphasis on quality as well as quantity in these sectors. In most sectors the size of the effect has diminished slightly but a clear exception is distribution, where the effect has grown. This covers the wholesale and retail sectors: use of collective forms of PBR may broaden out the incentives associated with

Table 11.8 *Poisson analysis of multiple contingent pay systems*

	1984	2004	1984	2004
Union	0.539	0.072	0.529	0.034
	(5.17)**	(0.89)	(4.58)**	(0.39)
Energy/water	0.044	0.643	−0.008	0.522
	(0.06)	(3.01)**	(0.01)	(2.11)*
Chemicals	0.861	0.599	0.805	0.476
	(2.93)**	(2.87)**	(2.51)*	(2.06)*
Engineering	0.362	0.293	0.135	0.198
	(1.25)	(1.29)	(0.41)	(0.82)
Other	0.354	0.408	0.240	0.273
	(1.25)	(1.82)	(0.76)	(1.11)
Construction	0.742	0.631	0.738	0.580
	(2.43)*	(2.48)*	(2.09)*	(2.12)*
Distribution	0.550	0.884	0.520	0.828
	(2.08)*	(5.27)**	(1.85)	(4.68)**
Transport	0.054	0.157	0.328	0.159
	(0.14)	(0.74)	(0.77)	(0.72)
Finance	0.732	0.731	0.802	0.713
	(2.64)**	(4.30)**	(2.64)**	(3.84)**
Size 50–99	0.270	−0.086	0.222	−0.092
	(2.42)*	(1.00)	(1.86)	(1.02)
Size 100–199	0.389	0.021	0.350	0.014
	(3.27)**	(0.21)	(2.59)**	(0.14)
Size 200–499	0.360	0.205	0.444	0.106
	(2.94)**	(2.46)*	(3.06)**	(1.19)
Size 500+	0.412	0.210	0.423	0.192
	(3.30)**	(2.08)*	(2.73)**	(1.84)
Foreign	−0.745	0.149	−0.931	0.166
	(3.72)**	(1.68)	(4.71)**	(1.80)
Single	−0.494	−0.403	−0.541	−0.458
	(3.50)**	(3.53)**	(3.27)**	(3.78)**
Female	0.103	0.194	0.145	0.241
	(0.43)	(0.91)	(0.55)	(1.10)
Part-time	−0.236	−0.422	−0.312	−0.509
	(0.66)	(2.48)*	(0.81)	(2.96)**
Non-manual	0.116	0.240	0.264	0.165
	(0.63)	(2.04)*	(1.13)	(1.36)
Workplace age: less than 5 years	0.193	−0.056	0.030	−0.039
	(1.29)	(0.35)	(0.17)	(0.22)
Workplace age: 5 to 9 years	0.030	−0.003	0.057	−0.011
	(0.24)	(0.03)	(0.39)	(0.11)
Briefing			−0.064	0.127
			(0.60)	(1.31)
Information			0.095	0.173
			(0.87)	(2.28)*
No competition			0.133	−0.607
			(0.68)	(2.07)*
Low competition			−0.002	−0.182
			(0.02)	(2.20)*
Constant	−1.177	−0.398	−1.094	−0.323
	(3.75)**	(1.94)	(3.10)**	(1.48)
Observations	1,081	1,056	717	849

Notes: Base: Columns 1 and 2: Private sector workplaces' columns 3 and 4: private sector trading workplaces. Regional dummies were included in the analysis but results are not shown. The count measure used for the dependent variable is based on the number of types of contingent pay scheme in place at a workplace, from 0 to 4 as presented on page 260.
Source: WIRS/WERS data.
*p < 0.05, **p < 0.01.

individual commission, thereby reducing the dysfunctional effects (e.g., over-zealous selling) often found with individual incentives.

In 1984, workplace and organisational size were associated with operating a larger number of contingent pay schemes, possibly because of the fixed costs of operating these schemes, and the costs of alternative forms of monitoring. By 2004, the relationship with establishment size had disappeared for most size categories. However, workplaces belonging to multi-site organisations were still more likely to operate multiple contingent pay schemes, indicating the continuing importance of organisational size. Whereas in 1984, workplaces with several schemes were likely to be domestically owned, in 2004 they were likely to be foreign owned. As for workforce composition, the only clear finding is that workplaces with fewer part-time workers were more likely to use several schemes in 2004, possibly because of the costs of operating these schemes for part-time workers.

The most interesting findings relate to the roles of information disclosure and competition in the private trading sector. Workplaces with more information disclosure in 2004 were more likely to use a greater number of contingent pay schemes, and this may be indicative of 'high commitment' work systems where management 'bundle' together a number of HR practices. This contrasts with the results for individual schemes where, as in earlier studies (e.g., Wood, 1996b; Long and Shields, 2005), there was no clear relationship between contingent pay and information disclosure. Finally, unlike earlier results in the chapter for specific forms of contingent pay, there is a clear relationship between the strength of product market competition and the propensity to use more than one form of contingent pay. Thus, the prediction that competition will lead to greater use of contingent pay seems to be borne out in this instance.

Conclusions

The findings of the analyses summarised in this chapter are both challenging to conventional wisdom and complex in nature. It is clear that the use of contingent pay in the twenty-first-century British workplace is very different from that in its early 1980s predecessor. For one thing, there is a much greater propensity to put multiple types of scheme in place; it is also more likely that collective forms of pay system will be used; furthermore, the distribution of such schemes is much broader now than it was in the 1980s so that it is less possible to talk of an archetypal contingent pay workplace.

There is also a strong suggestion that there has been a change of policy, perhaps even philosophy, among organisations about the nature and role of contingent pay at the British workplace. This is seen not just in the rise of collective (but not individual) forms of contingent pay and the changes in the characteristics of the 'typical' contingent pay workplace, but also in terms of the importance of within-sector (rather than sectoral-shift) factors in motivating the changes observed, and in relation to the growth of multiple forms of such schemes at the same workplace. This has been an area in the evolution of the modern British workplace in which there has been a great deal of flux over the WERS quarter century.

Appendix 11.1 *Variable construction of pay*
The appendix summarises the construction of each of the main pay variables used in the chapter.

The following questions about profit-related payments or bonuses were asked of companies with workplaces in the private trading sector	WERS 1984: 'Does the company operate any of the following schemes for any of the employees here: . . . a profit sharing scheme?' WERS 1990: 'Does the company operate any schemes on this card for employees here: . . . profit related payments or bonuses (including those covered by the 1987 Finance Act), deferred profit sharing scheme – where profits are put in a trust fund which acquires shares in the employing company for employees (sometimes under the 1978 Finance Act)?' WERS 1998: 'Do any employees at this workplace receive payments or dividends from any of the following variable pay schemes: . . . profit-related payments or bonuses; deferred profit sharing scheme?' WERS 2004: 'Do any employees at this workplace receive profit-related payments or profit-related bonuses?'
The following questions about share-ownership schemes with eligible employees were asked of companies with workplaces in the private trading sector	WERS 1984: 'Does the company owning this establishment operate a share-ownership or share option scheme?' (WERS 1984 and WERS 1990 make explicit mention of share *option* schemes.) WERS 1990: 'Does the company owning the establishment operate any of the schemes on this card for the employees here: . . . SAYE share option scheme; discretionary or executive share option scheme; other types of share-ownership scheme?' WERS 1998: 'Do any employees at this workplace receive payments or dividends from employee share-ownership schemes?' WERS 2004: 'Does the company operate any of the employee share schemes for any of the employees at this workplace (SIP, SAYE, EMI, CSOP, other)?' (WERS 2004 and WERS 1998: eligibility refers to non-managerial employees.)
The following questions on whether any employees receive individual-based, group, establishment or organisation-based payments by results were asked of companies with workplaces in the private trading sector	WERS 1984: 'Are any employees in any of the groups in this establishment paid by results?' The follow-up asks if they are paid on an individual, group, establishment or organisational basis. Not asked of managerial or senior white-collar workers. WERS 1990: Questions are only asked where there are 5+ employees for the single-digit occupation concerned. WERS 1998: 'Do any employees at this workplace receive payments or dividends from individual or group performance-related schemes?' The follow-up asks whether individual, group, workplace, or organisation schemes are for non-managerial employees only. WERS 2004: 'Do any employees at this establishment get paid by results?' The follow-up asks whether payment is linked to individual, group, workplace, or organisation measures of performance. Note that 1980 WIRS asks whether a *majority* of employees in seven occupational groups are paid by results. Reference to a majority is not comparable with later years, hence 1980 data are not used in the analysis here.

12 Foreign ownership and industrial relations

Tony Edwards and Janet Walsh

Introduction

The impact of increasing international competition on the management of labour is a recurring theme in this book. Thus far, it has been increased international competition in trade that has been the main concern. Across an increasing range of the British private sector, the past quarter century has seen employers struggling to meet the competitive threat from low labour cost producers elsewhere in the world. It is, however, arguable that what has been happening in capital markets has been at least as important an influence as what has been happening in product markets. The ownership of enterprises has also become much more international.

The rise of foreign ownership has been particularly important for Britain. The stock of foreign direct investment (FDI) had risen to $1,135 billion by 2006. In real terms, this represents a five-fold increase on the previous decade and a half. FDI flows as a percentage of gross fixed capital formation in Britain reached nearly 34 per cent in 2006, almost three times the world average. By then, there was a total of some 13,700 foreign-owned companies. A large part of this development has been the growth of mergers and acquisitions, which constitute around three-quarters of FDI. In 2006 alone, over 600 British firms were acquired by a foreign multinational, more than a quarter of the EU total and more than 10 per cent of the global total (UN, 2007). On the UK Stock Exchange, as was noted in Chapter 1, the proportion of shares listed that were owned by investors outside Britain rose, between 1981 and 2004, from 4 per cent to 36 per cent.

This chapter is concerned with the consequences of this internationalisation of ownership for the evolution of the contemporary workplace. One implication is simply that, as with internationalisation of product markets, competitive cost pressures are heightened. International owners are more footloose internationally than indigenous owners, and consequently more willing to consider shifting production abroad if they become unhappy about labour costs. But a more specific implication, on which this chapter will focus, is that the management practices of foreign companies are likely to have become more influential in shaping British workplaces. This may be because new practices arrive with the new overseas owners, as part of their management style. It may also be because native firms copy them as a potential source of competitive advantage. Whatever the route, Britain's position as one of the most open of the large developed economies in the world makes it particularly susceptible to influence by management practices from other countries. Thus foreign multinationals have the potential to drive the introduction of new practices into Britain, potentially acting as a force for change within the economy as a whole.

It has been established that the management practices of multinational companies (MNCs) tend to reflect, wherever in the world they set up operations, distinctive features that reflect those of their country of origin (Ferner, 1997). Their management style has a distinctive 'foreign accent'. The British operations of foreign MNCs, for example, have been shown to be under pressures to comply with company-wide policies, in what has been termed a tendency for 'corporate isomorphism'. We might expect this to result in the workplaces of foreign-owned firms being markedly different from those that are British-owned. However, these pressures are mediated by the requirements to adapt to the British system. Thus 'local isomorphic' influences, which arise from the legal, institutional and cultural context of employment relations in Britain, create a competing tendency for MNCs to resemble local firms in the practices that they operate.

It can be argued that the changes in British industrial relations in the last quarter of a century mean that pressures for local isomorphism have weakened. In particular, the decline in the constraints that employers face from trade unions might mean that it has become much easier for MNCs to introduce their desired practices. One illustration of the changing context in the 1980s came with the arrival of many Japanese-owned manufacturing workplaces, normally established on greenfield sites, which adopted a set of practices that marked them out from traditional patterns of industrial relations in Britain. For example, many such firms pioneered the use of practices such as single-status employment conditions and direct forms of employee involvement and either avoided unions altogether or signed single-union deals. While it was always clear that this type of workplace was never numerous, it raises the question whether over the last quarter of a century weakened collective bargaining has increased the scope for foreign-owned firms to implement employment practices that are in line with their national preferences.

There have also, on the other hand, been substantial new pressures for local conformity. However much traditional institutions have changed, there has been a wide range of legal innovations by both Conservative and Labour governments since 1980, many at the instigation of the European Union. These have related to many issues, from procedural matters, such as the recognition of employee representatives and requirements for employee consultation, to substantive matters, such as working hours. Thus it is not at all clear that the net effect of institutional constraints on management in foreign-owned firms is lighter than in the past. Moreover, as has been noted, most foreign MNCs enter Britain through merger or acquisition. As they do so, they acquire a set of pre-existing practices that may be costly to change.

In this chapter, we explore the extent to which MNCs in Britain are distinctive in terms of their employment practices. We do so by comparing British and foreign-owned workplaces and considering whether any such distinctiveness has become more pronounced over the last quarter of a century. We compare the practices of British- and foreign-owned workplaces in the early part of the period and again at the end. We address two particular questions. First, do foreign-owned firms operate practices that are distinctive from those of indigenous firms? Second, in so far as they do, has its extent increased over the last quarter of a century? We begin by reviewing the evidence from previous landmark studies of MNCs in Britain during this period.

Previous evidence on foreign multinational companies in Britain

Multinationals have been a focus of attention for analysts of British industrial relations for several decades. In the early 1970s, foreign-owned firms were examined on such issues as their strike proneness, and productivity in relation to British firms (for example, Gennard and Steuer, 1971). The 1980s witnessed many studies of Japanese-owned firms and of their apparently novel employment practices (for example, Oliver and Wilkinson, 1992). Building on these, there have been a number of studies of foreign-owned firms that have looked at such issues as employee involvement and post-acquisition integration (for example, Innes and Morris, 1995; Child et al., 2001). What do these tell us about how distinctive foreign-owned firms are and whether this has changed?

In the early 1980s, two major surveys addressed the question. One of these was the first of the WIRS series in 1980, which permitted Buckley and Enderwick (1985) to compare the British and foreign-owned workplaces among the 702 manufacturing sites. The second was the first Company Level Industrial Relations Survey (CLIRS), carried out in 1985, of 143 multi-plant firms employing a thousand or more (Purcell *et al.*, 1987). The two surveys were complementary; the former provided data on practice at establishment level while the latter shed light on policies at company level. What do they tell us of the distinctiveness of foreign-owned firms at the start of our period?

On some issues there was little difference between the two groups of firms. This was most notable on the issue of patterns of union recognition. Buckley and Enderwick (1985) found foreign-owned workplaces not to be significantly different from British-owned ones in this respect, nor were they more or less likely to be characterised by multiple unionism, to operate the 'check-off' and the closed shop or to have active shop stewards. Thus while there was some evidence in this period of American firms being hostile to unions and granting recognition only reluctantly, this did not result in overseas-owned firms as a whole being significantly different from British ones (Hamill, 1983; Beaumont and Townley, 1985). The similarities between the two groups were also in evidence when it came to patterns of consultation for manual workers, and to the propensity for managers to disclose information to their workforces on financial issues (Purcell *et al.*, 1987).

On three issues, however, there were significant differences between the two groups. The first was that, while the overall extent of trade union recognition was similar, the level at which bargaining took place did differ. Specifically, foreign-owned firms more commonly bargained with unions at the level of the establishment (Buckley and Enderwick, 1985; Purcell *et al.*, 1987). Second, while the existence of consultative committees for manual workers was largely the same, foreign-owned firms were distinctive in the way they communicated with their workforces. They were more likely to have formal channels for consulting with non-manual workers, and to do so by means of a range of direct forms of communication (such as quality circles, briefing groups, management–workforce meetings, newsletters, attitudes surveys and suggestion schemes). They were more likely to distribute information on investment plans and capacity utilisation to their workforces, and more likely to have a managerial style statement formalised in writing and distributed to employees. Purcell and his colleagues (1987: 136) used this evidence to argue that foreign-owned firms were 'more advanced in their adoption of human resource management techniques', and were more likely to encourage these through enterprise policy by monitoring and controlling managers.

The third area in which there were significant differences between British and foreign-owned firms was that of the nature of management organisation in personnel and human resources. Purcell *et al.* (1987)

found that the British headquarters of foreign-owned firms were more likely than their British counterparts to be involved in decision making on human resource issues at subsidiary level, and to monitor these subsidiaries. Moreover, in proportion to the size of the British workforce, foreign firms employed two and a half times as many personnel and human resource specialists as did British companies. This is consistent with Hamill's (1983) evidence that American MNCs – the biggest single nationality within the foreign-owned group – had more specialised and developed personnel departments at establishment level.

This picture of foreign-owned firms in the early 1980s being distinctive in some respects should be qualified. First, the four studies cited did not control for many independent factors that might have a bearing on the patterns of practice in question, such as company or workplace size. Second, the sample size was small in some of the studies. Third, the coverage of some of the studies did not provide the basis for an assessment of the national picture. For instance, Buckley and Enderwick (1985) examined manufacturing sites only, while Beaumont and Townley (1985) studied two particular regions.

What can we say about the picture in the early 1990s? Fortunately, the same two survey series were again used to analyse the issue of foreign ownership. The third WIRS, carried out in 1990, was analysed by Milner and James (1994) using all private sector workplaces with more than 25 employees, while the second Company Level Industrial Relations Survey, carried out in 1992, which covered 176 multi-plant firms which employed more than 1,000 people, 39 of which were foreign-owned, was also used for this purpose by Marginson *et al.* (1993). Once again, the two are complementary in the level at which data were gathered, and they enable us to examine the distinctiveness of foreign-owned firms at that time.

The similarities that were evident in the early 1980s were also in evidence in the early 1990s. Milner and James (1994) found no significant differences between British and foreign-owned workplaces in terms of union recognition. The evidence from the CLIRS 1992 confirms this picture on union recognition (Marginson *et al.*, 1993). It also found no significant difference between British and foreign-owned firms in the incidence of consultative meetings between management and employee representatives at company level. The studies from this period also demonstrated a similarity between foreign- and British-owned firms in the use of performance-related pay (Marginson *et al.*, 1993).

The differences in the early 1990s were also markedly similar to those of the previous decade. The first of these relates to the level of bargaining. Milner and James (1994) found foreign ownership to be positively and significantly associated with single-table bargaining in multi-union sites and with single employer bargaining. Moreover, Marginson *et al.*'s (1993) analysis showed that MNCs were more likely to bargain at establishment level than were what they called British domestics, though there was little difference between foreign and British MNCs. The second issue concerned communication. The CLIRS data allowed comparisons concerning the number of channels through which management communicates with their workforces. Foreign-owned firms were more likely to use four or more of these channels, and to use them consistently across the enterprise rather than at some sites only (Marginson *et al.*, 1993). The third area in which differences were evident was the nature of the human resource function. As had been the case earlier, CLIRS 1992 data showed that overseas-owned firms tended to have bigger human resource functions. In addition, just over half of foreign-owned firms had a member of the main British management board who had full-time responsibility for personnel and industrial relations, whereas just under a quarter of British firms did so. The authors concluded that 'since the 1990 WIRS found the same phenomena at the establishment level the conclusion is unmistakable that overseas-owned enterprises devote far more resources to personnel management than their indigenous counterparts' (Marginson *et al.*, 1993: 31–2).

The distinctiveness of foreign-owned firms in the early 1990s did not show up in the use of performance-related pay, but a difference was evident for profit-sharing and employee share-ownership schemes. These were much less likely to cover non-managerial workers in overseas-owned firms when compared with British firms (Marginson *et al.*, 1993).

The evidence for the early 1990s suggests a similar picture to the early 1980s. There were strong similarities between British and foreign-owned firms in terms of the extent of recognition and patterns of consultation with employee representatives in both periods. Where there were differences between the two groups of firms, they concerned the level of bargaining, the nature of direct communication and the organisation of the human resource function.

Research method

We were able to revisit the questions explored in the earlier research with the added advantages offered by the combined WIRS/WERS data set, a nationally representative sample and the opportunity for multivariate analysis. The key questions that enabled us to distinguish between British and foreign-owned firms differed slightly through the WIRS/WERS series. In the most recent survey, the question related to 'the ownership of the ultimate controlling company'. The 1980, 1990 and 1998

Table 12.1 *The extent of foreign ownership*

	1980 %	1984 %	1990 %	1998 %	2004 %
UK-owned	94	91	91	87	82
50/50 UK and foreign	0	2	1	1	4
Foreign-owned	6	7	8	13	14
N	1,362	1,265	1,370	1,425	1,508

Source: WIRS/WERS data.

surveys used slightly different concepts for identifying foreign-owned workplaces in such a way that probably underestimated the scale of foreign ownership.[1] While this makes direct comparisons across the entire series hazardous, the same concept of the ownership of the ultimate controlling company was used in the survey of 1984 and for this reason we concentrate on the data from 1984 and 2004. While this is not ideal, it does still enable a comparison to be made between British and foreign-owned workplaces in the early part of the last quarter of a century and at the end of this period.

Since MNCs have only recently become involved in the provision of public services, the analysis was restricted to the private sector. The numbers and percentages of workplaces in each of the categories for the five surveys are presented in Table 12.1. The increasing importance of foreign ownership shows through clearly, with the proportion of private sector workplaces in this category having more than doubled in the last quarter of a century. The numbers in the jointly British- and foreign-owned category are too small to stand up as their own category and so in the analysis that follows these are grouped together with fully foreign-owned firms. For the two surveys that are the focus of this chapter, therefore, foreign ownership constitutes 9 per cent of the sample in 1984 and 18 per cent in 2004.

The first step was to conduct bivariate analysis on those areas of employment practice for which direct comparisons could be drawn. There were six such areas: union recognition and collective bargaining; consultation and information disclosure; the character of channels

---

[1] The 1990 question on foreign ownership only goes as far as the ultimate controlling company (UCC) in Britain, whilst the 1980 and 1998 surveys do not introduce the concept of the UCC at all. One might expect the incidence of foreign ownership to rise with the level at which ownership is measured, so one might expect the 1980, 1990 and 1998 questions to underestimate the true incidence of foreign ownership, all other things being equal.

Table 12.2 *The control variables*

		Bivariate analysis		
		UK	Foreign	Significance
Manufacturing & extraction	1984	32%	43%	*
	2004	13%	28%	***
Age of establishment	1984	51%	31%	**
	2004	40%	38%	–
Size of establishment	1984	92	145	**
	2004	85	135	***

Notes: Age of establishment refers to proportion of workplaces which are more than 25 years old; Size of establishment refers to mean number of employees.
Source: WIRS/WERS data.
*p < 0.1, **p < 0.05, ***p < 0.01.

for communication; the organisation of the human resource function; the ways in which firms seek flexibility; and 'variable' pay. We present the data from the cross-tabulations and whether the differences were statistically significant using chi-square tests for each of these issues in columns 3, 4 and 5 in Tables 12.3 to 12.8.

The second step was to take each of the variables for which there had been a significant association in the bivariate analysis and carry out logistic regression analysis. Table 12.2 shows that foreign-owned workplaces were larger, on average, and more likely to be in the manufacturing sector when compared with British-owned sites. In 1984, they were also younger, though in 2004 the profile by age was the same. These findings are important because size, sector and vintage are key influences on many of the employment practices that we go on to examine, pointing to the need to include these three variables as controls in the regression analysis. This was carried out through separate regression models for the 1984 and 2004 data sets using the Complex Samples function to take account of the design of the surveys in the series. The direction of the coefficient on the foreign ownership variable is presented in the sixth column of Tables 12.3 to 12.8, and whether this is significant appears in the seventh column.

The third step was to examine whether the impact of foreign ownership had changed over time. In this respect, the approach of using separate models for the two years was limited, as it did not allow us to test whether the coefficients on foreign ownership had changed significantly between 1984 and 2004. Thus we carried out a pooled regression with cases from

Table 12.3 *Union recognition and the level of bargaining*

		Bivariate analysis			Multivariate analysis			
		UK	Foreign	Sig	Effect of foreign ownership	Sig	Interaction effects	Sig
Union Recognition	1984	47%	53%	ns				
	2004	22%	24%	ns				
Single-site bargaining	1984	30%	50%	***	+	***	−	
	2004	13%	36%	***	+	ns		

Source: WIRS/WERS data.
*p < 0.1, **p < 0.05, ***p < 0.01, ns = not significant.

both years and added a year dummy variable alongside the foreign ownership dummy and the control variables. By examining the interaction effects between the year and foreign ownership dummies, we were able to establish whether foreign ownership had a significantly different relationship with the dependent variable in each time period. The sign of the coefficient on the interaction effect appears in the eighth column of Tables 12.3 to 12.8 and the significance of this in column nine.

The results

The results for each of the six areas of employment practice are considered in turn. In each case, the results are presented in three steps: first, bivariate analysis of the associations between foreign ownership and the various issues; second, where the first step produced a statistically significant finding, we report the direction and level of significance of the foreign ownership variable in the multivariate analysis for each year; and, third, we present the direction and level of significance of the interaction terms between the year dummy and foreign ownership in the pooled regressions.

Union recognition and bargaining

There is little evidence of foreign-owned firms having a distinctive approach to union recognition. The bivariate analysis showed that they were no less likely to have a recognised union than British-owned firms,[2]

---

[2] It is possible that this is complicated by other factors, such as size, sector and vintage and that when these are controlled for it may be that foreign-owned workplaces are indeed less likely to grant recognition. For this reason a regression analysis was carried out

Table 12.4 *Consultation and information disclosure*

		Bivariate analysis			Multivariate analysis			
		UK	Foreign	Sig	Effect of foreign ownership	Sig	Interaction effects	Sig
JCC	1984	25%	36%	**	+	ns	–	ns
	2004	20%	28%	**	+	ns		
Disc of inv plans	1984	31%	36%	ns	–	ns	+	ns
	2004	44%	54%	*	+	ns		
Disc of finance	1984	55%	70%	**	+	ns	+	ns
	2004	54%	76%	***	+	***		
Disc of staffing	1984	57%	57%	ns				
	2004	62%	57%	ns				

Source: WIRS/WERS data.
*p < 0.1, **p < 0.05, ***p < 0.01, ns = not significant.

indicating that, despite the weakening of the pressures to grant recognition, this has not resulted in greater differences in practice between British and foreign-owned firms. In terms of the level of bargaining, though, foreign ownership did have a statistically significant effect. The bivariate analysis of those firms that had a recognised union shows that, across the period, foreign-owned firms were significantly more likely to operate single-site bargaining. This association holds for the multivariate analysis of the 1984 data, but the relationship falls just short of the 10 per cent level of significance in 2004. The sign on the interaction effect indicates that the influence of foreign ownership became less marked through time, though the change is not statistically significant. The findings in this area support the view of broad similarities between British and foreign-owned firms in terms of union recognition that was evident from earlier studies (Buckley and Enderwick, 1985; Milner and James, 1994), and that the distinctiveness of foreign firms in terms of level of bargaining is less evident at the end of the period.

Consultation

The second issue that we consider is that of consultation and information disclosure (Table 12.4), of which there were two elements. The first was the presence of a joint consultative committee at establishment level,

even though the bivariate analysis had not produced a significant difference. In fact, the foreign ownership variable was insignificant in both 1984 and 2004.

for which the bivariate analysis shows that joint consultative committees were significantly and positively associated with foreign ownership in both time periods. However, we know that joint consultative committees are more common in large manufacturing workplaces, and when these factors and plant vintage were controlled for in the regression analysis, the relationship was no longer statistically significant in either time period. Unsurprisingly given this, the interaction effect shows that the association with foreign ownership was not significantly different over time.

The second aspect was of information disclosure on three particular issues at establishment level. The bivariate analysis shows that foreign ownership had no association with the disclosure of information on staffing plans in either period. However, it was positively and statistically significantly associated with the disclosure of information on the site's financial position in both time periods, and with information disclosure on the investment plans for the site in 2004, where it had not been in 1984. The regression analysis shows that once controls were included, the relationship of foreign ownership with information disclosure on investment plans was no longer statistically significant. But it also shows that the impact of foreign ownership on information disclosure concerning the financial position of the establishment was statistically significant in 2004, where it had not been in 1984. The interaction associations between foreign ownership and the year dummies show that the influence of foreign ownership was, however, not significantly different over the two time periods.

Overall, the picture of partial distinctiveness of foreign-owned firms that emerged from earlier studies on this issue is largely intact at the end of the quarter century. Specifically, the incidence of joint consultative committees did not differ between the two groups of firms throughout the period, but foreign-owned firms were more likely to disclose information on certain issues at both the beginning and end of the period, albeit not on precisely the same issues.

Communication

There were four forms of direct communication that could be examined in both time periods (Table 12.5). One of these, suggestion schemes, was a bottom-up form of communication, which was slightly more common in foreign-owned establishments, but not statistically significantly so. A second, briefing groups, was a 'two-way' form of communication in that management can use these to pass information down the hierarchy; but the information flow can also be reversed. The bivariate analysis shows that the difference in the use of this practice between British and

Table 12.5 *Forms of communication*

		Bivariate analysis			Multivariate analysis			
		UK	Foreign	Sig	Effect of foreign ownership	Sig	Interaction effects	Sig
Suggestion	1984	22%	24%	ns				
schemes	2004	35%	37%	ns				
Briefing	1984	30%	39%	ns				
groups	2004	69%	75%	ns				
Management	1984	57%	68%	*	+	ns	−	ns
chain	2004	70%	75%	ns	+	ns		
Newsletters	1984	29%	43%	**	+	ns	+	ns
	2004	53%	68%	***	+	***		

Source: WIRS/WERS data.
*p < 0.1, **p < 0.05, ***p < 0.01, ns = not significant.

foreign-owned firms was not statistically significantly different. The other two forms of communication were top-down – systematic use of the management chain and newsletters. In the bivariate analysis, we see that foreign-owned firms were more likely to use both of these in 1984 and more likely to use newsletters in 2004, with these associations being statistically significant. In the regression analysis, the associations in 1984 became insignificant, and only newsletters in 2004 remains statistically significant (at the 1 per cent level). The direction of the coefficient on the interaction term for newsletters shows that, while foreign ownership had a stronger effect in the later period, the impact was not significantly different across the two periods. The general picture, then, is of only partial distinctiveness on the part of foreign-owned firms, with this not becoming markedly greater over time. Indeed, the WIRS/WERS data provide a rather different picture from the findings of the two company level surveys which pointed to rather more distinctiveness in the practices of foreign-owned firms (Purcell *et al.*, 1987; Marginson *et al.*, 1993).

Personnel or human resource organisation

The bivariate analysis indicates that foreign-owned firms had a distinctive approach to organising and resourcing the human resource function at establishment level. They were significantly more likely to have a human resource specialist at the site (at the 1 per cent level in 1984 and 5 per cent level in 2004) in both surveys, and there was a statistically significant link between this person spending more than a quarter of

Table 12.6 *The human resource function at establishment level and contact with higher levels*

		Bivariate analysis			Multivariate analysis			
		UK	Foreign	Sig	Effect of foreign ownership	Sig	Interaction effects	Sig
Pers/HR	1984	19%	43%	***	+	***	−	ns
specialist	2004	35%	51%	**	+	**		
+25% time	1984	47%	56%	Ns	+	ns	−	ns
on HR	2004	63%	76%	*	+	ns		
Formal HR	1984	28%	57%	***	+	***	−	ns
qualifications	2004	40%	58%	***	+	***		
Higher HR	1984	62%	63%	Ns	−	ns	−	**
contact	2004	82%	64%	***	−	**		

Source: WIRS/WERS data.
*p < 0.1, **p < 0.05, ***p < 0.01, ns = not significant.

his or her time on human resource issues in 2004, though not in 1984. The human resource specialist was also statistically significantly more likely to have relevant professional qualifications in foreign-owned firms in both periods. The regression analysis largely supports this picture. Foreign ownership was positively and significantly associated with the presence of a personnel specialist, and with this person having specialist human resource qualifications in both time periods. However, there is no statistically significant association with this person spending more than a quarter of his or her time on human resource issues. The interaction terms show that the distinctive influence of foreign ownership did not change over time.

The other aspect of the human resource function that was considered was the extent of contact with higher levels of management. Here, the bivariate analysis shows that, while there was no statistically significant difference between the two groups in 1984, there was in 2004, with British-owned workplaces being more likely to have contact with higher levels. This pattern holds in the regression analysis and the interaction effect is statistically significant, confirming that the impact of ownership changed over time. It is clear from Table 12.6 that the main change in the two time periods is among the British-owned workplaces, for which there was a sharp increase in the proportion of workplaces that have contact with a human resource specialist higher up in the organisation. These findings are congruent with previous analysis of data from the WIRS/WERS series, which has shown that there was a decline in

Table 12.7 *Numerical flexibility*

		Bivariate analysis			Multivariate analysis			
		UK	Foreign	Sig	Effect of foreign ownership	Sig	Interaction effects	Sig
Agency staff	1984	21%	39%	***	+	**	+	ns
	2004	21%	42%	***	+	***		
Freelancers	1984	19%	21%	ns				
	2004	14%	17%	ns				
Shift working	1984	32%	44%	**	+	ns	+	ns
	2004	42%	55%	**	+	ns		

Source: WIRS/WERS data.
*p < 0.1, **p < 0.05, ***p < 0.01, ns = not significant.

the autonomy of workplaces in multi-plant firms in the handling of employment relations issues between 1990 and 1998 (Millward *et al.*, 2000), and that foreign-owned workplaces generally have more autonomy from higher levels of management than their British-owned counterparts (Kersley *et al.*, 2006). This latter finding may reflect the absence of higher levels within Britain among the foreign-owned firms and it may well be that contact with higher levels of management in the foreign-owned workplaces is just as common but involves management outside Britain.

Flexibility

There are three types of numerical flexibility at workplace level that can be compared over time with WIRS/WERS data – the use of agency staff, freelancers and shift working (Table 12.7). The bivariate analysis shows that, while there was no statistically significant difference between British and foreign-owned firms in the use of freelancers, foreign MNCs were significantly more likely to use agency staff and shift working in both time periods.[3] In the regression analysis, the findings for the use of agency staff remain essentially the same, in that foreign ownership is positively and statistically significantly associated with this (at the 5 per cent level in 1984 and at the 1 per cent level in 2004). For shift working

---

[3] The 2004 data also allow us to consider the issue of subcontracting on seven issues. On all seven, foreign-owned firms were more likely to use subcontracting, and on four of them (cleaning, security, catering and transportation) the difference was significant at the 1 per cent level. This issue cannot be tracked over time, but it is consistent with the picture of foreign-owned firms being more likely to strive for numerical flexibility.

Table 12.8 *The use of variable pay*

		Bivariate analysis			Multivariate analysis			
		UK	Foreign	Sig	Effect of foreign ownership	Sig	Interaction effects	Sig
Share Ownership	1984	24%	12%	**	−	**	+	***
	2004	25%	47%	***	+	***		
Profit Pay/Sharing	1984	21%	6%	***	−	***		
	2004	41%	59%	***	+	*		

Source: WIRS/WERS data.
*p < 0.1, **p < 0.05, ***p < 0.01, ns = not significant.

the relationship is not statistically significant. The interaction terms show that there was no statistically significant change over time in the impact of foreign ownership on these three types of numerical flexibility.

Variable pay

We are able to consider two dimensions of 'supplementary' or 'variable' pay. It will be recalled that Marginson *et al.*'s previous (1993) work on the issue of performance-related pay revealed little difference between British and foreign-owned firms, but the WERS data reveal some interesting differences and trends on two other aspects of variable pay (Table 12.8). The first of these is share-ownership schemes, for which the bivariate analysis showed that foreign-owned workplaces were statistically significantly less likely than British-owned sites to have a share-ownership scheme in 1984, but more likely to have such a scheme in 2004. Indeed, the proportion of British-owned workplaces that had share-ownership schemes stayed almost exactly the same, at a quarter, with all of the growth accounted for by foreign-owned workplaces. The pattern for the regression analysis was exactly the same; foreign ownership was negatively associated with share-ownership schemes in 1984 but positively in 2004, with both relationships being statistically significant. The interaction term was also statistically significant, demonstrating that the impact of foreign ownership changed markedly over time.

The second type of variable pay concerned the extent to which profits were linked to pay. On this issue, the questions asked in the two surveys differed; in 1984 the survey asked about 'profit-sharing schemes' whereas in 2004 it asked about a 'profit-related pay scheme'. Thus the data should be viewed with caution and interaction effects cannot be assessed, because they are reliant on a pooling of the data from the two time periods. Nevertheless, the pattern was almost identical to that for share-ownership schemes. The bivariate analysis showed that foreign-owned workplaces were less likely than British-owned sites to have a profit-sharing scheme in 1984, but more likely to have a profit-related pay scheme in 2004, with both associations being statistically significant. Of course, the overall level of use of these practices cannot be directly compared across the time periods because the phenomena being asked about were slightly different. However, the key finding is that the differences between foreign and British workplaces changed direction across the twenty years. The pattern for the regression analysis was almost exactly the same: foreign ownership was negatively associated with profit-sharing schemes in 1984, but positively associated with profit-related pay in 2004, with both associations once again being statistically significant.

Assessment

These findings enable us to return to the questions with which we began this chapter. Are foreign-owned firms in Britain different from domestically owned workplaces in the character of employment practice at establishment level? And if they are distinctive, have the differences got greater?

Taking the first of these questions, the picture is mixed. In some respects, there is little to mark out foreign-owned from British-owned sites. For example, the incidence of union recognition is not significantly different between the two groups, nor is the incidence of joint consultative committees once controls are introduced into the analysis. There are also some similarities in terms of the way that the two groups consult and communicate with their staff, which shows up in the prevalence of information disclosure on investment and staffing plans, and the use of suggestion schemes and the management chain. There was little to distinguish the two groups in some aspects of numerical flexibility, such as the use of freelancers and the use of shift working. This may be interpreted as evidence of local isomorphism, with MNCs tending to adapt their practices to fit into a local pattern.

In other respects, however, there were marked differences. This shows up to a limited extent, even on those issues where we might expect the local isomorphic pressures to be strong, such as in the way in which management deals with employee representatives. For example, foreign-owned firms were significantly more likely to negotiate at site level in 1984 and to disclose information on the financial position of the establishment in 2004. They were also more likely to communicate with their workforces through the use of newsletters in the later part of the period and to use agency staff throughout the period. The most striking differences came in the nature of the human resource function and in the use of variable pay. In relation to the former, foreign-owned firms were significantly more likely to have a personnel or human resource specialist at site level, for this person to have formal human resource qualifications and to have less contact with higher level management in Britain. In relation to the latter, at the end of the period, foreign-owned firms more commonly ran share-ownership and profit-related pay schemes. These differences may be due to the pressures of corporate isomorphism, in that the sites belonging to foreign-owned firms had to fit into a set of company-wide human resource policies.

This picture of partial distinctiveness is consistent with much of the evidence from previous studies. As we have seen, previous analysis of the WIRS/WERS series in the early 1980s and 1990s, together with some other data sets, such as the CLIRS series, indicated that MNCs in Britain have tended to resemble local firms in areas such as union recognition and consultative structures, but to be distinctive on such issues as the way they resource the local human resource function. Arguably, however, we might have found a greater degree of distinctiveness had we been able to investigate those areas that are not subject to strong pressures for local isomorphism, such as management development and employee participation, many of which cannot be tracked across time through the WIRS/WERS series. This is supported by evidence from a major survey of MNCs carried out at company level in Britain in 2006, a successor to the CLIRS series in some ways though different in important respects.[4] This showed that over two-thirds of MNCs in Britain had a succession planning system, and 70 per cent have training programmes for 'high potentials'. Moreover, more than nine out of ten MNCs had at least one form of direct participation, such as teamwork (Edwards *et al.*, 2007). While this survey did not allow a comparison with a large sample of indigenous firms, the prevalence of policies on these issues in MNCs in Britain is strongly suggestive of international influence, which we might expect to lead to different policies in foreign companies, when compared with British companies.

This picture of partial distinctiveness was evident in both 1984 and in 2004. But what more can we say about the second question, concerning whether the differences between foreign- and British-owned firms were

---

[4] The survey was conducted in 2006 and incorporated overseas-owned MNCs with at least 500 employees worldwide and at least 100 in Britain and British-owned MNCs with at least 500 employees worldwide and at least 100 outside Britain.

greater in 2004 than they had been in 1984? The extent of distinctiveness was clearly not the same in the two years. Some associations that were significant in one period were not significant in the other. In some cases, the direction of the association was different at the two points in time. One crude way of assessing the change is to count the number of significant associations in each period. Of the nineteen issues in the six areas of employment practice for which we undertake comparison in this chapter, six were significantly different in 1984 and eight in 2004, suggesting that the overall distinctiveness of foreign-owned workplaces was only marginally greater at the end of the period than at the beginning. However, as we noted above, a better way of assessing this is to focus on what the interaction terms tell us about whether there has been a marked change in the influence of foreign ownership over time. On only two of the issues were the interaction terms significant. This suggests that changes in the context of British industrial relations were so substantial that they left little scope for the preferences of management in foreign MNCs to show through more strongly in shaping employment practices at site level at the end of the last quarter of a century compared with the beginning of it.

We can take the issue of whether the distinctiveness of foreign-owned firms has changed over time a little further by considering the data according to particular areas of employment practice. In this respect, we identify five patterns and consider whether each of these is consistent with a picture of a weakening of the constraints from the industrial relations context, leading to a changing distinctiveness of foreign-owned firms.

First, on many of the issues there was no significant association between foreign ownership and the practice in question in either 1984 or 2004. This is true for union recognition, the existence of a joint consultative committee, some aspects of information disclosure and some forms of communication and types of flexibility. There may be two causes for this continuing lack of distinctiveness on the part of foreign-owned firms. One is that foreign-owned firms continue to face significant constraints on those issues, arising from local traditions of collectivism, for example, and that management consider that departing from local practices entails costs that they deem not to be worthwhile. This gains credibility when we consider that the majority of foreign-owned firms in Britain have entered through acquisition and have, therefore, inherited a set of pre-existing practices that are costly to disrupt. Another possible cause, which is compatible with the first, is that senior management do not consider these issues to be ones that are of 'strategic' importance, in that they are not seen as contributing in a major way to the competitive position of the firm. Thus foreign-owned firms may prefer their practices to be different from those that are prevalent in the local environment, but do not see it as important enough to ensure that these preferences are translated into practice. Either way, this pattern of no significant associations throughout the period does not provide support for the argument that a weakening of the constraints posed by the British system has allowed foreign MNCs greater room for manoeuvre.

A second pattern, evident in some characteristics, is for there to be significant differences between the two groups throughout the period with the association being in the same direction. The tendency for foreign-owned firms to more commonly have human resource specialists at site level who hold formal human resource qualifications, and to more commonly use agency workers, were examples of distinctiveness that were apparent in the same direction across the time period. We might see these areas as ones in which local pressures to adapt to prevailing practices have been consistently weak. For example, it is difficult to identify significant obstacles to those foreign-owned firms that want to take a different approach to local firms in the resourcing of the local human resource function. Other than a shortage of qualified candidates in the labour market, there are no barriers to MNCs employing specialist human resource staff in greater numbers at site level. Once again, then, this strand of the data is not consistent with a 'weakening constraints leading to greater distinctiveness' thesis.

Third, on one issue, collective bargaining at site level, there had been significant differences between the two groups in 1984 that had dissipated by 2004. One explanation for this might be that, in the early part of the period, the organisational resources and negotiating power of unions meant that, where foreign-owned firms accepted that they had to grant recognition, they had distinctive preferences for the level at which they would do so. By contrast, in the later part of the period the influence of unions had declined for both the foreign-owned and the indigenous firms. This may have led those foreign-owned firms that continued to recognise unions to be less concerned about the nature of bargaining. It may also have permitted the indigenous firms to converge on the practices of foreign-owned firms. Thus it is possible that what we see on this issue is a change in the distinctiveness of foreign-owned firms that was brought about by a weakening of the constraints from the context. But it is a story of dissipating, not greater, distinctiveness. Moreover, the interaction term indicates that the influence of foreign ownership did not change significantly on this issue.

A fourth pattern is where there had been no statistical difference between the two groups in 1984, but one had emerged by 2004. On the face of it, this pattern is one that is most likely to be consistent with the 'weakening constraints leading to greater distinctiveness' thesis. However, this is unlikely to be the cause of the change for the three practices that fall into this category. Two of these are newsletters and the disclosure of financial information about the site. The problem with the weakening constraints thesis here is that it is unlikely that those managements in foreign-owned workplaces in 1984 who wanted to introduce newsletters and disclose more information about the financial position of the sites were prevented from doing so by unions or workforce opposition. In any event, the interaction terms show that the influence of foreign ownership did not change significantly over time on these two issues. On the third issue in this category, though, the interaction term was significant. The effect of foreign ownership on the incidence of contact with higher levels in the human resource function changed significantly over time. As already noted, it may be that the rise in the extent of higher level involvement from within Britain among indigenous workplaces was mirrored by a rise in interventions from higher-level management from other countries in the foreign-owned workplaces. While this is an intriguing finding, it is not evidently caused by a weakening of the constraints from the British industrial relations system.

The fifth pattern is perhaps the most interesting of all, and relates to those issues for which there were significant differences in both time periods, but with the direction of these effects changing over time. This was true for the two forms of variable pay. In 1984, foreign-owned firms had been less likely to operate share-ownership schemes and profit-related pay, but by 2004 they had become more likely to do so. A part of the explanation for this may lie in the 'weakening constraints' thesis. It may be that as the constraints of needing to negotiate pay with unions declined, so the distinctive preferences of foreign-owned firms began to show through in the greater use of share-ownership and profit-related pay schemes. But this can only be a part of the story. If it was merely a matter of their preferences to use these practices being constrained in 1984, then why were they significantly less likely to use them when compared with British firms which were facing the same constraints? Another part of the explanation may lie in the flurry of tax incentives for both share-option schemes (in 1980 and 1984) and profit-related pay (in 1987 and 1991, after which they were wound down), although it cannot be assumed that indigenous firms and foreign firms respond differently to these tax incentives. There must be another part of the story. One plausible account is that it has to do with changing patterns of integration across national borders within MNCs, and changing influences over employment practices associated with this. We elaborate on this in the conclusion.

Conclusion

This chapter has addressed two main questions. First, are foreign-owned firms different in the nature of their employment practices from indigenous ones? On this issue we have painted a picture of partial distinctiveness. Second, did this distinctiveness become greater over the last quarter of a century? Despite the a priori grounds for expecting this to be the case, the story was of the partial distinctiveness not being markedly different over time. In exploring this, we have seen that there is little evidence of the constraints from the context becoming less marked. This may be because the context in 1984 already allowed foreign-owned firms some room for manoeuvre. It may also be because most foreign-owned firms have come into Britain through acquisition and, therefore, have inherited pre-existing practices which constitute constraints of a different sort. More speculatively, in looking to understand the changing nature of employment relations practices of MNCs in Britain, it may be more productive to look at the way in which these are driven by changing strategies at least as much as by changing constraints.

There are good grounds for believing that many MNCs have built strong linkages between their operations across countries. The recent survey of MNCs referred to above provides evidence of this. For example, it shows that only 5 per cent of MNCs in Britain can be characterised as producing a range of unrelated products and services, indicating that the diversified conglomerate multinational is now rare. Moreover, three-quarters of MNCs were identified as producing a product or service that is standardised either across regions or globally, rather than adapting it to national markets. Four-fifths of companies exhibited a degree of integration of their operations across borders by means of British sites supplying those in other countries with components or services, sites in other countries supplying those in Britain, or both of these (Edwards et al., 2007). The British operations of MNCs evidently have much in common with their counterparts in other countries and are inter-dependent with them.

The position of British operations within the evolving nature of MNCs is also in evidence in other respects. The MNCs survey sheds light on the nature of corporate structures, showing them to be multi-layered in the sense that most firms possess more than one axis of internal organisation. Specifically, most firms in the survey identified at least one international axis of organisation, such as the region (82 per cent), global business functions (68 per cent) and international product divisions (66 per cent). By contrast, the national subsidiary was identified as a part of the corporate structure in a lower proportion of MNCs (60 per cent). The survey also shed light on the extent to which there is an international nature to the human resource function. For example, the monitoring of employment practices and outcomes in Britain by higher levels of management is widespread. Eighty-two per cent of MNCs collect data on three or more of nine issues listed. There was a worldwide company philosophy on how to manage staff in 61% of firms, and two-thirds brought human resource managers together across borders on a systematic basis (Edwards *et al.*, 2007).

This may offer an explanation of our findings. It is that the British operations of MNCs have over our period become increasingly integrated into the wider international firms. Given that this holds for the domestic operations of British MNCs, it may be as productive to search for an 'international accent', rather than simply a foreign one, when examining the nature of management style in MNCs. The globalisation of economic activity and the strengthening of regional trading blocks and forms of regulation have presented opportunities for MNCs to enhance the linkages between their operations across borders. It may be that this growing integration lies behind some of the changes that we have observed.

An example is variable pay. Employees in British subsidiaries of foreign MNCs in the early 1980s were less likely to have access to share schemes and profit-related bonuses. The explanation may be that these schemes were restricted to firms in domestic operations of the MNCs because the shares were generally only listed in the home country, and management structures across borders were not strong enough to provide a basis for international policies on such issues. In contrast, by 2004, many MNCs had pursued a policy of listing their shares on multiple stock markets, particularly in Britain. They had sought to integrate their British operations into the rest of the firm, not just through stronger international management structures, but also through the dispersion of the strategic responsibilities within the firm across countries. In this changed corporate context, some employees in Britain are more likely to experience such variable forms of pay as share-ownership and profit-related schemes.

The changing nature of the multinational firm thus provides important insights into understanding evolving employment practice in MNCs in Britain. The continuing distinctiveness of national business systems and the growing importance of international capital markets and of international ownership suggest that there are competing dynamics at play. On the one hand, there is a well-documented country-of-origin effect that gives rise to a national influence on management style that varies between multinationals according to where they come from. On the other, there is an 'international integration' effect that arises from the globalisation and regionalisation of markets and which is felt across a growing range of firms and industries.

13   The public sector in transition

Stephen Bach, Rebecca Kolins Givan and John Forth

Introduction

The last twenty-five years have seen momentous changes in public sector industrial relations. Successive governments have radically restructured the sector. They have privatised the former nationalised industries, encouraged more enterprise-specific patterns of employment relations, sponsored a management revolution and reduced the influence of public sector trade unions. The extent to which these reforms signal wholesale transformation or a more incremental process of transition has been widely debated (Bach and Winchester, 2003; Corby, 2000; Kersley *et al.*, 2006: 314–16). Convergence with the private sector is most evident in three ways: the diminished regulatory influence of industry-level collective bargaining; increased responsibility delegated to managers for local employment relations practice; and the spread of human resource management techniques. But the political and economic context in which these practices are enacted determines that state employment continues to differ in important respects from patterns prevailing in the private sector. For example, trade union density at the end of the period was three times the level of that of the private sector.

Some differences relate to the distinctive characteristics of the sector. The workforce has a higher proportion of women, has longer tenure and is older than the private sector workforce. In 2004, almost two-thirds (65%) of employees were women compared to 41% in the private sector (Hicks *et al.*, 2005: 21). This stems in part from the employment of more women than men in professional jobs (such as teaching, nursing and social work), but also from their employment in less-qualified and lower-status occupations, such as in secretarial and cleaning jobs. In the decade 1995 to 2005, the proportion of women employed in the public sector increased by 5% compared to a stable picture in the private sector. Job tenure is also longer. In 2004, 40% of public sector employees had been in their current workplace for ten or more years, compared to 28% of private sector workers (Hicks *et al.*, 2005: 29). Finally, almost three-quarters of public sector workers are over thirty-five, compared to just over 60 per cent in the private sector, and there are far fewer young workers (under twenty-four) compared to the private sector (Hicks *et al.*, 2005: 23).

These characteristics have influenced debates with regard to the extent to which pension provision and equal pay, for example, are major workforce concerns. In addition, the gender composition of the workforce has encouraged public sector employers to adopt equal employment and work–life balance policies. The high proportion of professionals, alongside a smaller managerial cohort than in the private sector, has facilitated investment in training and development.

The Workplace Industrial/Employment Relations Survey (WIRS/ WERS) series has played a valuable role in tracing the evolution of institutional arrangements in the sector, and the diffusion of human resource management practices. The publication of the first workplace survey in 1980 coincided with the end of relative institutional stability in the public sector, and interest in it was heightened by the subsequent reforms. A distinctive feature of public sector industrial relations has been the importance of national-level institutional structures, with both employers and trade unions traditionally oriented to the policies of government. Although these national drivers of change occur at a level beyond the workplace, the focus of WERS, their effects are experienced at the workplace.

This chapter draws on WIRS/WERS and other sources to examine changing patterns of employment relations in the public sector over the last twenty-five years. It considers the pattern of employment relations at the start of the period, and the reasons why the state was characterised as a model employer. The chapter then examines the restructuring of the sector, the decentralisation of employment relations and changes in human resources (HR) practice to assess the degree to which public sector employment relations have been transformed.

The public sector in 1980: a model employer?

In 1980, despite having been virtually ignored by the Donovan Commission a decade earlier, the public sector had become pivotal to debates about the economic and political crisis confronting Britain. The unexpected upsurge of strike action, triggered by incomes policies that were more readily enforced in the public sector, culminated in the 1978–9 'winter of discontent'. The increase in militancy during the 1970s placed the relationship between government and public sector trade unions at the centre of public policy, ultimately discredited the trade union movement and more immediately provided the legitimacy for Conservative governments to embark on major restructuring of the public sector. After a cautious start, whole industries were transferred from the public to the private sector, uprooting traditional patterns of employment relations and leading some commentators to highlight the transformation of the role of the state as an employer (Carter and Fairbrother, 1999; Fredman and Morris, 1989).

Until the end of the 1970s, this role had been characterised as that of a 'model employer'. The state set an example to the private sector by endorsing principles of fairness, involvement and equity in its treatment of its workforce, as discussed in the Priestley Report (1955). These principles were associated with the encouragement of trade union membership, support for centralised systems of collective bargaining and other forms of workforce participation. The main outcomes were relatively consensual employment relations and high levels of job security. Fredman and Morris (1989) acknowledge in their discussion that the model employer tradition was punctuated by pockets of low pay. Nonetheless, they suggested that Conservative governments departed radically from that tradition during the 1980s. This set in train a process of radical change marked by the adoption of private sector management practices, more equivocal support for trade unionism and the erosion of security in public sector employment.

In 1980, the high levels of job security that reflected the model employer tradition were underpinned by the growth in public sector employment. In health, the workforce increased from 522,000 in 1948 to 1.3 million in 1979, and this was accompanied by a surge in union density from 38 per cent in 1968 to 74 per cent in 1979. Local government and education employment also rose sharply from 1.2 million in 1948 to 2.9 million by 1979 (Bain and Price, 1983: 12–13). The immediate post-war period witnessed the nationalisation of the 'commanding heights' of the economy with gas, water, electricity, coal, steel, railways and telecommunications taken into state control, alongside a series of state-owned corporations, of which the most prominent were British Airways and Rolls-Royce.

The model employer concept was based on the assumption that employee participation should be underpinned by trade union membership and collective bargaining to foster co-operation and minimise industrial action. Joint committees between employer and employee representatives became the basis for national negotiating machinery, with extensive arbitration and consultation machinery to resolve disputes. These principles encouraged high levels of trade union membership, recognition and collective bargaining coverage, but also a complex

Table 13.1 *Employee representation*

	Public sector					Private sector				
	1980	1984	1990	1998	2004	1980	1984	1990	1998	2004
Workplaces with union members	99	100	98	97	97	64	57	47	35	36
Employees that are union members[a]	84	81	72	58	57	57	45	36	25	20
Workplaces with at least one recognised union	94	99	87	87	87	50	48	38	24	22
Workplaces with multiple recognised unions	–	–	75	45	51	–	–	16	8	6
Employees covered by collective bargaining	–	95	78	67	78	–	52	41	32	25
Workplaces with an on-site union representative	77	83	64	52	56	38	38	26	16	13

Note: [a] Figures for 1980 relate to full-time employees only.
Source: WIRS/WERS data. Workplaces with 25 or more employees.

pattern of multi-unionism (Table 13.1). Union presence in the public sector was virtually 100 per cent in 1980 and public sector union density was 84 per cent. In 1980, 94 per cent of public sector establishments recognised at least one trade union, compared to 50 per cent in the private sector. There was also a well-developed system of workplace union representation. There was a close correspondence between union recognition and collective bargaining coverage with 95 per cent of employees covered by a collective agreement in 1984. Although many of these assumptions about what constituted good employment relations were challenged from the 1980s onwards, public sector managerial attitudes towards union recognition have remained more supportive of trade unions than in the private sector.

Centralised and rather cumbersome bargaining arrangements were regarded as promoting orderly employment relations and ensuring adequate recruitment, retention and mobility. The emphasis on comparability criteria in pay determination also served to sustain relatively stable pay relationships (Winchester, 1983: 162–3). The increasing strife of the 1970s, however, highlighted the shortcomings of rigid national agreements. These required ministerial approval for the most minor variation in terms and conditions of employment, and did little to encourage greater efficiency at local level (Heald, 1983: 220). With hindsight, we can see that the first signs of a shift towards a more enterprise level of collective bargaining were emerging. To address productivity concerns and low pay, incentive bonus schemes were introduced for manual employees from the late 1960s. These required workplace managerial and workforce representatives to negotiate and monitor implementation (Howell, 2005: 122). This provided a key stimulus for the growth of shop steward organisation in public services, often sponsored by employers, which resulted in substantial coverage of shop steward organisation by 1980 (Terry, 1983: 79–81).

In 1980, it was the growth, complexity and militant character of public sector trade unionism that attracted most comment. An important dimension of unionisation was its multi-union character, with 72 per cent of those public sector establishments that recognised non-manual unions granting recognition to two or more such unions (the equivalent figure for manual unions was 45 per cent) (Millward and Stevens, 1986: 72, 74). In general, multi-unionism engenders complex bargaining and representation arrangements, and is frequently viewed by employers as impeding workforce flexibility. Multi-unionism reflected the occupational diversity of the public sector, and the unusually high proportion of professional workers and managers who were trade union members. These membership patterns had traditionally imbued public sector trade unions with a professional ideology that frequently precluded strike action. During the 1970s, however, repeated government attempts to bear down on wage inflation led to the radicalisation of public sector trade unions. In contrast to the private sector, it was strike action amongst non-manual workers that accounted for the increase in public sector strike action in the early 1980s (Millward and Stevens, 1986: 266–8).

A consequence of the distinctive model of public sector employment relations was that the development of the personnel function was slow and uneven. Public services developed as coalitions of separate professional hierarchies, each with its own set of values shaped by a lengthy training process and regulatory structures which established national occupational labour markets. The development of the personnel function was therefore stifled by traditions of self-regulation in other professions. Moreover, the development of standardised employment procedures assigned an essentially routine and administrative role to the personnel function, not least because there was little scope for local

Table 13.2 *Responsibilities of workplace personnel managers*

	Public sector					Private sector				
	1980	1984	1990	1998	2004	1980	1984	1990	1998	2004
Workplace has personnel specialist[a]	13	12	14	19	24	16	17	18	24	33
Person primarily responsible for personnel issues has responsibility for										
Pay and conditions	29	43	36	59	60	76	82	86	83	88
Recruitment and selection	92	88	93	94	95	90	90	91	91	92
Training	91	89	90	93	91	76	80	77	83	86
Systems of payment	63	69	73	61	–	18	23	24	41	–
Staffing or manpower planning	–	89	84	85	86	–	79	83	95	90

Note: [a] Workplaces in which the person primarily responsible for personnel issues has the title of personnel manager or employee/industrial/staff relations manager.
Source: WIRS/WERS data. Workplaces with 25 or more employees in which the respondent was interviewed at the sampled workplace.

interpretation of national agreements, whilst assertive trade unions were primarily oriented to national level developments. Reorganisations in local government and the health service in the 1970s stimulated the emergence of personnel officers, but still few public services workplaces employed on-site specialists as the public sector entered the 1980s (Table 13.2).

By 1980, there was a deep sense of unease about the state of public sector employment relations, rooted in the severe economic problems that confronted the country. Few commentators predicted the intensity of reform that cumulatively refashioned public sector employment relations over the next twenty-five years. Although Mrs Thatcher's Conservative administration had been elected on a manifesto committed to curbing public expenditure and the monopoly power of public sector trade unions, the government was cautious in reforming the public sector until the mid-1980s. In 1980, there was surprisingly little appetite amongst employers or trade unions for radical change in pay determination arrangements, despite some unexceptional moves to increase flexibility within national agreements. There were rudimentary signs of a more decentralised system of employment relations emerging, but this would require a significant boost to the capacity and authority of managers at local level, and the catalyst of organisational restructuring and altered funding regimes to stimulate managerial reforms of employment relations.

Restructuring of the public sector

At the heart of the reforms of public sector employment relations have been unprecedented organisational changes that have reduced its size and narrowed the scope of the sector. Looking back over the last twenty-five years, the contraction of the public sector is clearly visible. In 1981, 29% of all employees worked in the public sector, and this fell sharply during the 1980s and continued to decline, reaching a low point of 19.2% in 1999 (Hicks et al., 2005; Pearson, 1994). At the end of the 1990s the Labour government started to increase public expenditure substantially and this resulted in an increase in public employment after 1999, reaching just over 20% of the workforce in 2005 (Hicks et al., 2005). According to WERS, using a slightly different population base restricted to workplaces with twenty-five or more employees, around one-third (32%) of workplaces and 36% of employment was located in the public sector in 1980. After some expansion in the early 1980s, the size of the public sector declined thereafter, so that by 2004 it accounted for 22% of workplaces and 28% of employees. This decline has been less marked than the decline in manufacturing industry, and does not of itself merit the label transformation, but these aggregate trends tell us little about the underlying dynamics of employment relations in the sector.

Equally importantly, the WIRS/WERS series, using ownership criteria to distinguish between the public and the private sector, only imperfectly captures the complexities surrounding changes in regulation and control of the sector. While WIRS/WERS does identify recently privatised workplaces, it does not code separately those private companies which operate largely under contract to the public services. There has been a marked increase in public services provided wholly or partially by private firms, which have extended beyond traditional service functions (cleaning, catering, transport) to encompass, amongst others, independent sector treatment centres in the National Health Service, and private prisons. Private sector providers have frequently been castigated by trade unions as poor employers (Bach and Givan, 2005), but these providers are also subject to public sector systems of employment regulation. There is little systematic evidence on the employment practices of these private sector providers and, more generally, there is a degree of ambiguity in seeking to delineate the boundaries of public sector employment regulation which no longer corresponds precisely to ownership patterns.

Privatisation

From the mid-1980s, a far-reaching programme of privatisation led to most nationalised industries and public utilities covering gas, water, electricity, steel, coal and many parts of the transport sector (including the railways) being privatised. As Millward and Stevens (1986: 31, 78–9, 98–9) noted, the nationalised industries had the highest proportion of workers covered by a closed shop in any industry and virtually 100 per cent coverage of collective bargaining. One major attraction of privatisation for the Conservative government was the opportunity it presented to undermine entrenched trade union power. This goal was in the main achieved, although privatisation alone did not invariably promote convergence with private sector styles of employment relations. For example, the privatised energy and water supply industry retained 68 per cent union density in 1998, compared with 26 per cent across the private sector (Millward et al., 2000: 87–8).

Privatisation had a substantial impact, however, when in combination with liberalisation, deregulation and technological change. Collective bargaining remained the dominant form of pay determination in privatised companies, but it became more decentralised, and widespread enterprise restructuring was reflected in more disparate bargaining structures. The ability of trade unions to mobilise their members diminished, and senior-and middle-management grades were often excluded from collective bargaining. Senior managers emulated the economy-wide trend to increase direct communication, and in some cases (such as in water supply) adopted partnership agreements, whilst in others (such as British Airways) developed more abrasive styles of management designed to marginalise trade unions (Pendleton, 1997b).

Marketisation and outsourcing

Within the remaining public services, successive governments promoted the diffusion of market mechanisms using policies of compulsory competitive tendering in the health and local government sectors. In the civil service, the policy of market testing increasingly excluded in-house bids, ensuring that a higher proportion of work was contracted out. By 1990,

Table 13.3 *Sub-contracting of services*

	Public sector			Private sector		
	1990	1998	2004	1990	1998	2004
Workplaces that sub-contract						
Cleaning	32	53	56	48	62	64
Security	7	25	26	29	40	40
Catering	20	45	42	17	19	17
Building maintenance	30	59	62	57	62	64
Printing/photocopying	6	12	12	25	22	16
Payroll	3	22	35	11	15	23
Transport of documents	12	25	20	40	45	38
Workplaces sub-contracting any of these services	58	87	85	86	88	89
Workplaces that have brought any of these services back in-house in last five years	–	–	11	–	–	10

Source: WIRS/WERS data. Workplaces with 25 or more employees.

98 per cent of central government workplaces outsourced some services, a higher figure than for any other sector in the economy (Millward *et al.*, 1992: 346), indicating that the gap between public and private sector practice is smaller than is frequently assumed. There is a clear trend towards marketisation between 1990 and 2004, but this mostly occurred in the 1990s and the process has started to stabilise since 1998, as it has in the private sector (Table 13.3). There has also been a shift in the type of services being outsourced, which in the 1980s and 1990s focused on manual services (Ascher, 1987; Foster and Scott, 1998). More recently, attention has been directed at white-collar 'back-office' functions and, as Table 13.3 indicates, since 1998 the proportion of public sector workplaces that outsourced payroll has risen to a higher level than in the private sector.

The modest counter-trend towards increased in-house provision has been neglected in recent analysis of public sector employment relations. For much of the 1980s and 1990s increased managerial responsibility for employment relations was frequently combined with tight central directives promoting outsourcing. But this shift indicates that, by 2004, managers were granted more authority to decide whether they wished services to be provided on an in-house or outsourced basis. The attraction of outsourcing as a source of cost savings is receding, especially amongst services with a longer history of outsourcing. Managers' responses often suggested that in-house services provided cost savings (Kersley *et al.*, 2006: 107). In the public sector, this reason was cited by 49 per cent of those public sector managers in workplaces where services had been recently brought back in-house. This suggests that the high-water mark of privatisation may have passed. Back in 1990, 5 per cent of public sector managers specifically cited subcontracting as a reason for workforce reductions (Millward *et al.*, 1992: 323). Contracting out was therefore an important catalyst for workplace change in highly unionised environments. Public sector unions were least effective in resisting contracting out in the most highly unionised workplaces (Millward *et al.*, 1992: 342). The outcome was substantial employment reductions and worsening terms and conditions of employment, especially prior to the application of TUPE regulations (Foster and Scott, 1998). Consequently, by 2004, employers faced fewer constraints when reshaping the workforce to enhance flexibility and achieve cost savings in house. This is reflected in the fact that only 5 per cent of managers mentioned union pressure as a reason to return services in-house, despite union opposition remaining high.

Finally, within the remaining public services there has been a fragmentation of the sector. This was intended to ensure more agile, business-focused organisational units, exemplified by the establishment of civil service agencies, NHS trusts and grant-maintained (subsequently academy) schools. These reforms have led to a small reduction in both the size of public sector workplaces and the number of employees. In 1980, within the WERS population of workplaces with twenty-five or more employees, 29 per cent of workplaces in the public sector employed 100 or more employees, compared with 23 per cent in 2004 – in the private sector the proportion remained approximately unchanged at around 22 per cent. The size and degree of political and financial control differs markedly between these organisations, a fact that has implications for the capacity of local managers to shape their HR agenda. Many organisational units were reconstituted as employers. Increased managerial responsibility was assigned in order to establish pay and conditions on a more decentralised basis. The degree to which increased managerial responsibility has been translated into increased managerial authority for decision making has been at the core of debates about the degree of transformation in public sector employment relations, and about how far there has been a recalibration of the balance between centralised and decentralised decision making.

The decentralisation of employment relations: a management revolution?

It is not surprising that, as policy makers have looked to private sector 'best practice', increased emphasis has been placed on emulating its more enterprise-based systems of human resource management. Successive governments have encouraged closer alignment between HR policy and local managerial needs in order to foster more flexibility and enhance efficiency. In conjunction with organisational restructuring, a core component of the transformation thesis has been an assumption that the emergence of a 'new public management' has strengthened both managerial influence and managerial discretion in employment matters. It is assumed that this has reduced the emphasis on joint regulation with trade unions. This agenda could be expected to bolster the presence of employment relations specialists at workplace level, to enhance their responsibilities and to increase the amount of time they spend on employment relations matters. Countering this, it has been pointed out that increased responsibility for human resources cannot necessarily be equated with increased decision-making autonomy (Kersley *et al.*, 2006: 54–8).

Policy pronouncements emphasising decentralisation have not always been translated into increased managerial autonomy. This is especially important in relation to what we shall show has been the dramatic increase in the percentage of workplaces where local managers are responsible for pay and conditions. Between 1980 and 2004, the proportion of public sector workplaces with specialist HR managers increased from 13 to 24 per cent. But, reflecting the greater intensity of reform in the post-Thatcher years, this whole increase occurred after 1990 (Table 13.2). For some activities, even in 1980, workplace managers were largely responsible. Over 90 per cent of managers are responsible for recruitment and selection, a figure that has scarcely altered since 1980 (Table 13.2). What has changed in the intervening quarter of a century is that recruitment and selection and other areas of human resources policy have come to be viewed by employers as more strategic rather than solely operational matters. Consequently, increased decentralisation has been accompanied by tighter systems of central monitoring. Public sector managers are frequently required to consult higher level managers on a range of human resource issues, and this is reinforced by the presence of a human resource function at a higher level in the organisation (Kersley *et al.*, 2006: 54–8). On all human resource issues, local public sector managers are required to follow policies set by managers elsewhere in the organisation far more often than their private sector counterparts. Not surprisingly, local managers in public and private sector organisations have to follow organisational policy on issues such as pensions and holiday entitlement, but it is in relation to pay, working hours, recruitment and union recognition that local public sector managers have much less autonomy.

Employee representation and union organisation

The trend towards organisational decentralisation could also be expected to impact on employee representation because public sector trade unions have traditionally been organised on a centralised basis. It has been the traditions of collectivism, exemplified by higher union density and much greater coverage of collective bargaining, which marked out employment relations in the public sector as different from employment relations in the private sector. Contrary, however, to the expectations of those associated with the transformation thesis and its assumption of convergence, the gap between public and private sector in this respect has widened since 1980. Trade unions retain a strong presence in the public sector. Since 1980, the number of public sector workplaces with union members has remained almost universal, compared to a decline from around two-thirds to one-third of workplaces in the private sector (Table 13.1).

The fact that union density is three times greater in the public than the private sector is often used as the benchmark to indicate the relatively robust state of trade unionism in the public sector. Managerial attitudes do remain far more receptive to trade union involvement than in the private sector. Nonetheless, if attention is focused on the trend over the last twenty-five years, there are some indications that a process of transition is underway. Public sector trade unions cannot be complacent about their future. In particular, although trade unions as institutions retain a strong presence in the public sector, exemplified by high levels of union recognition, public sector trade union density has declined from 84% in 1980 to 57% in 2004. This aggregate picture disguises important differences between manual and non-manual workers, with trade union membership more prevalent amongst professional workers (Grainger and Crowther, 2007). It also hides variations between sub-sectors. WERS indicates that, in public administration and education, despite some decline, two-thirds of employees remain union members. In health, the sub-sector with the lowest density, there has been continuous decline between 1980 and 2004 from 85% to 48% union density. This sharp decline raises important questions about the effectiveness of trade union organisation.

There has also been a decline in the presence of workplace representatives between 1980 and 1998, although there was a small increase by 2004, in contrast to the private sector, which experienced continuous decline (Table 13.1). The complex process of pay reform in the public sector, undertaken on a social partnership basis, has encouraged some increase in workplace union representatives, although a degree of fragility remains in terms of workplace union organisation (Bach and Givan, 2008; Stuart and Martínez Lucio, 2000).

As with union membership, data on recognition also indicate substantial differences between the public and private sectors. They underline the reliance of the national union movement on its public sector presence. In 2004, the proportion of public sector workplaces which had at least one union recognised was 87%, which has altered little since 1980 (94%). In contrast, there has been a sharp decline in the private sector from 50% in 1980 to 22% in 2004. Collective bargaining coverage declined in the public sector from 95% coverage in 1984 to 78% in 2004 (Table 13.1). However, one reason was the growth of pay review bodies, which have traditionally not been considered a form of collective bargaining in the primary analysis of WERS. The decline is still modest when compared with the private sector, where bargaining coverage halved from 52% to 25% over the same period (Table 13.1).

The public sector experience of industrial action is in sharp contrast with that for the private sector. High levels of union organisation and collective bargaining coverage have traditionally been viewed as prerequisites for effective industrial action. It is well known that levels of industrial action have declined massively in the private sector since 1980. This trend was partially mirrored in the public sector, with 38% of workplaces reporting some form of industrial action in 1984, but with the proportion declining to 5% of workplaces by 1998. The underlying causes were in part the process of privatisation and marketisation described earlier. Since 1998, however, compared to stability in the private sector, there has been a substantial increase in public sector industrial action. In 2004, 14% of workplaces reported industrial action, three times the level of 1998. Official figures indicate that in recent years the public sector has become dominant in terms of the number of stoppages and the number of working days lost. A few very large national disputes in the public sector, especially in the civil service and local government, dominate the statistics. In 2006, 83% of working days lost arose from eighteen stoppages in public administration, indicating that collective labour disputes are becoming almost an exclusively public sector phenomenon (Hale, 2007).

Although public sector trade union density has declined since 1980, there has been relative stability in trade union recognition and collective bargaining coverage, and managers have continued to be supportive of negotiating and consulting with unions rather than directly with individual employees. The comparative strength of union presence is confirmed by the degree to which the public sector increasingly dominates the statistics on collective disputes. Although substantial changes have occurred in public sector unions, the gap with the private sector has widened, not narrowed, over the last quarter of a century. Public sector trade unions retain a strong presence.

Pay determination

The question of pay determination has aroused most controversy in terms of the shifting balance between centralisation and decentralisation. From the late 1980s, public sector managers were assigned greater responsibility for financial control and they questioned the relevance of prescriptive national arrangements. Organisational restructuring and more interaction with a variety of private sector partners added further weight to the arguments in favour of more decentralised systems of pay determination. The increased responsibility of workplace personnel specialists for pay and conditions was linked to the devolution of responsibility to managers as part of the fragmentation and marketisation of public services during the 1990s.

There was a dramatic increase from 36 per cent in 1990 to 59 per cent in 1998 in the proportion of public sector employee relations managers who were responsible for pay and conditions, before stabilising at 60 per cent in 2004. Despite the increase, this figure remained substantially lower than the private sector (Table 13.2). Significant reform in the 1990s gave way to less fervent support for decentralisation in recent years, and by 2004 in some parts of the sector a process of recentralisation is evident with a decline in the proportion of managers responsible for pay and conditions. In education, after a sharp rise from a quarter to almost three-quarters during the 1990s, by 2004 only just over half of employee relations managers had responsibility for pay and conditions. In health, the decline commenced earlier, and there has been a steady decline from almost 85 per cent (1990) to just under two-thirds in 2004. In public administration, the pattern is of a steady increase from just under half in 1990 to almost 60 per cent in 2004.

These trends indicate that there has been differentiation in the pattern of change. This has taken place within a broad government framework for public sector pay determination which has encouraged a shift away from a universal public sector model of pay determination. The reform of pay determination arrangements has been more comprehensive in public administration, mainly because government ministers have been able to exercise more direct control over the civil service than in other parts of the public sector. Following the creation of semi-autonomous executive agencies, the Treasury delegated its direct responsibility for negotiating pay and conditions to individual departments and agencies. This was followed in 1996 by the abolition of civil service-wide pay, and executive agencies established their own pay and grading structures. In health, at the start of the 1990s, the establishment of nominally independent NHS trusts, competing against each other for revenue in the 'internal market', raised expectations amongst managers of a much more extensive devolution of pay bargaining. These expectations were not realised, however, because of ambivalent signals from government which discouraged innovation in a context in which managers anticipated strong staff opposition to local pay (Bach and Winchester, 1994). In education, the creation of grant-maintained schools also shifted responsibility for pay and conditions from the local authority to the school level, but this occurred at a time when the pay review body for teachers was established, inhibiting school level discretion (Bach and Winchester, 2003).

As this discussion indicates, formal responsibility for pay and conditions does not always translate into local managerial authority over decision making for workplace pay and conditions. Indeed, in 2004, 92 per cent of local public sector managers had to follow policy on pay rates set elsewhere in the organisation, compared to just under two-thirds (64 per cent) in the private sector. Progress towards decentralised pay determination in the 1980s and 1990s was not as rapid as government rhetoric implied. Single-employer bargaining, an indicator of the degree of managerial autonomy, increased slowly during the 1980s and 1990s and declined after 1998 (Table 13.4). Despite multi-employer bargaining halving between 1984 and 1998, partly because of the growth of independent pay review bodies, it remains the dominant approach to pay determination in the public sector, covering half of all public sector workplaces in 2004.

Alongside the uneven progress towards decentralised pay determination, the system of independent pay review has become more important over the last quarter of a century, a process that has no equivalent in the private sector (excluding the minimum wage). The system of independent pay review was extended to nearly one million nurses and teachers in 1983 and 1991 respectively and in 2001 the Prison Service Pay Review Body was established. Independent pay review bodies make recommendations to government, mainly on pay, but also on other matters such

Table 13.4 *Locus of decision making within main type of pay determination in the public sector, 1984 to 2004*

	1984	1990	1998	2004
Collective bargaining	94	71	64	71
Most distant level of negotiations				
Multi-employer bargaining	82	58	40	50
Multi-site, single employer bargaining	11	12	18	15
Workplace bargaining	*	*	1	1
Don't know	1	1	5	4
Not collective bargaining	6	29	36	29
Most distant level of decision making				
External to organisation	3	16	29	23
Management at a higher level in organisation	1	6	5	6
Management at workplace level	*	*	2	*
Don't know	*	6	0	0
Weighted base	717	587	508	446
Unweighted base	812	617	579	452

* less than 0.5 per cent but not zero.
Source: WIRS/WERS data. Workplaces with 25 or more employees.

as workload, on an annual basis. The attraction of pay review bodies for governments is that they provide an arm's length way of dealing with sensitive public sector groups, distancing the government from unpopular public sector pay decisions. At the same time, the government retains more influence over the pay-bill than in traditional collective bargaining because it establishes the remit of each review body, and can choose to stage or reject the decisions of each review body. A recent official review also suggests that 'the history of the pay review body system as a whole shows that it is associated with improved employment relations where previously they were poor' (Booth, 2007: ix).

The existence of pay review bodies that make national recommendations has discouraged the decentralisation of pay bargaining, but it has not precluded local managers from exerting some influence over pay and conditions. There is a need to differentiate between centralised control over headline annual pay increases and the increased discretion of local managers, such as head teachers, over the actual pay and conditions of staff. This can be illustrated in the case of education, where the pay review body has delegated increasing levels of responsibility to head teachers to reduce the workload of teachers, to assess and award merit payments, and enhanced flexibility to decide on the grade of staff within national structures. For occupational groups such as teaching assistants with no national agreement, head teachers can shape pay and working practices to suit local requirements (Bach *et al.*, 2006).

The election of the Labour government in 1997 has been associated with a reassertion of centralised systems of pay determination and less official support for pay devolution, symbolised by the extension of the independent pay review system. Although the legacy of different patterns of reform in each sub-sector remains in place, the Labour government has attempted to develop more integrated and coherent systems of pay determination. These developments have been associated with a very significant increase in the use of job evaluation, the presence of which, according to WIRS/WERS, increased from 18 per cent to 44 per cent of public sector workplaces between 1984 and 2004, but remained around 20 per cent in the private sector. The use of job evaluation has been an integral component of the Labour government's modernisation of pay determination, designed to remove sex discrimination and ensure equal pay for work of equal value. In contrast to Conservative government emphasis on decentralised pay determination, the post-1997 Labour government has implemented reforms to pay determination which establish a national framework with some scope for local managerial flexibility. In local government, the stimulus of the 1997 'single status' agreement established a national framework, with each local authority seeking local agreement on a grading structure covering all staff, to address equal pay issues.

In health, these developments signal a sharper break with the early 1990s policy of trust autonomy. A more centralised national pay framework has emerged, arising from the Agenda for Change pay reforms, which established new pay structures, based on an NHS-wide job evaluation scheme. Because pay reforms such as Agenda for Change in the NHS have been agreed nationally with trade unions, and because managers were required to implement pay reform according to a national timetable, these managers not surprisingly perceived in WERS 2004 that they had diminished responsibility for pay determination. These agreements, however, do not mark a return to the prescriptive national agreements of the 1970s because they are framework agreements, such as in the universities, allowing some discretion for managers to shape implementation to fit local circumstances. Overall, there has been some rebalancing of the degree of centralisation and decentralisation since the election of the Labour government in 1997, but this does not signal a return to the status quo ante.

Examining the whole WERS quarter century, these uneven patterns of change signal transition rather than transformation in the process of pay determination. These trends can be attributed to the political and economic consequences associated with the size and prominence of the public sector pay-bill that places constraints on public sector managers. All governments have confronted potentially conflicting objectives: they seek to improve service standards by investing in the workforce whilst being mindful of the need for tight control of the public sector pay-bill. This has frequently resulted in inconsistent government policy, oscillating between the Treasury's determination to sustain centralised financial control and the exhortation of government ministers who support more devolved pay determination. In addition, the implementation of pay reform has been hindered by insufficient financial and human resource management to ensure effective implementation. This has been most apparent in local government, for which central government has provided insufficient funding to meet the cost of moving to single-status pay and conditions. Moreover, very few individual public sector workplaces are independent, but form part of a larger organisation which shapes pay determination decisions. Widespread reorganisation and decentralisation has also been accompanied by more intensive systems of performance monitoring. These place constraints on local management decision making (Givan, 2005).

Human resource practice

The dominant feature of the employment relations landscape over the last quarter of a century has been the emergence and diffusion of human resource management policies which have signalled a distancing from the collectivist traditions and centralised practices that had been integral to public sector employment relations. These shifts in policy indicate less emphasis being placed by policy makers on values of predictability and stability. Instead, there is a much greater focus on raising the efficiency of the public sector and its workforce, which we term a performance orientation. The utilisation of policies of performance appraisal and pay, the training and involvement of the workforce and the flexible deployment of staff all signal the extent to which HR policies are primarily performance-focused. A second strand, associated with the model employer legacy, may also foster improved performance, but is more oriented towards ensuring procedural justice and employee welfare. It is associated with grievance and disciplinary procedures and various work–life balance practices.

Performance-oriented practices

In contrast to the inconsistent patterns of change associated with pay determination, there has been a more clear-cut trend towards an increasing use of performance-oriented practices over the last two

Table 13.5 *Employment practices*

	Public sector				Private sector			
	1984	1990	1998	2004	1984	1990	1998	2004
Performance appraisals for non-managerial employees	–	68	79	88	–	80	70	81
Off-the-job training for some experienced employees in the largest non-managerial occupation	–	–	95	99	–	–	77	88
Briefing groups	46	62	61	77	31	42	49	70
Problem-solving groups	–	45	49	36	–	30	39	28
Systematic use of the management chain for communication	69	66	73	83	58	58	54	71
Newsletters	41	52	64	66	30	37	44	56
Suggestion schemes	31	31	38	33	22	26	30	36
Provides information about								
Investment plans	18	33	62	58	32	44	49	46
Establishment's financial position	52	70	79	80	56	56	60	58
Organisation's financial position[a]	56	58	63	58	64	63	63	60
Staffing plans	85	79	82	83	57	52	52	61

Note: [a] Workplaces that belonged to a larger organisation.
Source: WIRS/WERS data. Workplaces with 25 or more employees.

decades (Table 13.5). The increase in the use of these practices is evident in the case of performance appraisal, where, even by the mid-1980s, there was little tradition of appraisal in the public services, reflecting the self-regulatory ethos of professional staff (Long, 1986: 7). This position has altered markedly with the introduction of performance appraisal across the sector. This was initially controversial amongst occupations such as teachers, because it was viewed as a means to reinforce government priorities and erode professional autonomy (Healy, 1997). It is therefore noteworthy that by 1998 public sector workplaces were more likely to conduct performance appraisals than those in the private sector, and this remained the case in 2004. There is a similar gap in the area of off-the-job training, with almost all public sector workplaces providing off-the-job training for core employees during 2004, compared to 88 per cent of private sector workplaces.

Similar differences emerge in relation to employee involvement. The public sector has consistently communicated and involved its workforce more than the private sector, and has made greater use of methods such as briefing groups and newsletters. The exception relates to the use of suggestion schemes, although the gap in 2004 (36% compared to 33%) is relatively small. One of the largest increases of any practice between 1984 and 2004 (52% to 80%) relates to the provision of information about the establishment's financial position, which is in marked contrast to stability in the private sector (Table 13.5). This trend indicates that organisational restructuring and a more market-type environment has encouraged managers to disseminate financial information, including investment plans, to the workforce.

The use of these performance-oriented practices has been diffused widely across the public sector, but some differences emerge. These variations predominantly relate to education workplaces – the much smaller size of which enables more informal systems of communication and involvement. Overall, public administration has the most dense system of communication and involvement, followed closely by health, with generally a much lower prevalence of these practices in education. For example, in 2004, newsletters were used at 89% of workplaces in public administration and 82% of workplaces in health, but in only 54% of education workplaces.

The public sector typically has more performance-oriented human resource practices than the private sector. The slightly larger size of public sector workplaces and the higher proportion of professional and managerial employees enhances the presence of these practices. It is also important to note that, as in the private sector, the prevalence of one-way forms of communication from management to the workforce are much more widely available than two-way systems of involvement such as problem-solving groups, which encourage more active employee involvement. Nonetheless, these findings are intriguing when we consider the concerns amongst policy makers, who frequently lament the absence of a performance and involvement culture (Le Grand, 2007).

A degree of caution is needed in interpreting these results because they indicate managerial perspectives on the prevalence of performance-oriented practices, rather than providing more objective information about their implementation. These results can be complemented by examining responses from the WERS 2004 employee survey, which provides data on employees' evaluations of the degree to which managers are viewed as open to employee influence. When asked how good managers are at responding to suggestions from employees or workplace representatives, 44% of employees in the private sector rated their managers as 'good' or 'very good' compared to 40% in the public sector. The same gap (41% in the private sector compared to 37% in the public sector) emerged when private sector employees were asked about their satisfaction with their involvement in decision making at their workplace. Overall, these results suggest that although there has been a step change in the presence of performance practices in the public sector, it cannot be assumed this increased prevalence is necessarily translated into an effective high-involvement performance-oriented culture. It may also be the case that the higher proportion of professional staff in the public sector have higher expectations about the appropriate degree of involvement. This interpretation resonates with other research findings that mechanisms for employee voice are often quite hollow (Bach, 2004; McGivern and Ferlie, 2007).

Welfare-oriented practices

The second strand of HR practice relates to welfare-related practices. The model employer tradition has been associated with formal procedures to ensure that disputes and grievances are dealt with fairly, in conjunction with high levels of job security, a variety of equal employment opportunities and universal pension provision. Contrary to the assumption that the model employer tradition was set aside in the 1980s, the main practices associated with the model employer tradition have continued to be present across the public sector (Table 13.6).

Two main trends are evident. First, some practices which were already widely diffused across the public sector in the 1980s remain in place; the key change is that the private sector has emulated the public sector, indicating that the model employer tradition is being diffused more widely across the economy. The private sector has increasingly adopted individual grievance and disciplinary procedures, equal opportunities policies and, to a lesser degree, work–life balance policies. These trends stem partly from the expansion of employment legislation. The main exception relates to practices that have less resonance with HR practice in the private sector, especially collective disputes procedures, which have continued to decline in the private sector, in contrast to practice in the public sector.

A second trend is that, in the public sector, some aspects of the model employer tradition are being adjusted to the altered context of a more market-style environment. Public sector workplaces are now more likely to employ agency staff than the private sector. There has been a

Table 13.6 *Welfare-related practices*

	Public sector					Private sector				
	1980	1984	1990	1998	2004	1980	1984	1990	1998	2004
Collective disputes procedure (where some union members)	56	74	79	84	78	68	76	73	66	56
Individual grievance procedure	84	96	96	99	100	75	84	83	88	95
Disciplinary procedure	83	94	98	98	99	81	88	87	90	97
Job security guarantees	–	–	–	33	34	–	–	–	6	10
Any workforce reductions in past year	44	52	34	33	–	45	35	31	33	–
Methods of workforce reductions										
Natural wastage	–	–	70	68	–	–	–	66	53	–
Redeployment	–	–	46	34	–	–	–	49	30	–
Early retirement/ voluntary redundancies	–	–	46	62	–	–	–	29	26	–
Compulsory redundancies	–	–	4	14	–	–	–	42	32	–
Equal opportunities policy	–	–	–	97	98	–	–	–	60	83
Work–life balance practices (per cent of employees with access)										
Flexitime	–	–	–	38	44	–	–	–	30	35
Job-sharing	–	–	–	29	30	–	–	–	10	14
Homeworking	–	–	–	10	14	–	–	–	9	14
Financial assistance with child care or workplace nursery	–	–	–	7	10	–	–	–	2	5
Occupational pension scheme available to largest non-managerial occupation	–	–	–	93	95	–	–	–	62	67
Extra-statutory sick pay for largest non-managerial occupation	–	–	–	76	71	–	–	–	64	61

Source: WIRS/WERS data. Workplaces with 25 or more employees.

three-fold increase, with 35 per cent of workplaces using agency staff in 2004 compared to 10 per cent in 1980. These trends reflect, in part, increased budgetary uncertainties in the public sector, but also relate to recruitment and retention difficulties, which were very widespread in the later part of the 1990s (Audit Commission, 2002). More recently, recruitment and retention difficulties have eased, and this was reflected in a sharp slowdown in the rate of increase in agency staffing in the period leading up to the 2004 survey. The health sector, however, with its well-publicised shortages of professional staff, such as nurses, continued to be the sub-sector that was most reliant on agency staff.

Although in most of the WERS series there are only small differences in the relative proportion of public and private sector workplaces that have reduced their workforce, differences remain in the manner in which workforce reductions occur. In the public sector a more welfare-oriented approach is adopted, with a greater likelihood that reductions will be made on a voluntary basis, or through policies of redeployment, than on a mandatory basis. In 1998, only 14 per cent of public sector workplaces that made some workforce reductions used compulsory redundancies, compared to 32 per cent in the private sector. Nonetheless, in response to a more uncertain environment, the gap between sectors has reduced and workforce reductions are more likely to be on a mandatory basis in the public sector than in the past (Table 13.6).

Conclusions

Over twenty-five years the WIRS/WERS series has charted the radical changes in private sector employment relations, but there has been considerable uncertainty about the extent to which this process of institutional change has led to a transformation or a more gradual process of transition in the public sector. The process of interpreting these trends has been made more complex because WIRS/WERS uses the workplace as a unit of analysis, which only partially captures the consequences of the centralised systems of employment relations in the sector. In addition, the fragmentation and organisational restructuring of the sector has led to more divergence within the sector. Similar reform principles have been implemented in different ways in each sub-sector, generating more variation in outcomes between health, education and public administration.

The public sector certainly remains a unique employer with distinctive workforce characteristics that relate to occupation, gender, age and job tenure, and to the political and economic context in which the sector is managed. Employee perceptions of the public sector as an employer are shaped by this distinctive but changing context. Public sector employers have responded to the more efficiency-oriented context in which they are required to manage their workforce. They have strengthened their performance-oriented practices, whilst modifying some of their welfare practices. Some features of the model employer tradition have actually been diffused to the private sector by statute or government exhortation. However, there are indications that, despite the retention of many practices associated with the model employer tradition, public employees have substantial concerns about aspects of the employment relationship. This is evident in the increase in industrial action in recent years.

It has been the radical restructuring of the sector since 1980 that can be most closely associated with the transformation thesis. Large-scale privatisation, outsourcing and moves towards a more marketised public service sector have altered industrial relations practice in the sector. There has been a move away from standardised and relatively uniform systems of pay determination across the sector towards more fragmentation and diversity. Local employers at enterprise level have more influence over how they reward and utilise their workforce than twenty-five years ago. Public sector employment practices have also been influenced strongly by the emergence of a new public management which emulates human resource practice in the private sector. There has certainly been a growth of specialist human resource managers and a diffusion of performance-oriented human resource practices alongside an expansion of agency work. A willingness more recently to bring services back in-house also suggests that employers have increased discretion to shape enterprise-level employment practices. Despite these significant changes, the WIRS/WERS series also points to a more evolutionary and uneven process of institutional and managerial change, with a widening gap with practice in the private sector.

The clearest illustration of this process of transition is that, despite some decline in union density, trade union presence remains strong compared to the continuous decline in the private sector. The trade union movement has become increasingly dominated by its membership in the public sector, and collective labour disputes have become an almost exclusively public sector phenomenon. In these circumstances, whilst managers have embraced human resource systems of communication and involvement, public employers remain willing to engage in dialogue with public sector trade unions. A continuing acceptance of collective institutions may reflect the most effective way to work within these constraints (Howell, 2005). However, there is no room for complacency for the trade union movement as, although managerial attitudes towards trade unions remain much more positive than in the private sector, workplace union organisation shows signs of fragility.

There is also evidence of an evolutionary process of transition in relation to pay determination. All governments have been reluctant to delegate responsibility for such a large component of public expenditure to local employers, and the movement towards decentralised pay determination has been uneven and inconsistent. Over the last quarter of a century, central government has also increased its capacity to intervene directly and indirectly by extending the system of independent pay review and increasing the monitoring of practices at the workplace. The extension of the process of independent pay review to groups such as nurses and teachers has the attraction for government of discouraging industrial action and distancing government from direct pay setting. At the same time, the government continues to exert a strong influence over pay outcomes because it can accept, reject or stage the recommendations of the pay review bodies. Alongside these constraints, the growth of job evaluation systems in response to equal pay concerns has placed further controls on local employers. Consequently, the degree of autonomy that public sector managers have been granted rarely matches the formal responsibilities that they have been allocated.

Looking back over the last quarter of a century, there has been a transformation in the landscape of the public sector, and radical changes in its organisation and management. Despite these changes, the public sector remains a distinctive employer reflected in the public sector's attachment to institutions of joint regulation, its coverage of welfare and work–life balance policies and its more uneven implementation of performance-oriented practices. These changes signal a process of transition which has been discomforting for the workforce, but these human resource changes do not amount to substantial convergence with the private sector, or a transformation of the public sector model of industrial relations.

14 Legal regulation and the changing workplace

Linda Dickens and Mark Hall

Introduction

No account of the evolution of employment relations over the past twenty-five years can ignore the law. This chapter tells the story of the development of legal regulation in that period. We outline and discuss the dramatic changes that occurred in both the extent and nature of legal regulation. We identify what has driven these changes, and comment on whether and how legal regulation may have shaped the workplace developments analysed in earlier chapters.[1]

Legal regulation of employment relations is today centre stage in a way that would have been thought most unlikely at the time the first Workplace Industrial Relations Survey was being planned. In contrast to the position at the end of the 1970s, legal regulation plays a major role within a context of considerably weakened collective regulation. Protection at work now rests less on collective organisation than on individual legal rights, the number of which has expanded considerably. For some, 'British labour law has reached the stage where it can be said that we now have a comprehensive labour code', albeit one concerned primarily with minimum standards (Ewing, 2003:150).

Today, the policy of relative legal abstention – according primacy to, and support for, regulation through collective bargaining – which characterised the British voluntarist system, is dead and buried. Public policy no longer gives primacy to collective bargaining. Protection at work increasingly rests on individual statutory rights. Management policy is increasingly shaped and informed by law, and legal norms and values permeate industrial relations practice – a process termed the 'juridification' of employment relations. It is not simply a question of there being 'more law' twenty-five years on. The nature and scope of legal regulation has also shifted decisively, going to the heart of the employment relationship and providing more universal coverage.

---

[1] This chapter draws on the authors' earlier work (Dickens and Hall, 1995; 2003; 2005 and 2006), which provides more detailed references to relevant research.

We explore these developments by first sketching the position up to and around the first WIRS, a period characterised as one of state support for collective bargaining as the primary method of regulating the employment relationship. The twenty-five years that followed are then divided into two periods: 1979 to 1997, and post-1997. The first of these covers Conservative administrations under Thatcher (1979–90) and Major (1990–97), which we characterise as a period of restrictive law, deregulation and refusal to regulate. The second is the period of New Labour, under Tony Blair, characterised as a period of continuing restriction but re-regulation, legislating for fairness and flexibility. As this labelling implies, there are significant differences between these periods in terms of the nature of legal regulation, and its role within broader policy, but there are also continuities.

Up to 1979: supporting collective bargaining, gap-filling protections and attempts at reform

In Britain, for most of the twentieth century, the regulation of the employment relationship by means of collective bargaining between employers and unions was far more important than legal regulation through Acts of Parliament. This 'voluntarism', or 'collective laissez-faire', resting on autonomous self-regulation, was supported by both sides of industry. Unions saw the main role of legislation as preventing hostile intervention by the courts in industrial disputes. Employers were keen to avoid legislation that constrained their freedom to manage. Voluntarism involved a minimal role for legal regulation, permitting the free play of collective forces. Where law intervened, it did so to support and extend collective bargaining.

Legislation was not totally absent. It was necessary in the late nineteenth and early twentieth centuries to legalise trade union activity, notably to provide 'immunity' in order for unions to organise industrial action during disputes with employers, which would otherwise be unlawful under common (judge-made) law. Thus the freedom to take industrial action was embodied not in positive legal rights but in negatively expressed immunities. Outside special wartime provisions, these protected both primary and solidaristic industrial action, and activities such as picketing.

Legislation was used also to encourage and support voluntary collective bargaining through such measures as the provision of optional conciliation and arbitration machinery to assist in dispute settlement. Perceived gaps in the reach of collective bargaining were addressed through regulatory measures governing the terms and conditions of employment for certain groups. These included legally binding minimum wage rates set by wages councils in specified sectors where collective bargaining was underdeveloped (originally intended as a stopgap measure), and the statutory regulation of the working hours of women and young workers. There were also health and safety laws covering various occupations and industries. Such gap-filling, targeted measures were seen as supplementing rather than challenging collective organisation as the main source of worker protection.

The internal affairs of trade unions, such as the arrangements for selecting leaders and disciplining members, were regulated by their own rule-books rather than external legal regulation. The law did not protect freedoms to join or be active in trade unions; employers had freedom to decide whether or not they dealt with unions – either at all or any particular union. Where employers did recognise a union, any agreements reached through collective bargaining were not directly enforceable as contracts. Employers' hiring and firing decisions were not legally constrained. Choice of contractual form (for example, use of non-standard workers), and the setting of working time, pay and other terms and conditions of employment were generally unconstrained by statutory minimum conditions or legislative protections for workers. What protections workers enjoyed came from employer policy, including adherence to the 'good employer' model in the public sector, and/or from organisation in trade unions.

Compared with other industrialised countries, the crucial and distinguishing characteristic of British employment law from 1870 to the 1960s was its limited role, as highlighted in the oft-quoted comment made by a leading academic lawyer in the mid-1950s: 'There is, perhaps, no major country in the world in which the law has played a less significant role in the shaping of industrial relations than in Great Britain and in which today the law and legal profession have less to do with labour relations' (Kahn-Freund, 1954: 44).

By the 1960s, however, legal intervention was increasingly advocated to achieve a range of labour market and industrial relations objectives and to address perceived problems of low productivity, rigidities and inefficiencies in labour utilisation, high levels of (often unofficial) industrial action, abuse of union power and the inflationary consequences of earnings drift. Steps began to be taken which pushed the law beyond supplementing and supporting collective bargaining; for example, provision for compensation to be paid to workers made redundant. This redundancy payments legislation was intended to be an instrument of economic policy to encourage labour mobility.

Despite this growing pressure for the greater legal regulation of industrial relations, particularly strikes, a royal commission, established in 1965, argued against 'destroying the British tradition of keeping industrial relations out of the courts' (Royal Commission on Trade Unions and Employers' Associations, 1968: 47). It saw some further role for protective legislation (notably against unfair dismissal), but its emphasis was on the need to modify and reform collective bargaining, which it advised was to remain the prime regulatory mechanism.

This reaffirmation of voluntarism, however, did not prevent governments from attempting to use the law as an instrument of reform. Both the Labour government's 1969 White Paper *In Place of Strife* and the subsequent Conservative government's Industrial Relations Act 1971 accorded a central role to legal intervention in the reform of industrial relations. The 1971 Act, in particular, represented an ambitious radical attempt at the comprehensive legal regulation of industrial relations. But this controversial and union-opposed Act was short-lived. Although it provided a number of lessons for future attempts to regulate, it was little used, and had little impact on day-to-day industrial relations in most workplaces before its repeal in 1974. Only its statutory protections against unfair dismissal were re-enacted.

The remainder of the 1970s, under the Labour governments of 1974–9, saw further legal enactment, but in a form that could be presented as a return to a modified, supplemented form of voluntarism – although, with hindsight, in parts it represented a significant departure from it. Social regulation through voluntary collective bargaining was supported. The 1971 Act's abandonment of the traditional system of immunities for industrial action was reversed, and various auxiliary measures to support and extend collective bargaining were enacted, including a statutory procedure whereby a union refused recognition for collective bargaining by an employer could seek determination of the issue. A mass of piecemeal legislation in the health and safety area gave way to a more comprehensive system, but this emphasised self-regulation, within a framework of state inspection and enforcement, with safety representatives in unionised workplaces.

A statute in the mid-1970s (Employment Protection Act 1975) restructured much of the institutional framework of the industrial relations and employment law system, providing a statutory basis for the activities of the Advisory, Conciliation and Arbitration Service (Acas), which took over voluntary dispute settlement functions from the government, and establishing the Central Arbitration Committee to carry out statutory functions, including generalising collectively agreed terms of employment.

While all this reaffirmed the primacy of collective bargaining, the 1975 Act also introduced important new individual employment rights and strengthened others. Anti-discrimination legislation enacted in the 1970s furthered this, covering sex and race, and gender pay equality. The previous gap-filling role of the law gave way to a more 'universal' approach and, importantly for what has happened since, there began 'the crucial transition from a statutory floor of rights concerned primarily with the termination of employment to one concerned with the content of the employment relationship' (Davies and Freedland, 1984: 347).

1979–97: restrictive law, deregulation and refusal to regulate

The nature of the employment law reforms introduced by Conservative governments between 1979 and 1997 constituted a decisive shift away from the long-standing public policy view that joint regulation of the employment relationship through collective bargaining was the best method of conducting industrial relations. Restrictive legislation was used to curb union strength and to reduce social regulation. Indirect supports for collective bargaining were removed. The recently expanded scope of individual legal rights to be exercised against employers was curtailed. As employer freedom of action was enhanced, union autonomy was reduced.

The Conservative governments in the 1980s and 1990s made extensive use of the law. They did this with the aim of radically redressing the balance of power between employers and trade unions, the balance between individual liberty and collective interests, and between managerial prerogative and employee rights. In each case, the objective was to tilt the balance towards the first. The legislative agenda was strongly influenced by the government's neo-liberal economic and social objectives, with law being seen as a key instrument in facilitating labour market restructuring. Anti-unionism also provided a political resource for the Conservative Party in general elections.

Legislation was not the only tool used in this quest for a new balance, but it was an important instrument, with a major piece of industrial relations legislation every couple of years. A much greater emphasis was placed on law than in previous periods in the pursuit of government economic and social objectives. Particular fiscal and economic policies (for example, monetarism and reliance on the operation of the 'free market') helped shape the labour law agenda, and law was seen as a key instrument facilitating labour market restructuring. Co-ordination of the labour market through neo-corporatism (involving the CBI and TUC at state level) was not seen to offer a solution in the British context. The 'winter of discontent' – high profile national public sector strikes which heralded the end of the period of Labour government – testified to the failure of the 'social compact' between the government and TUC. Neo-liberalism emerged as a response to the problems of collective bargaining – wage militancy, inflation and poor adaptation to change – which had arisen under previous periods of full employment, exacerbated by growing international competition (Ludlam *et al.*, 2003).

The Conservatives' employment law programme included the dismantling of statutory supports for collective bargaining, including the abolition of the recognition procedure, and the legal restriction of industrial action.[2] Compulsory union membership was eradicated (with a step-by-step dismantling of the closed shop), and non-unionism promoted, with 'rights to disorganise', and an individual rather than functional approach to freedom of association (Lewis and Simpson, 1982). Internal union government, previously largely a matter for the union's rule-book, was to be regulated by statute. Labour law and social security measures that acted to provide a floor to wages were weakened or removed, including the wages councils, in the belief that downward pressure on wages would stimulate employment. Protections afforded by individual employment rights, many of them only recently introduced, were narrowed.[3]

In a comparative European context, even after the increased statutory intervention of the 1970s, the employment relationship was still relatively unregulated by statute law. Nonetheless, statutory rights were argued to be burdening business with additional costs, working to the disadvantage of job creation and entrepreneurship, and hampering labour market (external) flexibility. The few statutory employment rights were reduced and removed in order, it was argued, to promote employment and enhance the flexibility that was seen to be crucial to competitive success (see, for example, DE, 1986; 1989). Deregulation was embraced as a way of freeing employers to take the most effective measures as they

---

[2] Industrial action was restricted by a number of techniques in the 'step by step' legislative programme between 1979 and 1997. These involved removing immunity from certain types of industrial action (including making all secondary action unlawful) and limiting the issues about which industrial action could be lawfully organised. Unions were made liable for unlawful industrial action, posing a threat to union finances. Industrial action required majority support from workers to be lawful, as ascertained through an independently scrutinised postal ballot conforming to increasingly complex and detailed provisions. Social security measures also sought to deter individuals from taking industrial action and employers were able selectively to dismiss strikers.

[3] Tougher qualifying conditions, relating to length of continuous employment and minimum hours, were attached to various statutory rights, depriving many of protection, and changes to substantive law and tribunal procedures made it harder for those who were covered by the legislation to pursue their legal rights, and to succeed, and the available remedies deteriorated.

saw them. The nature of the break with voluntarism is thus seen in the reduction of trade union autonomy, and in the shift away from collective bargaining as the preferred method of regulating the employment relationship. But the desired shift was towards increased scope for the exercise of managerial prerogative. It was emphatically not towards an increased role for legal rules and procedures in shaping the content of the employment relationship.

Perversely, however, this period coincided with growing activity in employment regulation within the European Union, which the United Kingdom had joined in the early 1970s. This activity revolved around a 'social dimension', intended to accompany and facilitate economic integration into the single market. European legal instruments (usually legally binding Directives) were also used as a way of addressing disparities between levels and costs of employment protection legislation in different member states, as a political lubricant for the development of the free trade area. From the 1980s onwards, British legal intervention in the employment relationship reflected not only national concerns, but increasingly also this supra-national influence, which was driven by quite different continental European political ideologies and state legislative traditions.

Key aspects of the industrial relations agenda pursued by the Conservative governments of the 1980s and 1990s – especially the restriction of the freedom to take industrial action, and the statutory regulation of trade union governance – were unaffected by EU requirements. As it happened, they breached other, non-enforceable, international standards, such as those set by the International Labour Organisation, some of which were explicitly abandoned by Britain during this period. But the need to conform to EU law constrained the extent to which the government was able to pursue its deregulatory ambitions. It forced the enactment of some additional legal rights and protections. This occurred, for example, in relation to discrimination and pay equality, acquired rights and health and safety. Where it was forced to legislate to implement EU law, the government usually adopted a minimalist response, often coupled with deregulatory measures.

The government worked hard to block further European legislation, advocating liberalism and deregulation as the way to promote efficiency, employment creation and growth in the European Union rather than collectivism in labour market regulation with corporatist-style arrangements. It made some headway in arguing for an approach that left more scope for independent action by national governments, termed 'subsidiarity'. The British government refused to sign the 1989 Social Charter. In 1991, it negotiated exemption from the social policy provisions of the Maastricht

Treaty on European Union, which provided, among other things, for majority, rather than unanimous, decision making on a range of employment relations areas, fearing that this would further erode Britain's ability to block legislation it opposed.

Soon after attaining office in 1997, the New Labour government ended the Conservatives' so-called opt-out from the Social Chapter in the Maastricht Treaty, and in June 1997 accepted the Social Chapter of the European Union's Treaty of Amsterdam. In signing up to this, the New Labour government demonstrated a radically different attitude to that of its predecessor, and significant aspects of the legislative framework developed since 1997 flowed from this decision.

After 1997: continuing restriction; reregulation for fairness and flexibility

The Labour government elected in May 1997, and re-elected in June 2001 and May 2005, introduced substantial changes to employment relations legislation, affecting not merely the detail but the nature and extent of legal regulation of the employment relationship. The beginnings of juridification of aspects of the individual employment relationship had been discernible in the 1980s, and that period saw a decisive break with the traditional voluntary system. But, at the time of the 1997 election, central elements of British employment relations still remained largely outside the scope of statutory regulation. Crucially, the determination of employees' pay and other terms and conditions, and institutional relations between employers and trade unions or other employee representatives were regulated, if at all, through voluntary agreements.

From 1997, key elements in the Labour government's employment law programme, some of which was shaped by EU requirements, extended legal regulatory norms and statutory structures into these areas. Principally, these are the introduction of a National Minimum Wage (April 1999), legislation regulating working time and leave (from 1998), legislation on trade union recognition (a statutory recognition procedure, effective from 2000) and legislation on information and consultation of employees. Regulation of pay and working time goes to the centre of the employment relationship. Legal rights and statutory structures now help to shape the terrain and nature of workplace representation.

By 2004, Labour had achieved a much more comprehensive role for legislation in setting minimum standards and more 'universal' rights, extending protection to employees in non-unionised employment and to some 'non-standard' workers who might have difficulty establishing employee status. The narrowing of access to rights enforcement that occurred between 1979 and 1997 was reversed, and remedies improved. Further, the emergence of a work–life balance or family–friendly legislative agenda, with some stimulus from EU legislation, meant that the employment relationship was being required to address considerations which in the past might have been seen as external to the workplace, and to the concerns of employment relations.

However, the post-1997 period has not been one simply of re-regulation. The new framework of employment law was an amalgam of competing values, with continuities from the Conservative era of the 1980s and 1990s as well as new values. Important continuities are seen most notably in the continuing restrictive regulation of industrial action, and in legislative requirements relating to internal union affairs. There have been some important changes, but much of the web of complex legal restriction remains, even though the British legislation on the constraint of strikes has been adjudged to fall below the minimum international standards. New Labour sees industrial action very much as a remnant of the past. Secondary action, for example, was described in the government's first White Paper on industrial relations as 'anachronistic'. The Labour government was clear that there was to be no going back. 'The days of strikes without ballots, mass picketing, closed shops and secondary action are over' (DTI, 1998: 3).

The detailed legislative requirements relating to internal union affairs enacted by the Conservative administrations remained in place, as did the rights and protections given to members to be exercised against their trade unions, including the right not to be 'unjustifiably disciplined' by a union for refusing to take part in lawful industrial action. New Labour's 1998 White Paper said that the Conservatives' laws 'for increasing democratic accountability of trade unions' were among those which 'have helped to improve labour relations', and only minimal changes to them were introduced.

There were modest improvements in legal support for union organisation and security, but the extensive protections for non-unionists enacted by Conservative governments remained intact. There was some enhanced protection for trade union members and activists (for example from blacklisting by employers), but no return to compulsory union membership through the closed shop and no rights to organise as such for trade unions. However, the introduction of a statutory recognition procedure in 2000 clearly demarcated the government's approach from its predecessors, although there were no provisions for generalising the outcomes of collective bargaining more widely.

The 1998 White Paper *Fairness at Work*, which heralded the statutory recognition procedure, was described as 'the first major government document since 1981 to recognise and promote instruments of collective industrial relations' (Wedderburn, 1998: 254). Despite this, there was no return to the position of public policy prevailing up to the 1970s which, as noted earlier, had been to encourage and support collective bargaining as the best method of conducting industrial relations. There was some ambiguity in New Labour's attitude towards collective labour rights, and it was not clear that New Labour did see collective bargaining as the best method of conducting employment relations. There was an apparent reluctance to privilege collective bargaining and collective voice over more individualised methods. The New Labour legal framework was consequently one that sat well with the individualisation of employment relations which took place during the 1990s.

While there was no longer the hostility to collective bargaining which characterised its predecessor, there was also no sign from the Labour government of a general commitment to the democratic case for trade unionism and collective bargaining. What emerged instead was an acknowledgment that unions may demonstrate to employers, and employees, that they can add value. Thus, for example, collective representation and employee voice were not presented in terms of workplace democracy and fairness, but rather as fostering partnership (defined as co-operation) to help the business respond to customer and market requirements (DTI, 1998: 12; Wood, 2000: 130). Partnership was seen as a route to competitive success and received state support, including funding to support initiatives, but it tended to refer to enterprise-based partnership and did not necessarily have to involve collective representation. New Labour was reluctant to go for a European model of social partnership resting on representative structures with mechanisms for employee voice at workplace and strategic levels, even opposing EU social policy proposals designed to promote this. Its legislative programme was presented as promoting partnership between employers and employees, not between employers and unions.

New Labour showed a preference for ad hoc, one-off solutions rather than institution building, where it had to address the 'representation gap' in non-union workplaces in order to implement European legal requirements for employer consultation with worker representatives over issues such as redundancy and health and safety. As a result of the ending of the opt-out, Britain was required to implement a directive requiring European works councils in trans-national companies. But it opposed, unsuccessfully, proposals for similar consultation rights in companies at national level. These are now implemented in the Information and Consultation of Employees Regulations, although with provision for employers to fulfil their statutory duties by direct, individual-based, information and consultation and not exclusively through representative mechanisms.

As this suggests, although the post-1997 government was more open to European legislation than its predecessors, its implementation of directives at times has been reluctant and at a minimum level of compliance. This can be seen, for example, in the implementation of the working-time directive, with the inclusion of the ability to opt out of the maximum working week, and in the implementation of directives concerning non-standard employment and family-friendly rights (Barnard *et al.*, 2003; McColgan, 2000). The government takes pride in Britain being described in OECD reviews as being relatively unrestricted in both product and labour markets compared with other European countries, such as France and Germany.

There were tensions, ambiguities and compromises within the post-1997 legislative programme. To some extent, these reflect the different origins – EU as opposed to domestic – of particular pieces of legislation. But they are also the outcome of competing pressures: from employers to limit any burdens imposed by new regulatory requirements, and from trade unions for stronger statutory protections.

There is a marked change from twenty-five years ago, which is, in part, a reflection of increased union weakness. Trade unions, which once wanted nothing from the law other than that it leave them alone, and which opposed earlier proposals for legislative universal minimum standards or legislatively imposed workplace structures, now looked to legal regulation to provide worker protection and, increasingly, as a potential source of union renewal. During the 1980s, the trade unions learnt to live with the law, not only in terms of pragmatic adjustment to the restrictive reform of that period, but through a more fundamental reassessment of the role of law in industrial relations (Dickens, 1989). They accepted that there is a need for the state to do more than just provide a few procedural safeguards for a voluntary system and plug a few gaps. Although there was re-regulation post-1997, and a different balance between worker protection and management freedom was struck, this fell far short of what unions were asking for.

There are echoes of earlier Conservative arguments for deregulation in Labour's expressed concern with avoiding over-burdening employers, and with not hampering employers' flexibility (see, for example, DTI, 1998: para 1.13). The government sought to establish 'for the first time, a comprehensive framework of minimum employment standards', while seeking also to minimise the administrative and cost burden on businesses, and to avoid hampering employers' flexibility, which was seen as contributing to competitiveness (DTI, 2004a).

New Labour considered that an important role for regulation in the pursuit of competitiveness was to provide a skilled, educated and committed workforce that was conducive to 'internal' flexibility. Policy was intended to steer business towards the most efficient practices based on innovation in product and process, rather than depending on the exploitation of low cost labour. Some elements of this approach can be seen in the Labour government's thinking that the provision of minimum standards, such as the National Minimum Wage, could prevent a 'race to the bottom' and direct employers away from the 'low road' to competitiveness. Some legislative change was presented as encouraging 'a high skill, high productivity economy achieved through high performance workplaces, where employers and employees work together in partnership' (DTI, 2002).

The legislative programme was presented as a distinctive New Labour commitment to ensuring 'the fair treatment of employees within a flexible and efficient labour market' (DTI, 1998). Its 'cardinal principle' was that competitiveness could go hand in hand with fairness at work. The Labour government after 1997 made a different assessment to that of its predecessor in its attempt to balance the interests of social justice, curb abusive employer behaviour and provide minimum standards on the one hand, and the desire not to jeopardise entrepreneurship, growth and competitiveness on the other. New Labour's more nuanced approach to economic efficiency in employment regulation recognised the positive potential of the elevation of 'market friendly' labour standards (Davies and Freedland, 2007: 247). The attempt was a synthesis and mutual reinforcement of social goals, concerned with fairness, and economic goals reflecting the priorities of markets. In practice, however, there was a clear priority; fairness was to be pursued not as an end in itself, but to the extent that it was seen to promote competitiveness (Fredman, 2004; Dickens and Hall, 2006). New Labour's desire to be business-friendly exerted a brake on regulation.

Increasingly, the New Labour government required social rights to be legitimised in terms of their contribution to business competitiveness. The Employment Act of 2002, for example, grouped 'family-friendly rights' under 'participation, retention and development of skills', while, in a subsequent government policy statement, discrimination is described as 'economic drag'. Rather than equality being presented as a fundamental right, the 'economic imperative for more diverse workplaces' and the waste of talent caused by discrimination were stressed (DTI, 2004a: 9, 10). It was an approach that could frustrate legislative development as

short-term business interests were weighed against individual employment rights. In rejecting calls for compulsory equal pay audits, for example, the government's consultation paper *Framework for Fairness* asserted
that 'enforced equal pay reviews may... contravene better regulation
principles as the costs to employers may be out of proportion to the scale
of the problem they will address' (DCLG, 2007). Saying it 'would be
bureaucratic, burdensome on employers and costly to run and enforce',
it argued against taking the kind of monitoring and reporting approach
which elsewhere has been shown to be key in achieving desired outcomes
(McCrudden, 2007).

Another example of the importance of business-friendly considerations in New Labour thinking was its response to the steadily increasing employment tribunal case-loads that are described in Chapter 8.
The consequent reform of the tribunal system and increase in the statutory requirements of dispute resolution procedures at the workplace had
the effect of reducing the ease with which workers could access their
rights, again echoing action taken by previous Conservative governments
(Hepple and Morris, 2002).

New Labour's concern to reduce the regulatory burden on businesses
led to a minimal implementation of some European legislation. It was
committed to 'light-touch' regulation and to the use of 'soft law', such
as codes of practice and good practice exemplars, instead of 'hard' regulation through legislation. Light-touch regulation is more concerned
with process than with substantive rights. This was demonstrated, for
example, by the introduction of a statutory right of some parents and
other carers to make a request for flexible working, and to have it considered seriously by their employer. The law specified that the request
could be turned down only on reasoned grounds which were justifiable,
for example, in terms of business needs. This 'right to request' fell short
of a positive substantive right for employees, or a duty on employers,
for example, to set up family-friendly, employee-focused working time
arrangements.

Impact and influence

How have these substantial changes in the use of the law shaped the
evolution of the modern British workplace? Having discussed the development and nature of legal regulation over the twenty-five years, we turn
now to consider how far it is reflected in the changes described in earlier
chapters.

Addressing this question is not a straightforward task. As the sourcebooks for WIRS/WERS have commented, there has usually been

considerable legislative change in the period between surveys, but it has been difficult to attribute direct causal connection with any specific change in industrial relations behaviour. Although governments occasionally may point to surveys as demonstrating a direct impact of their legislative policy, most changes do not have a simple single-factor explanation. Legal innovation during our period was taking place alongside major economic and other changes.

In considering changes revealed by the 1980 and 1984 WIRS, for example, Millward and Stevens (1986) noted that, in addition to changes in legal regulation, there had been a fall in numbers of highly unionised manufacturing plants in 1980s recession, changes in the structure of the economy, a decline in male manual workers, a trend towards smaller workplaces, a rise of service sector employment, the contraction of the public sector, a rise in overseas-owned workplaces and a rise in part-time employment. Some of these changes would have had at least as great an impact as changes in the law. Surveys explore what has happened, but do not always illuminate why. For all their advantages, 'surveys are blunt and inappropriate instruments for understanding the social processes that underlie employer-employee relationships' (Millward *et al.*, 1998:137).

It is necessary to caution against over-estimating the importance of statute law as a cause of change. As Brown *et al.* (1977) observed, 'employment relations tend to change relatively slowly and often in ways independent of the law'. As our account of the legal framework illustrates, statute law operates alongside other aspects of government policy. In considering the 1980 to 1998 surveys, Millward *et al.* (2000) concluded that 'broadly speaking... government policy was an important source of change in employment relations over eighteen years of the Conservative administrations but on only a few specific matters could we clearly isolate it as a principal agent of change'.

In our earlier review of the period, we noted that assessing the impact of the legislative switch to individualist rather than collectivist relations is extremely difficult (Dickens and Hall, 1995). Survey evidence showed a declining proportion of workers covered by collective agreements, declining union membership and a decline in strike activity. There was also evidence of growth in more individualised techniques in managing labour. Our assessment was that legislative change could only be a part of the explanation for these developments, along with structural shifts in industry and labour markets and the inhospitable macroeconomic context, but that it had definitely played a role.

The legal framework between 1979 and 1997 was such that new entrant or greenfield site employers, particularly foreign multinationals, who wished to pursue a non-union strategy could do so, and that unions experienced difficulty in extending collective bargaining into new or traditionally under-organised areas. Alongside more general government hostility to collective bargaining, it legitimated and facilitated some employers' actions in derecognising unions, either completely or, more commonly, on particular sites or in respect of particular categories of staff. It was part of the context within which collective bargaining, where it remained in place, was decentralised and 'domesticated' and the quality or scope of bargaining deteriorated within continuing bargaining structures (Brown and Wadhwani, 1990: 64). A number of companies rolled back shop-floor organisation, with fewer rights and facilities being afforded to fewer shop stewards.

The proportion of establishments where any workers were covered by closed shops dropped from 23 per cent in 1980 to 18 per cent in 1984. Legislative change to this end had been made in the early 1980s, but the abolition of legal supports for compulsory union membership came at a time when the closed shop was declining in importance due to structural shifts (Brown and Wadhwani, 1990: 63). The changing structure of manufacturing employment, analysed in Chapters 2 and 3, provided an important context to the effects of the legislation. But Millward and Stevens concluded that it was 'difficult to argue that the incidence of the closed shop would have undergone such a dramatic decline had the promotion of involuntary union membership not been outlawed' (1986: 231). At a more detailed level, legislative influence could be seen clearly in changes that were made to closed shop agreements to keep up with the statutory exemptions from compulsory union membership, with most them containing 'verbatim quotations from the relevant legislation' (Millward and Stevens, 1986: 108).

The direct role of legislative change in the decline of industrial action is also not clear-cut, since various factors contributed to it, including an economic environment which tipped the balance of power in favour of management, and higher unemployment with associated fears over job security. New statutory provisions were used against unions in high profile, unsuccessful campaigns of industrial action in mining, print and publishing, as was the criminal law in the mining dispute, and this may have provided a demonstration effect. WIRS/WERS in the 1990s suggested that the clearest impact of statute law was on the conduct, rather than the level, of industrial disputes. Some forms of pressure expressly targeted by legal restrictions such as secondary blacking and secondary picketing almost disappeared, and unions became more likely to run formal strike ballots as required by the new legislation.

The experience of the requirement to hold pre-strike ballots is a useful reminder that legal regulation may not always have the intended impact.

By 1990, these ballots had become almost universal. Most have resulted in a vote in favour of industrial action, arguably strengthening the union's negotiating position, which was unlikely to have been the government's expectation when legislating on this issue. In the great majority of positive strike ballots, the dispute was then settled without recourse to industrial action, suggesting that unions frequently treat balloting as part of the negotiation process (Hale, 2007).

More individualist managerial approaches may have been assisted by the removal of positive legal support for unions and collective bargaining, but this is not the same as saying that legislative change caused such developments. What is clear, however, is that from 1979, at a time when sectoral and labour market change heightened the value of positive legal support to aid union organisation, such support was removed. At a time when unions were weakened by recession and declining membership, their economic and organisational security was reduced by legislative change. In a context where some employers were questioning the appropriateness or functional value of collective bargaining, some of the tactics that in the past had been part of the unions' legitimate armoury of persuasion were made unlawful, and non-unionism was increasingly supported by law.

In some cases, the symbolic function of the legislative change may have been as important as the change itself, helping to foster an anti-collectivist culture and emboldening management. This is arguably the case in some areas where tangible direct achievements of new rights were limited. The recognition procedure introduced in the mid-1970s had almost run aground at the time of its repeal in 1979, hampered by restrictive judicial interpretation and other problems, and it is therefore unlikely that its repeal played a direct role in the decline in union membership (Wood, 2000). In a similar vein, the impact of the statutory recognition procedure introduced by the Employment Relations Act 1999, in producing a significant growth in union recognition agreements and a reduction in the extent of de-recognition, appears to rests more on the shadow of law and symbolic effect than on its direct use (Gall, 2004a).

The changed legislative context since 1997 has encouraged voluntary, and pre-emptive, agreements. It has changed some employers' attitudes to trade unions. But, again, there are other related, but also independent, factors at work. These include an increased union emphasis on organising, and the preparedness of some unions to enter into particular partnership arrangements (Oxenbridge et al., 2003). There may also have been some employer recognition of efficiency benefits in recognising unions in order to provide an effective collective voice. Another instance of legislation altering employer attitudes may relate to consultation, discussed in Chapter 5. Although WERS 2004 showed that the then imminent prospect of the Information and Consultation Regulations had not resulted in an upturn in the proportion of workplaces covered by consultative committees, subsequent surveys have suggested considerable employer-led activity in terms of reviewing, modifying and introducing voluntary information and consultation arrangements (Hall, 2006; Hall et al., 2008).

Statutory intervention has encouraged the formalisation of recognition and collective agreements, which are now more often in writing. Research indicates that the content of such agreements, however, is fairly limited in depth and breadth (Moore et al., 2005). This reflects the restricted scope of statutory recognition (relating to collective bargaining over pay, hours and holidays) and provides an illustration of how statutory provisions may at times impose a 'ceiling' rather than act as a floor on which to build.

As reference to the shadow of law and symbolic effects of the legislation relating to trade union recognition implies, the impact of statutory enactment may be indirect and diffuse rather than directly ascertainable. This applies most obviously to behavioural and substantive impacts of legislative intervention. Impact may come gradually by effecting attitudinal change and helping shape the climate of employment relations. Legislation may provide levers, legitimacy and impetus for those wishing to act.

Rather than demonstrate a consequential change in employment practice, it is often easier to establish a more direct link between legal regulation and changes in procedures and espoused policies to comply with legislative requirements, and in the setting up of required institutions. This is the case, for example, in areas such as discipline and dismissal, equality and family-friendly rights. In the area of health and safety, the spread of health and safety committees and representatives can be linked to legislative intervention.

The unfair dismissal legislation introduced in the 1970s, for example, had a clear impact in terms of encouraging procedural growth and development. There has been formalisation and standardisation, with procedures reflecting legal provisions and codes of practice. There has also been generalisation, so that procedures are now almost universal across different employee groups and types of workplaces. The impact of the unfair dismissal legislation on employers has not been to weaken their control over hiring and firing. Indeed, it has served to legitimate it. But, rather, it has tended to foster improvements in managerial efficiency in the handling of job terminations, and the development of good employment practice or more professional personnel policies. This impact was seen quite early on, with greater care being taken over recruitment, and in the development and reform of disciplinary rules and procedures, which remained managerially determined. There were consequential restrictions on the freedom of action of lower-level management and enhanced importance, at least initially, of the personnel function (Dickens *et al.*, 1985: 264–5). Arbitrary hire and fire approaches to discipline were curbed, and due process and corrective procedures instituted, but the law does not go far in challenging managerial prerogative, and has afforded only limited job protection to employees.

Anti-discrimination legislation and statutory measures relating to work–life balance also demonstrate the positive role of statute law in shaping procedures and policies, and in agenda setting for employers and for trade union negotiators. Statutory rights can be seen to have encouraged the development and spread of equal opportunity policies, and shaped their nature and content, although substantive impact in terms of distributional outcomes is less apparent.

Accounting for variation in the impact of the law

Relative lack of impact may reflect weaknesses in the legislation in question, and in its enforcement. The lack of action on equality revealed by WERS 2004, for example, even by organisations with explicit equality policies, reflects the limitations in the approach of the British equality legislation (Dickens, 2007). For the most part, employers in Britain have been required not to discriminate rather than required to take action to tackle inequalities. The 'reasonable adjustment' provision in the disability legislation is a notable exception. The more recent public sector equality duties provide an example of a proactive positive duty approach within Britain's predominantly individualised, fault-based, discrimination legislation. Such approaches have been absent from much British employment legislation, which has limited its impact (Hepple *et al.*, 2000). The lack of attention to pay within many organisations' equal opportunity policies, at a time when aggregate data show continuing gender and racial pay gaps, needs to be seen in the context of the lack of any requirement for employers to undertake equality pay audits.

This links to a broader point about the impact of statute law. The impact can be expected to vary according to what the legislation requires of employers (or other actors), and to the consequences of non-compliance. Compliance may require action from employers only passively, that is, on request, or when challenged by someone claiming an infringement of rights, or it may require employers to take proactive steps. Impact may be individualised, or have collective or structural implications. That is to say, compliance may involve reactive adjustments relating to an individual employee; it may require proactive adaptation and adjustment relating to categories of workers or to organisational structures. Greater impact may be expected from the latter, proactive structural approach. Yet the approach generally adopted for individual employment rights in Britain is passive.

The use of an inspection regime for enforcement of aspects of the National Minimum Wage, which was seen as crucial to its effectiveness, stands in marked contrast to the individualised, passive, private law model characteristic of most of the individual rights legislation (Brown, 2006). Generally, individual workers are left to enforce their legal rights against employers at employment tribunals, with predominantly financial remedies. This regulatory approach places an emphasis upon awareness of rights, and a capacity and willingness to enforce them that is often lacking (Pollert, 2005). Survey research has found that awareness of rights varied by personal and job characteristics, with those relatively advantaged in the labour market – typically white, male, better qualified, white-collar employees in permanent full-time jobs with written employment particulars – being better informed (Meager et al., 2002). Such workers, however, were least likely to report that they had actually experienced violations of their rights. It was also notable that union members were found to be better informed about rights at work than non-members.

Union presence can act as a positive mediator of legislative rights. It affects the capacity to use and to comply with legislation, with unions potentially providing a mechanism for monitoring and enforcement. Union presence can also help translate formal rights into substantive outcomes at the workplace. Research studies of the influence that the growth of individual rights has had on contracts of employment suggest that the extent to which employers comply with their legal obligations depends to a significant extent on the presence of active trade unions (Brown et al., 2000). It should be recalled, in this context, how the WIRS/WERS series clearly documents the decline of active trade union presence at the workplace.

Proactive compliance also requires employer awareness of the duties and rights provided by legislation. Research indicates variability here too, with smaller firms often not aware of their obligations. Blackburn and Hart (2002) found knowledge varied by size of enterprise and business sector. It reflected the perceived relevance and experience of particular rights, rather than the length of time the legislation had been in existence. In summary, it is workers in situations where there is least awareness of employment rights, and least ability to remedy breaches of them, who are in most need of the proactive support that British employment law fails to offer.

Differences in the impact of legislation, and in the degree of resistance it generates, can be expected also according to whether the law is seeking to trail-blaze, on the one hand, or to underpin/generalise existing practice, on the other. Impact also depends on the extent to which legislation is concerned with setting specific, substantive standards, for example on the length of the working week, rather than setting broader objectives which may be met in different ways. Where, as is often the case, legislation reflects norms, the extent of its potential impact depends on the extent to which organisational practice already shows an affinity with the legislative objective.

Regulation interacts with the environment within which it falls to be implemented. We have suggested elsewhere that various external and internal factors mediate the influence of legal regulation on employment practice (Dickens and Hall, 2006). These include: market context; existing or desired competitive strategies, which may, for example, affect the persuasiveness of certain business arguments for compliance; organisation structures; management style and human resource strategies; social relations within the firm; and the presence and role of trade unions. These, rather than, say, the size of the firm per se, may account for perceived and reported differences among employers (see, for example, Edwards and Black, 2004).

Dire effects have been predicted to follow from many legislative proposals for workers' rights and protections, particularly by employers' groups. These predicted impacts have included, for example, job losses as a result of equal pay legislation and the National Minimum Wage, and a reluctance to hire, either in general or in relation to, say, part-time workers, as employees gain individual statutory rights. Such predicted adverse impacts have not been realised in practice. To some extent, this may reflect caution in the legislation as enacted, including business-friendly compromises. However, it also reflects problems with the evidence base upon which such predictions often rest. For example, some of the surveys of employers that are used to support such claims are problematic in terms of the representativeness of samples, and the validity and generalisability of findings (Edwards et al., 2004; Blackburn and Hart 2002). Timing is also an issue. Employer perceptions of adverse impact tend to recede once provisions have had time to bed down and be absorbed into practice (see, for example, Goodman et al., 1998; Edwards et al., 2004).

Conclusion

The voluntarist system is dead. Its underlying philosophy was one of relative legal abstention and of giving primacy to, and support for, the regulation of employment relations through collective bargaining. The changes discussed here, in the extent, nature and role of legal regulation, amount to a growing juridification of employment relations. Juridification varies in the breadth of what it encompasses. Early in the WIRS/WERS quarter century, it was proposed that juridification in the industrial relations context should be assessed by the extent to which 'behaviour on the shop floor determined by reference to agreed principles or to "custom and practice" has been replaced by that based on accepted legal (or what are believed to be legal) principles' (Wedderburn 1986: 857, see also Lewis, 1986). More broadly, it has been suggested that the way in which such principles and custom and practice are modified and informed by an awareness of legal provisions (even if not replaced) should also be seen as an aspect of juridification, with the implication that legal norms will be mediated (Dickens *et al.*, 1989: 252). The extent to which a party will be willing or able to call in aid legal norms, or will wish or be able to resist their importation, will vary with the political and economic context at both macro and workplace level. The implication is that juridification is likely to be experienced unevenly.

What this chapter has demonstrated is that industrial relations in Britain have undergone juridification. Its extent and nature differs between organisations and with respect to different aspects of employment relations. Today statutory minimum standards, legal rules and procedures inform what occurs within workplaces, replacing or reshaping voluntary norms. Legal regulation affects how employment relations are conducted, and how workers are treated. The line between state control and individual employer or union autonomy has shifted towards state intervention. Over the twenty-five year period under consideration in this book, legal regulation has come to play an increasingly influential role in the evolution of the modern British workplace.

15　Conclusion: the evolutionary process

William Brown, Alex Bryson, John Forth
and Keith Whitfield

'Things are the way they are, because they got that way', observed the evolutionary economist Kenneth Boulding.[1] In other words, an understanding of the present requires more than knowledge of regular relationships between phenomena, abstracted from time. Important though these may be, it also needs an awareness of history. For employment relations, in particular, a satisfactory account of the present calls for an analysis of what preceded it. The institutions of employment carry heavy legacies of past traumas, obsolete laws, unrealistic expectations, damaged trust and faded fads. Indeed, given such unavoidable inertia, it is remarkable that the change of the past quarter century in Britain has been as substantial as has been described in this book.

Evolution in the biological world is a process whereby species alter over successive generations in response to environmental change. They either adapt or fade away, dependent upon whether they can achieve incremental comparative advantage through small, inheritable mutations. In the world of employment relations, the metaphorical equivalents of species are the institutions and associated norms, practices and laws that regulate and constrain the employment relationship. The equivalent of inheritable mutations lies in the diversity of these institutions; in the extent to which successful features can be emulated and best practices introduced. The equivalent of environmental change facing workplaces is found primarily in the product, capital and labour markets in which they compete, and in the legal constraints imposed by governments. In this concluding chapter we consider first the broad nature of the institutional and other changes that the workplace has undergone, then suggest what might have initiated those changes and, finally, reflect on the environmental shocks that lie behind it.

---

[1] Quoted by A. Rapoport in Eatwell, J., Milgate, M. and Newman, P. (eds.), *The New Palgrave: A Dictionary of Economics*, vol. 1 (London: Macmillan, 1987), p. 266.

The workplace of the early twenty-first century has changed radically from that of a quarter century earlier. Some aspects of the change explored in this book stand out. The period of the surveys saw, in the private sector, the collapse of collective bargaining, which had been the principal means whereby labour standards had been maintained in the twentieth century. Its pace of decline was even greater than that of trade union membership. For both, changes in the composition of the economy accounted for only a small part of the explanation. What mattered much more were changes in behaviour within sub-sectors – by unions, workers and employers, and especially the last of these. There has been a fundamental shift in attitudes, towards individualism and away from collectivism.

Accompanying the decline of trade unions has been a diminution in their effectiveness for workers and in their influence on employers. Their success in enhancing their members' wages has faded. So also have the constraints they appear to have exercised over employers with regard to employment and the operation of workplaces. In terms of our evolutionary metaphor, wherever unions have become less able to protect, or to bargain improvements for their members, their prospects of survival have been impaired.

There have been important consequences for communications between workers and employers. The decline in the incidence of worker representatives elected through unions has not been compensated in either number or effectiveness by those elected without union affiliation. This does not mean that there has been a commensurate decline in communication between management and workers; four out of five workplaces have some form of 'voice' in this sense. But such voice has become increasingly dependent upon employers. It rarely still relies upon trade unions alone, as was once the case, although the utilisation of the employer's provision is greater where unions are present.

The workers' experience has been mixed. Computer technology has become ubiquitous in shaping the jobs, skills, roles, accountability and independence of workers. The diversity of the workforce has increased substantially, most notably in terms of gender and ethnicity. Some employers have taken positive steps to pursue equal opportunities and to facilitate more family-friendly work patterns. Although legislation has played a part in this, much of it can be attributed to the employers' need to manage an increasingly feminised workforce.

Overt conflict has diminished dramatically. In Britain, as in other countries, there has been a massive and sustained decline in strikes and other collective action, especially in the private sector. But the number of individual claims to employment tribunals by aggrieved workers has

increased. Expressions of covert conflict such as absenteeism and resignations have not diminished. Whatever responses related to conflict have
been, workers have generally experienced higher wages, greater use of
their skills, reduced job insecurity and reduced risk of accidents at work.
But the evidence is that this has been accompanied, at least up until
the 1990s, by intensified work effort and a decline in worker autonomy.
These improvements have been obtained at some cost.

What has initiated these developments? There are no signs that the
impetus has come from trade unions. They have become more reactive
than proactive as employer recognition has been diluted. Their workplace
representatives have seen a steady shift in their role from one of bargaining over work and wages to one of coping with individual members'
problems. Where bargaining continues it is, in contrast with twenty-five
or more years earlier, generally conducted at the organisational level
of the employer's choosing. Employers have more and more taken the
lead in managing the employment relationship. They have also ceased to
collude with each other at industrial or any other level; enterprises have
come to act independently. Within multi-site enterprises there has been a
tendency to devolve responsibility while tightening performance targets.

Deliberate innovation is far more evident in employers' methods of
managing employees. An example has been increased experimentation
with contingent pay, often with different forms of it within the same
workplace. More generally, the human resource practices associated with
high involvement management have become more popular, whether or
not trade unions are present. But the evidence does not suggest that
there has been an 'HRM revolution' as some have claimed. While the
incidence of some of the associated practices has increased, their growth
has been uneven. Only a minority of workplaces have adopted them
wholeheartedly. There has indeed been a substantial growth in the use
of trained personnel specialists at the workplace level. But the innovation
of human resource practices cannot, surprisingly, be attributed directly
to this growth. It has occurred just as much where specialists are not
present.

Part of the explanation lies with the rapid growth in foreign investment
in Britain, which has introduced new approaches to employee management. But so also has the increased internationalisation of British firms.
New ideas have come from overseas, both because outsiders have brought
them in and because indigenous firms have adopted them as they have
invested abroad.

Workplace change in the public sector has been very different, but not
as different as might have been anticipated. Trade unions have retained
their apparent position in the public sector more successfully than in

the private sector, but their influence on management has diminished. Standardised pay systems have given way to fragmentation and diversity, with public employers tending to imitate the human resource management techniques permeating the private sector. Performance-oriented practices have been strengthened and welfare practices modified. Direct government intervention has been the main stimulus here, irrespective of political party. Public services as a whole have experienced greater central government intervention, and their workplaces have been subjected to closer monitoring. An increased tendency for industrial action in the public services has been in part a reaction to these developments, and has been in sharp contrast to the private sector.

In looking for the sources of change in workplaces we must not ignore the role of government. Until the 1970s, relying on the legal tradition of collective laissez faire, governments had tried to stand back from employment relations. They upheld a tacit post-war settlement whereby employers and trade unions were left free to bargain over what levels of work and effort would prevail. By the beginning of our period this was being called into question. International economic pressures were triggering direct interventions with incomes policies. Membership of the European Economic Community demanded the regulation of labour standards by means of individual employment rights. Governments of the 1980s intervened to weaken the confrontational capacity of trade unions, changes that their New Labour successors did little to reverse, preferring instead to encourage unions to act in co-operative partnership with employers. As the provision of individual rights grew, they were shaped by governments to improve workforce flexibility and workforce diversity. The consequential juridification of employment relations has further encouraged the specialism of human resource management, albeit in a very different, and far more legalistic, way from that suggested by early proponents.

What environmental change has driven all this? The analysis outlined in this book leaves little doubt about the overwhelming importance of toughening competition in product markets, backed by increased legal intervention. The old institutions of British collective bargaining in the mid-twentieth century had been parented by the marriage of nationally bounded product markets and legal laissez faire. Both these parents changed fundamentally over our quarter century. Product market competition became, to varying extents, more international and more intense, thereby either moving profits beyond the organisational reach of trade unions, or denying the profit levels of which unions could bargain a worthwhile share. We have seen how increasing product market pressures were reflected in the retreat of collective bargaining, with privatisation playing an important role in those industries denied a natural monopoly for their services. We have also seen how legal intervention has been transformed over the period, with its role initially changing from one of passively propping up collective bargaining, to one of actively undermining it. In the 1990s it changed again, under European influence and New Labour, to one in which the law has come to be used to provide both a framework of minimum labour standards and a means to further business needs for flexible labour.

There is one profoundly important environmental change on which, because of their workplace focus, the surveys have been relatively silent. This is the liberalisation and deregulation of the financial markets within which so many employing organisations raise their capital. The quarter century of our study has seen increased levels of mergers and acquisitions within the British economy, and the exposure to hostile takeover of many hitherto sheltered firms. This has forced more managements to consider the implications of workplace organisational change for stock market valuations, and to seek funding in non-traditional and more open markets. The explanation of the tightening of the targets confronting managements, noted in earlier chapters, lies as much in the realm of capital markets as of product markets.

Our period has seen tightening economic and legal pressures erode or even destroy the collectivism that once prevailed across British employment relations. Enterprises now act more independently of each other in the paying, training and managing of employees. The collective support of trade unions has increasingly been eroded or denied to workers altogether. The workplace may have become more comprehensively managed than twenty-five years ago, and its workers might be more highly rewarded for their involvement, but it has also become a more pressured place to work.

What can we say about longer-term trends? We noted in Chapter 1 how poor had been the efforts of writers at the start of our period at predicting how the workplace would change in the years to come. This is enough to inhibit our attempting any forecasts of how the workplace might develop in the twenty-first century. We can be confident that forces external to the workplace will continue to drive change, and to do so in unexpected directions. It is, for example, of note that the 2004 WERS was being carried out at the very time when Britain was experiencing the largest influx of labour immigration on record, a major labour market development so little foreseen that no questions in the survey picked up on it. The implications of this unprecedented immigration for the employment circumstances of both the indigenous and immigrant workers are still obscure. Similarly, at the time of writing, the British economy is facing a world economic crisis and the end of the period of sustained growth that dominated the latter half of our quarter century. Again, the implications of recession for the conditions of the workforce, now with lower levels of unionisation than in the 1930s, are impossible to predict. It is, consequently, best not to describe the developments that this book has explored as 'trends', in the sense of changes that are expected to continue into the future. They are likely to turn out to have been surprisingly short phases in the continuing evolution of the workplace.

Technical appendix

John Forth and Alex Bryson

Introduction

This technical appendix describes the design and execution of each of the surveys in the Workplace Industrial/Employment Relations Survey (WIRS/WERS) series. The series comprises five national surveys of workplaces in Britain, in which the principal actors in the employment relationship provide information on the nature of employment relations at their place of work. The five surveys took place in 1980, 1984, 1990, 1998 and 2004.

A workplace is defined as comprising the activities of a single employer at a single set of premises; examples might include a single branch of a bank, a car factory, a department store or a school. The central focus of the survey series has been the formal and structured relations that take place between management and employees at the workplace, although this focus softened in the 1998 and 2004 surveys. The principal component of each survey in the WIRS/WERS series is a face-to-face interview at the establishment with the senior person dealing with industrial relations, employee relations or personnel matters. Within each of the five cross-sectional surveys in the series, interviews have also been sought with worker representatives, where present, and in 1998 and 2004 self-completion questionnaires were also distributed among employees. Individual cross-section surveys have also collected data from production managers (1984) and financial managers (1990 and 2004). Panel surveys of surviving workplaces from the previous cross-section have also taken place in 1984, 1990, 1998 and 2004.

Further details on the methodology of each of the surveys in the series are included in the technical appendices to each of the five sourcebooks (Daniel and Millward, 1983; Millward and Stevens, 1986; Millward *et al.*, 1992; Cully *et al.*, 1999; Kersley *et al.*, 2006) and in technical reports compiled by the National Centre for Social Research (formerly the Social and Community Planning Research, SCPR) who were responsible for conducting the fieldwork for each survey in the series (Airey and Potts, 1983; Airey *et al.*, 1992; Airey *et al.*, 1999; Chaplin *et al.*, 2005).[1]

The WIRS/WERS cross-section surveys

Sampling frames and samples

The samples for each of the five cross-section surveys have been taken from frames considered to be the best available at the time, namely the Censuses of Employment of 1977, 1981 and 1987 and the Inter Departmental Business Registers (IDBR) of 1997 and 2003. In each of the first three surveys, the sampling universe comprised all workplaces in Britain with twenty-five or more employees, except those in Division 0 (Agriculture, Forestry and Fishing) of the 1980 Standard Industrial Classification (SIC). In the fourth survey, the employment threshold was lowered to include workplaces with between ten and twenty-four employees, and in the fifth survey it was lowered again to include workplaces with between five and nine employees. However, analyses presented within the earlier chapters of this book often exclude workplaces with fewer than twenty-five employees in order to ensure a consistent basis for comparison across the series. The industrial scope of the fourth survey was slightly narrower than that of the first three surveys in the series, as it excluded workplaces in sections A to C (Agriculture, Hunting and Forestry; Fishing; and Mining and Quarrying), P (Private households with employed persons) and Q (extra-territorial bodies) of the 1992 SIC. The 2004 survey applied the same exclusions, albeit based on the 2003 SIC. However, workplaces engaged in deep coal mining had been withdrawn from the sample in 1984 prior to fieldwork, because of the industry-wide dispute taking place at the time, and in 1990, for reasons of consistency. The exclusion of SIC (1992/2004) Section C from the 1998 and 2004 samples thus ensured that consistency on this matter was preserved. Indeed, the proportion of workplaces involved in the variation of scope is not greater than 1 per cent in any one year.

In each of the five surveys, a stratified random sample was drawn from the file of eligible records. The total number of units drawn into the initial sample for each of the five surveys is shown in the first row in Table A1. The sample for the first three surveys was selected by, first, stratifying the sampling frame by workplace employment size and then employing differential sampling fractions within each stratum. In 1990, a second stage of sampling also took place, in which units in SIC

---

[1] A separate technical report was not published to accompany the 1984 survey.

Table A1 *Summary of fieldwork response for cross-section samples, 1980, 1984, 1990, 1998 and 2004 (number of workplaces, percentage of initial sample)*

	1980		1984		1990		1998		2004	
	Manual union	Non-manual union	Manual union	Non-manual union	Manual union	Non-manual union	Union	Non-union	Union	Non-union
Workplaces:										
Initial sample	3,332(100%)		3,209(100%)		3,023(100%)		3,192(100%)		4,293(100%)	
Ineligible/Out-of-scope/ Otherwise withdrawn	−606(18%)		−584(18%)		−531(18%)		−463(15%)		−706(16%)	
Total eligible and in-scope	2,726(82%)		2,625(82%)		2,492(82%)		2,729(85%)		3,587(84%)	
Non-productive addresses	−686(21%)		−606(19%)		−431(14%)		−538(17%)		−1,292(30%)	
Interviews achieved from selected sample	2,040(61%)		2,019(63%)		2,061(68%)		2,191(69%)		2,295(53%)	
Response rate	75%		77%		83%		80%		64%	
Worker representatives:										
Interviews achieved	1,040	1,016	910	949	726	670	877	70	735	249
Response rate	84%	85%	79%	82%	78%	79%	82%		80%	67%
Employees:										
Questionnaires returned							28,215		22,451	
Response rate							66%		61%	

Note: The scope of the survey varies over time, principally with respect to workplace employment size. See text for details.
Source: WIRS/WERS data.

(1980) Classes 91, 93 and 95 were under-sampled by a factor of 1 in 4. In 1998, the principle of differential sampling by employment size and industry was extended, but in a one-stage design: units were under-sampled in SIC (1992) Section D and over-sampled in sections E, F, H, J and O. The same broad approach was adopted in 2004, although restricted to over-sampling in SIC (2003) sections E, F, J and O. In each survey, sampling fractions increased with employment size in order to provide sufficient numbers of workplaces within each size band for separate analysis whilst permitting accurate employee-based estimates to be made. In each year, weights have been used in analysis to compensate for unequal probabilities of selection (see later section on coding, editing and weighting).

Questionnaire development and fieldwork

The interview schedules used in each of the five cross-section surveys were carefully developed and piloted before final versions were prepared for use in fieldwork. In 1990, 1998 and 2004, the development stages included specific contributions from academics, whilst for the 1990 and 1998 surveys much was also learnt from the Australian Workplace Industrial Relations Surveys of 1989/90 and 1995. Two pilot surveys were conducted in 1980, 1998 and 2004, whilst the 1998 and 2004 surveys also made use of cognitive testing prior to piloting. A single pilot was conducted in 1984 and 1990, when the changes that were made to the questionnaire between surveys were, in many ways, less radical.

The conduct of fieldwork has remained broadly the same throughout the series. Interviewers have attended a two-day briefing conducted jointly by the research team and the fieldwork contractor. Following these briefings, an initial approach letter has been sent to respondents from the government department responsible for the survey (the Department of Employment in 1980, 1984 and 1990; the Department of Trade and Industry in 1998 and 2004), describing the purposes of the survey, outlining the procedures for ensuring the anonymity of respondents and informing the recipient of the forthcoming request for an interview. In most cases, this letter has been sent directly to the sampled establishment. However, from 1984 onwards, certain types of establishment have been subject to a slightly different procedure whereby the initial contact was made at corporate, rather than establishment, level. This procedure is used in cases where head office approval has proved to be particularly crucial in securing establishment-level response to the survey. Such cases include central government, emergency services, the utilities and particular organisations engaged in telecommunications, postal services, banking and retail.

Following the initial contact, an interviewer has contacted the establishment by telephone and sought the main management respondent's agreement to be interviewed. The interviewer has then sent a letter of confirmation, together with a brief pre-interview questionnaire about the composition of the workforce at the sampled workplace,[2] the intention being that this short questionnaire should be completed prior to the interview, giving the respondent time to consult workplace records.

The main management interview is conducted face-to-face. Paper questionnaires were used in the first three surveys in the series, but computer assisted personal interviewing (CAPI) was introduced in 1998, with favourable outcomes in terms of data quality. Interviews have generally lasted around one hundred minutes on average, albeit with considerable variation around the mean in each year.

At the end of each management interview, the interviewer has sought permission to conduct interviews with worker representatives, where present, and in 1998 and 2004 also to distribute questionnaires among a random sample of employees. Interviews with worker representatives are conducted face-to-face and, in common with the management interview, migrated from paper questionnaires to CAPI in 1998. In 1980, 1984 and 1990, interviews were conducted with the senior union representative of the largest manual negotiating group, and equally for the largest non-manual negotiating group. In 1998 and 2004, interviews were sought instead with the senior representative of the largest recognised union and with the senior non-union representative, although in 1998 this non-union representative interview took place only when unions were not present. Worker representative interviews have lasted around forty minutes, on average. In 1998 and 2004, eight-page self-completion questionnaires were distributed to a random sample of twenty-five employees (or to all employees in smaller workplaces).

Fieldwork on each of the first four surveys in the series took around eight to ten months to complete, but this extended to fifteen months for the fifth survey in the series as a result of the more challenging fieldwork environment. The month of the median management interview has varied between February in 1998 and July in 2004. The fieldwork timetable for each survey is shown in Table A2.

---

[2] In 1980, 1984 and 1990 this was called the Basic Workforce Data Sheet (BWDS). In 1998, the name was changed to the Employee Profile Questionnaire (EPQ).

Table A2 *Fieldwork timetable for cross-section surveys, 1980, 1984, 1990, 1998 and 2004*

Survey year	Period of interviewing	Date of median management interview
1980	February 1980–September 1980	June 1980
1984	March 1984–October 1984	May 1984
1990	January 1990–September 1990	March 1990
1998	October 1997–July 1998	February 1998
2004	February 2004–April 2005	July 2004

Fieldwork outcomes: The initial sample averaged around 3,200 addresses in the first four surveys in the series, rising to around 4,300 addresses for the fifth survey (Table A1). Around one-sixth of each sample has proved to be ineligible for the survey or otherwise out of scope. Addresses are classified as ineligible or out of scope if, for example, the establishment has closed down between the last update of the sampling frame and the time of interview, the number of employees at the workplace has fallen below the survey threshold in that time or the premises indicated by the address are found to be derelict, vacant or demolished.

Around one-fifth of the addresses did not yield productive responses in the first four surveys, rising to 30% in 2004. The response rate for each survey – the number of cases yielding a satisfactory management interview and workforce profile questionnaire, expressed as a percentage of eligible and in-scope addresses – rose from 75% in 1980 to 77% in 1984 and 83% in 1990, but has since fallen back to 80% in 1998 and 64% in 2004 (Table A1).[3] Response rates in each of the surveys have varied by region, industry and size of establishment (as recorded on the sampling frame). Response rates have consistently been higher among larger units. Non-response has commonly been due to the respondent being unwilling to take part, but also, in a small number of cases, it has arisen because contact could not be made with the respondent, or because they were ill or away from the establishment for the duration of the fieldwork.

As stated above, the response rate is based on the achievement of a successful interview with a main management respondent and the satisfactory completion of the workforce profile questionnaire. However, interviews have not always been conducted with a manager based at the

---

[3] It should be noted that the 1998 and 2004 surveys have each included smaller workplaces, which are less likely to respond, on average, than workplaces with twenty-five or more employees. However, it is also the case that most surveys of businesses and individuals have experienced downward pressure on response rates in recent years.

sampled establishment. This might occur, for example, in cases where no-one at the sampled establishment has sufficient knowledge of personnel matters to answer the questions contained in the survey. In such cases, the interview is conducted at head office, at an intermediate regional or divisional office or, in some cases, interviewing is split between two respondents whose combined knowledge permits the completion of the questionnaire. Together, these types of interviews accounted for between 8% and 10% of the total in 1980, 1984 and 1998. However, the proportion was higher in 1990 (18%) and in 2004 (14%).

Worker representative interviews were conducted with a total of around 2,000 representatives in 1980 and 1984, falling to around 1,000 in 1998 and 2004. This decline partly resulted from the decision that was made in 1998 to interview only one union representative, and partly from the decline in the prevalence of union representation. Response rates have stood at around 80% in each year. A total of 28,215 employee questionnaires were returned in 1998, representing a response rate of 66%. In 2004, a total of 22,451 questionnaires were returned, representing a response rate of 61%.

Coding, editing and weighting the data: Data collected in each of the surveys has been coded and edited by experienced data-processing teams, with substantial involvement from research team members. In each survey, the verbatim answers to all open-ended questions have been coded to detailed frames, whereby similar answers are grouped under a single numeric code. Rigorous checks are also conducted on all of the questionnaires in order to identify inconsistencies and missing data. These include range checks to highlight extreme values, and logic checks to examine the internal consistency of answers given throughout the questionnaire. In cases where major problems are identified, the case may be referred back to an interviewer or direct contact may be made with the respondent by editors in an attempt to resolve the query. Significant discrepancies in the data, whether resolved at the editing stage or not, are flagged with appropriate codes.

The sampling procedures employed in each of the surveys mean that workplaces within the same survey, nonetheless, have differing probabilities of selection into the survey sample. The data arising from the survey therefore has to be weighted in order to adjust for the fact that, in the unweighted sample, certain types of workplace are either under-represented or over-represented in comparison with their representation in the population. For each workplace, the weight required to adjust for this is derived as the inverse of the estimated probability of selection of that case from the sampling frame (i.e., the inverse of the sampling fraction applied to the sample stratum from which the case originated). Additional weighting was also included for the first three surveys to compensate for the age of the sampling frame and its consequent under-inclusion of workplaces near the threshold of twenty-five employees. In 1998 and 2004, the sampling frame was considered sufficiently up to date to make this unnecessary. Non-response adjustments were also incorporated into the weighting schemes for the 1998 and 2004 Surveys of Employees to account for the fact that certain types of workplace were less likely to allow the Survey of Employees to take place, and also to account for differential rates of response by gender. All of the results presented in the main text of this volume have been produced using weighted data, unless otherwise specified.

The use of stratification and subsequent weighting in the design of a survey mean that the standard errors of estimates derived from the survey sample are generally larger than those pertaining to a simple random sample of the same size. The degree of inflation for a particular estimate is indicated by the 'design factor'. Design factors were calculated for a number of variables in each of the surveys at the time that each survey was conducted. The average design factor for each of the first three surveys was estimated to be 1.25 (indicating that the average design-based standard error in each survey was 25 per cent higher than the standard error from a simple random sample). The average design factor for the 1998 survey was estimated to be 1.70, whilst that for the 2004 survey was estimated to be 1.45. Some of the increase from the earlier surveys may reflect the more complex stratification of the 1998 and 2004 samples, but it may also partly reflect the more comprehensive nature of the calculations that were carried out in the derivation of the effect of survey design.

The most common statistical requirement when reading this volume will be to assess the statistical significance of changes in practice between different years. The statistical significance of such changes has been tested, and readers should assume that any changes noted in the text are statistically significant from zero at the ten per cent level unless otherwise stated.

The WIRS/WERS Panel Surveys

Accompanying the five cross-section surveys have been four panel surveys which have provided an insight into how employment relations may change within an establishment over time. Each cross-section sample is independent, and so it is not possible to track individual workplaces from one survey year to the next across the five cross-section surveys. Instead, the WERS Panel Surveys have been specifically designed to provide information on how workplace relations change within individual establishments from one period to the next. Each is a two-wave panel in which the respondents to a particular cross-section survey are re-contacted at the time of the next cross-section. There are four panel surveys in all: 1980–4, 1984–90, 1990–8 and 1998–2004. However, the 1980–4 panel was largely experimental and is not used for analysis.

Sampling frame and sample

As noted above, the sample of workplaces for wave two of each panel survey has been drawn from among those workplaces that participated in the previous cross-section survey. In the 1990–8 and 1998–2004 panels, the fieldwork company attempted to trace all workplaces from wave one in order to establish whether they survived the intervening period and, if so, also to establish their number of employees at wave two. Around two-thirds of workplaces from wave one were also pursued for interview at wave two (assuming that they survived). The 1984–90 panel took a slightly different approach, seeking only to trace workplaces in the private sector or trading public corporations, and then doing so only for around two-thirds of such workplaces. However, all survivors were then pursued for interview. In each panel, interviews were conducted only among 'continuing workplaces', that is, workplaces which had continued to operate throughout the intervening period and which also continued to be in-scope on the basis of the industry and size criteria applied in the cross-section at wave one.

Questionnaire development and fieldwork

A short telephone enquiry has typically been used to identify the survival status and employment of workplaces that are not being pursued for interview. However, those workplaces which have been pursued for interview have been allocated to interviewers, alongside their cross-section workload, and fieldwork has progressed in much the same way as for the cross-section survey. For these workplaces, the second wave of the 1980–4 and 1984–90 panel surveys simply utilised the questionnaire that had been designed for the cross-section survey in that year. However, the questionnaires used in the second waves of the 1990–8 and 1998–2004 panel surveys have been tailored instruments. Both have included a selection of questions from the original (wave one) cross-section survey, but have augmented these questions with others specifically designed to identify and enquire about changes in practice between the two waves. This has

Table A3 *Summary of fieldwork response for panel samples,*
1984–90, 1990–8 and 1998–2004 (number of workplaces,
percentage of initial sample)

	1984–90	1990–8	1998–2004
Eligible workplaces from wave one cross-section	1,385	2,061	2,191
Survival status established	704(51%)[a]	2,022(98%)	2,179(99%)
Interview achieved at wave two	537(39%)	846(41%)	938(43%)
Response rate	87%	82%	75%

Note: [a] 100% of all those for which the survival status was sought.
Source: WIRS/WERS data.

been facilitated by the use of CAPI technology, which makes it possible
to feed data collected at wave one directly into the wave two interview.

Fieldwork outcomes: The survival status of workplaces selected
for the panel survey was established in at least 98% of cases in each panel
(Table A3). This yielded survival data on around 700 workplaces in the
1984–90 panel and around 2,000 workplaces in the later panels. Around
15% of the selected sample was found to be out of scope for the purposes
of re-interview. These primarily consisted of establishments that had
closed down between waves one and two and those which, although still
in operation, no longer met the wave one employment threshold. Among
the remaining in-scope cases, the wave two interview achieved a response
rate of 87% in 1990, 82% in 1998 and 75% in 2004. This provided a
sample of 537 workplaces with wave one and wave two interview data in
the 1984–90 panel, and samples of around 900 workplaces in each of the
1990–8 and 1998–2004 panels.

Coding, editing and weighting the data: In common with the data
from the cross-section surveys, the data from the panel surveys were
coded and edited by experienced data-processing teams, with substantial
involvement from research team members. Rigorous checks were also
conducted to ensure that units met the definition of a workplace, and
that the history of the wave two unit could be clearly traced back to that
surveyed in wave one.

The weights to be applied to the panel data were calculated as the
inverse of the probability of being selected for and agreeing to take part in
the survey. This probability is the cross-product of the probability of being
in the wave one cross-section, the probability of being selected for wave

two and the probability of responding at wave two. The probability of responding at wave two was estimated by regression methods to identify non-response biases.

As with a cross-section survey, the various features of the design of a panel survey, such as sample stratification and weighting, must be taken into account when calculating estimates of standard errors. In the 1990–8 panel survey, the average design factor for differences in practice between the two waves was estimated to be 1.5. The equivalent figure for the 1998–2004 panel survey was 1.8. Again, the reader should assume that any differences noted in the text are statistically significant from zero at the ten per cent level unless otherwise stated.

Accessing the data used in this volume

It is an enduring principle of the WIRS / WERS series that the data collected in each of the surveys should be made publicly available to bona fide researchers wishing to conduct their own analyses. To this end, the data from each of the surveys in the series can be obtained from the UK Data Archive at the University of Essex.

A time-series data set has also been formed from the interviews with the main management respondent in each of the five cross-section surveys (1980, 1984, 1990, 1998 and 2004). The data set contains a wide range of data items from throughout the 1998 or 2004 management questionnaires, for which there are also comparable items in at least one other previous cross-section survey in the series. The time-series data set is also available from the UK Data Archive (study number 4511).

Bibliography

Ackroyd, S. and Thompson, P. 1999. *Organisational Misbehaviour*. London: Sage.

Acas. 2007. *Advisory, Conciliation and Arbitration Service 2007 Annual Report 2006/7*. London: Acas.

Addison, J. T. and Belfield, C. R. 2000. ' The impact of financial participation and employee involvement on financial performance: a re-estimation using the 1998 WERS', *Scottish Journal of Political Economy*, 47 (5): 571–83.

Addison, J. T. and Belfield, C. R. 2001. 'Updating the determinants of firm performance: estimation using the 1998 UK Workplace Employee Relations Survey', *British Journal of Industrial Relations*, 39 (3): 341–66.

Addison, J. T. and Belfield, C. R. 2004. 'Unions and employment growth: the one constant', *Industrial Relations*, 43 (2), April: 305–23.

Airey, C., Hales, J., Hamilton, R., Korovessis, C., McKernan, A. and Purdon, S. 1999. *The Workplace Employee Relations Survey (WERS) 1997–8: Technical Report*. London: National Centre for Social Research.

Airey, C. and Potts, A. 1983. *Survey of Employee Relations: Technical Report*. London: Social and Community Planning Research.

Airey, C., Tremlett, N. and Hamilton, R. 1992. *The Workplace Industrial Relations Survey (1990): Technical Report (Main and Panel Surveys)*. London: Social and Community Planning Research.

Anderson, T., Millward, N. and Forth, J. 2004. *Equal Opportunities Policies and Practice at the Workplace: Secondary Analysis of WERS98*, Employment Relations Research Series, No. 30. London: Department of Trade and Industry.

Appelbaum, E., Bailey, T., Berg, P. and Kalleberg, A. 2000. *Manufacturing Advantage: Why High-Performance Work Systems Pay Off*. Ithaca, NY: ILR Press.

Armstrong, P., Marginson, P., Edwards, P. and Purcell, J. 1996. 'Budgetary control and the labour force: findings from a survey of large British companies', *Management Accounting Research*, 7: 1–23.

Arthur, J. B. 1994. 'Effects of human resource systems on manufacturing performance and turnover', *Academy of Management Journal*, 7: 670–87.

Ascher, K. 1987. *The Politics of Privatisation: Contracting Out Public Services*. Basingstoke: Macmillan.

Atkinson, A. B. 2007a. 'The distribution of earnings in OECD countries', *International Labour Review*, 146 (1–2): 41–60.

Atkinson, A. B. 2007b. 'The long run earnings distribution in five countries: "remarkable stability," U, V or W?', *Review of Income and Wealth*, 53: 1–24.

Audit Commission. 2002. *Recruitment and Retention: A Public Service Workforce for the Twenty-first Century*. London: Audit Commission.

Autor, D. H., Levy, F. and Murnane, R. J. 2003. 'The skill content of recent technological change: an empirical exploration', *Quarterly Journal of Economics*, 118 (4): 1279–333.

Bach, S. 2004. 'Employee participation and union voice in the NHS', *Human Resource Management Journal*, 14 (2): 3–19.

Bach, S. and Givan, R. 2005. 'Union responses to public-private partnerships in the National Health Service', in S. Fernie and D. Metcalf (eds.) *British Unions: Resurgence or Demise?*. London: Routledge, pp. 118–37.

Bach, S. and Givan, R. 2008. 'Public service modernization and trade union reform: towards managerial led renewal?', *Public Administration*, 86 (2): 1–17.

Bach, S., Kessler I. and Heron, P. 2006. 'Changing job boundaries and workforce reform: the case of teaching assistants', *Industrial Relations Journal*, 37 (1): 2–21.

Bach, S. and Winchester, D. 1994. 'Opting out of pay devolution? Prospects for local pay bargaining in UK public services', *British Journal of Industrial Relations*, 32 (2): 263–82.

Bach, S. and Winchester, D. 2003. 'Industrial relations in the public sector', in P. K. Edwards (ed.), *Industrial Relations*, 2nd edn, Blackwell: Oxford.

Bacon, N., Blyton, P. and Dastmalchian, A. 2005. 'The significance of working time arrangements accompanying the introduction of teamworking: evidence from employees', *British Journal of Industrial Relations*, 43: 681–701.

Bain, G. S. and Price, B. 1983. 'Union growth: dimensions, determinants and destiny', in G. S. Bain (ed.), *Industrial Relations in Britain*. Oxford: Blackwell.

Baird, L. and Meshoulam, I. 1988. 'Managing two fits of strategic human resource management', *Academy of Management Review*, 13: 116–28.

Baker, G. 1992. 'Incentive contracts and performance measurement', *Journal of Political Economy*, 100: 598–614.

Baker, G. 2002. 'Distortion and risk in optimal incentive contracts', *Journal of Human Resources*, 37: 728–51.

Baker, G., Jensen, M. and Murphy, K. 1988. 'Compensation and incentives: practice vs theory', *Journal of Finance*, 43: 593–616.

Barmby, T., Ercolani, M., and Treble, J. 2004. 'Sickness absence in the UK 1984–2002', *Swedish Economic Policy Review*, 11 (1): 65–88.

Barnard, C., Deakin, S. and Hobbs, R. 2003. 'Opting out of the 48-hour week: employer necessity or individual choice?', *Industrial Law Journal*, 32 (4): 223–52.

Barney, J. 1991. 'Firm resources and sustained competitive advantage', *Journal of Management*, 17 (1): 99–120.

Barney, J. and Wright, P. 1998. 'On becoming a strategic partner: the role of human resources in gaining competitive advantage', *Human Resource Management*, 37: 31–46.

Bassett, P. 1986. *Strike Free: The New Industrial Relations in Britain*. London: Macmillan.

Batstone, E. 1985. *The Reform of Workplace Industrial Relations: Theory, Myth and Evidence*. Oxford: Clarendon.

Batstone, E., Boraston, I. and Frenkel, S. 1977. *Shop Stewards in Action: The Organisation of Workplace Conflict and Accommodation*. Oxford: Blackwell.

Beaumont, P. and Harris, R. 1990. 'Union recruitment and organizing attempts in Britain in the 1980s', *Industrial Relations Journal*, 21 (4): 274–86.

Beaumont, P. and Harris, R. 1995. 'The pattern of diffusion of employee share-ownership schemes in Britain: some key findings', *International Journal of Human Resource Management*, 6 (2): 391–409.

Beaumont, P. and Townley, B. 1985. 'Non-Union American plants in Britain: their employment practices', *Relations Industrielles*, 40 (4): 810–25.

Beer, M., Spector, B., Lawrence, P. R., Mills, D. Q. and Walton, R. E. 1984. *Managing Human Assets*, New York: Free Press.

Belfield, C. R. and Harris, R. D. F. 2002. 'How well do theories of job matching explain variations in job satisfaction across education levels? Evidence for UK graduates', *Applied Economics*, 34: 535–48.

Belfield, C. R. and Heywood, J. S. 2001. 'Unionization and the pattern of non-union wages: evidence for the UK', *Oxford Bulletin of Economics and Statistics*, 63 (5): 577–98.

Bender, K. A. and Heywood, J. S. 2006. 'Job satisfaction of the highly educated: the role of gender, academic tenure, and earnings', *Scottish Journal of Political Economy*, 52 (2): 253–79.

Bennett, J. T. and Kaufman, B. E. (eds.), 2007. *What Do Unions Do?: A Twenty-Year Perspective*. New Brunswick, Canada, and London, UK: Transaction Publishers.

Berthoud, R. 2006. *Work Rich and Work Poor: Three Decades of Change*. Bristol: Policy Press.

Bevan, S., Dench, S., Tamkin, P. and Cummings, J. 1999. *Family-Friendly Employment: The Business Case*. Research Report RR136. London: Department for Education and Employment.

Bewley, H. and Fernie, S. 2003. 'What do unions do for women?', in H. Gospel and S. Wood (eds.), *Representing Workers: Union Recognition and Membership in Britain*. London: Routledge.

Beynon, H. 1973. *Working for Ford*. London: Allen Lane.

Bird, D., Beatson, M. and Butcher, S. 1993. 'Membership of trade unions: an analysis of trade union membership based on latest information from the Certification Officer and the Labour Force Survey', *Employment Gazette*, 101 (5): 189–96.

Blackburn, R. and Hart, M. 2002. *Small Firms' Awareness and Knowledge of Individual Employment Rights*. Employment Relations Research Series, No. 14. London: Department of Trade and Industry.

Blanchflower, D. G. 1984. 'Union relative wage effects: a cross-section analysis using establishment data', *British Journal of Industrial Relations*, November: 311–32.

Blanchflower, D. G. 1986. 'What effect do unions have on relative wages in Great Britain?', *British Journal of Industrial Relations*, 24: 196–204.

Blanchflower, D. G. 2007. 'A cross-country study of union membership', *British Journal of Industrial Relations*, 45 (1): 1–28.

Blanchflower, D. G. and Bryson, A. 2003. 'Changes over time in union relative wage effects in the UK and the US revisited,' in J. T. Addison and

C. Schnabel (eds.), *International Handbook of Trade Unions*, Edward Elgar: Cheltenham and Northampton, MA.

Blanchflower, D. G. and Bryson, A. 2004. 'What effect do unions have on wages now and would Freeman and Medoff be surprised?', *Journal of Labor Research*, 25 (3): 383–414.

Blanchflower, D. G. and Bryson, A. 2007. *The Wage Impact of Trade Unions in the UK Public and Private Sectors*. Institute for the Discussion of Labour (IZA) Discussion Paper No. 3055.

Blanchflower, D. G. and Bryson, A. 2008. 'The wage impact of trade unions in the UK public and private sectors', *Economica*, 75: 1–18.

Blanchflower, D. G., Bryson, A. and Forth, J. 2006. *Workplace Industrial Relations in Britain 1980–2004*. Bonn: Institute for the Study of Labour (IZA), Discussion Paper No. 2518.

Blanchflower, D. G. and Cubbin, J. 1986. 'Strike propensities at the British workplace', *Oxford Bulletin of Economics and Statistics*, 48 (1): 19–40.

Blanchflower, D. G., Millward, N. and Oswald, A. J. 1991. 'Unionism and employment behaviour', *Economic Journal*, 101 (407): 815–34.

Blanchflower, D. G. and Oswald, A. J. 1987. 'Profit sharing – can it work?', *Oxford Economic Papers*, 39 (1): 1–19.

Blanchflower, D. G. and Oswald, A. J. 1988. 'Profit-related pay: prose discovered', *Economic Journal*, 98 (September): 720–30.

Blanchflower, D. G., Oswald, A. J. and Garrett, M. D. 1990. 'Insider power in wage determination', *Economica*, 57: 143–70.

Blanchflower, D. G. and Shadforth, C. 2007. 'Entrepreneurship in the UK', *Foundations and Trends in Entrepreneurship*, 3 (4): 1–108.

Bond, S., Hyman, J., Summers, J. and Wise, S. 2002. *Family-Friendly Working? Putting Policy into Practice*. York: York Publishing Services.

Booth, C. 2007. *Determining Pay in the Police Service: The Second Part of a Review of Police Service Pay Arrangements*. London: Home Office. police.homeoffice.gov.uk/publications/police-reform/Booth_Review_Second_Report.pdf. Last accessed 11 February 2009.

Boselie, P., Dietz, G. and Boon, C. 2005. 'Commonalities and contradictions in research on human resource management and performance', *Human Resource Management Journal*, 15 (1): 67–81.

Boxall, P. and Purcell, J. 2003. *Strategy and Human Resource Management*. Basingstoke: Palgrave Macmillan.

Brenner, M. D., Fairris, D. and Ruser, J. 2004. '"Flexible" work practices and occupational safety and health: exploring the relationship between cumulative trauma disorders and workplace transformation', *Industrial Relations*, 43 (1): 242–66.

Bronfenbrenner, K. and Juravich, T. 1995. *The Impact of Employer Opposition on Union Certification Win Rates: A Private/Public Sector Comparison*. Economic Policy Institute Working Paper No. 113. Washington, DC.

Brown, A., Charlwood, A., Forde, C. and Spencer, D. 2006. *Changing Job Quality in Great Britain 1998–2004*. London: Department of Trade and Industry.

Brown, C. 1984. *Black and White Britain*. London: Heinemann.

Brown, C. 1990. 'Firm's choice of method of pay', *Industrial and Labor Relations Review*, 43: 165–82.

Brown, C. and Gay, P. 1985. *Racial Discrimination: Seventeen Years after the Act.* London: Policy Studies Institute.

Brown, M. and Heywood, J. 2002. *Paying for Performance: an International Comparison.* Armonk, NY: M. E. Sharpe.

Brown, W. 1973. *Piecework Bargaining.* London: Heinemann.

Brown, W. (ed.), 1981. *The Changing Contours of British Industrial Relations: A Survey of Manufacturing Industry.* Oxford: Blackwell.

Brown, W. 2006. 'The Low Pay Commission', in L. Dickens and A. Neal, *The Changing Institutional Face of British Employment Relations.* The Hague: Kluwer.

Brown, W. 2008. 'The influence of product markets on industrial relations', in P. Blyton, N. Bacon, J. Fiorito and E. Heery (eds.), *Handbook of Industrial Relations.* London: Sage.

Brown, W., Deakin, S., Hudson, M., Pratten, C. and Ryan, P. 1998. *The Individualisation of Employment Contracts in Britain*, Employment Relations Research Series, No. 4. London: Department of Trade and Industry.

Brown, W., Deakin, S., Nash, D. and Oxenbridge, S. 2000. 'The employment contract: from collective procedures to individual rights', *British Journal of Industrial Relations*, 38 (4): 611–29.

Brown, W., Deakin, S. and Ryan, P. 1997. 'The effects of British industrial relations legislation 1979–1997', *National Institute Economic Review*, 161: 69–83.

Brown, W., Ebsworth, R. and Terry, M. 1978. 'Factors shaping shop steward organization in Britain', *British Journal of Industrial Relations*, 16 (2): 139–59.

Brown, W. and Nash, D. 2008. 'What has happened to collective bargaining under New Labour?', *Industrial Relations Journal*, 39 (2): 91–103.

Brown, W. and Wadhwani, S. 1990. 'The economic effects of industrial relations legislation since 1979', *National Institute Economic Review*, 131: 57–70.

Brown, W. and Wright, M. 1994. 'The empirical tradition in workplace bargaining research', *British Journal of Industrial Relations*, 32 (2): 153–64.

Bryson, A. 1999. 'The impact of employee involvement on small firms' financial performance', *National Institute Economic Review*, 169: 78–95.

Bryson, A. 2004a. 'Union effects on workplace closure, 1990–1998', *British Journal of Industrial Relations*, 42 (2): 283–302.

Bryson, A. 2004b. 'Unions and employment growth in British workplaces in the 1990s: a panel analysis', *Scottish Journal of Political Economy*, 51 (4): 477–506.

Bryson, A. 2005. 'Union effects on employee relations in Britain', *Human Relations*, 58 (9): 1111–39.

Bryson, A., Cappellari, L. and Lucifora, C. 2004. 'Does union membership really reduce job satisfaction?', *British Journal of Industrial Relations*, 42 (3): 439–59.

Bryson, A., Charlwood, A. and Forth, J. 2006. 'Worker voice, managerial response and labour productivity: an empirical investigation', *Industrial Relations Journal*, 37 (5): 438–55.

Bryson, A. and Dale-Olsen, H. 2008. *A Tale of Two Countries: Unions, Closures and Growth in Britain and Norway*. Centre for Economic Performance Working Paper No. 1655, London School of Economics, April.

Bryson, A., Forth, J. and Kirby, S. 2005. 'High-performance practices, trade union representation and workplace performance in Britain', *Scottish Journal of Political Economy*, 53 (3): 451–91.

Bryson, A. and Freeman, R. 2006. *Worker Needs and Voice in the US and the UK*. National Bureau of Economic Research Working Paper No. 12310, Cambridge, MA.

Bryson, A. and Freeman, R. 2007. *Doing the Right Thing? Does Fair Share Capitalism Improve Workplace Performance?*. Employment Relations Research Series, No. 81. London: Department of Trade and Industry.

Bryson, A. and Gomez, R. 2003. *Segmentation, Switching Costs and the Demand for Unionization in Britain*. Centre for Economic Performance Discussion Paper No. 568, London School of Economics, May.

Bryson, A. and Gomez, R. 2005. 'Why have workers stopped joining unions?: accounting for the rise in never-membership in Britain', *British Journal of Industrial Relations*, 43 (1): 67–92.

Bryson, A., Gomez, R., Kretschmer, T. and Willman, P. 2007. 'The diffusion of workplace voice and high-commitment human resource management practices', *Industrial and Corporate Change*, 16: 395–426.

Bryson, A., Gomez, R. and Willman, P. 2004. 'The end of the affair? The decline in employers' propensity to unionize', in J. Kelly and P. Willman (eds.), *Union Organization and Activity*. London: Routledge, pp. 129–49.

Bryson, A. and Wilkinson, D. 2002. *Collective Bargaining and Workplace Performance: An Investigation Using the Workplace Employee Relations Survey 1998*, Employment Relations Research Series, No. 12. London: Department of Trade and Industry.

Bryson, A., Willman, P., Gomez, R. and Kretschmer, T. 2007. *Employee voice and human resource management: an empirical analysis using British data*. Policy Studies Institute Discussion Paper No. 27.

Buckley, P. and Enderwick, P. 1985. *The Industrial Relations Practices of Foreign-Owned Firms in Britain*. London: Macmillan.

Budd, J. and Mumford, K. 2004. 'Trade unions and family-friendly policies in Britain', *Industrial and Labor Relations Review*, 57 (2): 204–22.

Burgess, S., Propper, C. and Wilson, D. 2000. *Explaining the Growth in the Number of Applications to Industrial Tribunals 1972–1997*, Employment Relations Research Series, No. 10. London: Department of Trade and Industry.

Callender, C., Millward, N., Lissenburgh, S. and Forth, J. 1997. *Maternity Rights and Benefits in Britain, 1996*. Research Report No. 67. London: Department of Social Security.

Cappelli, P. 2008. *Employment Relationships: New Models of White-Collar Work*. Cambridge University Press.

Cappelli, P. and Neumark, D. 2000. 'Do "high performance" work practices improve establishment-level outcomes?', *Industrial and Labor Relations Review*, 54: 737–75.

Card, D., Blundell, R. and Freeman, R. (eds.). 2004. *Seeking a Premier League Economy*. Chicago: University of Chicago Press for National Bureau of Economics Research.

Carter, B. and Fairbrother, P. 1999. 'The transformation of British public-sector industrial relations: from 'model employer' to marketized relations', *Historical Studies in Industrial Relations*, 7, Spring: 119–46.

Casebourne, J., Regan, J., Neathey, F. and Tuohy, S. 2006. *Employment Rights at Work: Survey of Employees 2005*. Employment Relations Research Series, No. 51. London: Department of Trade and Industry.

Cavendish, R. 1982. *Women on the Line*. London: Routledge & Kegan Paul.

Chaplin, J., Mangla, J., Purdon, S. and Airey, C. 2005. *The Workplace Employment Relations Survey (WERS) 2004: Technical Report (Cross-Section and Panel Surveys)*. London: National Centre for Social Research.

Charlwood, A. and Terry, M. 2007. 'Twenty first century models of employee representation: structures, processes and outcomes', *Industrial Relations Journal*, 38 (4): 320–337.

Chartered Institute of Personnel Development (CIPD). 2007. *The Changing HR Function*. London: CIPD.

Child, J., Faulkner, D. and Pitkethly, R. 2001. *The Management of International Acquisitions*. Oxford: Oxford University Press.

Clark, K. and Drinkwater, S. 2007. *Ethnic Minorities in the Labour Market: Dynamics and Diversity*. Bristol: Policy Press.

Clarke, J. and Wedderburn, K. W. 1987. 'Juridification – a universal trend?', in G. Teubner (ed.), *Juridification of Social Spheres*. Berlin: de Gruyter.

Clegg, H. A. 1979. *The Changing System of Industrial Relations in Great Britain*. Oxford: Blackwell.

Clegg, H. A., Killick, A. J. and Adams, R. 1961. *Trade Union Officers*. Oxford: Blackwell.

Colgan, F. and Ledwith, S. 2002. *Gender Diversity and Trade Unions*. London: Routledge.

Collins, H. 1999. *Regulating Contracts*. Oxford University Press.

Combs, J., Liu, Y., Hall, A. and Ketchum, D. 2006. 'How much do high-performance work practices matter? A meta-analysis of their effect on organizational performance', *Personnel Psychology*, 59 (3): 501–28.

Commons, J. R. 1909. 'American Shoemakers, 1648–1895: a sketch of industrial evolution', *Quarterly Journal of Economics*, November. Reprinted in Commons, J. R. 1969. *Labor and Administration*. New York: A. M. Kelley. 1909.

Confederation of British Industry (CBI). 2004. *Room for Improvement: Absence and Labour Turnover 2004*. London: CBI.

Conyon, M. and Freeman, R. 2004. 'Shared Modes of Compensation and Firm Performance: UK Evidence', in R. Blundell, D. Card and R. Freeman (eds.), *Seeking a Premier League Economy*. University of Chicago Press.

Corby, S. 2000. 'Employee relations in the public services: a paradigm shift?', *Public Policy and Administration*, 15 (3), 60–74.

Core, J., Guay, W. and Larcker, D. 2003. 'Executive equity compensation and incentives: a survey', *Federal Reserve Bank of New York Economic Policy Review*, April: 27–50.

Cox, A., Zagelmeyer, S. and Marchington, M. 2006. 'Embedding employee involvement and participation at work', *Human Resource Management Journal*, 16 (3): 250–67.

Creegan, C. and Robinson, C. 2007. 'Prejudice and the workplace', in A. Park, J. Curtice, K. Thomson, M. Phillips, M. Johnson and E. Clery (eds.), *British Social Attitudes: The 24th Report*. London: Sage.

Crompton, R. and Lyonette, C. 2007. 'Who does the housework? The division of labour within the home', pp. 53–80 in A. Park, J. Curtice, K. Thomson, M. Phillips, M. Johnson and E. Clery (eds.), *British Social Attitudes: The 24th Report*. London: Sage.

Cully, M., Woodland, S., O'Reilly, A. and Dix, G. 1999. *Britain at Work. As depicted by the 1998 Workplace Employee Relations Survey*. London: Routledge.

Dandridge, N. and Clarke, A. 2005. *TUC Guide to Equality Law*. London: Trades Union Congress and Thompsons Solicitors.

Daniel, W. W. 1976. *Wage Determination in Industry*. London: Political and Economic Planning.

Daniel, W. W. 1980. *Maternity Rights: The Experience of Women*. Policy Studies Institute Report No. 588. London: Policy Studies Institute.

Daniel, W. W. 1981. *Maternity Rights: The Experience of Employers*. Policy Studies Institute Report No. 596. London: Policy Studies Institute.

Daniel, W. W. and McIntosh, N. 1972. *The Right to Manage?* London: Macdonald & Jane's.

Daniel, W. W. and Millward, N. 1983. *Workplace Industrial Relations in Britain*. London: Heinemann.

Darlington, R. 1994. *The Dynamics of Workplace Trade Unionism*. London: Mansell.

Darlington, R. 1995. 'Restructuring and workplace unionism at Manchester Airport', *British Journal of Industrial Relations*, 33 (1): 93–115.

Davies, J. 2001. 'Labour disputes in 2000', *Labour Market Trends*, 109 (6): 301–15.

Davies, P. and Freedland, M. 1984. *Labour Law: Text and Materials*. London: Weidenfeld & Nicolson.

Davies, P. and Freedland, M. 1984. *Labour Legislation and Public Policy*. Oxford University Press.

Davies, P. and Freedland, M. 2007. *Towards a Flexible Labour Market: Labour Legislation and Regulation Since the 1990s*. Oxford University Press.

De Menezes, L. M. and Wood, S. 2006. 'The reality of flexible work systems in Britain', *International Journal of Human Resource Management*, 17: 1–33.

Deaton, D. 1985. 'Management style and large-scale survey evidence', *Industrial Relations Journal*, 16 (2): 67–71.

Delbridge, R., Turnbull, P. and Wilkinson, B. 1992. 'Pushing back the frontiers: management control and work intensification under JIT/TQM factory regimes', *New Technology, Work and Employment*, 7 (2): 97–106.

Delbridge, R. and Whitfield, K. 2001. 'Employee perceptions of job influence and organizational participation', *Industrial Relations*, 40 (3): 472–89.

Department for Business, Enterprise and Regulatory Reform (BERR). 2007. *Workplace Representatives: A Review of Their Facilities and Facilities Time*,

Consultation Document. London: Department for Business Enterprise and Regulatory Reform.

Department of Communities and Local Government (DCLG). 2007. *Discrimination Law Review; A Framework for Fairness: Proposals for a Single Equality Bill for Great Britain.* June.

Department of Employment (DE). 1974a. *Women and Work: A Statistical Survey.* Manpower Paper No. 9. London: HMSO.

Department of Employment. 1974b. *Women and Work: Sex Differences and Society.* Manpower Paper No. 10. London: HMSO.

Department of Employment. 1975a. *Women and Work: A Review.* Manpower Paper No. 11. London: HMSO.

Department of Employment. 1975b. *Women and Work: Overseas Practice.* Manpower Paper No. 12. London: HMSO.

Department of Employment. 1986. *Building Businesses . . . not Barriers.* London: HMSO.

Department of Employment. 1989. *Removing Barriers to Employment.* London: HMSO.

Department of Trade and Industry (DTI). 1998. *Fairness at Work.* Cm 2968. London: HMSO.

Department of Trade and Industry. 2002. *High Performance Workplaces: The Role of Employee Involvement in a Modern Economy.* London: Department of Trade and Industry.

Department of Trade and Industry. 2004a. *Success at Work.* London: Department of Trade and Industry.

Department of Trade and Industry. 2004b. *Fairness for All: A New Commission for Equality and Human Rights.* Cm 6185. London: Department of Trade and Industry, HMSO.

Desai, T., Gregg, P., Steer, J. and Wadsworth, J. 1999. 'Gender and the labour market', in P. Gregg and J. Wadsworth (eds.), *The State of Working Britain.* Manchester University Press.

Dex, S. and Scheibl, F. 1999. 'Business performance and family-friendly policies', *Journal of General Management,* 24 (4): 22–37.

Dex, S. and Scheibl, F. 2002. *SMEs and flexible working arrangements.* Bristol: Policy Press and Joseph Rowntree Foundation.

Dex, S. and Smith, C. 2002. *The Nature and Patterns of Family-Friendly Employment Policies in Britain.* Bristol: Policy Press and Joseph Rowntree Foundation.

Dex, S., Sutherland, H. and Joshi, H. 2000. 'Effects of minimum wages on gender pay gap', *National Institute Economic Review,* 173: 80–8.

Dickens, L. 1989. 'Learning to live with the law', *New Zealand Journal of Industrial Relations,* 14 (1): 37–52.

Dickens, L. 2000. 'Doing more with less: Acas and individual conciliation', in W. Brown and B. Towers (eds.). *Employment Relations in Britain: Twenty-five years of the Advisory, Conciliation and Arbitration Service.* Oxford: Blackwell.

Dickens, L. 2002. 'Individual statutory employment rights since 1997: constrained expansion', *Employee Relations,* 24 (6): 619–37.

Dickens, L. 2006a. 'Re-regulation for gender equality: from "either/or" to "both"', *Industrial Relations Journal*, 37 (4): 299–309.

Dickens, L. 2006b. 'Equality and work–life balance: what's happening at the workplace', *Industrial Law Journal*, 35 (4): 445–9.

Dickens, L. 2007. 'The road is long: thirty years of equality legislation in Britain', *British Journal of Industrial Relations*, 45 (3): 463–94.

Dickens, L. and Hall, M. 1995. 'The state, labour law and industrial relations', in P. Edwards (ed.), *Industrial Relations: Theory and Practice in Britain*. Oxford: Blackwell.

Dickens, L. and Hall, M. 2003. 'Labour law and industrial relations: a new settlement?', in P. Edwards (ed.), *Industrial Relations: Theory and Practice*. Oxford: Blackwell.

Dickens, L. and Hall, M. 2005. 'The impact of employment legislation: reviewing the research', in L. Dickens, M. Hall and S. Wood, *Review of research into the impact of employment relations legislation*. Employment Relations Research Series, No. 45: 7–72. London: Department of Trade and Industry.

Dickens, L. and Hall, M. 2006. 'Fairness – up to a point: assessing the impact of New Labour's employment legislation', *Human Resource Management Journal*, 16: 338–56.

Dickens, L., Hart, M., Jones, M. and Weekes, B. 1981. 'Re-employment of unfairly dismissed workers: the lost remedy', *Industrial Law Journal*, 10 (3): 160–75.

Dickens, L., Jones, M., Weekes, B. and Hart, M. 1985. *Dismissed: A Study of Unfair Dismissal and the Industrial Tribunal System*. Oxford: Blackwell.

Dickens, L. and Neal, A. C. (eds.), 2006. *The Changing Institutional Face of British Employment Relations*. The Hague: Kluwer.

Dickerson, A. and Stewart, M. 1993. 'Is the public sector strike prone?', *Oxford Bulletin of Economics and Statistics*, 55 (3): 253–84.

Disney, R., Gosling, A. and Machin, S. 1995. 'British unions in decline: an examination of the 1980's fall in trade union recognition', *Industrial and Labor Relations Review*, 48 (3): 403–19.

Donovan, T. 1968. *Royal Commission on Trade Unions and Employers Associations 1965–68*. Cmnd 3623. London: HMSO.

Drago, R. and Heywood, J. 1995. 'The choice of payment schemes: Australian establishment data', *Industrial Relations*, 34: 507–31.

Drinkwater, S. and Ingram, P. 2005. 'Have industrial relations in the UK really improved?', *Labour*, 19 (3): 373–98.

Dundon, T., Grugulis, I. and Wilkinson, A. 2001. 'New management techniques in small and medium-sized enterprises', in T. Redman and A. Wilkinson (eds.), *Contemporary Human Resource Management: Text and Cases*. London: Financial Times/Prentice Hall, 432–63.

Ebbinghaus, B. and Visser, J. 1999. 'When institutions matter: union growth and decline in Western Europe, 1950–1995', *European Sociological Review*, 15: 135–58.

Edwards, P. K. 1983. 'The pattern of collective industrial action', in G. Bain (ed.), *Industrial Relations in Britain*. Oxford: Blackwell.

Edwards, P. K. 1987. *Managing the Factory*. Oxford: Blackwell.

Edwards, P. K. 1995. 'Human resource management, union voice and the use of discipline: an analysis of WIRS3', *Industrial Relations Journal*, 26 (3): 204–20.

Edwards, P. K. 2003. 'The employment relationship and the field of industrial relations', in P. K. Edwards (ed.), *Industrial Relations: Theory and Practice*. 2nd edn. Oxford: Blackwell.

Edwards, P. 2008. 'The employment relationship in strategic HRM', in J. Storey, P. Wright and D. Ulrich (eds.), *Routledge Companion to Strategic Human Resource Management*. London: Routledge.

Edwards, P. and Black, J. 2004. *The Impact of Employment Legislation on Small Firms: A Case Study Analysis*. Employment Relations Research Series, No. 20. London: Department of Trade and Industry.

Edwards, P., Edwards, T., Ferner, A., Marginson, P. and Tregaskis, O. 2007. *Employment Practices of MNCs in Organisational Context: A Large-Scale Survey*. Research report, de Montfort and Warwick Universities and King's College London. police.homeoffice.gov.uk/publications/police-reform/Booth Review Second Report.pdf?view=Binary. Last accessed 11 February 2009.

Edwards, P., Ram, M., and Black, J. 2004. 'Why does employment legislation not damage small firms?', *Journal of Law and Society*, 31 (2): 245–65.

Elliott, R. and Murphy, P. 1986. 'The determinants of the coverage of PBR systems in Britain', *Journal of Economic Studies*, 13: 38–50.

Employment Gazette. 1986. 'Stoppages caused by industrial disputes in 1985', *Employment Gazette*, 94 (8): 323–33.

Employment Tribunal Service. 2008. *Jurisdiction List*, published online at: www.employmenttribunals.gov.uk/about_us/jurisdiction_list.htm. Retrieved 21st May 2008.

Ewing, K. 2003. 'Labour law and industrial relations', in P. Ackers and A. Wilkinson (eds.), *Understanding Work and Employment: Industrial Relations in Transition*. Oxford University Press.

Ewing, K., Moore, S. and Wood, S. 2003. *Unfair Labour Practices; Trade Union Recognition and Employer Resistance*. London: Institute for Employment Rights.

Fagan, C. and Burchell, B. 2006. 'L'intensification du travail et les différences hommes/femmes: conclusions des enquêtes européennes sur les conditions de travail, in P. Askenazy, D. Cartron, F. de Coninck *et al.*, *Organisation et intensité du travail*. Toulouse: Octarès Éditions, pp. 161–80.

Fairbrother, P. 2000. *Trade Unions at the Crossroads*. London: Mansell.

Felstead, A., Gallie, D., Green, F. and Zhou, Y. 2007. *Skills at Work, 1986 to 2006*. University of Oxford: SKOPE.

Ferner, A. 1997. 'Country of Origin Effects and HRM in Multinational Companies', *Human Resource Management Journal*, 7 (1): 19–37.

Ferner, A. 2000. 'The underpinnings of "bureaucratic" control systems: HRM in European multinationals', *Journal of Management Studies*, 37: 521–40.

Ferner, A., Edwards, P., Edwards, T., Marginson, P. and Tregaskis, O. 2007. 'The determinants of central control and subsidiary "discretion" in HRM and employment relations policies: findings from a large-scale survey in foreign multinational subsidiaries in the UK'. Paper to International Industrial Relations Association 8th European Congress, Manchester.

Fernie, S., Metcalf, D. and Woodland, S. 1994. 'What has human resource management achieved in the workplace?', *Economic Report*, 8 (3), May. London: Employment Policy Institute.

Fitzner, G. 2006. *How Have Employees Fared? Recent UK Trends*. DTI Employment Relations Research Series, No. 56. London: Department of Trade and Industry.

Forth, J., Bewley, H. and Bryson, A. 2006. *Small and Medium-Sized Enterprises: Findings from the 2004 Workplace Employment Relations Survey*. London: Routledge.

Forth, J., Lissenburgh, S., Callender, C. and Millward, N. 1997. *Family-Friendly Working Arrangements in Britain, 1996*. Research Report No. 16. London: Department for Education and Employment.

Forth, J. and McNabb, R. 2008. 'Workplace performance: a comparison of subjective and objective measures in the 2004 Workplace Employment Relations Survey', *Industrial Relations Journal*, 39 (2): 104–23.

Forth, J. and Millward, N. 2004. 'High involvement management and pay in Britain', *Industrial Relations*, 43: 98–119.

Foster, D. and Scott, P. 1998. 'Competitive tendering of public services and industrial relations policy: the Conservative agenda under Thatcher and Major, 1997–97', *Historical Studies in Industrial Relations*, 6: 101–32.

Fox, A. 1974. *Beyond Contract: Work, Power and Trust Relations*. London: Faber.

Fox, M. 2005. *Gender Differences in Enforcing Employment Rights*. Research Paper 07/05. London: Advisory Conciliation and Arbitration Service.

Fredman, S. 2004. 'Women at work: the broken promise of flexicurity', *Industrial Law Journal*, 33 (4): 299–319.

Fredman, S. and Morris, G. 1989. *The State as Employer: Labour Law in the Public Services*. London: Mansell.

Freeman, R. 1980. 'The exit-voice tradeoff in the labour market: unionism, job tenure, quits and separations', *Quarterly Journal of Economics*, 94 (4): 643–74.

Freeman, R. and Medoff, J. 1984. *What Do Unions Do?* New York: Basic Books.

Frege, C. 2007. *Employment Research and State Traditions*. Oxford University Press.

Fryer, R., Fairclough, A. and Manson, T. 1978. 'Facilities for female shop stewards: the Employment Protection Act and collective agreements', *British Journal of Industrial Relations*, 16 (2): 160–74.

Fuller, G. 2007. 'Equal pay for council workers: whose bill is it anyway?', *Personnel Today*, 27th March.

Gall, G. 2004. 'Trade union recognition in Britain, 1995–2002: turning a corner?', *Industrial Relations Journal*, 35 (3): 249–270.

Gall, G. and Hebdon, R. 2008. 'Industrial conflict', in N. Bacon, P. Blyton, J. Fiorito and E. Heery (eds.), *The Handbook of Employment Relations*. London: Sage.

Gall, G. and McKay, S. 1999. 'Developments in union recognition and de-recognition in Britain 1994–1998', *British Journal of Industrial Relations*, 37 (3): 601–14.

Gallie, D. 2006. 'L'intensification du travail en Europe 1996–2001?', in P. Askenazy, D. Cartron, F. de Coninck *et al.*, *Organisation et intensité du travail*. Toulouse: Octarès Éditions: 239–60.

Gallie, D., Felstead, A. and Green, F. 2004. 'Changing patterns of task discretion in Britain', *Work, Employment and Society*, 18 (2): 243–66.

Gallie, D., White, M., Cheng, Y. and Tomlinson, M. 1998. *Restructuring the Employment Relationship*. Oxford University Press.

Garahan, P. and Stewart, P. 1992. *The Nissan Enigma*. London: Mansell.

Gaunt, R. and Benjamin, O. 2007. 'Job insecurity, stress and gender', *Community, Work and Family*, 10 (3): 341–55.

Genn, H. 1999. *Paths to Justice: What People Do and Think about Going to Law*. Oxford: Hart.

Gennard, J. and Steuer, M. 1971. 'The industrial relations of foreign-owned subsidiaries in the United Kingdom', *British Journal of Industrial Relations*, 9 (2): 143–59.

Gerhart, B. and Rynes, S. 2003. *Compensation: Theory, Evidence, and Strategic Implications*. London: Sage.

Gibbons, M. 2007. *Better Dispute Resolution. A Review of Employment Dispute Resolution in Great Britain*. London: Department of Trade and Industry.

Gibbons, R. 1987. 'Piece-rate incentive schemes', *Journal of Labor Economics*, 5: 413–29.

Gibbons, R. 1998. 'Incentives in organisations', *Journal of Economic Perspectives*, 12: 115–32.

Gilman, M. W. 1998. 'Performance-related pay: organisation and effects' PhD dissertation, University of Warwick.

Gilman, M. W., Edwards, P., Ram, M. and Arrowsmith, J. 2002. 'Pay determination in small firms in the UK', *Industrial Relations Journal*, 33: 52–67.

Givan, R. 2005. 'Seeing STARS', *Personnel Review*, 34 (6): 634–47.

Godard, J. 2004. 'A critical assessment of the high-performance paradigm', *British Journal of Industrial Relations*, 42 (2): 349–78.

Goodman, J., Earnshaw, J., Marchington, M. and Harrison, R. 1998. 'Unfair dismissal cases, disciplinary procedures, recruitment methods and management style', *Employee Relations*, 20 (6): 536–50.

Goos, M. and Manning, A. 2007. 'Lousy and lovely jobs: the rising polarization of work in Britain', *Review of Economics and Statistics*, 89 (1): 118–33.

Gorman, E. H. and Kmec, J. A. 2007. 'We (have to) try harder: gender and required work effort in Britain and the United States', *Gender and Society*, 21 (6): 828–56.

Gospel, H. 1992. *Markets, Firms and the Management of Labour in Modern Britain*. Cambridge University Press.

Government Equalities Office. 2008. *Framework for a Fairer Future – The Equality Bill*. Cm 7431. London: HMSO.

Government Social Survey. 1968. *Workplace Industrial Relations*. SS 402. London: HMSO.

Grainger, H. 2006. *Trade Union Membership, 2005*. London: Department of Trade and Industry.

Grainger, H. and Crowther, M. 2007. *Trade Union Membership, 2006*. London: Department of Trade and Industry.

Green, F. 2003. 'The demands of work', in. R. Dickens, P. Gregg and J. Wadsworth (eds.), *The Labour Market under New Labour. The State of Working Britain 2003*. Basingstoke: Palgrave Macmillan.

Green, F. 2006. *Demanding Work. The Paradox of Job Quality in the Affluent Economy*. Princeton University Press.

Green, F. 2008a. 'Leeway for the loyal: a model of employee discretion', *British Journal of Industrial Relations*, 46 (1): 1–32.

Green, F. 2008b. 'Subjective employment insecurity around the world: Presented to the conference of the Cambridge Journal of Regions, Economy and Society: Transforming Work: a multi-disciplinary conference on new forms of employment and their regulation, St John's College Oxford 4–5 September 2008.

Green, F. (2008). 'Work effort and worker well-being in the age of affluence' in C. Cooper and R. Burke (eds.), *The Long Work Hours Culture: Causes, Consequences and Choice*. Bingley: Emerald Group Publications.

Green, F. and Tsitsianis, N. 2005. 'An investigation of national trends in job satisfaction in Britain and Germany', *British Journal of Industrial Relations*, 43 (3): 401–29.

Green, F. and Zhu, Y. 2008. *Overqualification, Job Dissatisfaction, and Increasing Dispersion in the Returns to Graduate Education*. University of Kent, Studies in Economics No. 0803.

Gregg P., Knight, G. and Wadsworth, J. 1999. 'The cost of jobs loss', in P. Gregg and J. Wadsworth (eds.), *The State of Working Britain*. Manchester University Press.

Gregg, P. and Machin, S. 1988. 'Unions and the incidence of performance linked pay schemes in Britain', *International Journal of Industrial Organisation*, 6: 91–107.

Griffin, M. A., Neal, A. and Parker, S. K. 2007. 'A new model of work role performance: positive behavior in uncertain and interdependent contexts', *Academy of Management Journal*, 50: 327–47.

Grimshaw, D. 1999. 'Changes in skills-mix and pay determination among the nursing workforce in the UK', *Work, Employment and Society*, 13 (2): 295–328.

Guest, D. 1989. 'Human resource management: its implications for industrial relations and trade unions', in J. Storey (ed.), *New Perspectives on Human Resource Management*. London: Routledge.

Guest, D. 1997. 'Human resource management: a review and research agenda', *International Journal of Human Resource Management*, 8 (3): 263–76.

Guest, D. and Conway, N. 1999. *How Dissatisfied Are British Workers? A Survey of Surveys*. London: Institute of Personnel and Development.

Guest, D. and Conway, N. 2004. 'Exploring the paradox of unionised worker dissatisfaction', *Industrial Relations Journal*, 35 (2): 102–21.

Guest, D. and Hoque, K. 1994. 'The good, the bad and the ugly: employee relations in new non-union workplaces', *Human Resource Management Journal*, 5: 1–14.

Guest, D. E., Michie, J., Conway, N. and Sheehan, M. 2003. 'Human resource management and corporate performance in the UK', *British Journal of Industrial Relations*, 41: 291–314.

Guest, D. and Peccei, R. 1994. 'The nature and causes of effective human resource management', *British Journal of Industrial Relations*, 32 (2): 207–36.

Hakim, C. 1979. *Occupational Segregation*. Research Paper No. 9. London: Department of Employment.

Hale, D. 2007. 'Labour disputes in 2006', *Economic and Labour Market Review*, 1 (6): 25–36.

Hall, M. 2006. 'A cool response to the ICE Regulations? Employer and trade union approaches to the new legal framework for information and consultation', *Industrial Relations Journal*, 37 (5): 456–72.

Hall, M., Hutchinson, S., Parker, J., Purcell, J. and Terry, M. 2008. 'UK trade unions response to the ICE regulations', *Bulletin of Comparative Labour Relations*, 67.

Hamill, J. 1983. 'The labour relations of foreign-owned and indigenous firms', *Employee Relations*, 5 (1): 14–16.

Harley, B. 2001. 'Team membership and the experience of work in Britain: an analysis of the WERS98 data', *Work, Employment and Society*, 15 (4): 721–42.

Haskel, J., Kersley, B. and Martin, C. 1997. 'Labour market flexibility and employment adjustment: micro evidence from UK establishments', *Oxford Economic Papers*, 49: 362–79.

Hassel, A. 2002. 'A new going rate? Co-ordinated wage bargaining in Europe', in P. Pochet (ed.), *Wage Policy in the Eurozone*. Brussels: PIE-Peter Lang S.A.

Hawes, W. R. 2000. 'Setting the pace or running alongside? ACAS and the changing employment relationship', in B. Towers and W. Brown (eds.), *Employment Relations in Britain: Twenty-five Years of the Advisory, Conciliation and Arbitration Service*. Oxford: Blackwell.

Hayward, B., Peters, M., Rousseau, N. and Seeds, K. 2004. *Findings from the Survey of Employment Tribunal Applications*. Employment Relations Research Series, No. 33. London: Department of Trade and Industry.

Head, J. and Lucas, R. E. 2004. 'Does individual employment legislation constrain the ability of hospitality employers to hire and fire?', *International Journal of Hospitality Management*, 23 (2): 239–54.

Heald, D. 1983. *Public Expenditure: Its Defence and Reform*. Oxford: Blackwell.

Healy, G. 1997. 'The industrial relations of appraisal: the case of teachers', *Industrial Relations Journal*, 28 (3): 206–20.

Hepple, B., Coussey, M. and Choudbury, T. 2000. *Equality: A New Framework*. Cambridge: University of Cambridge Centre for Public Law and Judge Institute of Management Studies.

Hepple, B. and Morris, G. 2002. 'The Employment Act 2002 and the crisis of individual employment rights', *Industrial Law Journal*, 31 (3): 251–69.

Heywood, J. and Jirjahn, U. 2006. 'Performance pay: determinants and conse-quences', in D. Lewin (ed.), *Contemporary Issues in Employment Relations*. Urbana-Champaign, IL: Labor and Employment Relations Association.

Heywood, J., Siebert, W. and Wei, X. 1997. 'Payment by results systems: British evidence', *British Journal of Industrial Relations*, 35: 1–22.

Hicks, S., Walling, A., Heap, D. and Livesey, D. 2005. *Public Sector Employment Trends 2005*. London: Labour Market Division and Employment of Earnings and Productivity Division, Office of National Statistics.

Hirschman, A. 1970. *Exit, Voice and Loyalty*. Cambridge, MA: Harvard University Press.

Hogarth, T., Hasluck, C., Pierre, G., Winterbotham, M. and Vivian, D. 2000. *Work–Life Balance 2000: Baseline Study of Work–Life Balance Practices in Great Britain*. Coventry: Institute for Employment Research.

Holmstrom, B. and Milgrom, P. 1994. 'The firm as an incentive system', *American Economic Review*, 84: 972–91.

Hoque, K. 1999. 'Human resource management and performance in the UK hotel industry', *British Journal of Industrial Relations*, 37: 419–43.

Hoque, K. 2003. 'All in all, it's just another plaque on the wall: the incidence and impact of the Investors in People standard', *Journal of Management Studies*, 40: 543–71.

Hoque, K. and Noon, M. 2001. 'Counting angels: a comparison of personnel and HR specialists', *Human Resource Management Journal*, 11 (3): 5–23.

Hoque, K. and Noon, M. 2004. 'Equal opportunity policy and practice in Britain', *Work, Employment and Society*, 18 (3): 481–506.

Howell, C. 2005. *Trade Unions and the State*. Princeton University Press.

Hubbuck, J. and Carter, S. 1980. *Half a Chance? A Report on Job Discrimination against Young Blacks in Nottingham*. London: Commission for Racial Equality.

Hunt, A. 1975. *Management Attitudes and Practices towards Women at Work*. London: HMSO.

Huselid, M. 1995. 'The impact of human resource management practices on turnover, productivity and corporate performance', *Academy of Management Journal*, 38 (3): 635–72.

Hutton, W. 1996. *The State We're In*. London: Vintage.

Hyman, R. 1972. *Strikes*. London: Fontana.

Hyman, R. and Price, R. 1983. *The New Working Class? White-Collar Workers and Their Organizations*. London: Macmillan.

Ichniowski, C., Shaw, K. and Prennushi, G. 1997. 'The effects of human resource management practices on productivity: a study of steel finishing lines', *American Economic Review*, 87 (3): 291–313.

Innes, E. and Morris, J. 1995. 'Multinational corporations and employee relations: continuity and change in a mature industrial region', *Employee Relations*, 17 (6): 25–42.

Institute for Employment Research. 1988. *Review of the Economy and Employment*. Coventry: University of Warwick.

Jefferson, M. 1985. 'Equal pay for work of equal value: a comment on Hayward v. Cammell Laird', *Industrial Relations Journal*, 16 (2): 76–80.

Jenkins, C. 1990. *All Against the Collar*. London: Methuen.

Jenkins, C. and Sherman, B. 1979. *White-Collar Unionism: The Rebellious Salatariat*. London: Routledge.

Jones, T. and Ram, M. 2007. 'Re-embedding the ethnic business agenda', *Work, Employment and Society*, 21: 439–58.

Jürgens, U. 1989. 'The transfer of Japanese management concepts in the international automobile industry', in S. Wood (ed.), *The Transformation of Work?*. London: Unwin Hyman.

Kahn-Freund, O. 1954. 'Legal framework', in A. Flanders and H. A. Clegg (eds.), *The System of Industrial Relations in Great Britain*. Oxford: Blackwell.

Kalmi, P. and Kauhanen, A. 2008. 'Workplace innovations and employee outcomes: evidence from Finland', *Industrial Relations*, 47 (3): 430–59.

Kandel, E. and Lazear, E. 1992. 'Peer pressure and partnerships', *Journal of Political Economy*, 100: 801–17.

Keegan, W. 1984. *Mrs Thatcher's Economic Experiment*. London: Penguin.

Kelly, J. 1998. *Rethinking Industrial Relations: Mobilization, Collectivism and Long Waves*. London: Routledge.

Kelly, J. and Gennard, J. 2007. 'Business strategic decision making: the role and influence of directors', *Human Resource Management Journal*, 17 (2): 99–117.

Kersley, B., Alpin, C., Forth, J., Bryson, A., Bewley, H., Dix, G. and Oxenbridge, S. 2006. *Inside the Workplace: Findings from the 2004 Workplace Employment Relations Survey*. London: Routledge.

Kingsmill, D. 2001. *Report into Women's Employment and Pay*. London: Women and Equality Unit.

Knight, K. G. and Latreille, P. 2000. 'Discipline, dismissals and complaints to employment tribunals', *British Journal of Industrial Relations*, 38 (4): 533–55.

Kochan, T. A. 1980. *Collective Bargaining and Industrial Relations*. Homewood, IL: Richard D. Irwin.

Kochan, T. A. and Osterman, P. 1994. *The Mutual Gains Enterprise*. Cambridge, MA: Harvard Business School Press.

Konzelmann, S., Conway, N., Trenberth, L. and Wilkinson, F. 2006. 'Corporate governance and human resource management', *British Journal of Industrial Relations*, 44: 569–96.

Latreille, P., Latreille, J. A. and Knight, K. G. 2007. 'Employment tribunals and Acas: evidence from a survey of representatives', *Industrial Relations Journal*, 38 (2): 136–54.

Lawler, E. E. 1986. *High Involvement Management*. San Francisco: Jossey-Bass.

Lawler, E. E. and Benson, G. S. 2003. 'Employee involvement: utilization, impacts, and future prospects', in D. T. Holman, T. D. Wall, C. W. Clegg, P. Sparrow and A. Howard (eds.), *The New Workplace: A Guide to the Human Impact of Modern Working Practices*. London: Wiley, pp. 155–73.

Lawler, E. E., Mohrman, S. A. and Ledford, G. E., Jr. 1995. *Creating High Performance Organizations*. San Francisco: Jossey-Bass.

Lawler, E. E., Mohrman, S. A. and Ledford, G. E., Jr. 1998. *Strategies for High Performance Organizations*. San Francisco: Jossey-Bass.

Lazear, E. 2000. 'Performance pay and productivity', *American Economic Review*, 90: 1346–61.

Le Grand, J. 2007. *The Other Invisible Hand: Delivering Public Services through Choice and Competition*. Princeton University Press.

Leach, D. J., Wall, T. D. and Jackson, P. R. 2003. 'The effect of empowerment on job knowledge: an empirical test involving operators of complex technology', *Journal of Occupational and Organizational Psychology*, 76: 27–52.

Leggatt, A. 2001. *Tribunals for Users Consultation Paper about the Report of the Review of Tribunals*. A Lord Chancellor's Department Consultation Paper.

Legge, K. 1978. *Power, Innovation and Problem-Solving in Personnel Management*. London: McGraw-Hill.

Lemieux, T. 2008. 'The changing nature of wage inequality', *Journal of Population Economics*, 21(1): 21–48.

LeRoy, M. H. 2006. 'The power to create or obstruct employee voice: does US public policy skew employer preference for "no voice" workplaces?', *Socio-Economic Review*, 4: 311–19.

Levine, D. and Tyson, L. 1990. 'Participation, productivity, and the firm's environment', in A. Blinder (ed.), *Paying for Productivity: A Look at the Evidence*. Washington, DC: Brookings Institution.

Lewis, R. 1986. 'The role of law in employment relations' in R. Lewis (ed.), *Labour Law in Britain*. Oxford: Blackwell.

Lewis, R. and Simpson, B. 1982. 'Disorganising industrial relations', *Industrial Law Journal*, 11 (4): 227–44.

Lipsky, D., Seeber, R. and Fincher, R. 2003. *Emerging Systems for Managing Workplace Conflict*. San Francisco: Jossey-Bass.

Long, P. 1986. *Performance Appraisal Revisited*. London: Institute of Personnel Management.

Long, R. and Shields, J. 2005. 'Performance pay in Canadian and Australian firms: a comparative study', *International Journal of Human Resource Management*, 16: 1783–811.

Ludlam, S., Wood, S., Heery, E. and Taylor, A. 2003. 'Politics and employment relations', *British Journal of Industrial Relations*, 41 (4): 609–16.

Lupton, T. 1963. *On the Shop Floor: Two Studies of Workplace Organisation and Output*. Oxford: Pergamon.

MacDuffie, J. P. 1995. 'Human resource bundles and manufacturing performance: flexible production systems in the world auto industry', *Industrial and Labor Relations Review*, 48 (2): 197–221.

Machin, S. 1995. 'Plant closures and unionization in British establishments', *British Journal of Industrial Relations*, 33 (1): 55–68.

Machin, S. 2003a. 'Trade union decline, new workplaces, new workers', in H. Gospel and S. Wood (eds.), *Representing Workers: Union Recognition and Membership in Britain*. London: Routledge.

Machin, S. 2003b. 'Wage inequality since 1975', in R. Dickens, P. Gregg and J. Wadsworth (eds.), *The Labour Market under New Labour*. Basingstoke: Palgrave Macmillan.

Machin, S. and Stewart, M. 1996. 'Trade unions and financial performance', *Oxford Economic Papers*, 48 (2): 213–41.

Machin, S. and Van Reenen, J. 2007. *Changes in Wage Inequality*. London School of Economics, Centre for Economic Performance, Special Paper No. 18.

Machin, S. and Wadhwani, S. 1991. 'The effects of unions on organisational change and employment', *Economic Journal*, 101: 835–54.

Machin, S. and Wood, S. 2005. 'Human resource management as a substitute for trade unions in British workplaces', *Industrial and Labor Relations Review*, 58 (2): 201–18.

Marchington, M., Goodman, J., Wilkinson, A. and Ackers, P. 1992. *New Developments in Employee Involvement*. Employment Department Research Paper Series, No. 2. London: HMSO.

Marginson, P. M. 1998. 'The survey tradition in British industrial relations research', *British Journal of Industrial Relations*, 36: 361–88.

Marginson, P. M., Armstrong, P., Edwards, P., Purcell, J. and Hubbard, N. 1993. *The Control of Industrial Relations in Large Companies: An Initial Analysis of the Second Company Industrial Relations Survey*. Warwick Papers in Industrial Relations No. 45. Coventry: University of Warwick.

Marginson, P. M., Edwards, P., Armstrong, P. and Purcell, J. 1995. 'Strategy, structure and control in the changing corporation: a survey-based investigation', *Human Resource Management Journal*, 5 (2): 3–27.

Marginson, P. M., Edwards, P., Martin, R., Purcell, J. and Sisson, K. 1988. *Beyond the Workplace: Managing Industrial Relations in the Multi-establishment Enterprise*. Oxford: Blackwell.

Marginson, P. M. and Sisson, K. 2004. *European Integration and Industrial Relations. Multi-level Governance in the Making*. Basingstoke: Palgrave.

Marginson, P. and Wood, S. 2000. 'WERS98 special issue: Editors' introduction', *British Journal of Industrial Relations*, 38: 489–96.

Martin, C. 2003. 'Explaining labour turnover: empirical evidence from UK establishments', *Labour*, 17 (3): 391–412.

Martin, J. and Roberts, C. 1984. *Women and Employment: A Lifetime Perspective*. London: Department of Employment and Office of Population of Censuses and Surveys.

Martin, J. and Roberts, C. 2008. 'Putting women on the research agenda: the 1980 women and employment survey' in J. Scott, S. Dex and H. Joshi (eds.), *Women and Employment: Changing Lives and New Challenges*. Cheltenham: Edward Elgar.

McCarthy, W. E. J. 1967. *The Role of Shop Stewards in British Industrial Relations*. Royal Commission on Trade Unions and Employers' Association Research Papers No. 1. London: HMSO.

McCarthy, W. E. J. and Ellis, N. D. 1973. *Management by Agreement*. London: Hutchinson.

McCarthy, W. E. J. and Parker, S. R. 1968. *Shop Stewards and Workshop Relations*, Royal Commission on Trade Unions and Employers' Association Research Papers No. 10. London: HMSO.

McColgan, A. 2000. 'Family-friendly frolics? The maternity and parental leave etc. Regulations 1999', *Industrial Law Journal*, 29 (2): 125–43.

McCrudden, C. 2007. 'Equality legislation and reflexive regulation: a response to the discrimination law review's consultative paper', *Industrial Law Journal*, 36 (3): 255–66.

McGivern, G. and Ferlie, E. 2007. 'Playing tick-box games: interrelating defences in professional appraisal', *Human Relations*, 60 (9): 1361–85.

McGovern, P., Hill, S., Mills, C. and White, M. 2007. *Market, Class and Employment*. Oxford University Press.

McIntosh, N. and Smith, D. 1974. *The Extent of Racial Discrimination*. Broadsheet No. 547. London: Political and Economic Planning.

McNabb, R. and Whitfield, K. 1997. 'Unions, flexibility, team working and financial performance', *Organisation Studies*, 15 (5): 821–38.

McRae, S. 1991. *Maternity Rights in Britain: The PSI Report on the Experience of Women and Employers*. London: Policy Studies Institute.

Meager, N., Tyers, C., Perryman, S., Rick, J., Willison, R. 2002. *Awareness, Knowledge and Exercise of Individual Rights*. Employment Relations Research Series, No. 15. London: Department of Trade and Industry and Institute for Employment Studies.

Menezes-Filho, N., Ulph, D. and van Reenen, J. 1998. 'R&D and unionism: comparative evidence from British companies and establishments', *Industrial and Labor Relations Review*, 52: 45–63.

Metcalf, D. 2003a. 'Trade unions', in R. Dickens, P. Gregg and J. Wadsworth (eds.), *The Labour Market under New Labour*. Basingstoke: Palgrave Macmillan.

Metcalf, D. 2003b. 'Unions and productivity, financial performance and investment', in J. T. Addison and C. Schnabel (eds.), *International Handbook of Trade Unions*, Cheltenham: Edward Elgar.

Metcalf, D. and Charlwood, A. 2005. 'Trade unions: numbers, membership and density', in S. Fernie and D. Metcalf (eds.), *Trade Unions: Resurgence or Demise?* London: Routledge.

Metcalf, H. 1990. *Retaining Women Employees: Measures to Counteract Labour Shortage*. Institute of Manpower Studies Commentary No. 43. Brighton: Institute for Manpower Studies.

Metcalf, H. and Forth, J. 2000. *Business Benefits of Race Equality at Work*. Research Report No. 177. London: Department for Education and Employment.

Meyer, H. 1976. 'Personnel managers are the new corporate heroes', *Fortune*, 93: 84–8.

Michie, J. and Sheehan, M. 2005. 'Business strategy, human resources, labour market flexibility and competitive advantage', *International Journal of Human Resource Management*, 16: 445–64.

Milgrom, P. and Roberts, J. 1992. *Economics, Organisation, and Management*. Englewood Cliffs, NJ: Prentice-Hall.

Milligan, S. 1976. *The New Barons*. London: Temple Smith.

Millward, N. 1994. *The New Industrial Relations?* London: PSI Publishing.

Millward, N., Bryson, A. and Forth, J. 2000. *All Change at Work? British Employment Relations 1980–1998, as Portrayed by the Workplace Industrial Relations Survey Series*. London: Routledge.

Millward, N., Marginson, P. and Callus, R. 1998. 'Large-Scale national surveys for mapping, monitoring and theory development', in K. Whitfield and G. Strauss (eds.), *Researching the World of Work*. London: Cornell University Press.

Millward, N. and Stevens, M. 1986. *British Workplace Industrial Relations 1980–1984*. Aldershot: Gower.

Millward, N., Stevens, M., Smart, D. and Hawes, W. R. 1992. *Workplace Industrial Relations in Transition*. Aldershot: Dartmouth.

Milner, S. 1993. 'Overtime bands and strikes: evidence on relative incidence', *Industrial Relations Journal*, 24 (3): 201–10.

Milner, S. 1995. 'The coverage of collective pay-setting institutions in Britain, 1895–1990', *British Journal of Industrial Relations*, 33 (1): 69–92.

Milner, S. and James, A. 1994. 'Foreign ownership, unionisation and collective bargaining.' Paper presented to British Universities Industrial Relations Association Annual Conference, Oxford, 1–3 July.

Mitchell, D., Lewin, D. and Lawler, E. 1990. 'Alternative pay systems, firm performance, and productivity', in A. Blinder (ed.), *Paying for Productivity: A Look at the Evidence*. Washington, DC: Brookings Institution.

Modood, T. 1997. 'Employment', in T. Modood, R. Berthoud, J. Lakey, J. Nazroo, P. Smith, S. Virdee and S. Beishon (eds.), *Ethnic Minorities in Britain: Diversity and Disadvantage*. London: Policy Studies Institute.

Moore, S. 2004. 'Union mobilization and employer counter-mobilization in the statutory recognition process', in J. Kelly and P. Willman (eds.), *Union Organization and Activity*. London: Routledge.

Moore, S., McKay, S. and Bewley, H. 2005. *The Content of New Voluntary Trade Union Recognition Agreements 1998–2002. Vol. 2, Findings from the Survey of Employers*. Employment Relations Research Series, No. 43. London: Department of Trade and Industry.

Nadeem, S. and Metcalf, H. 2007. *Work–life Policies in Great Britain: What Works, Where and How?*, Employment Relations Research Series, No. 77. London: Department for Business, Enterprise and Regulatory Reform.

Niven, M. 1967. *Personnel Management 1913–1963*. London: Institute of Personnel Management.

Noon, M. 2007. 'The fatal flaws of diversity and the business case for ethnic minorities', *Work, Employment and Society*, 21 (4): 773–84.

Office for National Statistics. 2008. 'Employee jobs, 1959–2007', ONS Time-Series Databank (series identifier BCAJ). Retrieved 20 June 2008 from: www.statistics.gov.uk/StatBase/tsdataset.asp?vlnk=496&More=N&All=Y

Office for Population Censuses and Surveys. 1982. *Labour Force Survey 1979*. London: HMSO.

Oliver, N. and Wilkinson, B. 1992. *The Japanisation of British Industry: New Developments in the 1990s*. Oxford: Blackwell.

Oxenbridge, S. and Brown, W. A. 2004. 'Achieving a new equilibrium? The stability of co-operative employer-union relationships', *Industrial Relations Journal*, 35 (5): 388–402.

Oxenbridge, S., Brown, W., Deakin, S. and Pratten, C. 2003. 'Initial responses to the Employment Relations Act 1999', *British Journal of Industrial Relations*, 41 (2): 315–34.

Oyer, P. 2004. 'Why do firms use incentives that have no incentive effects?', *Journal of Finance*, 59 (4): 1619–49.

Palmer, T. 2004. *Results of the First Flexible Working Employee Survey*. Employment Relations Occasional Paper. London: Department of Trade and Industry.

Parker, S. 1974. *Workplace Industrial Relations 1972*. London: HMSO.

Parker, S. 1975. *Workplace Industrial Relations 1973*. London: HMSO.

Pearson, N. 1994. 'Employment in the public and private sectors', *Economic Trends*, 43 (January): 92–8.

Pencavel, J. 2003. 'The surprising retreat of union Britain', in R. Blundell, D. Card and R. Freeman (eds.), *Seeking a Premier League Economy*. University of Chicago Press.

Pendleton, A. 1997a. 'Characteristics of workplaces with financial participation: evidence from the Workplace Industrial Relations Survey', *Industrial Relations Journal*, 28: 103–19.

Pendleton, A. 1997b. 'What impact has privatisation had on pay and employment? a review of the UK experience', *Relations Industrielles*, 52 (3): 554–79.

Pendleton, A. 2006. 'Incentives, monitoring, and employee stock ownership plans: new evidence and interpretations', *Industrial Relations*, 43: 753–77.

Pendleton, A. 2007. 'The study of employee share ownership using WERS: an evaluation and analysis of the 2004 survey', in K. Whitfield and K. Huxley (eds.), *Innovations in the 2004 Workplace Employment Relations Survey*. Cardiff: Cardiff University.

Pendleton, A., Brewster, C., and Poutsma, E. 2003. 'The development of financial participation in Europe', in T. Kato and J. Pliskin (eds.), *The Determinants of the Incidence and the Effects of Participatory Organisations, Advances in the Economic Analysis of Participatory and Labor Management*, vol. 7. Amsterdam: Elsevier/JAI Press.

Pendleton, A., Poutsma, E., Brewster, C. and Ommeren, J. 2001. *Employee Share Ownership and Profit Sharing in the European Union*. Dublin: European Foundation for the Improvement of Living and Working Conditions.

Penn, R. and Scattergood, H. 1996. 'The experience of trade unions in Rochdale during the 1980s', in D. Gallie, R. Penn and M. Rose (eds.), *Trade Unionism in Recession*. Oxford University Press.

Phizacklea, A. and Miles, R. 1987. 'The British trade union movement and racism', in G. Lee and T. Loveridge (eds.), *The Manufacture of Disadvantage*. Milton Keynes: Open University Press.

Pollert, A. 2005. 'The unorganised worker: the decline in collectivism and new hurdles to individual employment rights', *Industrial Law Journal*, 34 (3): 217–38.

Poole, M. 1988. 'Factors affecting the development of employee financial participation in contemporary Britain: evidence from a national survey', *British Journal of Industrial Relations*, 26: 21–36.

Poole, M., Brown, W., Rubery, J., Sisson, K., Tarling, R. and Wilkinson, F. 1984. *Industrial Relations in the Future*. London: Routledge & Kegan Paul.

Prais, S. 1978. 'The strike-proneness of large plants in Britain', *Journal of the Royal Statistical Society*, series A, 141 (3): 363–84.

Prendergast, C. 1999. 'The provision of incentives in firms', *Journal of Economic Literature*, 37: 7–63.

Priestley, R. E. 1955, *Royal (Priestley) Commission on the Civil Service 1953–55*. Cmd 9613. London: HMSO.

Protherough, R. and Pick, J. *Managing Britannia: Culture and Management in Modern Britain*. Denton, Norfolk: Brynmill Press.

Prowse, P. and Prowse, J. 2007. 'Is there still a public sector model of employment relations in the United Kingdom?', *International Journal of Public Sector Management*, 20 (1): 48–62.

Purcell, J. 1981. *Good Industrial Relations: Theory and Practice*. London: Macmillan.

Purcell, J. 1983. 'The management of industrial relations in the modern corporation', *British Journal of Industrial Relations*, 21: 1–16.

Purcell, J., Edwards, P., Marginson, P. and Sisson, K. 1987. 'The industrial relations practices of multi-plant foreign-owned firms', *Industrial Relations Journal*, 18 (2): 130–7.

Ramsay, H., Scholarios, D. and Harley, B. 2000. 'Employees in high performance work systems: testing inside the black box', *British Journal of Industrial Relations*, 38 (4): 501–31.

Ritzer, G. and Trice, H. 1969. *An Occupation in Conflict*. Ithaca, NY: Cornell University Press.

Robertson, J. and Briggs, J. 1979. 'Part-time working in Great Britain', *Employment Gazette*, 87 (7): 671–75.

Rose, M. 1996. 'Still life in Swindon: case-studies in union survival and employer policy in a "sunrise" labour market', in D. Gallie, R. Penn and M. Rose (eds.), *Trade Unionism in Recession*. Oxford University Press.

Rose, M. 2005. 'Job satisfaction in Britain: coping with complexity', *British Journal of Industrial Relations*, 43 (3): 455–67.

Rosen, S. 1969. 'Trade union power, threat effects and the extent of organization', *Review of Economic Studies*, 36 (106, April): 185–96.

Roy, D. 1952. 'Quota restriction and goldbricking in a machine shop', *American Journal of Sociology*, 9: 427–42.

Royal Commission on Trade Unions and Employers' Associations. 1968. *Report*. Cmnd 3623. London: HMSO.

Rubery, J. and Edwards, P. 2003. 'Low pay and the National Minimum Wage', in P. Edwards (ed.), *Industrial Relations: Theory and Practice*. Oxford: Blackwell.

Sabel, C. F. 1982. *The Division of Labor in Industry*. Cambridge University Press.

Scheuer, S. 2006. 'A novel calculus? Institutional change, globalization and industrial conflict in Europe', *European Journal of Industrial Relations*, 12 (2): 143–64.

Shackleton, J. R. 2002. *Employment tribunals: their growth and the case for radical reform*. London: Institute of Economic Affairs.

Siebert, W. S. and Addison, J. T. 1981. 'Are strikes accidental?', *Economic Journal*, 91: 389–404.

Sinclair, A. and Botten, N. 1995. 'Compensation for discrimination: cause for concern', *Employee Relations*, 17 (8): 46–59.

Sisson, K. 1993. 'In search of HRM', *British Journal of Industrial Relations*, 31: 201–10.

Sisson, K. (ed.). 1994. Personnel Management: A Comprehensive Guide to Theory and Practice in Britain. 2nd edn. Oxford: Blackwell.

Sisson, K. 2005. 'Personnel management and European integration: a case of indelible imprint?', in S. Bach (ed.), *Managing human resources: personnel management in transition*. Oxford: Blackwell.

Sisson, K. and Artiles, A. M. 2000. *Handling Restructuring: A Study of Collective Agreements on Employment and Competitiveness*. Luxembourg: Office for the Official Publications of the European Communities.

Sisson, K. and Marginson, P. 1995. 'Management: systems, structures and strategy', in P. Edwards (ed.), *Industrial Relations*. Oxford: Blackwell.

Skinner, W. 1981. 'Big hat, no cattle: managing human resources', *Harvard Business Review*, Sept.–Oct.: 106–14.

Sloane, P. J. and Williams, H. 2000. 'Job satisfaction, comparison earnings, and gender', *Labour*, 14 (3): 473–502.

Smith, D. 1981. *Unemployment and Racial Minorities*. London: Policy Studies Institute.

Snell, M. W., Glucklich, P. and Povell, M. 1981. *Equal Pay and Opportunities*. Research Paper No. 20. London: Department of Employment.

Spector, P. 2006. 'Method variance in organizational research: truth or urban legend?', *Organizational Research Methods*, 9 (2): 221–32.

Stewart, M. B. 1987. 'Collective bargaining arrangements, closed shops and relative pay', *Economic Journal*, 97 (385): 140–56.

Storey, J. 1992. *Developments in the Management of Human Resources*. Oxford: Blackwell.

Storey, J. and Sisson, K. 1993. *Managing Human Resources and Industrial Relations*. Buckingham: Open University Press.

Stuart, M. and Martínez Lucio, M. 2000. 'Renewing the model employer: changing employment relations and "partnership" in the health and private sectors', *Journal of Management in Medicine*, 14 (5/6): 311–25.

Taylor, R. 1978. *The Fifth Estate: Britain's Unions in the Modern World*. London: Pan.

Terry, M. 1983. 'Shop Steward Development and Managerial Strategies', in G. Bain (ed.), *Industrial Relations in Britain*. Oxford: Blackwell.

Terry, M. 1995. 'Employee representation: shop stewards and the new legal framework', in P. Edwards, *Industrial Relations: Theory and Practice*. 2nd edn. Oxford: Blackwell.

Terry, M. 1999. 'Systems of collective employee representation in non-union firms in the UK', *Industrial Relations Journal*, 30 (1): 16–30.

Thompson, P. 2003. 'Disconnected Capitalism', *Work, Employment and Society*, 17: 359–78.

Thompson, P. and Harley, B. 2007. 'HRM and the worker: labor process perspectives', in P. Boxall, J. Purcell and P. Wright (eds.), *The Oxford Handbook of Human Resource Management*. Oxford University Press.

Trades Union Congress. 2008. *Hard Work, Hidden Lives. The Full Report of the Commission on Vulnerable Employment*. London: Trades Union Congress.

Tsai, C. J., Sen Gupta, S. and Edwards, P. 2007. 'When and why is small beautiful? The experience of work in the small firm', *Human Relations*, 60 (12): 1779–807.

Turner, L. 2003. 'Reviving the labor movement: A comparative perspective', in D. Cornfield and H. McCammon (eds.), *Labor Revitalization: Global Perspective and New Initiatives. Research in the Sociology of Work*, vol. 11. Greenwich, CT: JAI.

Ulrich, D. 1997. *Human Resource Champions*. Boston, MA: Harvard Business School Press.

Ulrich, D. and Brockbank, W. 2005. *The HR Value Proposition*. Boston, MA: Harvard Business School Press.

Undy, R., Ellis, V., McCarthy, W. E. J. and Halmos, A. M. 1981. *Change in Trade Unions*. London: Hutchinson.

United Nations (UN) 2007. *World Investment Report: Transnational Corporations in Extractive Industries*. New York: United Nations.

US Department of Labor. 1993. *High Performance Work Practices*. Washington, DC: US Department of Labor.

Virdee, S. 2000. 'A Marxist critique of black radical theories of trade union racism', *Sociology*, 34 (3): 545–65.

Visser, J. 2003. 'Unions and unionism around the world', in J. T. Addison and C. Schnabel (eds.), *International Handbook of Trade Unions*, Edward Elgar: Cheltenham and Northampton, MA.

Waddington, J. 2003. 'Trade union organisation' in P. K. Edwards (ed.), *Industrial Relations: Theory and Practice*. 2nd edn. Oxford: Blackwell.

Wadsworth, J. 2003. 'The labour market performance of ethnic minorities in the recovery', in R. Dickens, P. Gregg and J. Wadsworth (eds.), *The Labour Market under New Labour: The State of Working Britain*. Basingstoke: Palgrave Macmillan.

Wall, T., Michie, J., Patterson, W., Wood, S., Sheehan, M., Clegg, C. and West, M. 2004. 'On the validity of subjective measures of company performance', *Personnel Psychology*, 57: 95–118.

Wall, T. and Wood, S. 2005. 'The romance of human resource management and business performance, and the case for big science', *Human Relations*, 58 (4): 429–62.

Wall, T. D., Wood, S. J. and Leach, D. 2004. 'Empowerment and Performance', in I. Robertson and C. Cooper (eds.), *International and Organizational Psychology*, London: Wiley.

Walton, R. E. 1985. 'From "control" to "involvement" in the workplace', *Harvard Business Review*, 63: 77–84.

Warr, P. 2002. 'The study of well-being, behaviour and attitudes', in P. Warr, *Psychology at Work*, Harmondsworth: Penguin.

Warr, P. 2007. *Work, Happiness, and Unhappiness*. Mahwah, NJ: Lawrence Erlbaum Associates.

Watson, T. 1977. *The Personnel Manager: A Study in the Sociology of Work and Employment*. London: Routledge & Kegan Paul.

Watson, T. 1986. *The Personnel Managers: A Study in the Sociology of Work and Industry*. London: Routledge & Kegan Paul.

Watson, T. 1995. *In Search of Management*. London: Routledge.

Webb, S. and Webb, W. 1902. *Industrial Democracy*. London: Longmans.

Wedderburn, K. W. (Lord). 1986. *The Worker and the Law*. 3rd edn. London: Pelican.

Wedderburn, K. W. (Lord). 1998. 'A British duty to bargain: a footnote on the end-game', *Industrial Law Journal*, 27 (3): 253.

Weitzman, M. and Kruse, D. 1990. 'Profit sharing and productivity', in A. Blinder (ed.), *Paying for Productivity: A Look at the Evidence*. Washington, DC: Brookings Institution.

White, M. 1981. *Payment Systems in Britain*. Aldershot: Gower.

Whitfield, K. and Huxley, K. (eds.). 2007. *Innovations in the 2004 Workplace Employment Relations Survey*. Cardiff: Cardiff University.

Wickens, P. 1988. *The Road to Nissan: Flexibility, Quality, Teamwork*, Basingstoke: Macmillan.

Williamson, O. E. 1973. *Markets and Hierarchies: Analysis and Antitrust Implications*. New York: Free Press.

Willman, P. 2005. 'Circling the wagons: endogeneity in union decline', in S. Fernie and D. Metcalf (eds.), *Trade Unions: Resurgence or Demise?* London: Routledge.

Willman, P. and Bryson, A. 2006. *Accounting for Collective Action: Resource Acquisition and Mobilization in British Unions*. Centre for Economic Performance Discussion Paper No. 767. London: London School of Economics.

Willman, P. and Bryson, A. 2007. 'Union organization in Great Britain', *Journal of Labor Research*, 28 (1): 93–115.

Willman, P., Bryson, A. and Gomez, R. 2006. 'The sound of silence: which employers choose "no voice" and why?', *Socio-Economic Review*, 4: 283–99.

Willman, P., Bryson, A. and Gomez, R. 2007. 'The long goodbye: new establishments and the fall of union voice in Britain', *International Journal of Human Resource Management*, 18 (7): 1318–34.

Winchester, D. 1983. 'Industrial relations in the public sector', in G. Bain (ed.), *Industrial Relations in Britain*. Oxford: Blackwell.

Womack, J., Jones, D. and Roos, D. 1990. *The Machine That Changed the World*. New York: Rawson Associates.

Women and Work Commission. 2006. *Shaping a Fairer Future*. London: Women and Equality Unit, Department of Trade and Industry.

Wood, S. 1989. 'The Transformation of Work?', in S. Wood (ed.), *The Transformation of Work?*, London: Unwin Hyman.

Wood, S. J. 1993. 'The Japanization of Fordism?', *Economic and Industrial Democracy*, 14: 538–55.

Wood, S. 1996a. 'How different are human resource practices in Japanese "transplants" in the UK?', *Industrial Relations*, 35 (4): 511–25.

Wood, S. 1996b. 'High commitment management and payment systems', *Journal of Management Studies*, 33: 53–77.

Wood, S. 1996c. 'High commitment management and unionization in the UK', *International Journal of Human Resource Management*, 7: 41–58.

Wood, S. 1999. 'Human resource management and performance', *International Journal of Management Review*, 1: 367–413.

Wood, S. 2000. 'Learning through Acas: the case of statutory recognition' in B. Towers and W. Brown (eds.), *Employment Relations in Britain: Twenty-five Years of the Advisory Conciliation and Arbitration Service*. Oxford: Blackwell.

Wood, S. 2008. 'Job characteristics, employee voice and well-being in Britain', *Industrial Relations Journal*, 39 (2): 153–68.

Wood, S. and Albanese, M. T. 1995. 'Can we speak of a high commitment management on the shop floor?', *Journal of Management Studies*, 32 (2): 215–47.

Wood, S. and de Menezes, L. 1998. 'High commitment management in the UK: evidence from the Workplace Industrial Relations Survey and Employers' Manpower and Skills Practices Survey', *Human Relations*, 51 (4): 485–515.

Wood, S. and de Menezes, L. 2008a. 'Comparing perspectives on high involvement management and organizational performance across the British economy', *International Journal of Human Resource Management*, 19, 639–83.

Wood, S. and de Menezes, L. M. 2008b. 'High involvement management, work enrichment and well-being'. Paper presented at the Academy of Management Annual Meeting, Institute of Work Psychology, University of Sheffield. Mimeographed.

Wood, S., Stride, C. B., Wall, T. D. and Clegg, C. W. 2004. 'Revisiting the use and effectiveness of modern management practices', *Human Factors and Ergonomics in Manufacturing*, 14: 415–32.

Wood, S. and Wall, T. 2007. 'Work enrichment and employee voice in human resource management-performance studies', *International Journal of Human Resource Management*, 18: 1335–72.

Wood, S., van Veldhoven, M., Croon, M. and de Menezes, L. M. 2008. 'High involvement management, work enrichment and well-being: mutual gains or conflicting outcome?' Paper presented at the IWP2008 Conference, Institute of Work Psychology, University of Sheffield. Mimeographed.

Wrench, J. 1987. 'Unequal comrades: trades unions, equal opportunity and racism', in R. Jenkins and J. Solomos (eds.), *Racism and Equal Opportunity Policies in the 1980s*. Cambridge University Press.

Wright, P., Gardner, T., Moynihan, L., Park, H., Gerhart, B. and Delery, J. 2001. 'Measurement error in research on human resources and firm performance: additional data and suggestions for future research', *Personnel Psychology*, 54: 875–902.

Yeandle, S., Wigfield, A., Crompton, R. and Dennett, J. 2002. *Employed Carers and Family-Friendly Employment Policies*. Bristol: Policy Press.

Zabalza, A. and Zannatos, Z. (eds.). 1986. *Women and Equal Pay: The Effect of Legislation on Female Employment and Wages in Britain*. Cambridge University Press.

Index

absenteeism
accidents 205
Advisory, Conciliation and Arbitration
 Service (Acas) 8, 188, 335
 Annual Report (1998) 185
African men, employment rates 248
age
 and dissatisfaction 226–7
 and lack of influence 221
 rights in respect of 248
 see also workplace age
agency staff 298
Agenda for Change 32, 323
Albanese, M. 165
Alpin, C. 123, 126, 140, 150, 195, 197
Anderson, T. 243
Annual Business Inquiry 20
anti-discrimination legislation 230, 231,
 248, 336, 349
anxiety 173–4, 205–6
approved profit-sharing plan 265
Armstrong, P. 289–90, 299
Associated British Ports 45

Bacon, N. 226
Bangladeshi men, employment rates 248
Batstone, E. 187–8
Beaumont, P. 289
Beer, M. 73
Belfield, C. R. 227
Bender, K. A. 225
Benjamin, O. 226
Bewley, H. 123, 126, 140, 150, 195, 197
Blackburn, R. 350
Blair, Tony 333
Blanchflower, D. G. 181
Blyton, P. 226
Boraston, I. 187–8
Boulding, Kenneth 353
Boxall, P. 120
breach of contract 185
briefing committees 227–8

briefing groups 136–7, 140, 295–6, 326
British Aerospace 45
British Airports Authority 45
British Airways 45, 309
British Gas 45
British Household Panel Survey 193
British Leyland 80
British Petroleum 45
British Social Attitudes Survey (BSAS)
 90–1, 192–3, 194
British Steel 45
British Telecom 45, 241
Brown, W. 9
Bryson, A. 29, 49, 51, 99, 104, 123, 126,
 140, 150, 195, 197, 228, 345
Buckley, P. 287–8, 289
Bundesbank 189
Burgess, S. 190

Cable and Wireless 45
Canada, trade union membership 49
Cappellari, L. 228
Casebourne, J. 191
CBI (Confederation of British Industry) 7,
 10, 336
Central Arbitration Committee 335
Central Statistical Office (CSO) 234
Chamber of Commerce 165
Chartered Institute of Personnel and
 Development (CIPD) 121, 123,
 127, 129, 150
 2007 survey 127
Citizens Advice Bureau 191–2
Clegg, H. A. 10, 75, 77
climate of employment relations 145
closed shops 59, 346
coal industry 45
Colgan, F. 246
collective bargaining 4–5, 22–47, 76, 88,
 189, 345–6
 and changing economy 30–1
 coverage of workers 31–3

397